FORAGERS OF THE TERMINAL PLEISTOCENE IN NORTH AMERICA

Foragers of the Terminal Pleistocene in North America

Edited by

RENEE B. WALKER

and

BOYCE N. DRISKELL

University of Nebraska Press
Lincoln & London

Library of Congress Cataloging-in-Publication Data
Foragers of the terminal Pleistocene in North America /
edited by Renee B. Walker and Boyce N. Driskell. p. cm.
Some chapters originally presented at a Society for American Archaeology symposium in 2000.
Includes bibliographical references and index.
ISBN-13: 978-0-8032-4802-1 (cloth: alk. paper)
ISBN-10: 0-8032-4802-4 (cloth: alk. paper)
ISBN-13: 978-0-8032-3286-0 (paper: alk. paper)
1. Paleo-Indians—Antiquities. 2. Hunting and gathering societies—North America.
3. Excavations (Archaeology)—North America. 4. North America—Antiquities. I. Walker,
Renee Beauchamp, 1968– II. Driskell, Boyce N.
E61.F67 2007
970.01—dc22
2006032043

CONTENTS

PREFACE

This volume grew out of a Society for American Archaeology symposium (2000) organized by Renee Walker on Paleoindian subsistence. The chapters by Fiedel, Yesner, Kuehn, Walker, Hollenbach, McWeeney, and Dunbar and Vojnovski are revised from earlier versions presented in that symposium. Although we did not attempt to provide comprehensive regional or topical coverage in the book, we solicited several other essays (Dent, Collins, Kornfeld) to provide more even regional representation. As a group, these chapters present intriguing new data on Paleoindian subsistence garnered often from excavated faunal remains but in some cases from preserved floral remains. These essays generally report data and interpretations just out of the trenches. By that we mean that most of the data considered are less that a decade in existence and therefore have been generated from modern, meticulous investigations and recovery techniques. One additional chapter was commissioned, so to speak, by the editors to provide background and additional insight into Paleoindian subsistence strategies. The chapter by Randall and Hollenbach examines the potential role of ethnographic models of hunter-gatherers in our studies of Paleoindian subsistence.

We would like to thank our colleagues who have penned these chapters, each contributing significantly to our continuing enlightenment concerning Paleoindian subsistence. We go to press with the recent sad news of the passing of our mentor, colleague, and friend, Paul Parmalee, who supported and assisted us in many ways in our careers and research. We'll certainly miss his energy, his smile, and his kind words. Our direct experience in this research subject has come primarily from the "trenches" at Dust Cave, located in northwest Alabama. We certainly want to express our appreciation for all the students, volunteers, and collaborators at Dust Cave whose labor has made several chapters in this volume possible. Thanks also to our copyeditor, Robert Burchfield, and the University of Nebraska Press staff for bringing this volume to fruition. Most important, we want to dedicate this book to our spouses, Charles Walker and Susan Driskell, who endured all the problems of absentee spouses during the many seasons of fieldwork at Dust Cave. Their sacrifice was indeed the largest.

INTRODUCTION

New Developments in Paleoindian Subsistence Studies

Renee B. Walker and Boyce N. Driskell

The discovery and excavation of stone artifacts, including distinctive, fluted projectile points, in direct association with a species of bison known to have become extinct at the end of the Pleistocene at the Folsom site in New Mexico in the mid-1920s (Cook 1927; Figgins 1927) stimulated the popular imagination and professional inquiry about the nature of North America's earliest inhabitants and began a controversy in American archaeology that, if anything, is more heated today than at any time in the past. What nature of people were these?

Eventually to be called Paleoindians (Wormington 1957:3), these early people appeared to be quite efficient and successful hunters, downing large animals with simple stone-tipped spears. Other sites investigated in western North America in the ensuing years supported the pattern of predation on Pleistocene megafaunal species. Additionally, judging from the sources of the materials from which the Clovis people made their tools, archaeologists came to realize that these "hunters" also ranged widely in pursuit of their prey.

As research continued through the twentieth century, the broad chronological and spatial patterns of the Paleoindian Stage in North America formed. The Paleoindian Stage conventionally began with the rapid spread of a tool complex referred to as the Clovis manifestation, dominated by distinctive fluted projectile points and, often, blade technologies. However, with the general acceptance of a pre-Clovis dating for Monte Verde (Dillehay 1997), in southern Chile, and reports of a number of possible pre-Clovis sites in North America, some archaeologists now include a pre-Clovis manifestation as the earlier of several periods of the Paleoindian Stage. In addition to pre-Clovis (before ca. 11,500 BP), the Paleoindian Stage has been divided into early or Clovis (11,500–10,900 BP), Middle 10,900–10,500 BP, and Late (10,500–10,000 BP) (Anderson et al. 1996:7–15).

Although pre-Clovis manifestations in North America are poorly understood and controversial, claimed antecedents to the Clovis manifestation are some early artifacts (bifacial and blade technologies) found in Alaska, including the probably quite early Bluefish Cave Complex (Cinq-Mars 1979) and the later Nenana Complex (Powers and Hoffecker 1989). Similarly, the Miller Complex found at Meadowcroft Rockshelter (Adovasio 1993:205–213) in Pennsylvania exhibits early blade and biface technologies. Claims for pre-Clovis materials have come from the excavators of Little Salt Spring and Page-Ladson in Florida (Anderson et al. 1996:8–9). None of these early complexes exhibit fluting as a technique for shaping bifaces or projectile points.

In spite of growing data in support of earlier cultural expressions in North America, the first clearly defined archaeological manifestation is the Clovis complex. This manifestation includes a variety of traits but is principally defined by association with the Clovis projectile point, a lanceolate fluted artifact often considered the apogee of New World flint knapping. Clovis projectile points are highly valued by artifact collectors because they are very finely flaked, often from the highest quality raw materials. As Collins (1999b:35) notes, these projectile points have been recovered from unglaciated parts of Canada and the Great Lakes area, every part of the continental United States, and as far south as Central America.

Only a few dozen radiocarbon dates from across North America are available for Clovis (Morrow and Morrow 1999:226; Haynes 1993). These suggest a rather brief Clovis period in the west from ca. 11,200 to 10,900 BP; however, Frison (1993:238) dates Clovis on the high plains as beginning by 11,500 BP. Clovis sites in the Northeast seem generally younger, ranging from ca. 10,600 to 10,200 BP (Haynes 1993:220–223, table 1), but these available dates are not in areas where the oldest dates would be expected (Dincauze 1993a:279). Anderson et al. (1996:11) places Clovis in the Southeast between 11,500 and 10,800 BP, as early as Clovis in the West, but lasting longer in the Southeast.

During the Middle Paleoindian period, the Clovis manifestation precedes a similar lithic technology but with derivative variants of Clovis projectile points for most regions of the continent. On the high plains, the Goshen point may be derivative from Clovis (Frison 1993:242). Also, across much of the west, Clovis is succeeded by the Folsom projectile point and associated assemblage, apparently popular from ca. 10,800 to ca. 10,200 BP (Haynes 1993:220). Similar lanceolate or weak-shouldered points, including Midland, Agate Basin and Hell Gap, probably date slightly later than Folsom.

In the Southeast, Middle Paleoindian assemblages (dated from ca. 10,900 to ca. 10,500 BP) are also similar to, and no doubt derived from, Clovis prototypes. Regional types include Cumberland, Clovis Variant, Redstone, and possibly Ross County. Projectile points in Justice's (1987:34–44) Dalton cluster, including Quad, Beaver Lake, Dalton, Greenbrier, and Hardaway Side Notched, apparently follow Cumberland-style points in the greater Southeast. These latest Paleoindian point styles (characteristic of the Late Paleoindian period) date between 10,500 and 10,000 BP (Goodyear 1982). Radiocarbon dates from Dust Cave support this date range (Driskell 1994; Sherwood et al. 2004).

While Clovis projectile points may be somewhat younger in the Northeast (Dincauze 1993a; Spiess et al. 1998), Clovis is followed by Cumberland and in turn succeeded by the so-called short stubby points referred to by Justice (1987:44–46) as the Hi-Lo cluster. These points seem to be coeval, more or less, with the Dalton cluster to the south dating between 10,500 to 10,000 BP.

Paleoindians were probably highly mobile, moving often in order to follow large-mammal herds. This lifestyle would require Paleoindian people to limit the essential material items they carried from place to place (Walthall 1980). Tool kits were generally highly curated, and there was extensive use of high-quality materials (Goodyear 1983). In addition, groups would have been small, but also highly cooperative. Often archaeologists (Bamforth 1988; Cassells 1997; Dixon 1999; Todd and Rapson 1999; Wedel 1961, 1986) went so far as to define Paleoindians (particularly fluted point makers) as hunting specialists, meaning that exploitation of one or a few large terrestrial animal species dominated settlement and subsistence decisions and practices.

There are theoretical issues about the ability of hunting specialists to exploit each of the diverse environments on the continent (but particularly in the eastern United States) at the end of the Pleistocene. In addition, recent new data from faunal and floral remains and recent challenges to the Paleoindian hunter model emphasize the likely importance of collected plant and animal foods, and the settlement and subsistence decisions associated with this approach to livelihood (Hollenbach 2005).

Possibly the most popular recent reification of the Clovis hunter hypothesis is by Kelly and Todd (1988). They postulate the following: The North American continent was devoid of human population prior to the Clovis colonization in the twelfth millennium BP. Clovis peoples entered a rapidly changing environment at the end of the Pleistocene. Faunal biomass was high but dropping rapidly. By 10,000 radiocarbon years BP, the extinction of over 30 mammalian genera was complete or nearly so (Haynes 1984). Seasonal climate, possibly also year-to-year climate, was becoming variable. Preadapted to hunting of terrestrial fauna, "early Paleoindians probably were generalists in relation to large terrestrial faunal resources and opportunists in relation to all other food resources" (Kelly and Todd 1988:233).

The model proposed by Kelly and Todd (1988), often referred to as the high-technology forager (HTF) model, portrays the Clovis settlement/subsistence system as one of high residential mobility, based primarily on resource abundance and availability and the lack of stored resources, and dominated by use of search-and-encounter hunting tactics. According to them, early Paleoindians were technology oriented rather than place oriented; while other resources (collectible plants, animals) were exploited as opportunity permitted, Clovis peoples moved across the landscape motivated primarily by availability of large terrestrial and/or megafaunal resources. Accordingly, this settlement/subsistence practice accounts for the rapid colonization of the continent, accomplished, it would seem, in only several hundred years (Kelly and Todd 1988: 238).

While there is little doubt concerning the association of Clovis people with the exploitation of large animals, it is not entirely clear how usual this practice was in the course of subsistence activities. Meltzer (1993a) points out that in spite of the high profile of kill sites in the literature and among archaeologists, there are not really many of these sites known, even in the West. This is particularly the case when compared to the hundreds of known Pleistocene bone (fossil) finds from North America that do not exhibit evidence for Clovis or other human predation. However, even though soil conditions and environment east of the Mississippi River have not been conducive to bone preservation (Dincauze 1993a), Pleistocene bone finds and bone beds are known. Some evidence of Clovis association is seen at Little Salt Spring in Florida (Dunbar and Webb 1996; Hemmings 1999), the Kimmswick site in Missouri (Graham et al. 1981), and the Coats-Hines site in Tennessee (Breitburg et al. 1996). This indicates that Clovis people hunted megafauna, but perhaps not to the extent one would expect given the provisions of the HTF model.

Nor is it entirely clear that there was generally a great abundance of large terrestrial animals available to Clovis peoples in any, or most, of the environments in which they existed. Meltzer (1993a) points out that the changing environments of the terminal Pleistocene were generally species rich but may have been, in relative terms, "individual" poor. The huge bison herds of the Great Plains was a Holocene event.

In a survey of aboriginal groups documented in the Human Relations Area Files, Meltzer (1993a) found that hunting specialists were quite rare in North America. Hunting or fishing specialists (those groups basing more that two-thirds of their subsistence efforts on this single activity) are found only in areas offering little alternative potential for subsistence, such as areas of the Arctic and open plains. Seemingly, hunting specialists always specialize on gregarious herd animals in treeless environments (Meltzer 1993a). Obviously, these requirements were not uniformly available in North America during the terminal Pleistocene; conditions and resources were quite different in the eastern woodlands. "Ecological theory strongly favors the expectation that Paleoindian forest dwellers were generalist foragers, taking large herbivores opportunistically but not risking their futures by disdaining the great diversity of smaller game and vegetable foods around them" (Dincauze 1993a:285). Meltzer (1993a:305) turns the popular phrase by Kelly and Todd (1988) to say, "Clovis groups were opportunists in relation to large terrestrial faunal resources and generalists in relation to all other species"; bison herd sizes probably expanded greatly during the early Holocene. This may have also been the case for caribou in the Northeast (Dincauze and Curran 1983:4; Dincauze 1993a).

The essays in this volume explore the lesser-known crevices of North American Paleoindian studies to present fine-grained analyses and evidence for patterns of collecting, as well as hunting, associated with Paleoindian cultures. Paleoindian subsistence studies are hampered by the lack of archaeological contexts where faunal and floral specimens are preserved. With diligence, some of these contexts are now coming to light, as reported by essays in this volume.

As new data becomes available, the monothetic stereotype of the late Pleistocene hunter will be replaced by chronometrically grounded regional models of subsistence and mobility that more realistically relate constraints and possibilities for resource exploitation within each region to evidence for human response. No doubt, collecting activities will loom large for most prehistoric groups in most regions of North America, and future research will suggest the importance of broad-spectrum foraging and extricate the diverse nature of Paleoindian subsistence strategies.

To this end, we have included recent research on Paleoindian sites that have produced data necessary to answer questions about subsistence strategies. We have included sites from a variety of regions and environments to better amplify the variation in Paleoindian adaptations. Sites discussed in this volume represent Paleoindian occupations in several regional contexts. Particular sites are from the following states: Alaska, Wisconsin, Texas, Alabama, Florida, Ohio, Pennsylvania, Maine, New Hampshire, Massachusetts, Connecticut, and Virginia, as well as sites in the western Plains and Rocky Mountains (see map on page xv). They range in antiquity from 12,000 to 10,000 radiocarbon years ago, and dates are provided in years before present (BP) unless otherwise noted.

This volume is not intended as a comprehensive survey of the evidence for Paleoindian subsistence; however, sites discussed in this volume represent Paleoindian occupation in several regional contexts. The first two chapters examine the northern section of North America. Stuart Fiedel first proposes migratory waterfowl routes as one impetus for human migration into the Americas. David Yesner then presents the faunal extinctions, foraging strategies, and subsistence diversity among eastern Beringian Paleoindians. In the next chapter, Marcel Kornfeld illustrates the unique nature of Paleoindian hunting in the western plains and Rocky Mountains, with a reinvestigation of mammoth and bison bone beds, in addition to camps, workshops, and task-specific sites. Michael Collins discusses subsistence strategies during the terminal Pleistocene in Texas through his research at the Gault site.

The north-central portion of North America is represented by Steven Kuehn's study of late Paleoindian subsistence strategies in the western Great Lakes region, through an examination of five terminal Pleistocene sites. Similarly, subsistence analyses from eastern North America, discussed in Renee Walker's interpretations of subsistence strategies at Dust Cave, Alabama, indicates a well-established, generalized foraging strategy by the end of the Pleistocene. Richard J. Dent presents a reanalysis of the subsistence research from the Shawnee-Minisink site and highlights the interconnectedness of seed collecting and fishing.

Our understandings of gathering activities during the Paleoindian period are generally poor, because plants remains are so rare from these contexts. However, investigations of Late Paleoindian botanical remains from Dust Cave by Kandace Hollenbach provide important new information about Paleoindian subsistence. In addition, Lucinda McWeeney has revised the scheme of Paleoindian-period environmental changes in the eastern United States through an analysis of plant remains from sites in Maine, New Hampshire, Massachusetts, Connecticut, Virginia, and Ohio.

James Dunbar and Pamela Vojnovski combine faunal and lithic data from Paleoindian campsites in Florida. They discuss the complex relation-

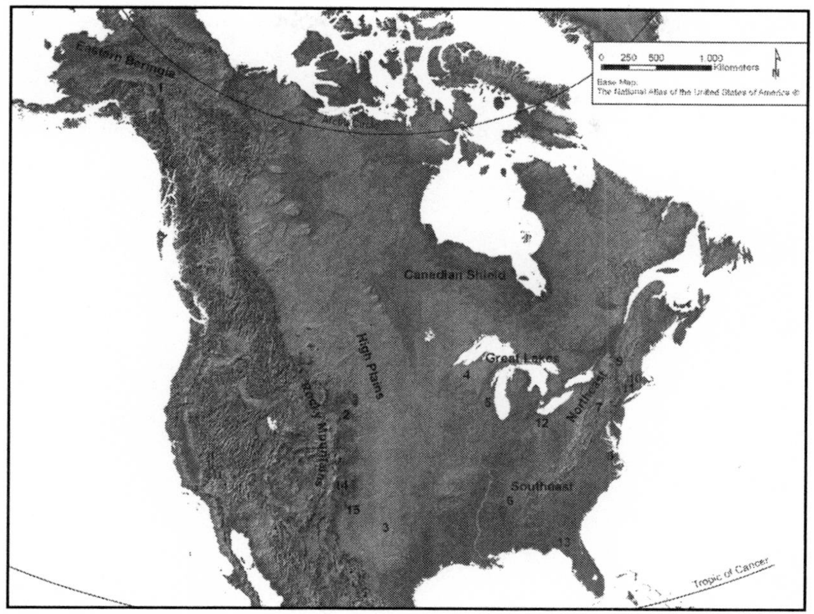

Locations of sites mentioned in the text. 1, Swan Point and Broken Mammoth AK; 2, Indian Creek, Barton Gulch, Allen, Ray Long, Hell Gap WY; 3, Gault TX; 4, Deadman Slough, Sucices WI; 5, Kiesow Grove, Wohlt, Russell Wohlt WI; 6, Dust Cave AL; 7, Shawnee Minisink PA; 8, Cactus Hill VA; 9, Jefferson, Whipple NH; 10, Bull Brook, Willmantic Kettle MA; 11, Pequot CT; 12, Sheridan Cave OH; 13, Ryan-Harley, Louis-McQuinn, Norden, Dunnigans Old Mill FL; 14, Folsom NM; 15, Clovis NM. Map prepared by Stephen Yerka.

ship between early Floridians, their subsistence technologies, and late megamammals.

We have included a chapter by Kandace Hollenbach and Asa Randall on the role of ethnographic analogy in Paleoindian subsistence research. This chapter underscores the importance of ethnographic data for explaining patterns of subsistence observed in the archaeological record. The pattern of high mobility foraging (Kelly and Todd 1988) no longer fits the archaeological data (at least for many of the archaeological examples presented in this volume), and we need to find better ethnographic analogues.

We conclude the volume with a discussion of the relative contributions of the chapters to the study of Paleoindian subsistence. The topics examined in this volume will, we hope, stimulate similar research on myriad questions about Paleoindian peoples in North America.

ONE

Quacks in the Ice

Waterfowl, Paleoindians, and the Discovery of America

Stuart J. Fiedel

The ice-free corridor between the Laurentide and Cordilleran ice sheets has long been regarded as the most likely route by which the Beringian ancestors of Paleoindians entered North America. Despite recent advocacy of an alternative coastal migration route, I contend that the corridor remains a viable option (see also Ives et al. 1993; Wilson and Burns 1999). I further suggest that observation and pursuit of migratory waterfowl may have provided the impetus for Paleoindian exploration of the corridor.

Migration Routes: Coast or Corridor?

Although the late Pleistocene geology of western Canada is still somewhat debatable, there appears to be a consensus that the Laurentide and Cordilleran glaciers coalesced during the Last Glacial Maximum (20,000–17,000 cal BC). Ice-core records from Greenland show no significant change in late glacial Northern Hemisphere climate prior to the rapid warming at the onset of the Bølling/Allerød at 12,700 cal BC. This temperature rise caused dramatic melting of northern ice sheets; meltwater poured into the ocean, probably causing a global sea level rise (known as meltwater pulse IA). In the southern Pacific, meltwater pulse IA is manifest as a 16-meter rise in sea level between 12,600 and 12,300 cal BC (Hanebuth et al. 2000). A recent reanalysis of New England varves demonstrates that recession of Laurentide ice began there at 12,600 BP (ca. 12,700 cal BC), and the ice had receded into Quebec by 11,600 BP (11,500 cal BC) (Ridge et al. 1999). It seems a safe assumption that the western edge of the Laurentide ice sheet also retreated dramatically between 12,600 and 12,000 cal BC, exposing an ice-free corridor. The basal sediments in Boone Lake, in the Peace River district, date from 12,000 BP (White 1983).

Knut Fladmark (1979, 1983) described the corridor, newly unglaciated about 12,000 BP (12,000 cal BC), as an inhospitable landscape, "harsh, raw, and primitive . . . unpleasant and oppressive." It was even colder than today, when winter temperatures are severe. The remnant ice sheets blocked drainage, creating huge shifting lakes in which fish could not live. Mandryk (1992, 1998) has concluded that hunter-gatherers could not sustain themselves in this environment prior to 12,000 BP. In contrast, recent research along the Pacific coast (Fedje et al. 1996; Josenhans et al. 1997; Mathewes 2000; Fedje and Josenhans 2000) shows that coastal ice had receded from most areas of British Columbia and Alaska by 14,000 BP (ca. 14,500 cal BC). Bears were living on Prince of Wales Island by 12,300 BP (Heaton et al. 1996). If they could thrive on the coast, so too, perhaps, could people. Fladmark, followed by other scholars (e.g., Gruhn 1988, 1994; Dixon 1999), suggested that humans had moved south along the coast, rather than through the corridor.

Monte Verde, a peculiar site in southern Chile (Dillehay 1997), is often cited by advocates of a coastal migration (e.g., Dixon 1999:249). It appears to date to about 12,500 to 12,000 BP (ca. 12,100 cal BC). Even if we ignore the glaring omissions and contradictions in the provenience data for the handful of definite artifacts (Fiedel 1999a) and provisionally accept MV-II as a human encampment, Monte Verde offers no evidence of a marine orientation. It sits beside a creek, some 30 kilometers from the Pacific shore. The faunal assemblage contains about 400 bones from seven mastodon-like gomphotheres, one scapula of a paleo-llama, and a few unidentifiable scraps of smaller animals. There are no fish and no marine shellfish (Dillehay 1997:674). Only the presence of seaweed suggests that the inhabitants ever visited the shore. Not the subsistence pattern, but only the early date of Monte Verde might imply a coastal route, because it leaves so little time for the long journey from a just-opened corridor almost to the tip of South America. Furthermore, the absence of any similar sites of comparable antiquity in North America can be conveniently explained by supposing a journey by boat that left no traces on the land.

Two sites found recently in coastal southern Peru, which seem to present much clearer evidence of a truly marine adaptation, also have been cited in support of a coastal migration model. At Quebrada Tacahuay, a hearth dated to ca. 10,500–10,800 BP (ca. 10,100–10,900 cal BC) was associated with bones of cormorants, boobies, anchovies, and seals (Keefer et al. 1998;

deFrance et al. 2001). Quebrada Jaguay 280, 220 kilometers to the north, has dates of ca. 11,100–9850 BP (ca. 11,000–9300 cal BC), with remains of drumfish and clams (Sandweiss et al. 1998; Sandweiss et al. 2000). The anchovies and drumfish imply the use of nets; indeed, probable net fragments were recovered at Quebrada Jaguay, and a polished marine mammal rib from Quebrada Tacahuay is interpreted as a possible net mesh gauge (deFrance et al. 2001). At Quebrada Jaguay, obsidian was found that can be traced to a source in the Andes, 130 kilometers inland. It was probably acquired there during the interior phase of a seasonal round that included terrestrial hunting as well as periodic visits to the shore.

Comparably early dates of ca. 11,000 BP have been obtained from Fell I or fishtail point occupations in Patagonia and the Pampas of Argentina (Nami 1996; Flegenheimer and Zarate 1997), where terrestrial hunting of horses and other Pleistocene fauna is attested. As Dillehay (2000:155–156) observes, the early Peruvian sites possessed the rudiments of a coastal marine technology, but "Quebrada Tacahuay and Quebrada Jaguay do not represent the first migrants moving south along the Pacific coast. Given the fact that older and contemporaneous sites exist in other parts of the continent, these Peruvian sites most likely represent interior groups adapting slowly to a stabilized environment shortly after 11,000 years ago."

In North America, there is, at present, no archaeological evidence for early coastal migration preceding Clovis occupation of the interior. Excavations at Daisy Cave (Erlandson and Moss 1996; Erlandson et al. 1996; Erlandson 1998) show that the Channel Islands off southern California were occupied by 10,400 BP (perhaps as early as 10,800 cal BP), and recent dating of Arlington Springs Woman to ca. 10,950 BP (Stafford et al. 2002) pushes this occupation back several centuries into the Clovis era, but not earlier. Farther north, the earliest known lithic industries on the coast of Alaska or British Columbia date to 9800 BP (ca. 9300 cal BC) (Ackerman 1992; Carlson 1998). A human mandible of about the same age was found in On-Your-Knees Cave on Prince of Wales Island (Fifield 1996; Dixon 1999). This is 2,000 years after Clovis expansion throughout North America at 11,500–11,000 BP (11,500–11,000 cal BC) (Fiedel 1999b). The Clovis complex had a thoroughly terrestrial hunting orientation, although these hunters did net or spear the occasional fish, as demonstrated by fishbones from Shawnee-Minisink, on the Delaware River (McNett ed. 1985).

In view of the weak evidence from the coast, the ice-free corridor deserves another look. It seems clear that it was not a prime choice for long-term occupation. Although people were living permanently in this area by

10,800 BP (ca. 10,800 cal BC), as shown by occupations at Charlie Lake Cave (Fladmark et al. 1988) and Vermilion Lakes (Fedje et al. 1995), that is too late to represent the first entry by Clovis ancestors (it should be noted, however, that the Charlie Lake Cave dates were run on bone collagen and may be underestimates). Sites marking the route of these pioneers should date to ca. 11,600 BP.

The Importance of Birds in Upper Paleolithic Siberia and Beringia

Who were these ancestors? Recent genetic data, lending support to the conclusions reached years ago by physical anthropologists (e.g., Hrdlička 1913), point to the area around Lake Baikal in southern Siberia as the ancestral homeland (Kolman 1996; Karafet et al. 1999; Santos et al. 1999). The Mal'ta-Afontova Upper Paleolithic culture (Gerasimov 1958) probably represents the ancestral population of ca. 25,000 BP (Haynes 1982, 1987). From the Baikal region, Clovis ancestors trekked northeast, across the land bridge, to eastern Beringia, now Alaska and the Yukon. As things now stand, there are two or three distinct cultures in that region that are plausible candidates for Clovis ancestry.

In northern Alaska, surface finds of fluted points cluster to the north of the Brooks Range. A dubious residue analysis (Loy and Dixon 1998) has reportedly identified mammoth blood and DNA on some of them (see Fiedel 1996). This could indicate that a mammoth-hunting culture, with fluted points, had already developed north of the ice sheets. Two fluted points from Sibbald Creek and similar "stubby" points from other loci in Alberta (Gryba 1983; Ives et al. 1993; Roberts and Julig 1997) are reported to resemble the Alaskan points, rather than Clovis or Folsom, and might indicate a southern extension of this early Alaskan proto-Clovis culture. However, the Alaska and Alberta points are not dated, and it is generally assumed that they represent a late reflux migration of Clovis people from the plains northward. Since there is no evidence that mammoth or even bison or caribou herds moved north when the ice sheets retreated, the impetus for this hypothetical migration is unclear.

A second candidate is the Nenana culture, which was present in central Alaska by 11,800 BP (ca. 11,900–11,400 cal BC). The Nenana lithic assemblage is characterized by macroblades, scrapers, and small triangular and teardrop-shaped points. The emphasis on large blades is shared with Clovis (Goebel et al. 1991) and appears to distinguish Nenana from the contemporaneous Paleoarctic or Denali tradition, characterized by microblade technology. However, a Nenana assemblage at Swan Point (Holmes et al. 1996) appears to include microblades. This has been attributed to mixing of deposits (Hamilton and Goebel 1999), but direct dating of residue on a microblade core fragment to 11,770±140 BP (AA-19322) (Holmes 1998) would appear to be conclusive evidence that the Nenana and microblade components at Swan Point are at least contemporaneous, if not elements of the same assemblage. So, Nenana may not be a distinctive culture after all, but only a seasonal or functional facies of the Paleoarctic tradition. If Nenana is a separate entity, its Siberian roots are not yet clear, but the Paleoarctic is clearly derived from the widespread Dyuktai culture of Siberia.

The Broken Mammoth site has provided the clearest picture of Nenana subsistence. The Nenana people seem to have collected and worked ivory from long-dead mammoths, leaving it an open question whether there were any mammoths still alive in central Alaska at 11,500 cal BC. They actually hunted elk, bison, sheep, and smaller game. But 40 percent of their meat came from waterfowl, mostly tundra (whistling) swans, as well as brants, various geese, and dabbling ducks such as mallard and teal (Yesner 1998). At Swan Point, seven kilometers away from Broken Mammoth, bones of geese (*Branta* sp.) and a large cervid were recovered (Holmes et al. 1996). Bird gastroliths, of a size suggestive of ptarmigan, were recognized at Dry Creek, in the Denali component (II), ca. 10,600–9300 BP (Hoffecker et al. 1996). In western Beringia, at Ushki 1 in Kamchatka (on the southern shore of Great Ushki Lake), Level VII (ca. 11,300 BP) (Goebel et al. 2002) contained pebbles identified as duck gastroliths (Dikov 1996). Level VI, the overlying microblade component (ca. 10,800 BP), yielded bones of ducks as well as fish, presumably salmonids (Goebel and Slobodin 1999:133, citing Dikov 1990). Within the ice-free corridor, Charlie Lake Cave contained bones of a large dabbling duck, in association with a stubby fluted point and collagen-derived dates of ca. 10,500 BP (Fladmark et al. 1988).

Not long after 12,000 cal BC (12,000 BP), the probable ancestors of Clovis were living in Alaska, often feasting on ducks and geese. Blocking their way to the south was a mile-high sheet of ice. But the great ice sheet was melting every year, as the warmer weather that had suddenly set in seven centuries earlier continued to prevail. A huge chasm was opening in the midst of the ice. Each year, as winter came on, the people would look skyward and watch the swans and the smaller birds fly south, across the ice. Eight months later (usually in April or early May, based on the behavior of their modern descendants), the birds would return. Where had they been? Obviously, there was habitable land somewhere to the south, beyond the ice. What the people didn't know was that they would have to walk 2,000 kilometers to get there.

Were Beringian people fascinated by birds in flight? Among the carved ivory figurines from Mal'ta, near Lake Baikal, are flying swans (Gerasimov 1958; Jelinek 1975:360, 429) (Figure 1.1A, B). Most of the identifiable birds depicted in European Upper Paleolithic art are ducks or geese; attention may have been focused on these species as harbingers of seasonal change (Mithen 1990). An ethnographic analog is provided by the Kutchin of central Alaska, who awaited the arrival of waterfowl as an indication of the beginning of warm spring weather (Nelson 1973). The people of Mal'ta probably derived 25 to 50 percent of their dietary protein from freshwater fish and waterfowl, based upon the results of a recent analysis of skeletal nitrogen isotopes (Richards et al. 2001). But their interest in birds was not merely pragmatic. An ancient belief in bird-human transformation is manifest in Eurasian mythology (e.g., the motif of the swan maiden [Leavy 1994]) and in shamanic practices. To this day, Siberian shamans are thought to take the form of birds during their spirit journeys, and specialize in mimicry of bird calls (La Barre 1972:176, 421). La Barre (1972:175–178, 419–422) theorized that there were two kinds of shamans in European Upper Paleolithic bands (as also in recent Siberian groups such as the Tungus): reindeer shamans and bird shamans. A juxtaposition of swans and possible shamanic figures is depicted on an Upper Magdalenian carved bone from Teyjat, France (Marshack 1972:260). A few millennia later, at 10,290±100 BP, a raven appears to have been ceremonially deposited in Charlie Lake Cave (Driver 1999). Driver notes that various native peoples of western Canada believed that they could communicate with ravens. In the Cree vision quest, men sometimes perched on platforms to make contact with bird spirits. The Cree believed that a manito, a supernatural master, controlled the migrations of geese and ducks (Brightman 1993). Northern peoples clearly have long had an aesthetic and even spiritual focus on birds.

Did birds fly over the ice sheets? Williams and Webb (1996) suggest that the present-day flight paths of migratory birds in North America are not significantly different from those of the Last Glacial Maximum. Darlene McCuaig-Balkwill has recently identified skeletal remains of 18 species of migratory birds in the Bluefish Caves in the Yukon, near the Alaskan border. They date between ca. 25,000 and 10,000 BP, that is, during the Last Glacial Maximum. The caves also contain possible evidence of a human presence by 12,500 BP, perhaps even as early as 23,500 BP (Cinq-Mars and Morlan 1999). The birds include swallows, plovers, snowy and hawk owls, red-

FIGURE 1.1A. Ivory figurine (Jelinek 1975:429) depicting swan(?), from Mal'ta, Siberia, ca. 25,000–21,000 BP.

FIGURE 1.1B. Ivory figurines (Jelinek 1975:360) depicting swans(?) in flight, from Mal'ta, Siberia, ca. 25,000–21,000 BP.

tailed hawk, fly-catcher, redpoll, waxwing, snow bunting, phoebe, snow goose, and American wigeon (Anonymous 1999). These last two species are particularly notable because, unlike the various small birds and predators, they might have been of economic interest to Nenana people. Today, the Mackenzie–Great Lakes–Mississippi flyway is traversed by more birds than any other migration route in the world (Lincoln 1950). The present-day migration routes of the two main breeding populations of tundra swans recently have been delineated by satellite-tracking of individual birds (Bird Studies Canada n.d.; Ely et al. 1997) (Figure 1.2). The swans that breed in the Yukon-Kuskokwim Delta follow a route that is very similar to the least-effort route through the corridor hypothesized for Paleoindians (Anderson and Gillam 2000). The Mackenzie Delta swans follow a parallel route, beyond the eastern edge of the one-time corridor. This flight path would have taken them across glacier-covered terrain in the terminal Pleistocene, so one may suppose that their route at that time may have shifted westward and southward, to permit brief stops at proglacial lakes in the corridor. Swans must make frequent stops to accommodate the limited flight capability of their fledglings (Ely et al. 1997:689). Not all birds survive the trip; about 20 percent die during migration.

The mountain glaciers that now stretch between the Yukon and Alaska have swallowed up numerous stray animals over the years, including many birds: "Dozens of bird species migrate over the ice fields and surprisingly often crash by the flockful, later to turn up in snowbanks like raisins in a fruitcake." Among the well-preserved items currently emerging from melting 8,300-year-old ice in the Yukon are "whole freeze-dried birds and rodents." Within hours after exposure, these carcasses may be scavenged by ravens that "may not mind eating even 8000-year-old meat" (Krajick 2002:454).

The use of birds as scouts to discover distant, unseen lands is a motif of some of the most ancient recorded myths. In the Akkadian Epic of Gilgamesh, Utnapishtim, afloat on the waters of the great flood, sent out first a dove, next a swallow, and finally a raven, in search of dry land (Speiser 1958:69–70). In the book of Genesis, Utnapishtim's counterpart, Noah, sent a raven, followed by a dove, on the same errand. Such observation of birds is probably a very ancient Eurasian tradition, with which Paleoindians would have been familiar (both archaeological and genetic evidence point to a lineal relationship between the southern Siberian ancestors of Paleoindians and the Russian branch of the pan-European Upper Paleolithic). The flying birds of the Akkadian and Hebrew myths have

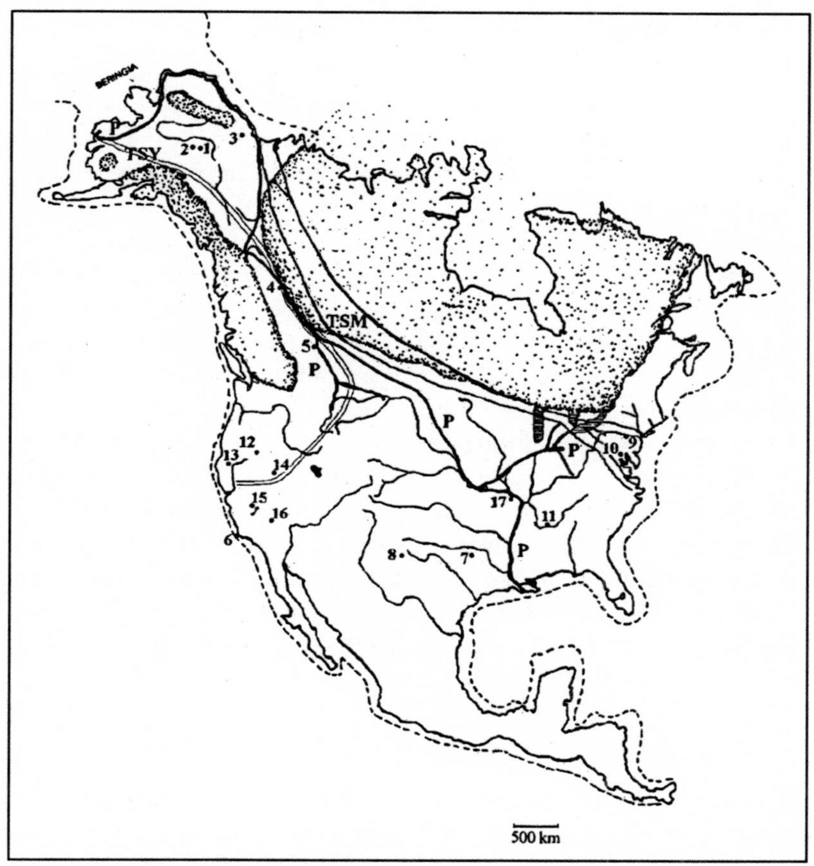

FIGURE 1.2. Annual fall migration routes of the tundra swans (TSY = Yukon-Kuskowim Delta population, TSM = Mackenzie Delta population) compared to least-effort Paleoindian route from Alaska through ice-free corridor (solid black line P) (after Anderson and Gillam 2000) and selected Paleoindian sites mentioned in text. 1, Broken Mammoth and Swan Point; 2, Nenana sites; 3, Bluefish Caves; 4, Charlie Lake Cave; 5, Sibbald Creek; 6, Daisy Cave; 7, Aubrey; 8, Lubbock Lake; 9, Shawnee-Minisink; 10, Higgins; 11, Dust Cave; 12, Dietz; 13, Borax Lake; 14, Fishbone Cave and Pyramid Lake; 15, Tulare Lake; 16, China Lake; 17, Kimmswick. Stippled areas represent ice sheets ca. 12,000 BP (12,000 cal BC).

swimming counterparts in several versions of the "Earth-Diver" story that was widespread among North American and Central and Northeast Asian native peoples (Count 1935). A culture-hero, afloat on the waters of the primordial world, delegates a series of aquatic animals to dive in search of the bottom-mud from which the earth will be formed. In the Arapaho version of this tale, ducks, geese, and swans, diving successively, fail in this quest, but turtle succeeds (Marriott and Rachlin 1975). In the Amur Basin version, three swans and three unspecified animal divers undertake the same task (Okladnikov 1981:19). A remarkable Paiute tale, which seems to be a variant of the Earth-Diver story, was recently quoted in the *National Geographic* (Parfit 2000:43): "Ice had formed ahead of them and it reached all the way to the sky. The people could not cross it. . . . A Raven flew up and struck the ice and cracked it. Coyote said, 'These small people can't get across the ice.' Another Raven flew up again and cracked the ice again. Coyote said, 'Try again, try again.' Raven flew up again and broke the ice. The people ran across." Did the Paiutes retain an oral tradition, for 13,000 years, of their ancestors' passage through the corridor? The detail of sky-high ice is difficult to explain otherwise. In view of the central role of the ravens in this story, the discovery of a carefully interred raven at Charlie Lake Cave acquires an eerie resonance. Haynes (2002a) suggests that Paleoindian hunters may have developed big game–tracking strategies involving observation of, and even active collaboration with, ravens and wolves. Perhaps survival during the corridor trek hinged upon discovery of ravens gathering to feast upon flocks of recently crashed and freeze-dried waterfowl.

Paleoindians and Waterfowl: The Archaeological Evidence

Obviously, northern hunting peoples have always been acute observers of the natural world; they could hardly have survived otherwise. It requires no new stretch of the imagination to attribute such awareness to ancestral Paleoindians. However, we do have to change our traditional view of Paleoindian migration strategies and motivations. They were not drawn south in hot pursuit of thundering herds of megafauna. If they had waited until the ice-free corridor was a pleasant place to live, filled with lush meadows that invited herds of caribou, elk, and bison, they might still have been sitting in Alaska at a time when we know that they had already inhabited North and even South America for centuries.

The earliest seemingly reliable Clovis dates (from the Aubrey site in Texas) are 11,540±110 and 11,590±90 BP (Ferring 1995), or ca. 11,500 cal BC; a comparable unpublished date for the Anzick burial is 11,550±60 (CAMS35912) (Dixon 1999:121, citing Stafford, personal communication 1997). However, the Aubrey dates might be outliers (as argued by Roosevelt et al. 2002), as the precise association with Clovis activities in the area is unclear; and Stafford (personal communication 2002) now would discard the early date for Anzick as inexplicably erratic. For the moment, a safe initial date for Clovis would be 11,100 BP, probably equivalent to 11,250 cal BC.

It appears that eastern Beringian grazers may not have found the corridor passable prior to ca. 10,000 BP (ca. 10,000–9300 cal BC), when a northern species, *B. bison occidentalis*, abruptly replaced *Bison antiquus* in the northern plains (Wilson 1996). This bison migration obviously occurred too late to have any connection with Clovis movements. In contrast, meltwater lakes accessible to waterfowl had already formed within the corridor prior to 11,600 BP. For example, ducks could have fed on the blue-green algae, which was most abundant between about 13,000 and 11,600 BP in Fairfax Lake, in west-central Alberta (Hickman and Schweger 1991). When the Paleoindian emigrants emerged from the southern opening of the corridor, they would have found similar meltwater lakes hosting waterfowl in the northern plains (Beaudoin 1998).

The Paleoindians must have ventured into the corridor when it was still rugged, barren, wet, and inhospitable—yet passable. This was not a slow, gradual, budding growth and expansion of hunters moving 80 kilometers per generation. I envision instead a rapid, planned, directed migration—rather like Moses leading the Israelites through the parted waters of the Red Sea (see also West 1996:555–556). We will never know the exact details of this epic trek across 2,000 kilometers in perhaps three months. Did a bird-shaman have a vision of the new land, imparted by his spirit familiar? Was a troop of adolescent boys sent into the void as an initiation ordeal? Was some sort of supply line established, passing packets of dried elk or bison pemmican down the line to the forward camps? Did the advance party sustain itself by netting injured or fatigued migrating birds on the shores of the proglacial lakes? Or did they depend upon discovery of freeze-dried carcasses emerging from the melting ice? All of these are plausible scenarios, well within the likely range of cultural capabilities of eastern Beringian proto-Paleoindians.

Was the allure of potentially habitable lands to the south enough to warrant exploratory probes, or might some "push" factor have lent some urgency to this quest? A recent study of paleo-lake levels in central Alaska (Abbott et al. 2000) indicates a sudden decrease in precipitation around 11,600 BP. Perhaps this drought severely affected the lake-edge resources on which Paleoindians relied, and economic stress drove them to undertake a desperate journey into the corridor. An additional exacerbating factor may have been a "domino effect" created by competition in Beringia between Nenana congeners and expanding Paleoarctic microblade makers.

Roberts and Julig (1997) have suggested that Paleoindians in the Great Lakes region, ca. 11,000–10,500 BP, retained a littoral adaptation that had been developed in eastern Beringia and employed along the proglacial lakes of the ice-free corridor. They infer a mixed economy, similar to that of recent boreal forest hunters, emphasizing caribou hunting and fishing (see Custer and Stewart [1990] for a similar reconstruction of Eastern Paleoindian lifeways). Dincauze and Jacobson (2001) propose that Paleoindians may have first entered northern New England by following waterfowl along a string of proglacial lakes. This route could explain the seemingly early discovery by fluted point-makers of the Munsungun chert source in Maine. The Aubrey site in north-central Texas, which has yielded the oldest credible Clovis-associated dates, was a camp on the eastern shore of a spring-fed pond. Burned turtle bones demonstrate consumption of these reptiles. The remainder of the faunal assemblage found at the pond edge is only loosely associated with the Clovis cultural material and may be mainly a natural accumulation. In any case, the 40 taxa recognized here include bison, deer, squirrel, bog lemming, muskrat, and "several kinds of rabbits, fishes, and birds" (Ferring 1995:277). Lakeside settlements of western Clovis are known at the Dietz site on Alkali Lake in Oregon (Willig 1996) and beside several pluvial lakes in California (Borax Lake, China Lake [Davis 1978], Tulare Lake) and Nevada (Lake Hubbs and Tonopah Lake). Dansie and Jerrems (1999) have identified a multibarbed harpoon made of ivory, directly dated to ca. 10,380 BP, from a site near Pyramid Lake in the western Great Basin; a Clovis association is likely for this probable fishing device. Indeed, it has been suggested recently (Stanford 1998; Boldurian and Cotter 1999; Dixon 1999) that the Clovis point-and-foreshaft weapons system may have been developed from a harpoon prototype.

We know from rare finds of preserved fauna that Paleoindians in North America collected turtles and fish. But fish may have been scarce in the proglacial lakes of the corridor. The earliest vegetation and insects, however, might have served as food for waterfowl; if these birds were alighting on the lakes, the Paleoindians evidently knew how to take them. In the recent past, Subarctic people typically used blunt-headed arrows (McKennan 1981:566; Hosley 1981:535) or, less often, snares (Honigmann 1981:220; McLennan and Denniston 1981:377), to hunt birds. Paleoindians did not have the bow yet, but they almost certainly used spearthrowers. In the 1940s, the Tarascans of Lake Patzcuaro, Mexico, still hunted ducks from canoes, using atlatls and multipronged spears (Stirling 1960). The Nunivak Eskimo of the Bering Sea hunted sea birds in the same way (Lantis 1984:214), and the

Caribou Eskimo used a double-pointed dart when hunting waterfowl from a kayak (Arima 1984:449). Paleoindian use of watercraft is not improbable (Engelbrecht and Seyfert 1994; Jodry 1999a), so they could have used this method. It is also likely that Paleoindians took birds in nets. This technique is attested in the Contact period in the Great Basin (Fowler 1986:82–87), New England (Salwen 1978:162), and Alaska (Lantis 1984:214). As noted above, marine birds appear to have been netted by Paleoindian inhabitants of the Peruvian coast ca. 10,700 BP (de France et al. 2001). Netting is known from East European Upper Paleolithic sites (Adovasio et al. 1996). Cordage is attested by impressions on 12,000 BP pottery in Japan and the Russian Far East, and fiber technology is evident at Great Basin sites at ca. 11,000 BP (Lysek 1997; Hyland et al. 2000). A partial human skeleton in Fishbone Cave, in western Nevada, was accompanied by fine netting and pieces of baskets, cordage, and matting. The textile fragments yielded radiocarbon dates of 11,555±500 and 10,900±300 BP (Orr 1956; Dixon 1999:132–133; Lysek 1997) (however, Jerrems and Dansie [2002] have redated this context and indicate a more recent age). A Late Paleoindian net from northern Wyoming, presumed to have been used in hunting large game such as pronghorn, deer, or mountain sheep, has been directly dated at 8860±170 BP (ca. 8050 cal BC) (Frison et al. 1986).

Remains of waterfowl and other birds have been identified at many Paleoindian sites. An ostensibly cut-marked swan bone was found at the base of the stratified cultural deposits, and just above Glacier Peak tephra (ca. 11,200 BP), in the Marmes Rockshelter in Washington. This bone was directly dated to 11,230±50 BP (Beta-156698) (Hicks 2004:391–392). Bones of unidentified avian species were associated with a Clovis-era mastodon kill at Kimmswick, Missouri (Graham and Kay 1988). At Lubbock Lake, Texas, a turkey leg-bone found at a probable Clovis processing station (FA 2–1) bore cutmarks. Folsom-age bone piles (FA 6–8) contained wing and pectoral bones of ducks, which seem to have been pulled apart at the joints, leaving no butchering marks. The Late Paleoindian (ca. 8600 BP, or 7600 cal BC) Firstview component at Lubbock Lake yielded remains of mallard, cinnamon teal, gadwall, pintail, and grouse (Johnson 1977, 1987:123–131). In the Great Basin, bones of birds, along with fish and marmot, were found in an early context at Fishbone Cave; at the Old Humboldt site, waterfowl eggshells were recovered (Willig 1991, 1996). Apparent turkey feather fragments were recovered from a possible Clovis feature (it might be Archaic) at the Higgins site in Maryland (Ebright 1992:410). The lowest, Late Paleoindian levels of Dust Cave, Alabama (ca. 10,500 BP), contain mainly bones of small game and waterfowl (Walker 2000; Walker et al. 2001). Lynch (1983:121) noted the frequent occurrence of bones of the partridgelike *tinamou* in South American Late Paleoindian contexts: "Archeologists have probably underemphasized birds (a duck was also identified in Guitarrero II) and especially ground-dwelling birds, as potential early game animals." In fact, the lowest levels of Fell's Cave in Patagonia contained, in addition to horse, guanaco, and ground sloth, bones of several geese, ducks, and other birds (Borrero and Franco 1997).

The apparent ceremonial interment of a raven at Charlie Lake Cave (Driver 1999) has already been mentioned. The recently reported discovery of a Late Paleoindian cache of goose humeri in Dust Cave (Walker and Parmalee 2004) suggests some nonutilitarian function was intended for these bones—perhaps as flutes or, with feathers attached, as ornaments or fans. In Fishbone Cave, the human burial contained also "the well-preserved skin of a young pelican" (Dixon 1999:133). Similar evidence of the ritual treatment of birds was reported recently from Quebrada Jaguay in Peru, where gulls or terns were wrapped in fiber and deposited in postholes of a domestic structure, shortly after 10,000 BP (ca. 9400 cal BC) (Sandweiss et al. 2000).

The importance of aquatic birds in Paleoindian subsistence should not be exaggerated. The large and exquisite fluted points that characterize classic Clovis assemblages clearly were not designed to bring down or butcher fowl. Once they emerged from the corridor into a hunter's paradise of naive megafauna, the Paleoindians probably preferred mammoth to mallard. Even so, they often found proboscideans and other large game, perhaps under the compulsion of extended drought conditions (Haynes 1991), at lake or swamp edges. Paleoindian hunting tactics may even have derived from the Subarctic or Arctic, where caribou were often taken by spearing them from canoes or kayaks as they crossed lakes or rivers (see Rogers and Smith [1981:132] for the Naskapi and Chipewyan and Arima [1984:448–449] for the Caribou Eskimo). Overall, Paleoindian subsistence and settlement patterns probably retained a lacustrine focus, which could be extended with minimal innovation to the sea coast. We should not be surprised to find that the earliest people in South America could dine alternately on horse, mastodon, and deer at Tagua Tagua, a lakeshore kill site in Chile (Nunez and Santoro 1990), and on cormorants, anchovies, and clams at Quebrada Tacahuay.

TWO

Faunal Extinction, Hunter-Gatherer Foraging Strategies, and Subsistence Diversity among Eastern Beringian Paleoindians

David R. Yesner

Until recently, the lifeways of the earliest immigrants to eastern Beringia (Alaska and the Yukon Territory) have been largely a matter of conjecture, based upon vegetative reconstructions and the limited paleontological record. Furthermore, reconstructions based upon the paleontological record are affected by the fact that the greatest abundance of fossils date to the Last Glacial Maximum or earlier (i.e., 20,000–30,000 BP; Harington 1978; Pewe 1975), while the current archaeological record for eastern Beringia is no older than the terminal Pleistocene. This fact is important, because the initial human occupation of interior Alaska—defined as the region of unglaciated valleys extending northward from the Alaska Range—apparently took place during the period of relatively rapid climatic amelioration from around 14,000 to 9,000 BP. This period is characterized as the "Birch Interval," during which scrub birch and willow colonized the xeric "tundra-steppe" of the Last Glacial Maximum (Ager 1975; Ager and Brubaker 1985; Hopkins 1979; Edwards et al. 2001). This probably resulted in a shift from a more continental to a maritime climate associated with inundation of the Bering Land Bridge (Young 1982), which more recent data (Elias et al. 1992;) suggest was not completed until after 12,500 BP.

These climatic and vegetational transformations resulted in "immediate and profound effects on the other elements of the ecosystem, including particularly the large mammals" (Young 1982:191). The limited zooarchaeological record associated with the oldest sites in eastern Beringia may track this change: for example, at the Trail Creek site in western Alaska and Bluefish Caves in the Yukon Territory, both of which contain a fossil record that dates to ca. 14,000 BP. At these sites, as in most paleontological and archaeological contexts from eastern Beringia, bison fossils are the most abundant (Matthews 1982:140), along with a variety of other late Pleistocene taxa, including *Rangifer* (caribou), *Cervus elaphus* (wapiti), *Ursus* (bear), and *Ovis* (mountain sheep) (Vinson 1993; Morlan and Cinq-Mars 1982). Perhaps most notable is the presence at both Trail Creek and Bluefish Caves of *Mammuthus* (mammoth) and *Equus* (horse) fossils, which are absent from sites dated after 12,000 BP, and both may have become extinct by the time of the "Poplar Rise." Two late paleontological dates on mammoth include 10,050 BP at Lost Chicken Creek (Harington 1978) and 11,360 BP at Trail Creek Caves (Vinson 1993), but questions have been raised about the validity of both of these dates. As a result Guthrie and Guthrie (1990:41) argued that mammoth extinction occurred shortly before human occupation of eastern Beringia, and that "Asian immigrants . . . probably walked Alaskan mammoth trails that were still tracked and dusty."

At the Dry Creek archaeological site in the Nenana Valley south of Fairbanks, dated as early as 11,100 BP, excavations during the mid-1970s uncovered tooth fragments of bison, wapiti, and mountain sheep, but not mammoth or horse. This was particularly important, because many have doubted the archaeological status of earlier sites such as the Trail Creek or Bluefish Caves. The overall impression from the scanty remains of Dry Creek was that the landscape into which the earliest known hunters of interior Alaska moved was a mosaic of grassland and shrubs, generally associated with more mesic precipitation and warmer temperatures than during the LGM (Last Glacial Maximum), and supporting a fauna of gregarious herd species such as bison and wapiti. These herd populations would have found refugia in areas such as the broad outwash floodplains of the Nenana and Tanana river valleys, where high-quality grazing forage would have been maintained, and increasing snowfall would have been counteracted by high wind velocities (Guthrie 1982, 1983b; Guthrie and Guthrie 1990).

Unfortunately, because of the scanty preservation associated with Dry Creek and other Nenana Valley sites, little else could be said about the nature of the foraging strategies, settlement patterns, or overall dietary diversity of the earliest settlers of interior Alaska (Hoffecker 1988; Thorson 1990). However, the discovery of the Broken Mammoth site in the Shaw Creek Flats region of the central Tanana River valley, east-central Alaska (Holmes and Yesner 1992; Holmes 1996; Yesner 1996, 2001), along with the subsequent discovery of the nearby Mead and Swan Point sites, has presented new opportunities to evaluate the nature of late Pleistocene/early Holocene lifeways in interior Alaska. Excavations at these sites during the period from 1990 to 2005 have revealed the first well-preserved evidence of late Pleistocene human subsistence in eastern Beringia. Loess deposits at these sites contain a series of archaeological components, the earliest of which date to late Pleistocene and early Holocene times. These components are contained within paleosols that have preserved an excellent record of late Pleistocene/early Holocene human occupation. Included in these deposits are lithic artifacts and features referable to the Nenana Complex of late Pleistocene times (Goebel et al. 1991; Hoffecker et al. 1993). Also included, however, are well-preserved organic materials, including bone artifacts, faunal remains (including mammal, bird, and fish bone; mammoth tusk fragments; terrestrial snail shell; and insect carapaces), and plant macrofossils. The study of these materials is greatly amplifying our understanding of the subsistence, foraging strategies, settlement patterns, domestic activities, and material disposal patterns of early occupants of eastern Beringia.

The Broken Mammoth Site

The Broken Mammoth site (Figure 2.1) is located on a 30-meter bluff overlooking the confluence of Shaw Creek and the Tanana River, ca. 100 kilometers southeast of Fairbanks, Alaska. It represents a typical interior Alaskan "overlook" site from which game could easily be sighted and a variety of microenvironments could be exploited (Hoffecker 1988). Basal paleosols at the Broken Mammoth site have preserved two archaeological components that have been labeled Cultural Zones 3 and 4 (Holmes and Yesner 1992; Holmes 1996; Yesner 1996, 2001). Cultural Zone 3 is separated from the upper cultural zones by 75–90 centimeters of culturally sterile loess and sands. It is associated with the Middle Paleosol Complex within the basal site stratigraphy, and has provided radiocarbon dates ranging from 9,300 to 10,300 BP, including one hearth dated to 10,300 BP. Several large hearth smears with associated hearth stones were uncovered in Cultural Zone 3, with artifacts and butchered faunal material scattered in and around the hearths. Diagnostic artifacts include basally thinned, edge-ground bifacial projectile points; other small bifaces; large blades; flake cores; choppers; hammerstones; and anvils. Most of the formal bone tools recovered from excavations at the Broken Mammoth site were also found in this cultural zone, including several ivory and bone rods, an eyed needle, a bone toggle or fastener, and a cache of mammoth ivory hunting tools, including a rod and possible atlatl handle.

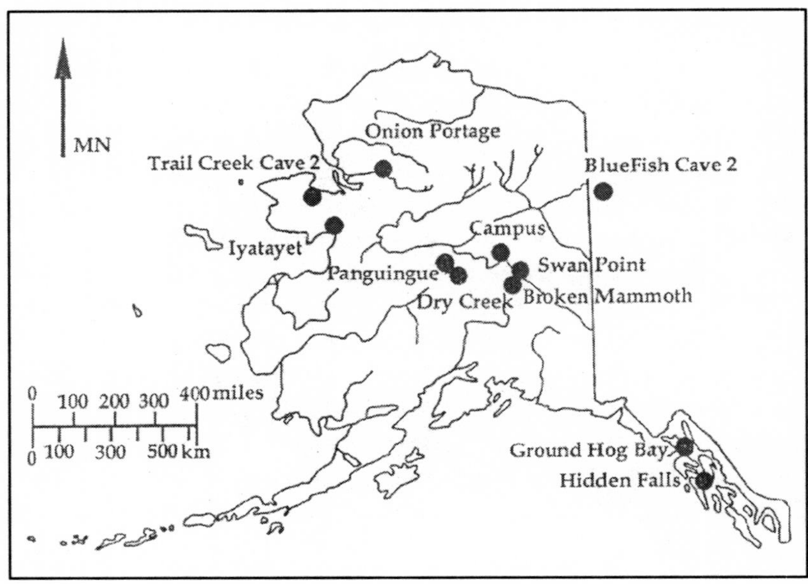

FIGURE 2.1. Late Pleistocene/Early Holocene archaeological sites in Alaska, indicating the location of the Broken Mammoth site.

Cultural Zone 4 at the Broken Mammoth site comprises the oldest cultural material found there. It is associated with the Lower Paleosol Complex, located around 15–25 centimeters below Cultural Zone 3 and above a 50-centimeter-thick late Pleistocene sterile sand unit. Radiocarbon dates for Cultural Zone 4 range from 11,000 to 11,800 BP. Several large hearth smears were also excavated for Cultural Zone 4. Here, too, abundant butchered faunal remains, including a large number of avian remains, were found scattered in and around the hearths. Artifacts include large unifacial core-scrapers, flake cores, and other unifacial and bifacial materials, as well as choppers, anvils, and hammerstones. Large workshop areas were also uncovered, particularly for the reduction of local quartz ventifacts and river cobbles. Only one mammoth ivory tool has been recovered from this unit.

Faunal Remains

In addition to the artifactual remains, over 10,000 faunal elements have been recovered from the Broken Mammoth site (Table 2.1), and 1,000 faunal elements were recovered from the Mead and Swan Point sites. Ninety percent of the faunal sample from these sites derives from the late Pleistocene/early

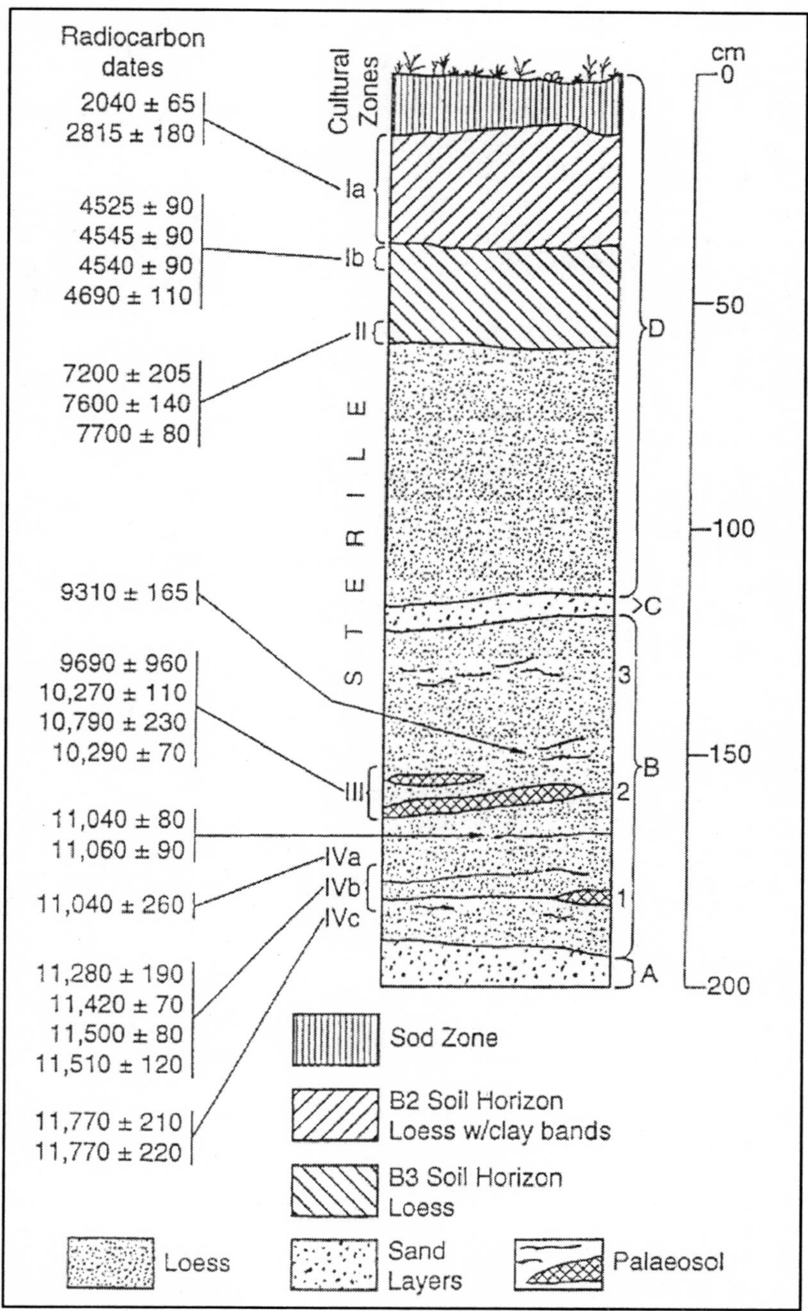

FIGURE 2.2. Stratigraphy and radiocarbon dates from the Broken Mammoth site.

TABLE 2.1. Numbers of identified species (NISP) from the Broken Mammoth archaeological sites, Cultural Zones 3 and 4 (1990–1991 data).

Taxon	Common Name	Zone 3	Zone 4	Total
FISH				
Cycloid/salmonid	trout/salmon	28		28
BIRD				
Cygnus columbianus	tundra swan	41	525	586
Branta canadensis	Canada goose	2	22	24
Anser albifrons	white fronted goose	12	54	66
Chen caerulescens	snow goose	5	35	40
Anas platyrhynchos	mallard	6	24	30
Anas acuta	pintail	2	36	38
Anas strepera	gadwall		4	4
Anas americana	widgeon		2	2
Anas carolinensis	green-winged teal	6	22	28
Lagopus lagopus	willow ptarmigan	23	77	100
Subtotal	identified birds	97	801	898
Unidentified bird		117	363	480
MAMMAL				
Bison priscus	super bison	87	21	108
Cervus elaphus	elk, wapiti	133	44	177
Rangifer tarandus	caribou	6		6
Alces alces	moose		4	4
Ovis dalli	mountain sheep	11		11
Mammuthus primigenius	woolly mammoth	?	?	(tusk)
Subtotal	identified large mammals	237	69	306
Ursus arctos	brown bear		1	1
Canis sp.	wolf	1		1
Alopex lagopus	Arctic fox	13	18	31
Lutra canadensis	river/land otter		6	6
Subtotal	identified carnivores	14	19	39
Unidentified large/medium mammals		639	329	968
Lepus sp.	hare	33	44	77
Marmota flavescens	hoary marmot	8	5	13
Ochotona collaris	collared pika	3		3
Subtotal	identified small mammals	44	49	93
Spermophilus parryi	Arctic ground squirrel*	298	305	603
Sorex arcticus	Arctic shrew*	9	11	20
Subtotal	microtine rodents*	165	151	316
Unidentified small mammal		108	173	281
Unidentified mammal		203	111	314
Unidentified fragments		1,067	976	2,043
Total Identifiable (NISP)		**420**	**938**	**1,358**

* These taxa assumed not used by humans, not included in NISP

Holocene strata, largely because of better preservational conditions. The sample from the Broken Mammoth site, which has been best studied to date, includes a diverse spectrum of large animal species, including large game, mostly bison (*Bison priscus*) and wapiti (*Cervus elaphus*), with smaller amounts of caribou (*Rangifer tarandus*), moose (*Alces alces*), and mountain sheep (*Ovis* cf. *dalli*). The size of the bison and wapiti remains from the Broken Mammoth site suggests that both represent the larger Pleistocene forms. Woolly mammoth (*Mammuthus Pnmigenius*) remains were also retrieved from the site, but these were limited exclusively to tusk fragments. Whether these mammoth ivory remains represent animals hunted by contemporaneous human populations is still an open question.

Direct AMS (Accelerator Mass Spectrometry) radiocarbon dates on remnant collagen in mammoth ivory from the Broken Mammoth, Mead, and Swan Point sites have provided divergent results. Most dates from the Broken Mammoth and Mead sites were between 17,000 and 15,000 BP, but two specimens from the Broken Mammoth and Swan Point sites have provided dates of 11,500 and 12,000 BP, respectively, suggesting possible contemporaneity with the earliest dated human occupation at these sites. However, no postcranial mammoth remains have been uncovered from any of the Tanana Valley sites, and the recovery of mammoth ivory points, sections of split mammoth tusk, and a microchip embedded in a groove within one piece of mammoth ivory suggests a well-established ivory-based industry, and that mammoth tusks were being scavenged primarily for tool production (Yesner 2000).

In addition to large game, small mammal remains are abundant in the late Pleistocene/early Holocene strata. The most abundant remains are from hare (*Lepus*), marmot (*Marmota*), beaver (*Castor*), otter (*Lutra*), pika (*Ochotona*), and ground squirrel (*Spermophilus*). Also present throughout the site are large numbers of microtine rodent and insectivore bones, including three species of *Microtus* (voles), as well as *Sorex* (shrews) and *Dicrostonyx* (lemmings). Many of these are found articulated in krotovina rodent burrows or other noncultural contexts, and none are burned, suggesting that they are intrusive. Ground squirrel bones occur in similar contexts, but are also found in association with occupation surfaces, and are occasionally burned, suggesting utilization.

The remains of two carnivores have been found in the deposits: *Alopex* (Arctic fox), known from a number of specimens, and a possible distal humerus of *Canis lupus* (timber wolf). In general, there is little evidence of interest in the taking of either large or small carnivores, as a source of either food or furs. There was, however, great interest in the taking of a wide variety of species of birds, principally waterfowl (swans, geese, and ducks), evidently already abundant in late Pleistocene times. This suggests that the North Pacific flyway had already been reestablished following dissolution of the Bering Land Bridge, and that the Tanana Valley may have been an important nesting area. They include *Cygnus columbianus* (tundra swan), *Branta canadensis* (Canada goose), *Anser albifrons* (white-fronted goose), *Anser caerulescens* (snow goose), *Anas platyrhynchos* (mallard), *Anas acuta* (pintail), and *Anas crecca* (green-winged teal). In addition, the willow ptarmigan (*Lagopus lagopus*) was extensively used, constituting about 15 percent of the avian remains. Fish are also represented in the assemblage by a species of salmonid, possibly grayling. Both mammal and bird remains from the lower strata at the Broken Mammoth site were characterized by a high degree of fragmentation, much of which appears to be intentional, since it is associated with impact marks on meat-bearing bones.

Patterns of Dietary Diversity

Microenvironments Utilized

The taxa represented in the Broken Mammoth faunal assemblage indicate wide utilization of paleomicroenvironments adjacent to the site: dry steppe/tundra (bison, elk, caribou); wetlands (fish, waterfowl, beaver, otter); and uplands (marmot, ground squirrel, Dall sheep, ptarmigan). As today, extensive wetlands were probably present in the Tanana Valley immediately below the site; their exact location and extent probably depended on the postglacial dynamics of the Tanana River. Upland species would have been available to the north of the site, with more extensive areas to the south, in the foothills of the Alaska Range. Large grazing mammals were probably found both in the Tanana Valley floodplain and in adjacent Shaw Creek Flats, an important refugium for these taxa. The change from open savanna to scrub parkland in these areas may have been associated with changes in animal adaptations, including reductions in herd size and gregarious behavior, reductions in herd migration distances, and reductions in male aggressiveness and agonistic competition. All of these can be expected to have had important impacts on human populations colonizing that landscape.

Foraging Strategies and Dietary Breadth

Although analyses of faunal remains from the Broken Mammoth site remain incomplete, there are some general observations that can be made about subsistence patterns and diet. The wide range of species represented at the site and other sites in the central Tanana Valley suggests a broad-spectrum diet that probably included most animals available to the human population. If the difference in the relative importance of large mammals and birds in Cultural Zones 3 and 4 is not attributable to shifts in avian flyways or changes in the location or flow patterns of the Tanana River or backwater lakes and tributaries within its floodplain, then it is most likely due to changes in foraging strategies, including seasonality of site occupation. In any case, the abundance of bird remains in Cultural Zone 4 suggests that this food resource may have been a key factor in attracting human populations to the site. In addition, the recovery of fish remains in Cultural Zone 3 may indicate the establishment of fish populations, a further broadening of the diet, or a shift in seasonality of site occupation.

Measures of Species Diversity

In order to quantify the diversity of the faunal assemblages in the late Pleistocene/early Holocene units at the Broken Mammoth site, a variety of measures were used, including standard diversity measures based simply on species "richness" (the total number of species exploited, standardized by the total numbers of individuals, or, in this case, the Number of Identified Specimens [NISP]), and "heterogeneity" measures that include species "evenness" (the degree to which exploitation was concentrated on some species or was more evenly distributed among the total range of species). Thus, more "homogeneous" exploitation patterns showing a greater degree of concentration on individual species would be numerically less "diverse," even if the total number of species exploited were greater. The latter statistics are the most meaningful for examining the overall diversity of the total assemblage, because they allow expression of that diversity on a scale from 0 to 1. On that basis, the modified Simpson Index (e.g., Whittaker 1972) shows a value of 0.791, suggesting high overall diversity. Similarly, the Shannon-Weaver statistic, based on information theory (e.g., Pielou 1975; see also Walker, this volume) shows a value of 0.825, again reflecting a highly diverse assemblage. An attempt was also made to calculate species diversity after "partitioning" unidentifiable large mammal, small mammal, and bird bones among the various identified taxa within each one of those categories. The results showed a marginal increase in overall taxonomic diversity, resulting in a Simpson Index of 0.818 rather than 0.791.

Temporal Changes in Dietary Diversity

The faunal assemblage recovered from the Cultural Zone 3 at the Broken Mammoth site is dominated by large ungulates. This is reflected by the dominance of large mammal bone fragments from this unit (around 60 percent of both the identifiable and nonidentifiable specimens), followed by small mammal and bird remains. Among the identifiable large mammal remains, wapiti are numerically dominant (around 50 percent), followed by bison (35 percent) and caribou (15 percent). A few elements of caribou and mountain sheep are also represented, as well as woolly mammoth in the form of ivory tools. Carnivores included are the Arctic fox and timber wolf. Small mammals contributed about 30 percent of the total assemblage and were numerically dominated by the Arctic ground squirrel (around 50 percent of the assemblage), followed by insectivores, rodents, hare, hoary marmot, and collared pika. Finally, birds contributed only about 10 percent of the faunal assemblage in Cultural Zone 3 and were attributable to three genera of waterfowl: *Anas* sp. (dabbling ducks), *Anser* sp. (geese), and *Branta* sp. (brants). Salmonid fishes, however, were also represented in Cultural Zone 3 by a dozen vertebral elements as well as two fish scales. These elements may represent the Arctic grayling, currently present in the area.

The character of the faunal assemblage from Cultural Zone 4 differs significantly from that of Cultural Zone 3. In particular, while only 20 percent of the taxonomically identifiable elements in Cultural Zone 3 were from birds, approximately 70 percent of the elements from Cultural Zone 4 were from birds. Thus, the Cultural Zone 4 assemblage was dominated by bird bones and bone fragments (60 percent of both the identifiable and nonidentifiable specimens), followed by large mammal remains (around 25 percent of the assemblage) and small mammal remains (around 15 percent of the assemblage). Among the identifiable large mammal remains, bison were numerically dominant (ca. 60 percent), followed by wapiti (32 percent) and moose (10 percent). No definitive elements of other large game species have been recovered from Cultural Zone 4, except for woolly mammoth, represented exclusively by ivory (tusk fragments). Carnivores included the Arctic fox and brown bear. The small mammal assemblage was similar to that of Cultural Zone 3 and was numerically dominated by the Arctic ground squirrel (ca. 50 percent of the assemblage), followed by insectivores/rodents, hare, and hoary marmot. River otter was also represented. In general, there was a lower species diversity of mammalian taxa in Cultural Zone 4 than in Cultural Zone 3. One possibility is that it is a result of shifts in seasonality of site occupation or other aspects of changing foraging strategies, or simply a by product of the smaller sample site of mammalian fauna present in Cultural Zone 4.

As noted above, birds contributed about 60 percent of the faunal assemblage in Cultural Zone 4 and represented a wider diversity of species than found in any of the other site components. The avian assemblage was dominated by the tundra (whistling) swan (*Cygnus columbianus*), which constituted 45 percent of identifiable bird remains. Since this was the only large bird represented in the assemblage (with the exception of a single distal mandible fragment that may be attributable to a large accipiter), it can be assumed that the large bird long-bone fragments that dominate the unidentifiable bird remains (also around 45 percent) are similarly attributable to this species. Approximately 20 percent of the identifiable bird remains are attributable to three species of geese (*Branta canadensis*, *Anser albifrons*, and *Anser caerulescens*), and 20 percent are attributable to three species of dabbling ducks (*Anas platyrhynchos*, *Anas acuta*, and *Anas crecca*). The willow ptarmigan (*Lagopus lagopus*) is represented in 15 percent of the assemblage. As noted above, the abundant remains of waterfowl in Cultural Zone 4 at the Broken Mammoth site testify to the fact that already by 12,000 BP, the North Pacific avian flyway had been reestablished, following the dissolution of the Bering Land Bridge, and perhaps that modern breeding areas had become established in backwater areas along the braided Tanana River floodplain (for discussion, see Fiedel, this volume). All of the avian remains recovered in Cultural Zones 3 and 4 reflect extant species, with the possible exception of the mandible of an unidentified large raptor. No fish remains have been identified in Cultural Zone 4.

Richness and Evenness

Applying both the "richness" and "evenness" measures of diversity discussed above was even more useful in distinguishing the relative diversity of the faunal assemblages associated with the late Pleistocene and early Holocene occupations. The two "richness" measures used showed similar results: Margalef's statistic ([S-1]/ln N) showed an overall species richness of 3.824 for Cultural Zone 3 and 2.901 for Cultural Zone 4, while Odum's statistic (S/log N) showed an overall species richness of 7.450 for Cultural Zone 3 and 5.407 for Cultural Zone 4, indicating the greater number of taxa recorded for Cultural Zone 3 (mean values for the site as a whole were 3.361 for Margalef's statistic and 6.548 for Odum's statistic). Measures of species heterogeneity, which include "evenness" as well as "richness" measures, showed relatively less difference between the occupations: Simpson's Index showed a value of 0.852 for Cultural Zone 3 and 0.795 for Cultural Zone 4, while the Shannon-Weaver Index showed a value of 0.895 for Cultural Zone 3 and 0.814 for Cultural Zone 4. In both cases, however, the overall diversity of Cultural Zone 3 was greater.

Paleoenvironmental Change

One explanation for the changes in dietary diversity seen in the late Pleistocene and early Holocene cultural zones at the Broken Mammoth site is that they are related to paleoenvironmental change. Based on sediment size and accumulation rate, Bigelow et al. (1990) have suggested that the time interval between the basal components at Dry Creek and other Nenana Valley sites, representing several centuries to a millennium at the end of the Pleistocene, may represent a cold, windy period of climatic deterioration equivalent to the European Younger Dryas episode. On the basis of radiocarbon date distributions from late Pleistocene sites, Kunz and Reanier (1994) have suggested that the Younger Dryas interval is represented in the interior as well as northern Alaska. However, sedimentological analysis at the Broken Mammoth site does not confirm this, since there is no perceptible change in sediment size until after the earliest Holocene cultural zone (3), and accumulation rates do not appear to alter significantly until that time. Spruce and alder colonized the region after 4,000 BP (Ager 1973), but this is probably the result of a similar process and not clearly interpretable climatically. In the faunal record from Broken Mammoth, one could cite only the greater presence of Arctic species such as caribou, Arctic fox, timber wolf, Arctic hare, Arctic ground squirrel, collared pika, and collared lemming continue to be present in Cultural Zone 3 in defense of this hypothesis. Nevertheless, it is likely that interior Alaska was first occupied during a somewhat warmer and wetter period, and was affected to some degree by the Younger Dryas cooling.

Seasonality

Perhaps a more profitable analysis of changes in species diversity between Cultural Zones 3 and 4 at the Broken Mammoth site relates to changes in seasonality of site occupation and its relation to overall settlement patterning. For Cultural Zone 4, the abundant remains of migratory waterfowl suggest either a spring or late summer/fall utilization of the site. Several immature elements from geese and ducks suggest that spring may be a more likely scenario. Spring occupation of the site may help to explain the high degree of comminution of the large mammal bones found in Cultural Zone 4, suggesting a major utilization of long bones, in particular, for marrow extraction and bone grease/soup production during a more difficult time of year. These activities may be correlated with the high number of large cobble tools known from this occupation. Alternatively, the latter may reflect either a very short period of site occupation or a lack of knowledge of lithic resources, resulting in the manufacture of expedient tools for primary carcass reduction.

For Cultural Zone 3, a similar analysis of both wapiti and bison teeth suggests a primary occupation in late fall/winter. In addition, tooth eruption patterns from a juvenile bison mandible in that component are consistent with late fall/winter occupation at 17 months of age. Perhaps it is noteworthy that these mammalian remains cluster at the western end of the site, in association with a large hearth feature; in fact, bone dispersal in this part of the site reflects the characteristics of a "toss zone" (Binford 1978a, 1978b: Krasinsky 2005; Yesner and Stone 2001). In contrast, fewer large mammal and more small mammal and bird remains cluster at the eastern end of the site, in relation to a smaller hearth area near which was found the eyed needle. The fish remains found in Cultural Zone 3 were from this area, suggesting that this somewhat distinct portion of the site may represent a different season of occupation. Alternatively, it may represent a difference in households occupying the site or male-female activity areas.

The abundance of large ungulate bones at the Broken Mammoth site suggest that these species were of considerable importance as concentrated, storable, high-biomass resources. There is good evidence to suggest that some of the primary butchering and much of the secondary butchering of game took place on site. Although cranial fragments are not well represented, mandibles are well represented, along with axial skeletal elements (ribs and vertebrae), which are nearly as well represented as meat-bearing carcass segments. In addition, although hind limbs are slightly better represented than forelimbs, the difference is not statistically significant. Elements frequently removed from kill sites (e.g., distal metapodials, carpals/tarsals, phalanges) are well represented. Cutmarks are infrequent because of surface erosion of the bone, but spiral fractures and impact points are common. Eventually, refitting experiments will be undertaken to reconstruct butchering and bone dispersal patterns, and to determine whether the latter represent toss zones, household middens, or merely palimpsests of bone accumulations in a deflated paleosol surface.

On the other hand, the great diversity of taxa recovered, particularly from the lowest levels at the Broken Mammoth site, suggests that waterfowl and other birds, small mammals (including aquatic mammals), and possibly fish may have been among the most important resources that attracted humans to the area. Techniques for mass harvesting such resources may have included nets or traps, evidence for which is apparently present in the European Upper Paleolithic. In areas farther from the Tanana River, where such resources were unavailable (e.g., at the Mead and Swan Point sites, as well as the newly excavated Gerstle River Quarry site about 80 kilometers to the southeast), large game appears to have predominated in the diet.

Paleoindian Dietary Diversity in Interior Alaska

Current interpretations of the artifactual, and particularly the faunal, data from the Broken Mammoth site suggest the following tentative conclusions:

1. In spite of changing environments of the Pleistocene/early "Holocene Birch Interval" and "Poplar Rise" in interior Alaska, as tundra/steppe gave way to open parkland, foraging strategies of the earliest human occupants continued to focus on large game whenever possible. However, by the time of the Broken Mammoth site occupation, some obligate grazers such as horse and mammoth may have been extinct. Other herd species such as bison and wapiti apparently survived in the refugia of the Nenana and Tanana valleys, where wind-cleared grasslands would have been maintained on the floodplain outwash. Some elements of the Pleistocene megafauna therefore survived—at least until the early Holocene period—and had apparently not yet undergone substantial size diminution. However, declining herd size and reduced herd gregariousness would have increased search and pursuit times, and therefore energetic return rates, of species such as bison and wapiti. The result of both of these phenomena would have been an increased relative advantage for mass harvesting of smaller, higher-cost game and fish, which are found in large seasonal aggregations. Thus, an increased exploitation of small game, birds, and fish apparently took place.

2. The high dietary diversity reflected at the middle Tanana Valley sites such as Broken Mammoth is also a reflection of their location and the nature of resources obtainable in the vicinity. From these sites, it was possible to scan for and intercept large game

migrating through the valley below, as well as to obtain large and small mammals from uplands surrounding the sites, and waterfowl, fish, and aquatic mammals from surrounding wetlands. In this regard, Broken Mammoth and other bluff-top encampments in interior Alaska probably represent "outlier spike camps" linked to a semipermanent base camp, perhaps in the river valley below (Guthrie 1983b:268). Such an "orb model," with "a moderately stable base camp and numerous outlier spike camps . . . in a radiating pattern away from the main hub" (Guthrie 1983b:269), would have maximized the use of large game resources, which by the end of the Pleistocene were "thinly distributed [and] only moderately predictable" (Guthrie 1983:269), and at the same time it would have allowed the use of a broader spectrum of lower-return but more predictable resources such as small game, birds, and fish (Kelly and Todd 1988; Wilmsen 1974).

3. Some changes in dietary diversity can be observed between the late Pleistocene and early Holocene occupations of the Broken Mammoth site. The faunal record itself, as well as the palynological and sedimentological records, suggests that paleoenvironmental change in the form of a Younger Dryas climatic deterioration may represent one explanation for these changes in dietary diversity. However, they are probably best explained by a combination of paleoenvironmental change and changes in foraging strategies and settlement patterns, likely related to longer-term site occupation.

4. The season of the year most likely to have been favored for the exploitation of large game would have been autumn/winter, when migratory herds of species such as bison and wapiti could have been intercepted when they left their higher altitude summer feeding grounds in the Alaska Range or Tanana Uplands to overwinter in the windy, relatively snow-free grasslands of the middle Tanana Valley. If the animals were taken with the use of coarse-grained "encounter" strategies (rather than drives), they would also have been easiest to hunt at this time of year. In addition, they would have developed maximum concentrations of body fat; hides would have been in prime condition for winter clothing and skin tent manufacture; and limited frozen meat caches could have been developed. Migratory waterfowl and fish,

in contrast, may have been taken primarily during the spring and summer. Thus, differences in site seasonality observed between the late Pleistocene and early Holocene occupations, as well as within the early Holocene occupations at the Broken Mammoth site, may reflect the use of "spike camps" specifically addressed toward harvesting large game at some times and waterfowl or fish at others.

5. Paleosol surfaces containing occupational evidence may in fact represent a conflation of seasonal activities taking place over a period of decades to hundreds of years. As such, localized occupation of portions of the site will have occurred at discrete time intervals within the overall period of site occupation. These localized occupations appear to be characterized by discrete archaeological signatures, including different types of fauna related to different seasons of occupation, as well as different patterns of animal/bird butchery, food caching and consumption, and bone discard and dispersal. In the artifactual record, localized occupations are reflected in different artifact types, tool manufacturing sequences, and source materials for artifact production, as well as patterns of tool maintenance (repair/replacement) and discard, hearth construction, small-scale caching of artifacts, hide preparation, skin sewing and clothing manufacture, and other "maintenance" activities.

6. Late Pleistocene/early Holocene occupations of these sites contain large amounts of animal bone but do not represent "kill" or "butchering" sites, even though numerous butchering activity areas are present. As noted above, elements frequently removed from kill sites are well represented at the Broken Mammoth site. These "spike camps" appear to be processing stations where "kills were brought to process the meat and hides for transport elsewhere" (Guthrie 1983b:269). This is indicated in part by the retrieval of both axial and meat-bearing segments of animal carcasses, indicating that some of the primary butchering and much of the secondary butchering did take place on site. In fact, these "spike camps" probably reflect the activities of supra-nuclear family groups (band segments or multiple household units). This is also reflected by the technological inventories at these sites, which exhibit a combination of expedient and curated

tool assemblages, but with a greater emphasis on the former. Indications of this include the use of a greater percentage of local stone sources for lithic tool manufacture, the use of heavy cobble industries for bone reduction for expedient tool manufacture (as well as for cooking, marrow extraction, and bone grease production), and the use of other readily available materials such as scavenged mammoth tusk for tool manufacture.

7. Hunting procedures based out of these camps probably utilized "opportunistic, heterogeneous hunting strategies," rather than specialized techniques such as drives and impoundments (Guthrie 1983b:265). No evidence is found at Broken Mammoth for large, catastrophic accumulations of animals, as reflected in numbers of bones, in unprocessed bone piles, or in animal age distributions (mortality profiles). Thus, techniques for obtaining herd species such as bison or wapiti probably involved the use of javelins or spears for taking individual animals, rather than the use of animal drives. At the same time, technologies involving nets or traps made of perishable materials may well have been used for mass harvesting of aquatic resources, particularly waterfowl.

In the absence of well-preserved fauna from early archaeological sites in Alaska (ca. 12,000–9,000 BP), a big-game hunting model has been developed. This model has been based on a full-glacial tundra/steppe environment, which supported large gregarious herds. However, the zooarchaeological data from the Broken Mammoth site in interior Alaska challenge this model, and provide evidence that the earliest populations had a diverse diet, including large and small mammals, birds, and fish. This broad-spectrum diet arose in response to the environmental conditions of the Birch Interval and Poplar Rise, which included the replacement of tundra/steppe by an open parkland; the local extinction of mammoth and horse; the survival of restricted bison and elk herds on outwash plains in the northern foothills of the Alaska Range; the development of stable seasonal wetlands; and the reestablishment of the modern North Pacific avian flyway. Although the Yanger Dryas climat episode may have had some impact on human populations, the apparent greater sedentism and/or density of populations suggests its effect was minimal.

THREE

Are Paleoindians of the Great Plains and Rockies Subsistence Specialists?

Marcel Kornfeld

Paleoindians in both North and South America are frequently portrayed as specialist big-game hunters, emphasizing communal hunting strategies. In western North America, such an economy is seen as first oriented toward mammoth hunting (Clovis), followed by a series of bison-dominated economies (the cultural complexes from 11,000 to 7,500 years ago). To succeed on such a big-game diet, Paleoindian groups have been portrayed as highly mobile. This model is most elegantly presented by Kelly and Todd (1988) for the first migrants, but it has been commonly extended to the rest of the Paleoindian period (e.g., Bamforth 2002; Jodry 1999c). Based on the plains evidence, the big-game specialization has also been extended to other regions (Caldwell 1958; Willey 1966; Jennings 1989; Spencer et al. 1965). In the past 20 years, a few voices have been raised in opposition to this dominant paradigm (Dincauze and Curran 1983; Kornfeld 1988; Meltzer 1988; Meltzer and Smith 1986; Olsen 1990), but few detailed studies are yet available to support a generalist view of Paleoindian subsistence (e.g., Bamforth 1991; Collins and Bousman 1995; and Hamilton and Goebel 1999; cf. Bamforth 2002; and Landals 1990 for a non-Paleoindian case). However, explicit models are beginning to appear (Collins, this volume; Dincauze 1993b, 2000; Lepper 1999; Fiedel, this volume).

Were western Paleoindians specialized big-game hunters or broad-spectrum generalist foragers? To begin to answer this question, I consider the following topics:

1. A review of the history of Paleoindian studies to demonstrate how the false consciousness of big-game hunting specialists

developed and became entrenched in the scientific literature and public minds;

2. a brief discussion of the bone midden sites that dominate so much of the Paleoindian literature; and

3. a summary of the overlooked and underinterpreted literature of the non-big-game Paleoindian sites.

My study focuses on the western plains and Rocky Mountains, the region from New Mexico to southern Canada and from western Kansas to eastern Utah (Figure 3.1). However, due to sparse Paleoindian evidence, I occasionally rely on studies from a wider area.

Before addressing these topics, however, it is useful to provide a definition of the terms "generalist" and "specialist." A generalist is an organism that procures food in roughly similar proportions to that available in the procurement habitat, while a specialist procures only some resources and excludes others (Winterhalder 1981:23). Hence, to demonstrate that an organism is a generalist or specialist, we must know the nature of the environment as well as the nature of the procurement. I have argued elsewhere that the Great Plains and Rocky Mountains provide a wide array of resources (Kornfeld 2003). Thus, a generalist procurement strategy would include these in a forager's diet, while a specialist diet would concentrate on only a portion of the resources available.

Another dimension of generalized versus specialized procurement strategy is the effect of each on the overall economy and indeed the structure of the cultural system. Thus, on the plains it is often said that bison is such an important resource that all life is organized around this species and its by-products (Bamforth 1988; Wedel 1986). Bison is emphasized to such an extent that technological organization (e.g., gearing up for bison hunts; Reher and Frison 1980), ritual (e.g., Frison 1971), and ideology (e.g., Sundstrom 2003) revolve around this single species. With a generalized economy, on the other hand, technology and ritual would not be driven by any single resource.

How Did We Get into This Rut?

The origin and persistence of the view of Paleoindians as specialists and (communal) big-game hunters are commensurate with the origin of Paleoindian studies. At the end of the nineteenth century, after the demolition of the moundbuilder myth by Cyrus Thomas, questions regarding the

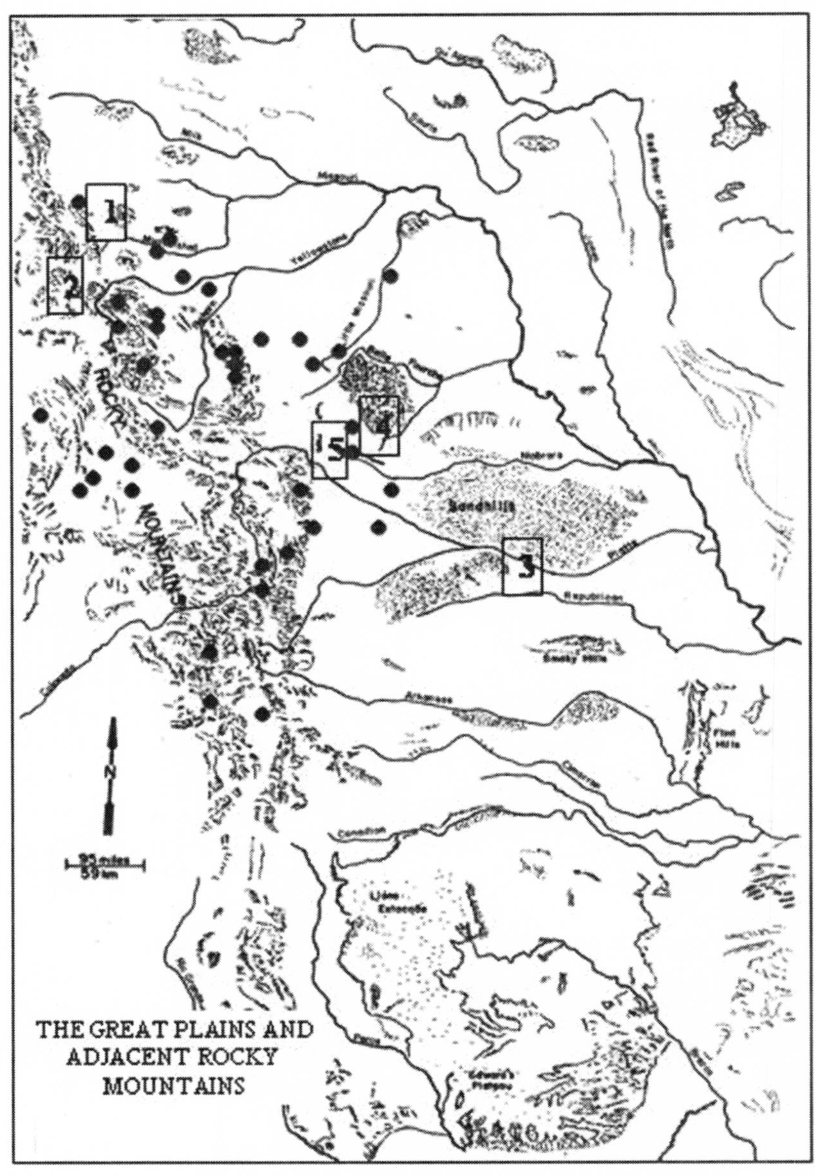

FIGURE 3.1. Western plains and Rocky Mountain region showing location of Paleoindian sites discussed in the text and listed in table 3.1. 1, Indian Creek; 2, Barton Gulch; 3, Allen; 4, Ray Long; and 5, Hell Gap.

origin and antiquity of American Indians dominated American archaeology (Willey and Sabloff 1993; Trigger 1989). Initially, the concept of the American Paleolithic suggested great antiquity for the first inhabitants of the continent, and the data was buttressed by the poorly known quaternary geology of the Americas (Willey and Sabloff 1993:54). After a few years the idea was soundly trounced by rigorous research demonstrating that the supposed Paleolithic artifacts were in fact production debris, not primitive, crude, and old tools, and the sediments in which they were contained were recent (Holmes 1892; Richards 1939).

From the last part of the nineteenth century and into the first part of the twentieth century, several sites were discovered that suggested great antiquity of American Indians, but none of these convinced the scientific community, until the affirmation of association of projectile points and extinct bison at the Folsom site in New Mexico in 1927 (Meltzer et al. 2002; Wormington 1957). Folsom was a watershed that initiated subsequent Paleoindian studies. Given the general skepticism of claims of great antiquity coupled with a poor grasp of quaternary geology, few options were available to early-twentieth-century scientists to demonstrate the antiquity of their discoveries. However, since paleontologists had worked out a preliminary historic sequence of extinct fonules and specifically extinct species of bison (Leidy 1852; Wilson 1975), direct stratigraphic association of human artifacts with extinct fauna was virtually the only option for demonstrating a site's antiquity. At the Folsom site, unquestionable human artifacts were discovered in the context of an extinct species of bison (Figgins 1927; Roberts 1935). In fact, at least one Folsom point photographed was in a bison rib cage (Figgins 1927), and a similar point now preserved *in situ* at the Denver Museum of Nature and Science, can be considered the crucial piece of evidence that changed the course of Paleoindian studies (Meltzer 1993b).

Almost immediately following the Folsom finds, pundits claiming antiquity of American Indians also in the same breadth proposed their primary diet derived from the hunt (e.g., Roberts 1940; see also Todd and Rapson 1999:481–482). This situation continued for nearly half of the history of Paleoindian studies or well into the 1960s, but the precedent set in the first half of the twentieth century continues to affect Paleoindian studies.

The notion that extinct bison middens represented kill sites preceded the Folsom discovery, as Cook (1925) interpreted Lone Wolf as a Pleistocene kill location. Stanford later noted that "the association of fluted projectile points with extinct fauna at kill sites demonstrated the relative antiquity of early North Americans and *elucidated aspects of their diet*" (Stanford (1999:283, emphasis added). Or as Todd and Rapson (1999:481–482) observed: "a large number of dead bison indicated a large communal kill from which a very large quantity of food products were derived."

This interpretation certainly should not be surprising because it occurred in the context of many other Upper Paleolithic peoples, particularly Eurasians, who were also viewed as single-species specialists (e.g., mammoth hunters, reindeer hunters, cave bear hunters, and others; Trigger 1989:95).

The Folsom link to communal big-game hunting was of course made that much easier and apparently logical by the very recent (within memory of nearly all participating scientists) presence of historic bison-hunting peoples of the plains (e.g., Wissler 1916). It was but a short leap from Pleistocene bison bone beds with cultural objects, specifically spear heads, to communal bison hunts of recent memory.

Subsistence orientation was obvious, and to some it still is. Dixon, for example, uses the Folsom projectile point at the Denver museum as the basis for his assertion that "the *primary focus of Folsom economy was hunting*. The archaeological evidence indicates that Folsom hunters commanded exceptional knowledge of bison behavior. Although other species were hunted, from Folsom times until the end of the Plano tradition, taking bison in mass kill settings became the *single most important subsistence strategy* on the North American Great Plains" (Dixon 1999:223, emphasis added). Similar statements can be seen in much of the plains Paleoindian literature (e.g., Bamforth 1988; Cassells 1997; Wedel 1961, 1986). However, it should be noted that, to others, it is far less obvious. Frison, for example, who has excavated many bison bone middens, including some of the best known and most intensively studied (e.g., Frison and Todd 1987; Frison 1996), and who is often cited as the champion for the big-game hunting emphasis (Gero 1993; Hudaceck-Cuffe 1998), is actually far more cautious. In the conclusion to a volume on the oldest Paleoindian bison midden in North America, Frison and colleagues (1996:209) say "archaeologists may have tended to place Paleoindian bison hunting groups into lifeways with subsistence strategies that are too narrowly focused towards bison procurement alone." He further suggests that the best-known communal kills "may represent only a small increment of the total range of subsistence activities and only those that are the most visible archaeologically" (Frison et al. 1996:210; see also Frison 1977; Kornfeld 1988:212, 1994:8; Kornfeld and Francis 1991).

After the Folsom site was accepted by the scientific community and the public, other similar discoveries followed at Blackwater Draw, Lindenmeier, Scottsbluff, and Plainview, to name a few (e.g., Stanford 1999). Again, the association of human artifacts with extinct fauna played a crucial role in demonstrating the antiquity of these finds. As many of the localities contained artifacts quite unlike those at previously accepted sites, the only certain demonstration of antiquity was the association with Pleistocene fauna. In other words, unless they contained extinct fauna, sites were generally not defined as Paleoindian in age. In fact, the lag in eastern North American Paleoindian studies is partially because faunal preservation is poor to nonexistent in that region, and few extinct fauna were recovered to date the artifacts relatively (Jennings 1989; Spencer et al. 1965). It was only later, when Paleoindian diagnostic artifacts were recognized as index fossils and as ancient (dating to the Pleistocene/Holocene transition) that Paleoindian occupation of the East was accepted. Once accepted by eastern archaeologists years later, eastern Paleoindians were assumed to be, like their western cousins, hunters of large game (e.g., Fisher 1987; Funk 1978; Willey 1966; Jennings 1989; Caldwell 1958; Spencer et al. 1965).

Furthermore, because these early studies relied on association with extinct fauna, possibly representing kill sites, projectile points were the artifacts recognized as index fossils of this period, rather than other artifact classes. Hence, sites with these points were recognized as Paleoindian, while others were not. Essentially, this restricted the types of sites entering the Paleoindian literature (further discussed below) and created a vicious circle from which Paleoindian researchers have yet to extricate themselves. Although a few other artifacts are now accepted, albeit reluctantly, as evidence for Paleoindian occupation (blades, blade cores as some examples), a frequent question concerns whether an 11,200-year-old site is Clovis if it doesn't have Clovis points.

As a result of the limited dating options before midcentury, virtually all Paleoindian sites discovered contained extinct Pleistocene fauna, usually mammoth and bison and only rarely other species, enhancing the big-game hunting scenario of Paleoindians. If sites did not contain Pleistocene fauna—and a few recognized as Paleoindian did not—their significance to the overall understanding of Paleoindian lifeways was muted (e.g., Sellards 1952; Wormington 1957), and indeed they remained either minimally published or unpublished (e.g., Allen and Lindenmeier).

To exacerbate the problem, far fewer small Pleistocene mammals and avifauna became extinct (Grayson 1991:194), meaning that few of these remains could be used as an index of Pleistocene age. If the object was to demonstrate antiquity, the large mammals provided the critical data. Consequently, the earliest known Paleoindian sites, interpreted as representing human-induced kills and resource procurement locations, were plains sites with excellent preservation of large quantities of bison or mammoth bone.

While animals other than mammoth and bison occurred occasionally, especially in Clovis sites, in post-Clovis contexts bison were virtually the only animals recovered and extensively reported. And while the mammoth and its extinct status would be recognized from a variety of skeletal elements and fragments, extinct bison species were at the time recognized largely on the basis of horn core shape, skull morphology, and measurements (Frison 1991b:267; Leidy 1852; Skinner and Kaisan 1947). Use of postcranial measurements to distinguish *Bison antiquus* from *Bison bison* is a relatively recent development (e.g., McDonald 1968; Wilson 1975:37). Generally, bison skulls were found at large-bone middens where many animals were buried in the same location. Consequently, demonstrating the antiquity of a site meant finding a bison bone midden with skulls sufficiently well preserved to make qualitative and quantitative observations to prove that the bison were of the extinct Pleistocene species.

Clearly this research orientation favored sites with large quantities of bison bone, interpreted as communal kill locations. Only a few sites, such as Lindenmeier, were not primarily kill sites, but even here bison remains comprised a large portion of the assemblage. Interestingly, use of postcranial remains were not well reported (Roberts 1935; Wilmsen and Roberts 1978). In fact, a curious lack of reporting exists on the bison remains in middens, except for the all-important skulls. Rather, until the 1970s (Wheat 1972), reports primarily emphasized projectile points.

After the advent of radiocarbon dating, the requirement for associated extinct Pleistocene fauna diminished, and the development of preliminary chronological sequences of diagnostic Paleoindian artifacts provided alternative means of dating and identifying sites as Paleoindian (Roberts 1940; Wormington 1949; 1957). Radiocarbon dating, associational seriation, and stratigraphic excavations fostered the development of the chronological sequence of Paleoindian complexes by the mid-1950s (Sellards 1952; Wormington 1957). However, sites with few bison bones, such as the Medicine Creek Complex (Roper 2002), rarely made a big impact on Paleoindian studies (Roper 2002). The lack of impact of such sites could be because they were never fully analyzed and published (Knudson 2002:135). Obviously, the fact that these sites were the ones not published, while the results of many bone middens excavated at the same time were published and widely disseminated, reflected priorities of scientists studying Paleoindians.

In summary, events and circumstances throughout the history of Paleoindian studies in a sense predetermined that: (1) sites identified as Paleoindian would be associated with great quantities of extinct Pleistocene fauna, a definition that Wormington (1957) uses to identify Paleoindian sites; (2) large mammals would be the major component of the fauna; (3) skulls must be part of the recovered faunal inventory (particularly in the bison bone beds); and (4) projectile points were the main artifacts linking the sites to each other and eventually providing the chronological sequencing of Paleoindian complexes. The initial interpretation of these sites as communal kill events of the first North Americans is not surprising. The surprise is that despite the discovery and investigation of a large number of non-big-game Paleoindian sites since the early 1950s, the economic specialization view persists.

Bone Middens

A pile of bison bone geologically associated with artifacts does not unambiguously indicate a kill or procurement site. Such an interpretation should only be made after a thorough and intensive study of the recovered remains. Enough of the bison bone middens have now been studied, or in most cases restudied, to demonstrate Paleoindian procurement and use of these megafaunal resources of the late Pleistocene. It is not my intention to question careful assessments, but rather to advocate an approach to interpretation, which utilizes all of the data, including the bison bone middens. When considered fully, a broad-spectrum generalist forager scenario (e.g., Kornfeld 1996) fits the data better than the conventional specialist big-game hunting orientation.

Approximately 30 Paleoindian megafaunal kill sites have been found within my chosen study area. Human association through direct evidence for procurement and handling practices has been demonstrated for some of the sites through intensive analyses, but others have not been investigated, and indeed in some instances cannot be investigated, as only selected or virtually no faunal remains are curated—for example, James Allen (Mulloy 1959) and Finley (Howard et al. 1941). At the recently reinvestigated Hudson-Meng site, human involvement with the bone midden may be minimal or nonexistent (Todd and Rapson 1999).

How would generalist foragers procure and use big game? What may be the role of ambush and communal hunting among such groups? Is the data from bone middens consistent with such practices? It may not be possible to rely on already-analyzed assemblages, but it may be necessary to reanalyze the assemblages with these questions in mind.

The Mammoth Middens

Three well-known mammoth bone middens exist in the western plains and the Rocky Mountains. At the relatively well excavated, analyzed, and reported Colby site, mammoth remains form the bulk of the recovered material, along with a few stone tools and two features (Frison and Todd 1986). The Dent site data suffers from the site being excavated early in the history of Paleoindian studies, largely by amateurs. Dent contained 14 mammoths and three projectile points, but relatively little else is known about the locality (Figgins 1933). Haynes and colleagues (1999) leave open the possibility that much of the mammoth bone may be redeposited; hence the bone's association with the projectile points remains ambiguous. Finally, the Lang-Ferguson site represents a Clovis mammoth association, but the site is highly eroded with little evidence of human activity remaining (Hannus 1990). Mammoth bone has been found at other archaeological sites, such as Claypool; however, the eroded and deflated nature of the deposit precludes robust statements regarding human association or the nature of procurement efforts (Stanford and Albanese 1975). At other locations, human involvement with mammoth is tenuous and is based on ambiguous evidence (Davis 1971; Holen 1995).

Of these sites, Colby provides the most information regarding Paleoindian lifeways (Frison and Todd 1986). Here the remains of seven mammoths were discovered in an arroyo bottom that contained a seasonal stream, which later changed course, and the gully filled with sediment burying and preserving the remains. Along with the mammoths were four Clovis projectile points, one tool, one probable channel flake, several pieces of chipped stone that may represent tool fragments, 30 flakes, and several cobble tools. At least some of the projectile points exhibit cutting functions (Kay 1996), suggesting they were used in butchering of the mammoth.

Perhaps the most significant aspect of the Colby site are two piles of mammoth bone. Frison and Todd (1986:139) suggest that they may represent meat caches; however, after an exhaustive taphonomic analysis, they were unable to confidently rule out the possibility that the bone piles were noncultural phenomena (Frison and Todd 1986:27–90). Caching food supplies has significant implications for foragers, including their interaction with the natural environment and the complexity of their lifeway and economic strategies. Such complex cultural features are not unexpected at this late date in the Paleolithic continuum, but the evidence is scanty in the Americas. Colby thus suggests that the earliest inhabitants of the Americas may have participated in more complex and diverse socioeconomic systems than generally portrayed for highly mobile, big-game specialists. More specifically, it suggests seasonal economic variation limiting mobility for at least part of the year.

The Bison Middens

The 27 bison bone middens from the study area range from the Goshen to James Allen complexes, or in time from approximately 11,000 to 7,500 years ago. Bison bone constitutes the major portion of the assemblage at these sites, along with small quantities of chiefly chipped stone specimens, although resharpening flakes may count in the thousands. These associated artifacts, generally dominated by projectile points, include scrapers, spokeshaves, gravers, a variety of flake tools, and debitage. Stone tool raw materials sometimes include distant sources, but more often are local. Furthermore, the distant raw materials generally form a small proportion of the entire assemblage, although in a few instances a small amount (a nodule, biface, or preform) of distant raw material was reduced at the locality, accounting for a relatively large proportion of the debitage assemblage by count.

The chipped stone tools at the middens are dominated by projectile points; indeed, at some sites other tool classes are virtually nonexistent. Scrapers, spokeshaves, gravers, and other flake tools occur, but generally in low proportions. However, given a wide range of variation of bone midden sites—from small to large, from kill to processing locations, from kill to kill-associated camps, and from occupations at different seasons—a variable assemblage is expected. Variation in stone tools and stone tool inventories would be expected, but analyses have recently been dominated by variation in the bone component rather than the chipped stone component of the assemblage.

The projectile point assemblage is variable, from a few specimens at some sites (Agenbroad 1978; Kornfeld et al. 1999), to over 100 at others (e.g., Stanford 1978:92; Frison and Stanford 1982a:80). The projectile points are often broken and in several instances where studies have been completed, many have been used as knives (Greiser 1977; Stanford, personal communication 2002).

As noted earlier, the bulk of the recovered material at each of the bison bone middens is bison bone. The minimum number of individuals ranges from 5 at the Jerry Craig site (probably a sample; Richings-Germain 2002) to a total of 250 at the Jones-Miller site and over 600 if Hudson-Meng is included (Stanford 1984; Todd and Stanford 1992; Agenbroad 1978; cf. Todd and Rapson 1999). For sites that have been relatively completely excavated (unlike Jerry Craig), numbers in the upper teens seem to be the lower limit of the minimum number of individual animals represented (Hill 2002).

At some of the sites, butchering is minimal, with virtually no evidence of removal of any body parts from the kill, or dismemberment, or other modification of the carcass (Hill 2001; Todd 1983). At others, significant butchering and use of marrow are evidenced by point impact fractures and bone shaft fragments (Hill 2001; Todd et al. 1997). No sites contain evidence for extremely extensive processing such as seen in the Archaic and Late Prehistoric grease-boiling features in the vicinity of kill sites (e.g., Reeves 1990; Brink and Dawe 1989; Frison 1967).

While the original analyses of bison remains vary, recent studies of the taphonomic processes at many of these sites use similar methodologies (e.g., Kreutzer 1996; Todd 1987; Hill 2001; Hill 2002), as do the studies reevaluating season of bison mortality (e.g., Todd et al. 1990; Todd et al. 1996; Todd 1991). The current evidence suggests that bison mortality at over half of the sites (14 out of 25 with available data) occurs in just over a third of the year, from very late fall to early spring (Figure 3.2). Although this inference may change as more sites are found and/or reanalyzed, the pattern of winter use of bison appears constant through prehistory from the Paleoindian to Late Prehistoric times (e.g., Frison 1991b). Was bison the main resource exploited by Paleoindians at this time of the year? What were Paleoindians consuming the rest of the year? And how does this seasonal bison procurement relate to earlier seasonal storage strategies such as those at the Colby site?

For a perspective on the dietary contribution of bison, as reflected from archaeological data, consider the following calculations. These 27 Paleoindian bison bone middens contain approximately 1,380 individual bison (Hill 2002). At an approximate dressed weight of 300 kilograms/individual (225 kilograms/individual for modern bison, plus 1/3 to account for the larger body size of the extinct species), bison at these sites would have

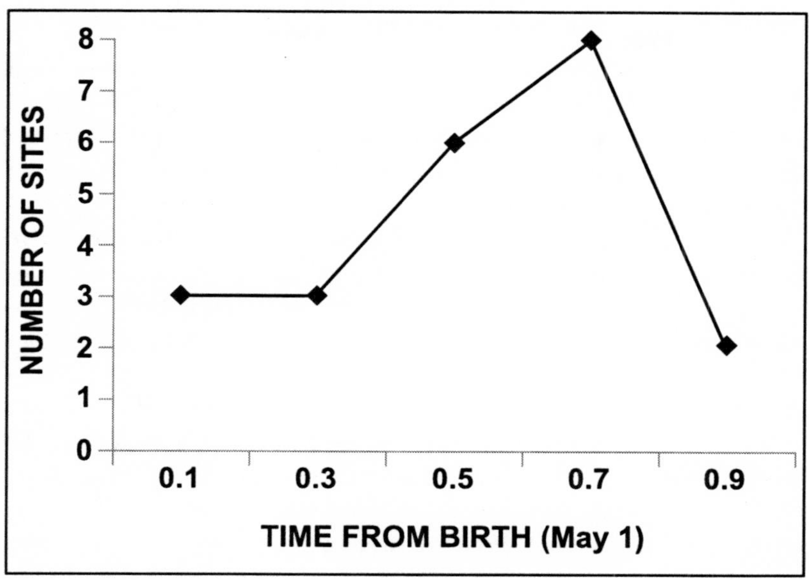

FIGURE 3.2. Seasonality summary of Paleoindian bison bone middens. Note the winter and early spring (0.55 to 0.75 from mean birthing season of May 1) peak in bison mortality. Data from Todd 1991; Todd et al. 1996; Todd et al. 1990; Hill 2002.

yielded a total of 414,000 kilograms of edible meat product, or 869,400,000 calories (at 2,100 cal/kilogram). To feed one connubium (approximately 500 people) for a year at 3,000 cal/individual/day (FAO 1974), 547,500,000 calories are required. Consequently, the calories represented by all the bison from the western plains and Rocky Mountain Paleoindian bone middens represent 1.588 years of subsistence for one connubium. For the duration of the later Paleoindian time period (approximately 3,500 years), the known and investigated bison kills represent 0.045 percent of the required diet. As the area covered by this study likely includes a number of connubia, the proportion of total Paleoindian subsistence represented by the sample is substantially less. From this one must conclude that Paleoindian bison bone middens represent a very small portion of human dietary needs for over 3,500 years.

Camps, Workshops, Task-Specific Localities, and Other Paleoindian Sites

Numerous Paleoindian sites other than the animal bone middens are known. These are often classed as camps, caches, burials or human remains, workshops, or some type of task-specific location (see Table 3.1).

Camps are locations of relatively long-term residence with evidence of food consumption, craft manufacturing, social activity, and ritual. Workshops are locations of intense craft production, which could involve different materials and result in a variety of goods, but on the western plains and the Rocky Mountains are represented solely by chipped stone. Camps and workshops sometimes occur together, such as at the Hanson site, where chipped stone manufacturing is the dominant activity (Frison and Bradley 1980). Limited-activity sites are common, but how many of these really represent task-specific localities rather than resulting from limited sampling or poor preservation of once larger or multifunctional sites (e.g., Rocky Foolsm)? That is, task-specific localities are often difficult or impossible to differentiate confidently from camps because these localities may be inadequately sampled camps. Conversely, sites interpreted as camps may be nothing more than frequently and redundantly occupied task-specific locations. Without detailed studies—virtually none of which have been performed, and indeed data may not exist for such studies—it is not possible to unambiguously differentiate camps from some task-specific locales. Only a few caches, or locations of stored objects, are known for the region. These frequently occur isolated from other evidence of human activity, and most, if not all, on the western plains and Rocky Mountains may actually constitute burial offerings (e.g., the Fenn Cache) rather than caches. The bone at these locations either was not recovered or not preserved. Intentionally or unintentionally buried human remains, like caches, are often spatially separated from other activities and constitute a distinct site type (e.g., Gordon Creek). Most of these Paleoindian sites are open-air localities; however, some are in caves or rockshelters (e.g., Bighorn Canyon Caves).

Below is a brief review of perhaps the most significant Paleoindian camps on the plains and in the Rocky Mountains: Barton Gulch, Indian Creek, Allen, Ray Long, and Hell Gap. However, several other sites, specific features, and artifacts are mentioned, along with their archaeological assemblages, as these sites are particularly indispensable for reaching a comprehensive understanding of Paleoindian subsistence.

Camps and Camp Workshops

The five campsites discussed below are dispersed over the study area from mid Nebraska in the east to western Montana in the west and from southern Wyoming in the south to central Montana in the north. The sites are not particularly unique; rather, they provide the best contrast to the better known bone middens. Although minimally analyzed and published, we know quite a bit about these five localities; however, in this review I concentrate only on those observations relevant to the understanding of broad-spectrum diets.

BARTON GULCH

Barton Gulch in southwest Montana was discovered in 1972 and was tested by archaeologists from 1979 through the 1980s (Davis et al. 1988; Davis et al. 1989). Located on a tributary of the Ruby River, Barton Gulch is the type site of two Paleoindian complexes, Barton Gulch and Alder, dated to 8700 and 9400 RCYBP, respectively. Both components contain a range of fauna and features interpreted as representing domiciles. The older, Alder Complex has a fuller artifact and feature inventory and is briefly discussed.

Davis and colleagues (Davis et al. 1988; Davis et al. 1989) excavated 37 features arranged into four similar, discrete aggregations. Each aggregation contains a central, shallowly excavated, unlined, heavily oxidized pit. One or two unlined, 30-centimeter-deep, charcoal-filled features surround each basin. A series of 10-centimeter-deep, small (20–30 centimeters in diameter) features form a two-meter-diameter circle around each oxidized basin. These circles are interpreted as living floors and are characterized as domiciles.

The fauna includes cottontail, undifferentiated rabbit, mink, and deer. The deer bone has been heavily utilized, as indicated by hammerstone impacts and the small, reduced, burned, and calcined fragments of the majority of the specimens. The chipped stone artifact inventory includes preforms, points, knives, flake tools, and end scrapers. One abrading stone was also recovered.

INDIAN CREEK

Indian Creek is a series of deeply buried, stratified, Paleoindian localities in the southern Elkhorn Mountains of west-central Montana. Both fluted and later unfluted components are present dating from 11,000 to 8000 RCYBP (Davis and Greiser 1992:239–266). Most analysis has concentrated on the older levels.

The downstream locality contains 15 end scrapers, 13 side scrapers, three projectile points, three flake knives, two gravers, one bifacial core, seven channel flakes, and 2,504 pieces of debitage. The tools exhibit microwear evidence from scraping hides; from working soft, pliable material such as

TABLE 3.1. Selected sample of Paleoindian sites in the western plains and Rocky reference is usually indicated. Site type is my interpretation.

Site	Major Component	Localities for Components
Adobe	Folsom	1
Anzick	Clovis	1
Barger Gulch, Loc. B	Folsom	1
Barton Gulch	Alder, Ruby	2
Betty Green	Lusk, LP	2
Bighorn Canyon Caves	Lovell, Pryor	multiple
Bighorn Mountain Shelters	Folsom to LP	multiple
Black Mountain, Colorado	Folsom	1
Blue Point	Folsom to Alberta	multiple
Caribou Lake	LP-Lanceolate	2
Cattle Guard	Folsom	1
Charlie Lake	Fluted	2
China Wall	Folsom to LP	several
Deep Hearth site	Deception Creek	1
DjPo-47	LP	1
Duckett	PI	?
Drake	Clovis	1
Eclipse	Fluted, LP	2
Fenn	Clovis	1
Hanson	Folsom	1+
Hell Gap	Goshen to Lusk	16+
Indian Creek	Folsom, Hell Gap	20+
James Pass	Fluted (Clovis)	2
Krmpotich site	Folsom	1
Laddie Creek	Cody	1
Lindenmeier	Folsom, Cody	2
Lookingbill	Haskett, Alder, Fishtail	3
MacHaffie	Folsom, Plainveiw	2
Medicine Creek	Plainview to LP	15 approximately
Medicine Lodge Creek	Goshen, Cody, LP	9+
Mill Iron Camp	Goshen	1
Mummy Cave	Various mid PI to LP	14
Minnewanka	Fluted	?
Myers-Hindman	LP	multiple?
Niska	10,880	1
North Fork site(s)	Cody, LP	several
Pictograph Cave	LP	several?
Pine Spring	Goshen to	several
Pretty Creek	Mid PI to LP	6+
Ray Long	Angostura	2
Rocky Foolsm	Folsom	1
Schiffer Cave	LP	1
Schutte Creek	Folsom, other	multiple
Sheep Mountain Net	LP	1
Sibbold Creek	Fluted, other	several
Signal Butte		1
Simons	Clovis	1
Sinks Canyon	Pryor Stemmed	1
Sister's Hills	Hell Gap	1
Southsider Shelter	LP	several
Vail Pass	LP	1
Vermillion Lakes	10,800-9,000	6+
Yellowstone Cody	Cody	several

PI = Paleoindian, LP = Late Paleoindian.

Mountains. Many sites have multiple references; the original or the most complete

Site Type	Reference
limited activity	Hofman and Ingbar 1988
cache	Lahren and Bonnichsen 1974
camp/workshop	Surovell et al. 2001
camp	Davis et al. 1988
camp	Greene 1967; Frison 1991b
limited activity	Husted 1969
various	Frison 1991b
limited activity	Jodry et al. 1996
limited activity	Pastor, personal communications, 2003
limited activity	Benedict 1992
camp	Jodry 1999b
limited activity	Fedje 1996
camp? limited activity?	Waitkus, personal communication, 2003
limited activity (camp?)	Rood 1993
limited activity	Driver 1982
?	Wilson and Burns 1999
cache	Stanford and Jodry 1988
	Fedje 1996
cache	Frison and Bradley 1999
camp/workshop	Frison and Bradley 1980
camp/limited activity	Irwin-Williams et al. 1973
camp, limited activity?	Davis and Greiser 1992
limited activity?	Wilson and Burns 1999
camp/workshop	Peterson 2001
limited activity	Larson 1990
camp, other	Wilmsen and Roberts 1978
camp/workshop	Larson et al. 1995
camp	Forbis et al., n.d.
camp/workshop/limited activity	Davis 1954; Bamforth 2002; Knudson 2002
limited activity	Frison 1976
camp	Frison 1996
limited activity	Husted and Edgar 2002
	Fedje 1996
limited activity	Lahren 1976
limited activity	Wilson and Burns 1999
limited activity, cache	Eakin, personal communication 2003
limited activity	Mulloy 1958
workshop/camp	Sharrock 1966
camp?	Loendorf 1973
camp	Wheeler 1995
limited activity	Kornfeld 1988
camp	Frison 1973
limited activity	personal observation
cache	Frison et al. 1986
camp	Gryba 1983
limited activity	Forbis et al., n.d.
cache	Butler 1963
limited activity	Sanders, personal communication 2003
limited activity	Agogino and Galloway 1965
limited activity	Frison 1991b
camp	Gooding 1981
limited activity, camp	Fedje et al. 1995
limited activity	Sanders, personal communication 2003

hide or vegetable fiber; and from working hard materials such as wood or bone. Cutting tools are underrepresented. Faunal material includes bison, bighorn sheep, marmot, cottontail, jackrabbit, ground squirrel, and microtine-size rodents. Spring occupation is suggested. Domestic activities indicate a short-term, spring-to-early-summer base camp.

The upstream locality includes fluted (Folsom), Agate Basin, and Hell Gap complexes. The Folsom component includes 2,407 pieces of debitage, 9,025 bone specimens, two bone tools, and seven chipped stone tools, all recovered through 1/16-inch mesh screening. These artifacts occurred in a very restricted space interpreted as a discard location from a nearby living floor.

The fauna in the upstream locality includes bison, medium-size artiodactyls (deer/antelope), marmots, rabbits/hares, prairie dogs, and voles. Only one bone shows butchering marks; however, most bones are burned or calcined. Chipped stone includes two projectile points, nine channel flakes, three end scrapers, one side scraper, and one flake tool. Two anvil stones were also associated with the feature on this floor.

Davis and Greiser (1992) interpret the Indian Creek site as a camp, on the basis of domestic activities such as food processing and cooking, and on a variety of craft activities such as hide, wood, and bone working. A tentative spring-to-early-summer period of occupation is inferred from a small sample of faunal seasonality indicators. A broad-spectrum economy is suggested by a number of small and medium-size mammalian species represented.

ALLEN

Three sites along Medicine Creek (Lime Creek, Allen, and Red Smoke) were excavated in the early 1950s, but received little notice in Paleoindian studies (Davis 1954). Part of the reason was suspicious dating and a poor fit with the then known Paleoindian pattern, that of large-game bone middens. The Medicine Creek sites contained insignificant quantities of large-animal bones, projectile points that were not typical of the known Paleoindian complexes, a variety of small to medium-size animals, and a large number of features (hearths, many recovered through casting). The sites were deeply buried in alluvial, colluvial, and eolian sediment, interrupted by periods of soil formation (May 2002). However, details of sedimentation varied between the sites as well as between the occupations. Recent redating indicates that the occupations ranged from nearly 11,000 to after 8000 RCYBP, or the entire Paleoindian period (Bamforth 2002:58).

Knudson (1983, 2002), the first to analyze the Red Smoke assemblage, focused primarily on bifacial technology and compared the assemblage to other Paleoindian sites, namely Plainview and MacHaffie. Bamforth began a reinvestigation into the Allen site in the 1980s and has since completed a wide variety of spatial, radiocarbon, zooarchaeological, use wear, and other studies (Bamforth 1991, 2002, in press). The Allen site had been divided into three occupations; however, Bamforth's studies suggest that the cultural use of the locality has been continuous, but intermittent, throughout the Paleoindian period.

The Allen site contains 101 bifaces, 16 preforms, six points, 113 flake tools, 19 cores, four perforators, 12 hammerstones, eight pieces of ground stone (hand stones and slabs), several bola stones or net weights, 94 bone tools, 20 hearths, 2,319 specimens of unmodified bone, and over 10,000 pieces of debitage. The artifacts are spatially clustered and suggestive of dumps, not activity loci. The faunal species include bison, deer, antelope, jackrabbit, cottontail, prairie dog, freshwater mussel, catfish, birds, predators (wolf and bear), turtles, beaver, and others. Although not in the same proportions in all components and at each of the Medicine Creek sites, the Allen artifact and feature classes characterize most of the Medicine Creek occupations. The hearths vary in their firing intensity, with some classified as lightly, others as heavily fired. Hackberry seeds were recovered, but their associational and behavioral implications are questionable.

Bamforth (in press) sees a continuity in Paleoindian landscape use within this drainage. The Allen site, located on the main Medicine Creek drainage, represents a longer-term residential camp at which a variety of tasks occurred, while Lime Creek and Red Smoke (in tributary drainages) are locations of various task-specific activities organized around procurement of local raw material for chipped stone manufacture or bison procurement.

RAY LONG

The Ray Long site was excavated as a part of the River Basin Surveys in the 1940s and the 1950s; however, the report was not available until recently (Wheeler 1995). Adrian Hannus began reinvestigating the site in the 1980s (Hannus 1986). The Ray Long site is located on a tributary of the Cheyenne River in thick alluvial sediments. As at Medicine Creek, the early dates were considered unreliable since they used the composite solid carbon dating technique, the projectile points (Angostura) were not known to be chronologically diagnostic of the Paleoindian period, and the overall site pattern, including numerous hearths, did not fit the other known Paleoindian sites (large-bone middens).

The Ray Long site consists of three areas and three components. Two of the components, B and C, date to the Paleoindian period, 7073 and 9380 RCYBP, respectively. The Paleoindian components contained unprepared (i.e., surface), lightly and heavily fired hearths, with 12 hearths in component B and 13 in component C. A charred mass of vegetal material indicates a possible storage feature. The chipped stone tool inventory, dominated by debitage (n = 1,253), includes projectile points, bifaces, preforms, drills, cores, and a variety of flake tools. Ground stone was present in the form of choppers, milling stones, and palettes. Burned bone was present, but is not discussed in any detail. The site is interpreted as a "seasonal hunting camp of extended family or small band units" (Wheeler 1995:449), and represents one of the first cases of Paleoindian use of plants based on the presence of grinding implements. I do not think Wheeler means this to be literally a hunting camp, but rather a hunter-gatherer camp where hunting, gathering, and other activities took place. Such an interpretation is presented elsewhere in his study (Wheeler 1995:444–446).

HELL GAP

Hell Gap in east-central Wyoming is at the eastern edge of the Hartville Uplift and at the ecotone between the open plains to the east and foothills of the Rocky Mountains to the west. Information on the site was never fully published, but the most significant information is available in one article and a dissertation (Irwin-Williams et al. 1973; Irwin 1967). Although frequently mentioned in Paleoindian studies, its significance was largely the contribution to Paleoindian chronology (e.g., Frison 1991b:50; Irwin-Williams et al. 1973; Irwin and Wormington 1970). The archaeological record beyond the diagnostic artifacts made little impact, although the site is one of a few Paleoindian localities with hearths, domestic structures, and ornaments. Especially ignored were the large quantities of bone now under study at the University of Wyoming (Rapson and Niven 2000; Byers 2001). Although dominated by bison, the site is not a communal bison kill. Along with bison, deer- or antelope-size artiodactyl bone was more common in the upper, Frederick components, but smaller animals were also present, as was freshwater shell.

The Hell Gap site stretches for over a kilometer along an internally drained arroyo, probably a creek during Paleoindian times and possibly a tributary to the North Platte River. At least four localities were identified and tested, each containing multiple Paleoindian components, up to 9 at

Locality I, with a total of 16 known for the valley. Hearths were present in the Frederick components, while structures identified on the basis of the circular distribution of postholes or stone circles were defined in Frederick, Midland, and Agate Basin components.

Several domestic structures were discovered during the original Hell Gap investigation. These include a stone ring in the late Paleoindian Frederick component, two series of overlapping postholes interpreted as two superimposed structures in the Agate Basin component, and a series of postholes interpreted as a structure in the Midland component (Irwin-Williams et al. 1973). Structures, presumably domestic, have also been found at least at the Agate Basin site in the Folsom component, at the Hanson site, at the Barton Gulch site, and at the Vermilion Lakes site (Davis et al. 1989; Fedje et al. 1995; Frison and Bradley 1980; Frison and Stanford 1982a).

All components contained an abundance of chipped stone, inclusive of projectile points, preforms, bifaces, cores, end scrapers, side scrapers, perforators, an abundance of flake tools, and dominated by debitage. Activity areas and workshop locations were present in some components as indicated by high-density concentrations of debris. The components vary a great deal in size, artifact density, and distribution. It is likely that some components represent palimpsests, while others may be living floors (e.g., Irwin-Williams et al. 1973; Sellet 1999). Hammerstones, palettes, shaft abraders, bone needles, and bone and stone beads indicate that a variety of activities occurred at the site.

The site was originally interpreted as a base camp; however, some of the components were interpreted as task-specific loci (e.g., Hell Gap and Alberta). Generally, this interpretation is still valid. Animal bone recovered indicates a variety of individual or small-group hunting strategies, although the animal bone assemblage in a few of the 16 components may represent animals transported from a multiple kill.

Task-Specific Sites

Task-specific or limited-activity sites are those probably occupied for a short period of time for a specific purpose such as, but not limited to, extraction of a resource (plants, animals, rocks, or minerals), a short-term camp en route to a resource, or a hunting overlook. Archaeologically, these types of sites are recognized by an artifact inventory limited in both quantity and variety, suggesting a single activity or few activities. Bone middens, in fact, should be viewed as task-specific locations in the context of the wider settlement and mobility strategies. Because of their very well known archaeological manifestations, I deal with them separately. I also discuss a few localities that likely represent other, limited Paleoindian behaviors that are important to the overall economic systems of these early peoples.

Hofman and Ingbar (1988) describe a very small assemblage of Paleoindian artifacts found on a surface of a prominent topographic feature. The artifact inventory includes only three unmodified flakes, one graver, one biface, one tested pebble, one projectile point base, one formal flake tool, and one minimally modified flake. Hofman and Ingbar (1988) argue that the site represents a Folsom complex hunting overlook. This site is particularly interesting since no similar localities are described for the region. In fact, such small sites are very rarely found or adequately analyzed and reported, resulting in the appearance that all Paleoindian sites are large. If the identification is correct, is this an overlook for a communal hunt or for pursuit of individual animals? Is it for pursuit of bison or some other prey species? While it is likely not possible to provide answers to these questions at present, we must pursue data to deal with such issues.

Another site with a limited artifact inventory is Rocky Foolsm, located in the northwestern Black Hills (Kornfeld 1988). The tool inventory consists of one projectile point, one graver, possibly one biface, and several dozen pieces of debitage. Discovered in an overflow channel of a reservoir, the exact context of the assemblage was never identified. Nevertheless, the specimens seem related and represent the remains of a small Folsom occupation.

The Laddie Creek site is well known for its Early Plains Archaic components (Larson 1990; Frison 1991b). However, a Cody occupation was below the Archaic components (Larson 1992). This mid-to-late-period Paleoindian occupation consisted of one Cody knife, a biface, several flake tools, and debitage. Although only a small excavation area was completed in the Cody component, the assemblage nevertheless suggests a limited set of activities.

Sister's Hill, located in north-central Wyoming on the eastern flank of the Bighorn Mountains, is at the ecotone between the mountains and the Powder River Basin to the east (Agogino and Galloway 1965). The assemblage includes a Hell Gap projectile point indicating the age and relative cultural context of the site. The small chipped stone assemblage likely represents a limited set of Paleoindian behaviors.

Caribou Lake is a multicomponent site at 3,400 meters above mean sea level, near the continental divide in the Colorado Front Range (Benedict 1992). The Paleoindian component consists of a hearth, two concentrations of resharpening flakes, several projectile points, and several bifacial and unifacial chipped stone tools. The artifact inventory again suggests a limited set of activities carried on at the site. Benedict (1992) suggests that these activities likely occurred in the process of travel from the plains into the mountain basins.

In summary, numerous spatially and artifactually limited localities of Paleoindian finds are scattered in the western plains and the Rocky Mountains. The sites mentioned above are a pale reflection of what constitutes the Paleoindian archaeological record and likely an even paler reflection of what the Paleoindian peoples of 12,000 to 7,500 radiocarbon years ago left behind. Other regions are likely not any different in this respect and contain numerous small localities. However, the synthetic literature rarely incorporates these sites into the overall discussion of early American lifeways. I suspect that these sites are exceedingly underrepresented in the literature and consequently biase the way we view Paleoindian economic systems.

Other Significant Sites, Features, and Artifacts

A series of caches, storage features, and various midden deposits known from the study area also illustrate aspects of Paleoindian lifeways. Specifically, the Sheep Mountain net (Frison et al. 1966), the storage pits at the Medicine Lodge Creek site (Frison 1991b:343), and the rodent midden at the Medicine Lodge Creek site (Walker 1975) are discussed below. However, similar observations at other localities are introduced that place these three sites in a more complete context of Paleoindian subsistence.

The Sheep Mountain net, cached on a prominent ridge west of Cody, Wyoming, represents one of a few perishable objects from the Paleoindian period (Frison et al. 1986). The net was discovered in a limestone alcove at an elevation of 2,440 meters at the confluence of the North and South forks of the Shoshone River. Today, Sheep Mountain is a wintering area for mountain sheep, and this species was likely included in the prehistoric faunal inventory. The net is estimated to be 50 to 65 meters long and 1.5 to 2.0 meters high. It was constructed from juniper bark cordage from 1.0 to 5.2 millimeters thick, with a mesh ranging from 0.71 centimeter to 3.01 centimeters. Wooden stakes were incorporated into the net, a sample from which yielded a date of 8800 RCYBP. Frison (1991b:258) suggests the net was stored for seasonal use by a small group (n = 2) of laborers to hunt sheep. Later in prehistory, similar artifacts associated with sheep remains were discovered in Mummy Cave (e.g., Husted and Edgar 2002:86–87).

The Medicine Lodge Creek site is the location of a number of unique and significant Paleoindian discoveries (Frison 1976; 1991b). Located near the confluence of Medicine Lodge and Paint Rock creeks, major drainages of the western Bighorn Mountains, the site is in a large flat floodplain protected by a high sandstone cliff. Beginning approximately 10,000 RCYBP, the occupation of the Medicine Lodge Creek site spans much of the Paleoindian period. Similar to most other mountain and foothill localities, except for the Cody occupation, most of the complexes differ from the classic Paleoindian sequence. Of specific interest at the site are a series of pits and their content located in three layers dated to about 8,300 radiocarbon years ago. At least 14 elaborately prepared pits were found in one two-meter-square area, while 6 other pits were found in another part of the site. The globular, 25–50-centimeters-in-diameter pits are filled with trash (Frison 1991b:341–342).

Frison (1991b:343) thinks the purpose of the trash fill was to protect the Paleoindian pits from collapse during periods of nonuse and suggests that the pits were for dry storage of seeds, such as the recovered charred juniper and prune seeds. Similar storage facilities filled with dried and charred *Helianthus*, *Opuntia*, *Amaranthus*, *Prunus*, *Pinus*, and *Juniperus* seeds from the Paleoindian period were recovered at Schiffer Cave (Frison 1973, 1991b:342). It has been suggested that a large number of seeds were stored here. A number of fire pits were recorded in the lower, Paleoindian levels of the Bighorn Canyon cave sites (Husted 1969). Frison (1991b:343) suggests that a number of these may be storage features, such as those of the Medicine Lodge Creek site and Schiffer Cave. Finally, Southsider Shelter in the Bighorn Mountains also held similar facilities; however, these date to the Paleoindian to Archaic transition period (Frison 1991b:343).

In addition to the Late Paleoindian storage facilities, the Medicine Lodge Creek site also had a wide variety of fauna represented, including an extensive rodent bone midden. The fauna consists of cottontail, jackrabbit, and fish (chub, sucker, and whitefish or trout) in two Paleoindian strata. The extensive bone midden, dated to 9,500 radiocarbon years ago (Frison 1991b:285), contained 101 pocket gophers, 135 bushy tailed woodrats, 134 montane voles, and 180 prairie voles. Based on tooth eruption and wear, the woodrats died in late July or August (Walker 1975). This unique Paleoindian feature, along with the wide variety of fauna at the Medicine Lodge Creek site, certainly speaks of a very different subsistence strategy than communal big-game hunting.

Several other observations are relevant to the understanding of

Paleoindian subsistence strategies. First, in many of the sites mentioned in the preceding portions of this section, bison remains are noticeably rare or even absent. This is the case at the Medicine Lodge Creek site, the Bighorn Canyon caves, Mummy Cave (Husted and Edgar 2002), and Pine Spring (Sharrock 1966). Conversely, bighorn sheep remains are very common at many of these same sites, as are a wide variety of plant and other animal resources. Second, grinding stones, suggesting use of plant material, are present at a number of sites already discussed as well as at several others (e.g., Betty Green, Lookingbill, and Myers-Hindman).

Discussion

Commonly, discussion of Paleoindian subsistence strategies revolves around implications and inferences from the large-animal bone middens. Prehistorians have relied on these middens because they are easy to find, are generally well preserved, and quantitatively contain the bulk of Paleoindian archaeological material. While of lesser bulk and more difficult to extricate and quantify, the evidence for numerous subsistence activities other than big-game hunting has been reviewed above.

Even so, I have emphasized a very selective sample of the Paleoindian sites that do not contain bone middens. The 50+ sites or localities (see Table 3.1) include over 150 components, with an even greater number of occupations. However, this does not begin to exhaust Paleoindian manifestation in the western plains and Rocky Mountains. I reviewed only a few of the many salvage reports containing information on Paleoindian occupations. Additionally, the "isolated surface finds," many of which prove only the tip of the iceberg if followed up by testing and excavation, are not included. As an example, in the Middle Park of Colorado, a small intermontane basin, intensive research has been carried on for 10 years (for a preliminary summary, see Kornfeld and Frison 2000). Approximately 100 Paleoindian components have been recorded, and the area does not seem to be unusual (see Jodry 1999c; Pitblado 1999; Wimer 2001). While bison bone swamps our storage shelves with material from 27 sites (the bison bone middens), more numerous occupations from hundreds if not thousands of poorly published and minimally studied sites tell "the rest of the story."

The 5 sites chosen for this discussion, the other 14 sites mentioned, and those listed in Table 3.1 are not necessarily representative of the non–bone midden occupations, activities, or Paleoindian diets and subsistence strategies. Indeed, we currently have no way of knowing what might be representative. Rather, these sites provide a point of departure for a discussion of the breadth of Paleoindian economies. In these sites, we see evidence that Paleoindian economies were not focused on large game (mammoth or bison), but rather included, likely in significant quantities, a wide variety of plant and animal resources.

In addition to the few sites discussed, most of those mentioned in Table 3.1 contain a variety of fauna, including but not limited to rodents, birds, and shellfish. Chipped stone artifacts are found at each of the sites, often in significant numbers. Bone can vary from being a dominant class at some sites (e.g., the Indian Creek–Upstream locality) to a few scraps or fragments at other sites or other components of the same site (e.g., the earliest occupation at the Lookingbill site). While preservation is an important factor in the overall bone quantity, other factors play a role: most significantly, subsistence and manufacturing activities that produced bone debris. The remains of smaller animals (smaller than mammoth and bison) are remarkably common at Paleoindian sites, even at large-animal bone middens. Interest in smaller fauna is also evidenced by equipment such as the Sheep Mountain hunting net. Finally, rare features, such as the rodent bone middens with hundreds of processed animals at the Medicine Lodge Creek site, add significant and indispensable information about Paleoindian subsistence strategies and dietary variety.

Plant remains are rare, but seeds have been found in storage, processing, and discard facilities, leaving no doubt about Paleoindian use of these resources. Other classes of objects are rare at most non-big-game sites but can include at least ground stone tools, bone tools, bone ornaments, ochre, clothing accoutrements/buttons, incised bone objects, and cordage netting. Ground stone objects consist of at least the following: shaft smoothers, handstones, slabs, and ornaments.

Domestic structures are inferred from patterns found at several sites. Hearths or heating facilities, while less rare than structures, are generally ephemeral, described as surface hearths, usually consisting of a thin line of burned sediment. In some instances, hearths have only been defined by a patterned distribution of burned objects (e.g., Cattle Guard site; Jodry 1987, 1999b).

Other features at Paleoindian localities include storage pits, several of which were recovered in the Bighorn region rockshelters (e.g., Schiffer Cave; Frison 1991b:242). Storage, which was undoubtedly already well developed in Paleolithic economies of the Old World (e.g., Gamble 1986:390), was a significant component of Paleoindian systems from the earliest times. In fact, there is every reason to think that the first peoples crossing into

North America stored food reserves. Storage, a means of buffering against fluctuating food availability, is a critical strategy in northern regions (e.g., Binford 1980).

Use of storage features and caching behavior imply tethering to a particular location (the equipment or food cache). Plant and animal storage facilities, reoccupations, domiciles, and other characteristics suggest that Paleoindians often reutilized places and were far more "place oriented" than implied by the bone midden view of their lifeways.

Impressed by the distances apparently traversed by Paleoindians to acquire raw material for some chipped stone tools, archaeologists have usually interpreted this phenomenon as support for high mobility. For instance, for the Folsom period, Stanford (1999:302) states that "raw materials were quarried at locations that were many miles distant." Such generalizations, however, miss the fact that most raw material at most Folsom sites (big-game middens as well as others) is local. If, however, we assume that bone middens are communal hunting locations and aggregation locales for multiple bands (e.g., Fawcett 1987), exotic material may not be a function of high mobility, but may reflect exchange practice when different bands converged.

In conclusion, when the Paleoindian archaeological record from the western plains and the Rocky Mountains is examined closely, it shows incredible variability in subsistence strategies and diets. Paleoindian groups responded to environmental fluctuations, neighboring groups, resource characteristics (such as resource size, seasonality, distribution, and abundance), and other factors, similarly to other hunter-gatherers at the Pleistocene/Holocene transition (Strauss et al. 1996). Certainly, the first wave of people into North America found a continent empty of people, but this process was not significantly different from groups colonizing other previously unoccupied regions such as northern (previously glaciated) Europe.

Although the 4,500-year span of Paleoindian prehistory in the western plains and the Rocky Mountains may have seen changes in the economic strategies, the limited data set currently available is not yet complete enough to delineate these changes. Nor is it clear that all Paleoindian economic strategies practiced in the study area are represented in the archaeological record. However, the data clearly indicates the significant contribution of a wide variety of resources to Paleoindian subsistence strategies as well as their seasonal variation. In all likelihood, the Sheep Mountain net, the Medicine Lodge Creek rodent bone midden, and other features and artifacts described above point to the focus of Paleoindian economy, from 12,000 to 7,500 years ago.

Acknowledgments

Several colleagues improved the quality of this chapter, although they may not agree with its conclusions. Matthew E. Hill was kind enough to provide his unpublished data on Paleoindian bison bone middens to augment my own data collection. Todd Surovell and Nicole Waguespack clarified my thinking on several significant arguments. Finally, I thank George Frison and Mary Lou Larson for improving this chapter, and additional thanks go to Mary Lou for improving the clarity of my thoughts and for major editorial assistance.

FOUR

Discerning Clovis Subsistence from Stone Artifacts and Site Distributions on the Southern Plains Periphery

Michael B. Collins

Subsistence data are sparse at most Clovis sites on and near the southern Great Plains as they are throughout North America. Exceptions, of course, are the so-called kill sites (e.g., Miami, Domebo; see Table 4.1 for references). At best, the bones of a variety of animals are preserved at campsites, and these certainly afford direct evidence for the faunal aspect of subsistence (e.g., Aubrey, Kincaid, and Lewisville). However, because of differential preservation among the various animal species and the near total absence of preserved plant remains of Clovis age, prehistorians are often left with only indirect evidence as the basis for inferring Clovis subsistence (e.g., Pavo Real, McFaddin Beach).

The Gault site in central Texas presents a case-study opportunity to investigate Clovis subsistence behavior where poorly preserved faunal remains tell a fraction of the story, plant remains were not recovered, and stone artifacts constitute the primary avenue for research (Collins 2002). This chapter offers a preliminary attempt at using the context, configuration, and condition of the Clovis lithic assemblage at Gault as they compare to other archaeological patterns on the Southern Plains Periphery to infer aspects of the subsistence stance of the site's Clovis occupants.

Gault is a large site with an extensive and highly visible Archaic midden of burned rocks some 800 meters long by 200 meters wide that ranges in thickness from ca. 0.2 meters to 2.0 meters (Collins 2002; Collins and Brown 2000). Temporally diagnostic artifacts in the midden indicate periodic occupations from Early Archaic through Late Prehistoric times (ca. 8,800 to 500 RCYBP). Relic collecting for more than 70 years has decimated this midden, but underlying deposits bearing a stratified sequence of Paleoindian com-

TABLE 4.1. Bibliographic references for sites mentioned in text. Map numbers correspond to numbers on Figure 4.14

Map	Site	References
1	Aubrey TX	Ferring 2001
—	Anzick MT	Lahren and Bonnichsen 1974; Wilke et al. 1991
2	Barton TX	Ricklis and Collins 1994
3	Blackwater Draw NM	Boldurian and Cotter 1999; Hester 1972; Holliday 1997
4	Blue Hole TX	Mueggenbourg 1991
5	Bonfire TX	Dibble and Lorrain 1968
—	Carson-Conn-Short TN	Broster and Norton 1993
—	Dent CO	Figgins 1933
6	Doc Bell TX	Collins 1968, 1971
7	Domebo OK	Leonhardy 1966
—	Drake CO	Stanford and Jodry 1988
—	East Wenatchee WA	Gramly 1993; Mehringer 1988, 1989; Mehringer and Foit 1990
—	Fenn UT?	Frison 1991a; Frison and Bradley 1999
8	Frazier OK	Spivey et al. 1994
9	Gault TX	Collins 1998, 1999, 2002; Collins and Brown 2000; Collins et al. 1992; Collins and Lohse 2004
10	Keven Davis TX	Collins 1999b
11	Kincaid TX	Collins 1990; Collins et al. 1989
12	Lamar OK	Neal 1994
13	Landslide TX	Sorrow et al. 1967
—	Lehner AZ	Haury et al. 1959
14	Lewisville TX	Crook and Harris 1957; Holliday 1997; Stanford 1982, 1983; Story 1990
15	Lubbock Lake TX	Johnson 1987
16	McFaddin Beach TX	Long 1977; Turner and Tanner 1994; Stright 1999
17	Miami TX	Sellards 1938, 1952; Holliday et al. 1994
—	Murray Springs AZ	Haynes 1993; Hemmings 1970
—	Naco AZ	Haury 1953
18	Pavo Real TX	Collins et al. 2003
—	Sailor-Helton, KS	Mallouf 1994
—	Simon, ID	Butler 1963; Woods and Titmus 1985
19	Sitter Ranch TX	Collins 1968, 1971
20	Spring Lake TX	Shiner 1983; Takac 1991
21	Stillman Pit OK	Bartlett 1994
—	Thunderbird, VA	Gardner 1974
22	Twilla Ranch TX	Collins 1968; Tunnel and Hughes 1955
23	Vara Daniel TX	Ricklis et al. 1991; Collins et al. 1990
24	Wilson-Leonard TX	Collins, ed. 1998
25	Yellow Hawk TX	Mallouf 1989

ponents (pre-Clovis[?], Clovis, Folsom, Wilson, Cody, Golondrina-Barber, St. Mary's Hall, and Angostura) largely escaped this destruction and have been the object of intense archaeological investigations under my direction in 1991 (with codirector T. R. Hester), in 1998 (with codirector Hester), and from 1999 to 2002 (with codirectors Hester, H. J. Shafer, and M. R. Waters). Among the Paleoindian components, Clovis is by far the best represented and has been the primary focus of the investigations. Preliminary tabulations indicate a count of approximately 650,000 Clovis specimens (mostly debitage but including cores, bifaces, unifaces, and several categories of formal tools) recovered and cataloged from Gault. Detailed analyses of this assemblage have just begun, but enough information is at hand to support a number of preliminary conclusions. In my view, the evidence points clearly to the basic conclusion that the Clovis archaeological manifestation represents generalized subsistence, probably organized around foraging a wide array of resources.

Context of the Assemblage

Gault occupies the constricted head of the valley of a small stream at the place where reliable springs flow and abundant Edwards chert of extraordinary quality crops out. Today, the valley floor at this locality is well watered and supports a diverse array of trees and other vegetation on deep soils. This is in stark contrast to sparse xeric vegetation on thin, rocky soils on the immediately surrounding uplands of the Lampasas Cut Plains (part of the Edwards Plateau). At a larger scale, this setting is in the Balcones ecotone, where resources of limestone uplands mingle with contrasting ones occurring on adjacent coastal plains (Figure 4.1). The Edwards Plateau differs in its geology, soils, flora, and fauna from the Black Prairie region of the Gulf Coastal Plain. This edge between the southernmost extent of the high plains and the prairie land of the Gulf Coastal Plain is one of the great ecotones of North America. Gault today is a special place and evidently has been for a very long time.

Excavations in eight areas of the site (Figure 4.2) penetrated intact Clovis-bearing geologic deposits, where the depositional environments can be inferred to have been fluvial channels, overbank floodplains (with possible colluvial toe slope contributions), and an alluvial fan. Except in the fluvial channels, modest rates of deposition, roughly estimated to have been on the order of 0.2 to 0.8 millimeter per year, prevailed in these settings before, during, and briefly after Clovis times. The essential characteristics of

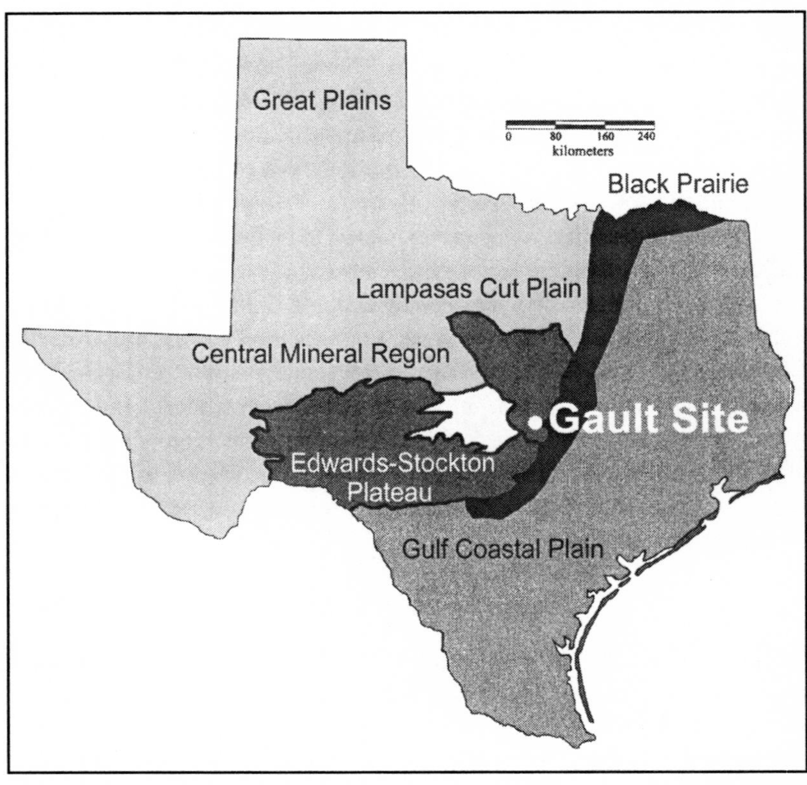

FIGURE 4.1. Physiographic setting of the Gault site in the ecotone along the juncture of the Edwards Plateau and the Gulf Coastal Plain ecozones.

these geologic contexts are summarized in Table 4.2. Excavation controls in the Clovis components were in 0.05-cubic-meter units (1 meter square by 5 centimeters thick). Most objects larger than 2 centimeters across were piece-plotted to 1-centimeter accuracy in the three-dimensional site grid.

Clovis materials vary in their concentrations from fewer than 10 to more than 300 pieces per 0.05-cubic-meter unit. This variance is expressed horizontally as areas of high artifact density separated by relatively artifact-free areas and, in one area of the site (Area 8), vertically as multiple Clovis components of great density separated by nearly sterile zones. Features include numerous tight clusters and small piles of debitage, a large concentration of initial reduction cores and flakes, one small pit of unknown function, a well, and a 2-by-2-meter patch of gravel that appears to have been partly shaped by humans. This gravel square has a scattering of Clovis blades, debitage, biface fragments, core fragments, and several bones on and

TABLE 4.2. Simplified geological contexts and archaeological sequences in eight excavation areas of the Gault site, Texas.

Excavation Area*	Geomorphological Setting	Strata	Cultural Content**
Area 4	alluvial fan w/ clay drapes	surface soil/midden	mixed L Paleoindian, E,M,L Archaic, and L Prehistoric
		carbonate-rich, iron-stained clay	Clovis
		lenses of clay and gravel	nondiagnostic flakes
Area 5	overbank floodplain; toe of alluvial fan	surface soil/midden	mixed L Paleoindian, E,M,L Archaic, and L Prehistoric
		carbonate-rich, iron-stained clay	Clovis and Clovis-like
		gravel lenses	sterile
Area 7	overbank floodplain, fluvial channel	surface soil/midden	mixed Archaic?
		paleosol	E Archaic
		calcareous clay	E Archaic
		iron-stained clay	Clovis
		iron-stained clay w/ gravel	Clovis
		iron- and manganese-stained gravel	sterile
Area 8	overbank floodplain, colluvial slope	surface soil/midden	mixed E, M, L Archaic, L Prehistoric
		calcareous clay	E Archaic, L Paleoindian
		paleosol	L Paleoindian
		iron-stained clay	Folsom
		iron-stained clay	Clovis
		iron-stained clay w/ gravel	Clovis
		iron- and manganese-stained gravel	sterile
Area 10	overbank floodplain	dense midden	mixed Archaic
		rubified soil	E Archaic, L Paleoindian
		iron-stained clay	Clovis
Area 11	overbank floodplain, colluvial toe slope, channel cut-and-fill	dense midden	mixed Archaic
		rubified soil	E Archaic, E,L Paleoindian
		iron-stained clay	Clovis
Area 12	overbank floodplain and colluvial toe slope	dense midden	Mixed E,M,L Archaic, L Prehistoric
		rubified clayey soil	L Paleoindian
		iron-stained clay	Folsom
		iron-stained clay	sterile
		iron-stained clay	Clovis
		iron-stained, carbonate-rich clay	sterile
		limonitic clay and gravel	sterile
Area 13	overbank floodplain and colluvial toe slope	midden	Mixed Archaic
		rubified soil	E Archaic?
		iron-stained clay	Clovis

* See site map for locations of excavation areas. ** Abbreviations: E = Early; M = Middle; L = Late.

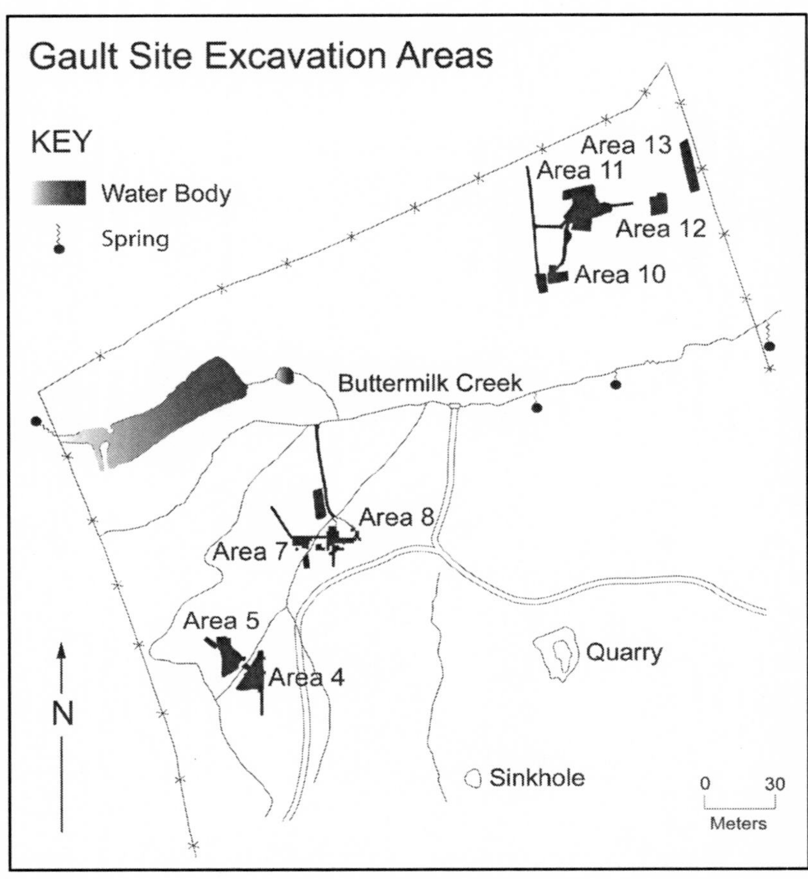

FIGURE 4.2. Map of the Gault site showing Buttermilk Creek and the major excavation areas. Clovis materials were recovered in Areas 4, 5, 7, 8, 10, 11, 12, and 13.

around it. Nothing that could be identified as a Clovis hearth or fireplace was observed at the site, but burned bone and heat-damaged chert occur throughout the Clovis components, and upon detailed distributional analysis these burned items may reveal concentrations indicating the location of simple, open campfires (comparable to those at the Aubrey site).

Lithic Assemblage Configuration

Clovis lithics at the Gault site are dominated by debitage that resulted from production and maintenance of bifaces, blades, flakes, and a variety of tools made on each of these kinds of blanks. Bifaces include large discoidal cores, choppers, projectile point preforms, projectile points, adzes, and

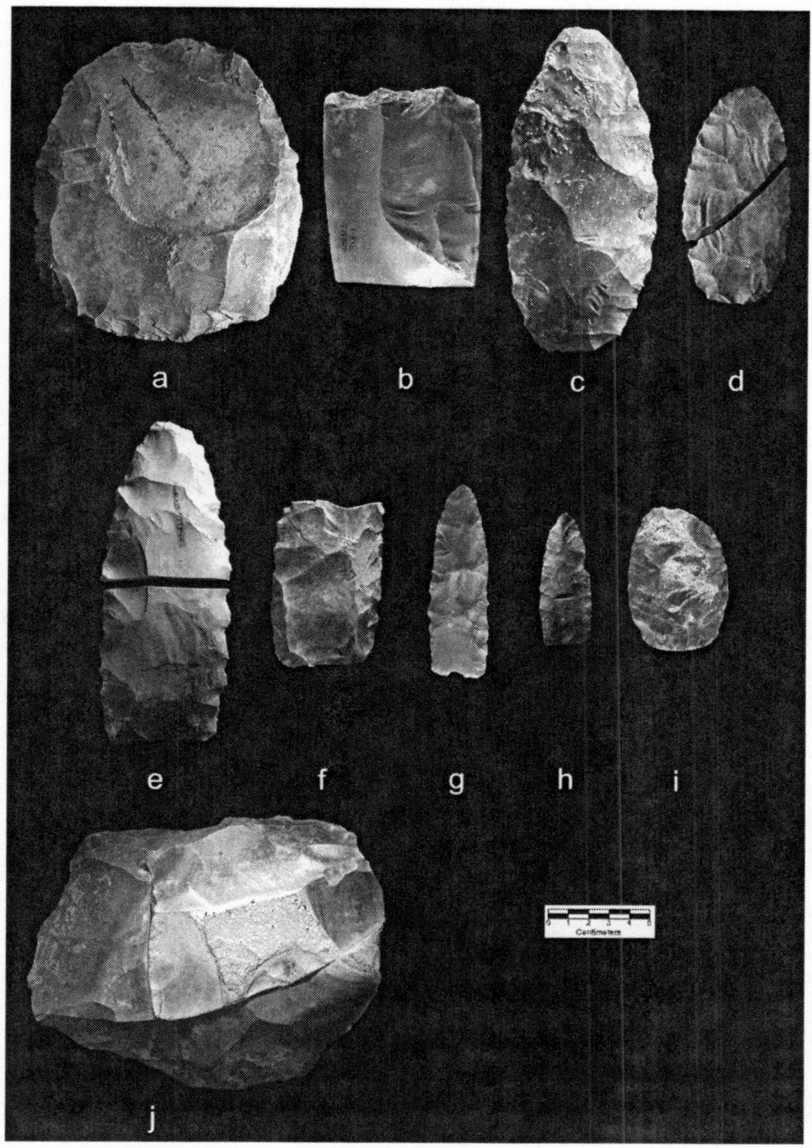

FIGURE 4.3. Representative Clovis bifacial artifacts. a, discoidal core; b, chopper; c–g, projectile point preforms; h, projectile point; i, adze; j, large early stage biface.

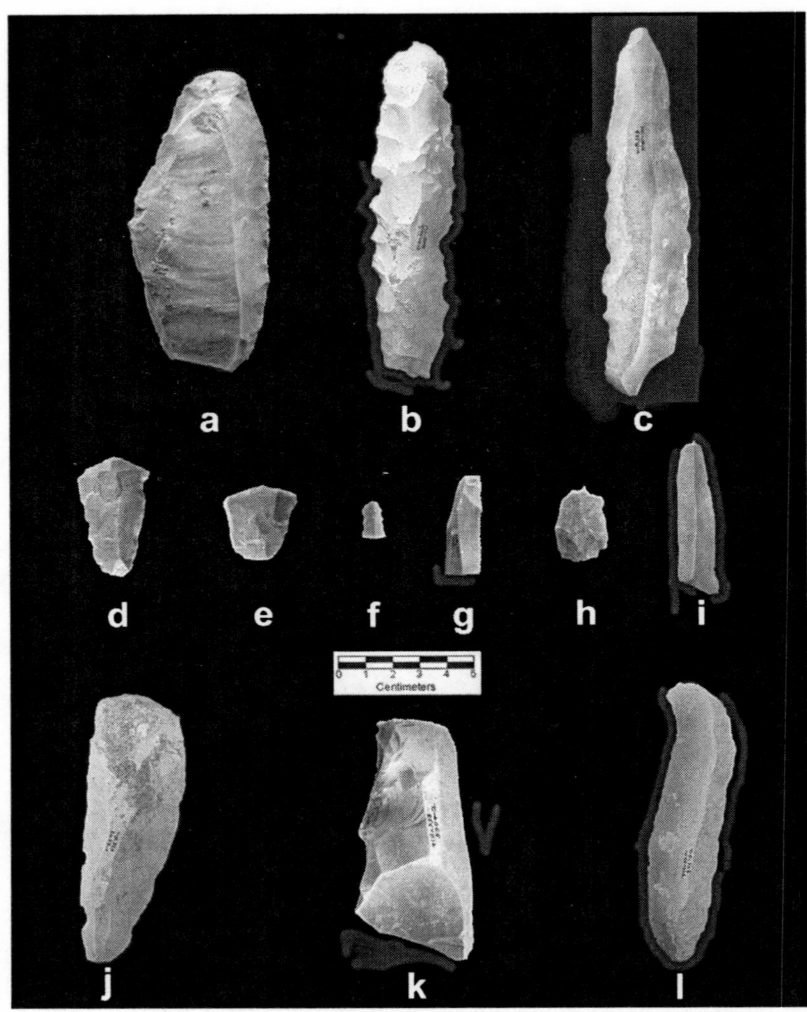

FIGURE 4.4. Clovis tools made on flakes and blades and a utilized flake. a, flake knife; b, c, serrated blades; d, end scraper on blade; f, end scraper on flake; f, tool on blade; g, serrated blade; h, graver on flake; i, graver on blade; j, end scraper on blade; k, utilized flake; l, utilized blade.

large, thick objects that could be reduced either as bifaces or as blade cores (Figure 4.3). Projectile point preforms are present in all stages of reduction, and projectile points are found in various conditions, from just produced to heavily resharpened or broken and discarded (see Figure 4.3). Large, flat flakes struck from the discoidal cores and other large bifaces were made into unifacially retouched cutting tools (Figure 4.4). Blades (and occasionally blade segments) were generally used without edge modification (see Figure 4.4). Modified blades—including end scrapers, side scrapers, denticulates, and gravers—are numerous but less frequent than unmodified blades (see Figure 4.4). Unmodified flakes exhibit utilization and occur along with various forms of unifacially retouched flakes (see Figure 4.4).

At the Gault site, a small proportion of the projectile points (ca. 8 percent) are made of nonlocal stones (chert, jasper, or quartz crystal). Some of these "nonlocal" stones are tentatively identified as coming from nearby sources (within 70 kilometers of the site). All of the remaining projectile points and well over 99 percent of the other chipped materials are of the immediately local chert (meaning the on-site source). The assemblage affords a rich and comprehensive sample of manufacturing debris for all categories of Clovis artifacts. From this debris, it is clear that biface and blade production were distinctive aspects of the technology except in the initial reduction of some large bifaces. Much of the local chert occurs in large, flattish nodules, and Clovis knappers began reduction of these nodules by removing large flakes across the faces. If the results of this initial step were satisfactory, the piece continued to be reduced as a biface (core or preform). If flaws or other difficulties interfered with this initial reduction, the bifacial piece might be reconfigured into a blade core. From this stage on, the reductive steps of bifaces and of blade cores were entirely different, and the two kinds of debris produced are quite distinctive (Callahan 1979; Bradley 1982; Collins 1999b; Morrow 1995).

Condition of the Assemblage

Debitage at Gault is prolific and largely pristine. Among unmodified blades and flakes are numerous specimens exhibiting use wear. All categories of retouched blade, flake, and biface implements include specimens showing evidence for use and are found in all stages of depletion and refurbishment; many are broken. The overall pattern is one of tool production, use, and maintenance leading ultimately to exhaustion and discard. Specimens in most formal implement categories can be seriated into stages of use-attrition.

Use actions and contact materials have been discerned on stone tools using microscopic techniques. Marilyn Shoberg of the Gault research staff has examined a sample of Clovis artifacts from the site under magnifications up to 500X and related the microscopic evidence of each individual piece to its inferred stage of resharpening or breakage (Shoberg 2001; Shoberg and Beers 2004). These pieces demonstrate the diversity of activities evidenced at the site and are particularly compelling evidence in the argument that Gault is a multifunctional campsite. It is also clear that it was occupied repeatedly during Clovis times and that at least occasionally Clovis occupants stayed long enough to completely wear out locally made stone tools. Alternatively, tools made at the site may have been carried afield, used, and returned before being abandoned.

Cutting of soft material, inferred to be meat in most cases, is indicated for serrated blades, blades, thin unifaces, and thin bifaces (Figures 4.5, 4.6). Hide-working wear is seen on modified and unmodified flakes and blades (Figure 4.7). Wear consistent with woodworking appears on small adzes and on blades (Figure 4.8). Bone working is inferred on a utilized blade (Figure 4.9). One large, notched flake exhibits wear tentatively interpreted to have resulted from digging (Figure 4.10). Well-developed polish from cutting silica-rich grasses appears on blades and flakes (Figure 4.11). Silica polish on the Clovis artifacts matches the two forms of wear (from green grass and from dry grass) produced experimentally by Bettison (1985). The two forms of polish may indicate cutting of grass in the growing season and the dry season or the harvesting of green grass that was then dried and worked again.

Clovis points are the hallmark of the archaeological manifestation generally called Clovis culture (Stanford 1991, 1999). It is doubtful, however, that the makers of fluted Clovis points would conform to any social entity that ethnologists would recognize as an ethnic group, or "a culture." There is not a consistent artifact assemblage that recurs at sites across the geographic range of Clovis points, and available dates suggest that these points were in vogue for at least 300 and perhaps as much as 600 years or more (Collins 1999b; Fiedel 1999b; Meltzer 1993a; Morrow and Morrow 1999; Stanford 1991, 1999). There is no ethnographic analog for the existence of such a long-term and so widely dispersed hunter-gatherer cultural unit. Nor is there ethnographic support for the notion that Clovis subsistence could have been in the highly specialized big-game-dependent mode of popular theory (Meltzer 1993a).

In spite of indications of cultural plurality, the technology of Clovis point manufacture is remarkable for its uniformity over a vast range (Collins 1999a, 1999b). If point morphology alone were similar everywhere, the fact would be interesting but not perplexing. What is perplexing is that Clovis point preforms in all stages of reduction reflect highly similar sizes, shapes,

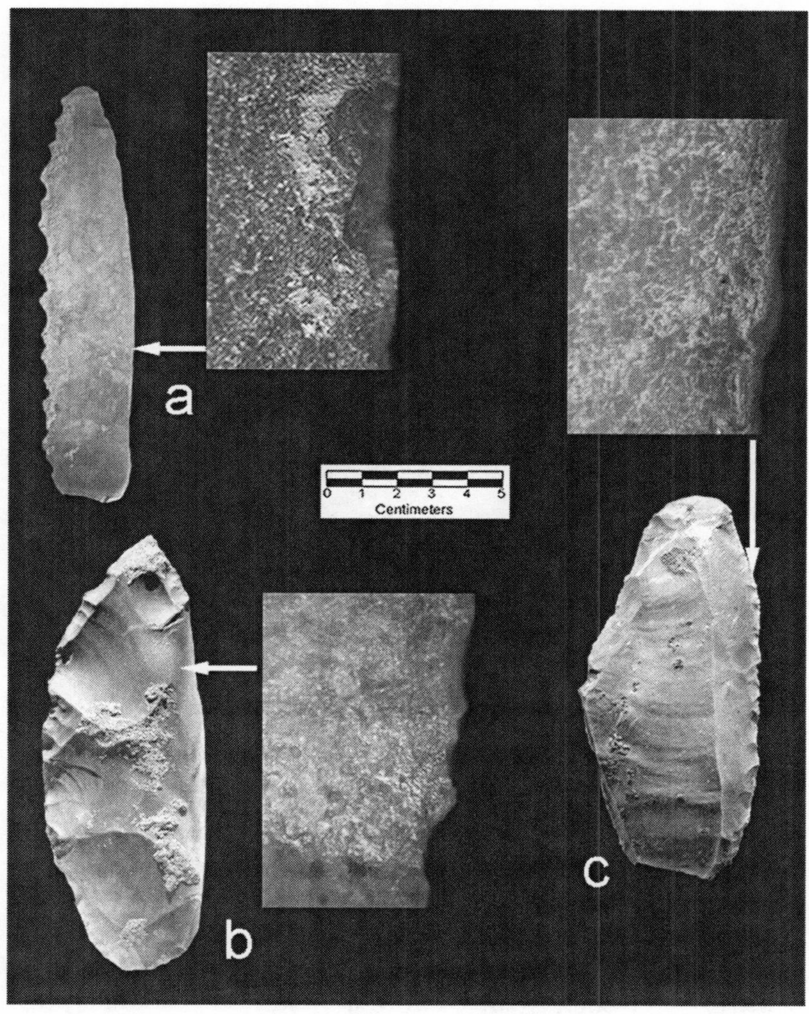

FIGURE 4.5. Clovis tools inferred to have been used in cutting meat. a, serrated blade; b, biface with very sharp edge created by overshot flake scar; c, retouched flake.

and details of flaking behavior, and seriate into a similar sequence of reduction steps everywhere from the Atlantic to the Pacific, from the southern fringe of Canada to Central America. We do not know what compelled these artisans to adhere to this technology, but the fact that Clovis points with a preponderance of shared attributes and manufactured using a similar technology occur so widely leads to formulation of the null hypothesis

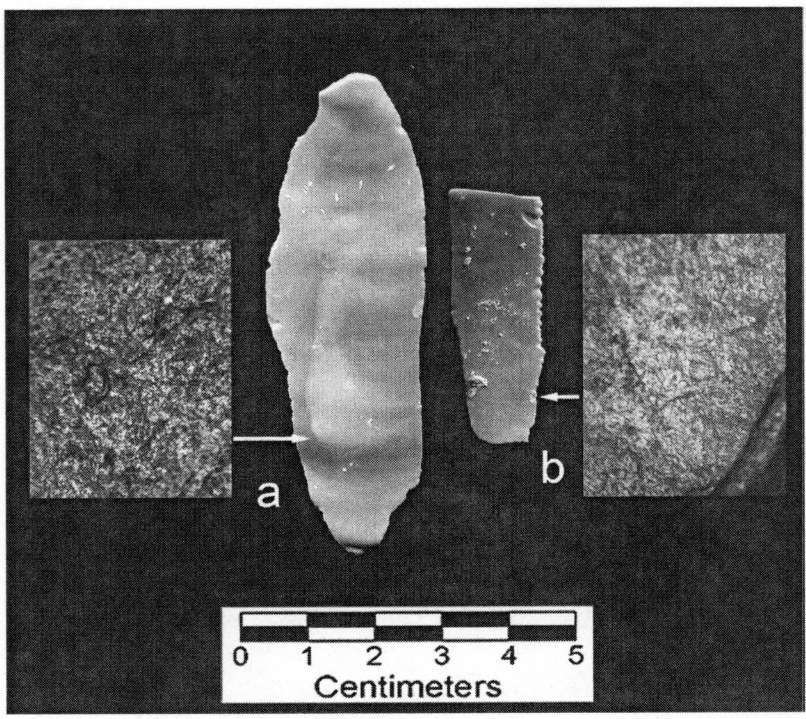

FIGURE 4.6. Clovis blade tools inferred to have been used in cutting meat. a, blade; b, finely serrated blade.

that their function(s) was (were) also similar. What was that function, or what were those functions?

Archaeologists have long placed great emphasis on Clovis big-game hunting (e.g., Haynes 1966; Frison and Bradley 1999; Wormington 1957), viewed the Clovis point as part of a lethal armature capable of killing mammoths and other large animals (Frison 1989; Frison and Bradley 1999), and even suggested that this lethality brought about the extinction of much of the North American megafauna (Martin and Klein 1984; Martin and Wright 1967; see Haynes 2002b for a recent discussion). For these reasons, a close look at Clovis points is obligatory in any consideration of Clovis subsistence behavior.

Archaeological contextual evidence, Clovis point morphology, some theoretical parameters, and comparisons with other styles of points raise questions about the ways in which these tools were employed. From the time they were discovered among the bones of mammoths at Dent, Colorado;

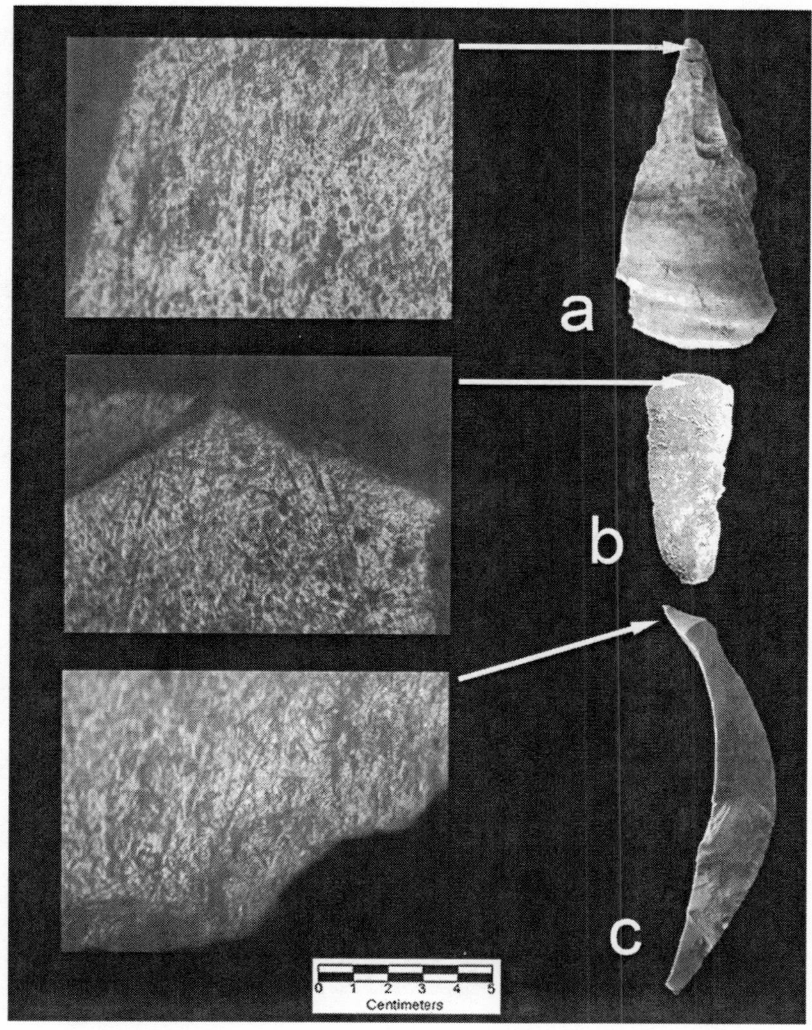

FIGURE 4.7. Clovis tools inferred to have been used in hide working. a, flake; b, end scraper on blade; c, blade.

Blackwater Draw, New Mexico; and Miami, Texas, Clovis points have generally been assumed to be weapon tips. Recently, most investigators acknowledge that they probably also served as knives (Frison and Bradley 1999; Kay 1996; Stanford 1999). This dual pattern is seen on points from the Gault site (Figure 4.12). A persisting question is whether there are more specific indications of function and mode of deployment.

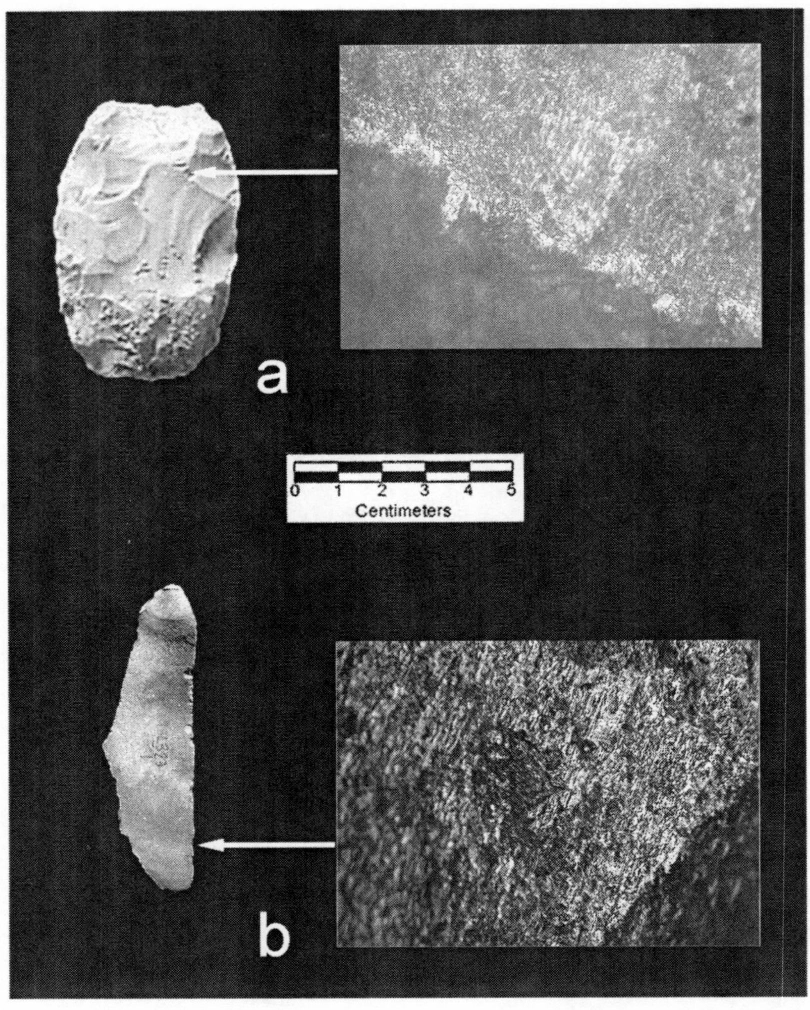

FIGURE 4.8. Clovis tools inferred to have been used in woodworking. a, bifacial adze; b, blade.

Scholars for years have assumed that Clovis hunters propelled darts with the atlatl, or spearthrower (Frison 1989). It has also been common to infer that Clovis points were hafted onto foreshafts of wood (Frison 1989; Frison and Bradley 1999) or bone or ivory (Lahren and Bonnichsen 1974). In absence of preserved atlatls, shafts, and unequivocal foreshafts, indirect means are needed to test these ideas.

Design and function of the Clovis point emphasize bilateral symmetry,

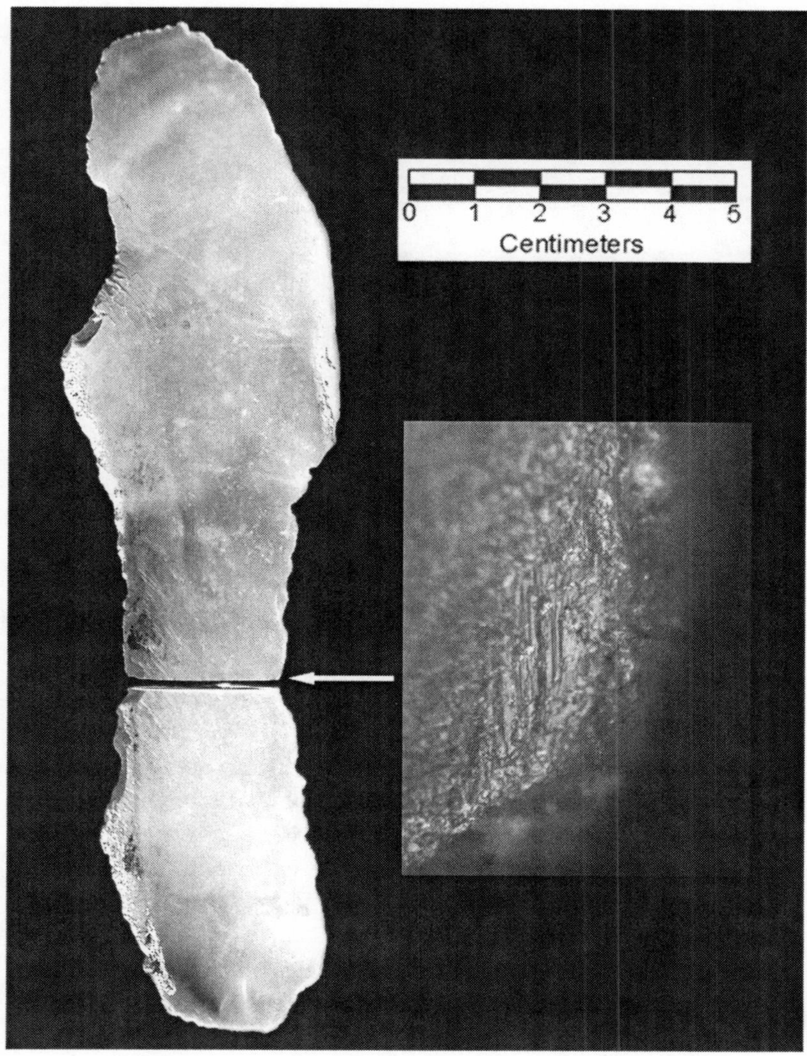

FIGURE 4.9. Clovis blade inferred to have been used in bone working.

strength, and sharpness. These are integrated traits consistent with the identification of it as a weapon tip. These attributes were maintained as Clovis points were resharpened (typically from lengths of 100 millimeters or more to 50 millimeters or slightly less [Collins 1999a, 1999b]). If the point's intended function was solely as a knife, symmetry would be less important, and impact damage would not occur. There is appeal to the con-

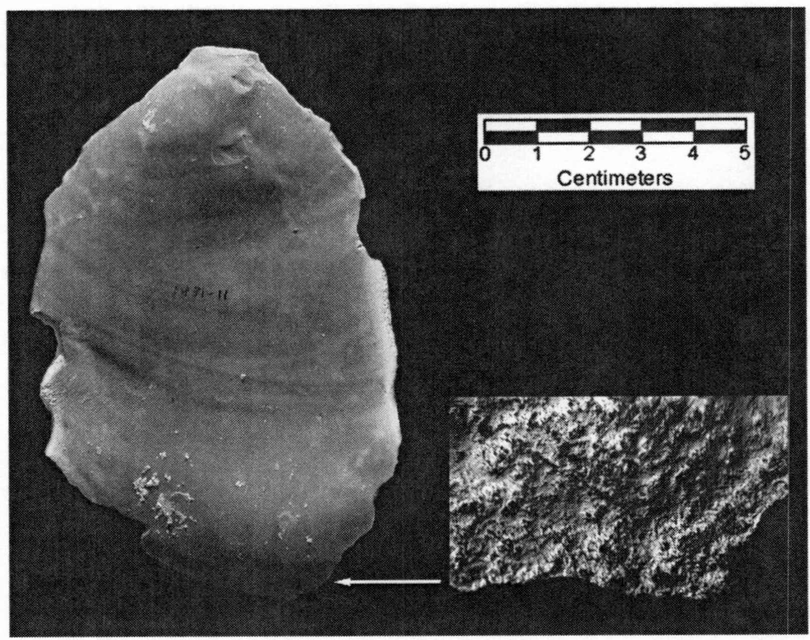

FIGURE 4.10. Clovis flake inferred to have been used in digging.

cept of Clovis points hafted onto short rods of bone, ivory, or wood that served dually as foreshaft in the spear or as a handle when the assembly was used as a knife. If bone or ivory foreshafts were in common use, it would seem that by now at least one would have been found articulated with a point among the animal bones of a kill site; the same cannot be said for wooden foreshafts, of course.

There are four basic weapon systems that might employ chipped stone–tipped projectiles (Cattelain 1997; Dial et al. 1998; Knecht 1997): javelins, lances, atlatls, and bows and arrows. Simplest of these is the javelin that is propelled by hand. Javelin tips could be either attached directly to a shaft or mounted in a foreshaft. Lances are thrusting weapons that are not propelled; commonly, they are thrust, withdrawn, and thrust again in multiple stabs. These, too, are comparatively simple weapons. Although foreshafts are a possibility on lances, the juncture of shaft and foreshaft would seem to add an unnecessary point of potential failure when withdrawing the point. Mechanical advantages of the atlatl and the bow and arrow make these complex systems superior in terms of force. The bow and arrow also has the advantage of great accuracy.

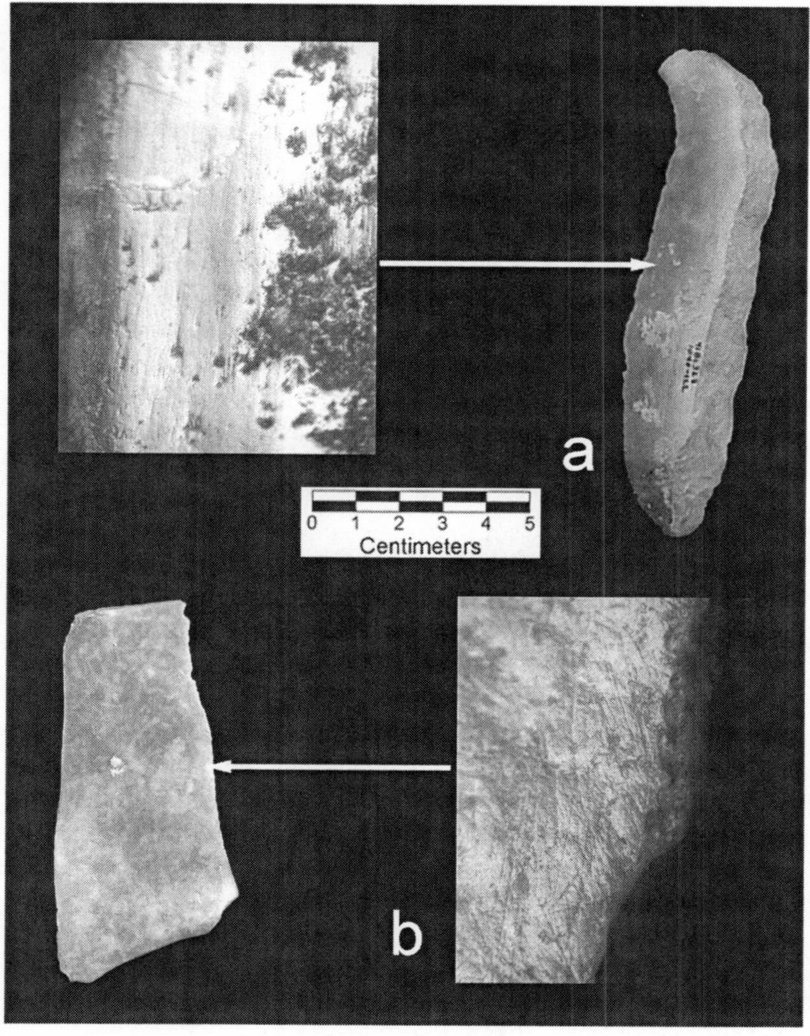

FIGURE 4.11. Clovis flake and blade inferred to have been used to cut grass. a, blade; b, flake.

We are probably safe in eliminating from consideration the bow and arrow based on widespread evidence that this system was not introduced into North America until late in prehistory (Hamilton 1982). Javelins offer an advantage of being relatively accurate in the hand of an experienced hunter, but this is offset by limited range and low impact force. Limited force probably excludes the javelin as a weapon capable of efficiently killing mammoths with their thick, tough skin. Even with javelin accuracy, it is to be expected that many such spears would hit bone. Damage to stone tips on a javelin should be seen relatively frequently, but it should not indicate high-speed impacts.

Hunting large animals with the lance would necessitate strategies for immobilizing the quarry enough to allow hunters to get in close and inflict one or more wounds. In such a case, the lance has the advantage of being highly accurate and capable of making deep wounds. By controlling the point of entry, direction of force, and orientation of the blade relative to the skeleton of the prey animal, the hunter armed with a lance could reach the vital organs (heart and lungs) of the thorax and often do so without hitting bone. Tips of stone lance points should show comparatively infrequent damage from high-speed impacts.

The atlatl is capable of transferring enough force to a dart to carry it a considerable distance and still inflict a potentially lethal wound (cf. Frison 1989). Accuracy is a potential limitation of the atlatl dart, although several hunters might quickly hit an animal with numerous darts and compensate for this, and do it from a safe distance. Because atlatl darts travel at high rates of speed, hit with considerable force, and cannot be thrown with enough precision to reliably avoid hitting bone, atlatl dart points should commonly show evidence for substantial impact damage.

Without preservation of all of the components, weapon systems are an elusive part of the archaeological record (cf. Cattelain 1997). Scarce examples of preserved bows and atlatls, or their parts, along with abundant data on projectile point sizes and weights for North America seem to indicate a late shift to the bow and arrow following a long history of use of the atlatl (Christenson 1986; Fenenga 1953; Hamilton 1982; Thomas 1978). There is limited direct evidence for the atlatl in Clovis times, that being in the form of three inferred atlatl hooks of bone and ivory and a bannerstone of bone, all of apparent Clovis age (Hemmings 2004:151, 165–171). Much effort has gone into attempts to discern arrows from atlatl darts using stone or organic projectile points with no absolutely reliable outcome (cf. Cattelain 1997; Dial et al. 1998; Patterson 1985).

In a sample of 112 Clovis points (13 from Gault and 99 from the Texas Clovis Fluted Point Survey data base made available by David Meltzer [see Meltzer and Bever 1995]), data were gathered on evidence for resharpening and impact damage (Table 4.3). A small subsample of these was also examined under the microscope for evidence of use wear. These data confirm the prevailing notion that Clovis points were both piercing and cutting imple-

TABLE 4.3. Frequencies of impact damage on Clovis, bifurcate stem, Andice, and Montell/Castroville projectile points.

Type	Complete/no damage		Tip impact damage		Blade edge damage		Total
	N	%	N	%	N	%	
Clovis	85	76	14	12	13	12	112
Bifurcate stem	25	44	28	49	4	7	57
Andice	12	39	10	32	9	29	31
Montell/Castroville	47	62	22	29	7	9	76

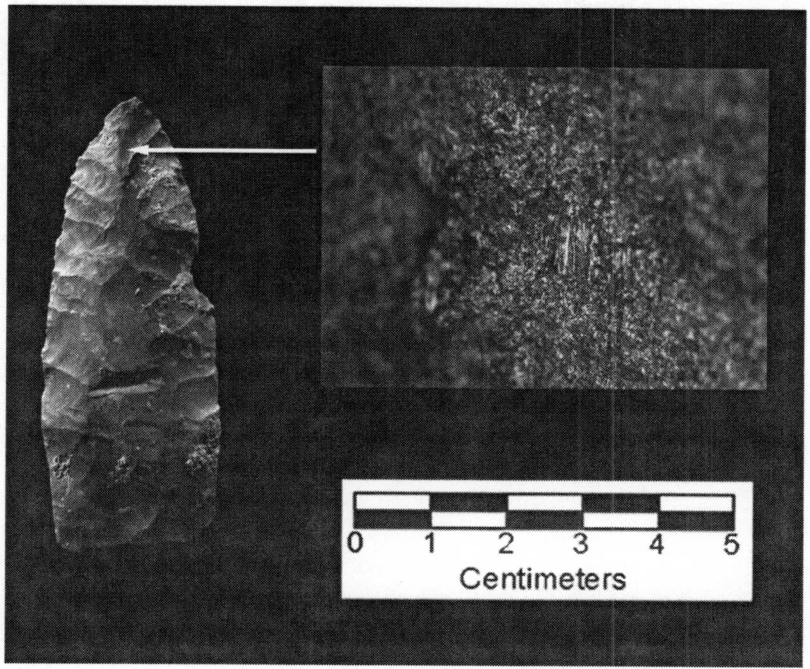

FIGURE 4.12. Clovis point exhibiting wear inferred to derive from piercing and from cutting.

ments (see Figure 4.12) but place some doubt on the interpretation that they were tipped darts propelled by the atlatl.

Compared to several styles of Early Archaic dart points, the occurrence of impact damage on Clovis points is a low 27 out of 112 (24 percent). Of these 27 impact features, 14 are at the tip, and 13 are along blade edges (Figures 4.12, 4.13a). In a sample of 57 Early Archaic, bifurcate-stemmed dart points (types Gower, Hoxie, Jetta, Martindale, and Uvalde) from the

FIGURE 4.13. Examples of impact damage on selected types of projectile points. a, resharpened Clovis point with blade edge damage; b, Hoxie point with extensive tip impact damage and blade edge damage; c, resharpened Andice point with minor edge damage; d, heavily resharpened Andice point with tip impact damage; e, resharpened Montell point with minor tip impact damage; f, resharpened Castroville point with minor tip impact damage.

Gault site, 32 (56 percent) manifest impact damage, predominantly at the tip, but in a minority of cases (4 out of 57, or 7 percent) along the edge of the blade (Figure 4.13b). Of 31 Andice points from Gault, 19 (61 percent) exhibit impact damage, 10 (32 percent) to the tip and 9 (29 percent) to the edge (Figure 4.13d).

The Calf Creek/Andice dart point type is broad bladed with large barbs (Figure 4.13c). Widely distributed in the south-central United States (Justice 1995; Prewitt 1995; Wyckoff 1995), it is found in association with bison at certain sites (e.g., Landslide, Barton, and Frazier) and in Texas falls into one of the times when bison populations were relatively plentiful (ca. 5500 RCYBP). During another interval of bison relative abundance in Texas (ca. 2500 RCYBP), two other large, broad-bladed dart point forms (Montell and Castroville) were in vogue. One of the distinctive characteristics of all of these point forms is extreme resharpening. These forms, like the Clovis point, seem to be weapon tips well suited for use on big game and have some of the attributes that might be expected of a lance point. This is a hypothesis worth further investigation in that only 2 of the 16 reasonably intact Montell and Castroville points found among the bison bones of Bone Bed 3 in Bonfire Shelter (Dibble and Lorrain 1968) have impact fractures—minor ones at that (Dibble and Lorrain 1968:figure 21a, c). These points were evidently used in killing bison, yet the incidence of tip damage is minimal, possibly indicating the use of lances, where hitting bone could be largely avoided.

Microscopic wear on Clovis points includes striations parallel to the long axis of the point and originating from the distal end (see Figure 4.12; see also Kay 1996:figure 9). These are consistent with use as a projectile tip. These same points as well as others exhibit the characteristic diagonal and V-shaped striations and polish of knife use. Haft wear is consistently present on Clovis points, and ochre staining is often seen on the haft area of these points, strong evidence that these were securely hafted, although the nature of the haft is not known. Clovis points were reused multiple times, with frequent resharpening between uses.

This evidence favors an inference of hunting live animals over one of scavenging meat from dead ones. Mammoth kill sites are typically at water holes (Miami, Blackwater Draw) or in stream beds (Domebo, Dent, Naco, Lehner, Murray Springs). Ambushing healthy animals and killing sick or injured ones at water are equally effective strategies that might account for this pattern. If Clovis hunters were killing mammoths at water, it is possible that the combination of soft ground and sloping banks afforded enough advantage for close-range use of the atlatl dart or perhaps even the lance, especially if the animals were impaired by dehydration, illness, or injury. Whatever the method, it seems clear that the Clovis point was part of an armature capable of killing mammoths and that Clovis hunters were, in fact, doing just that. Equally clear is the fact that this was far from being the mainstay of Clovis subsistence.

Faunal Evidence

Wherever faunal evidence is recovered in Clovis campsites, mammoth remains are only part of a diverse array of small, medium-size, and large animals (Cannon and Meltzer 2004). These include fish, amphibians, reptiles, birds, and mammals (Cannon and Meltzer 2004). At Aubrey, Gault, Kincaid, and Lewisville, for example, the faunal lists (Table 4.4) include game ani-

TABLE 4.4. Informal list of vertebrate fauna from Clovis components at four sites.

Taxon	Aubrey	Gault	Kincaid	Lewisville
Fish	X			X
Frog/Toad	X			
Salamander	X			
Alligator			X	
Turtle	X	X	X	X
Snake	X	X		X
Bird	X	X		X
Mammoth	X	X	X	
Horse		X	X	X
Bison	X	X		
Deer	X	X		X
Cottontail rabbit	X	X		X
Jackrabbit	X			
Rat	X			X
Mouse	X		X	X
Prairie dog				X
Vole	X			
Lemming	X			
Gopher	X	X		
Mole	X			
Muskrat	X			
Ground sloth	X			
Wolf				X
Canid		X		
Badger			X	
Raccoon			X	X

mals that were undoubtedly hunted (probably by the able-bodied males). Also recovered were numerous species that could be caught, trapped, or collected (probably by almost everybody else in the group); these are, respectively, such game as mammoths, deer, horse, bison, ground sloth, and alligators, on the one hand, and fish, salamanders, turtles, snakes, frogs, birds, mice, rats, moles, voles, lemmings, and rabbits, on the other hand.

At Gault, there is evidence to suggest that mammoth, horse, and bison were hunted early in the Clovis interval but that only bison were hunted near the end of that time (Collins 2002; Timperley et al. 2003). This is tenta-

TABLE 4.5. Informal list of vertebrate fauna for the early, middle, and late Archaic at the Wilson-Leonard site, central Texas (from Baker 1998).

Taxon	Early Archaic	Middle Archaic	Late Archaic
Fish	X	X	X
Frog/Toad		X	X
Turtle	X	X	X
Snake	X	X	X
Bird	X		X
Rabbit	X	X	X
Squirrel		X	X
Gopher		X	X
Rat		X	X
Raccoon			X
Canid			X
Deer		X	X
Antelope			X
Deer/Antelope	X	X	X
Bison			X

tively taken to indicate that, locally, the mammoth and horse became extinct during Clovis times. There is no evidence that any technological change in Clovis weaponry accompanied a shift to bison as the primary large-game animal.

Comparisons with other archaeological data put these Clovis faunal assemblages in perspective. It has long been popular to generalize Paleoindian subsistence as reliant upon the hunting of big game (Cannon and Meltzer 2004). This mode of subsistence clearly seems to apply to Folsom, Cody, and possibly Plainview adaptations. Evidence is best in the case of Folsom, where there is a consistent occurrence of bison kill sites, a preponderance of bison remains in all Folsom sites where faunal remains are preserved, and a nearly perfect concordance between the distribution of Folsom sites and the open grassland environments favored by bison (Bamforth 1985; Largent et al. 1991; Hofman 1991). Clovis evidence stands in stark contrast to the Folsom data. Clovis faunal evidence, as noted above, is far more diverse, and Clovis site distributions do not correspond to the environmental preferences of any particular fauna.

Archaic archaeological faunal assemblages, on the other hand, compare closely to those of Clovis. On and near the southern plains, Archaic sites with comprehensive faunal records consistently include diverse small, medium-size, and large animals. Wilson-Leonard fauna (Baker 1998) offers a representative comparison to Gault in that it is in the same environment and setting, the culture-bearing deposits are similarly clay-rich, and bone preservation is almost as poor as at Gault (95 percent of the bone from Gault is unidentifiable; 70 percent at Wilson-Leonard). In spite of these limitations, Wilson-Leonard provides an indication of the typical diet breadth in the Early, Middle, and Late Archaic of the region (Table 4.5). Bison, deer, and antelope are common among the larger animals; medium-size animals that occur frequently include canids and raccoons; and such small animals as fish, frogs/toads, turtles, snakes, birds, rabbits, squirrels, gophers, and rats are typical.

Faunal data show that Clovis subsistence more closely matches that of the long Archaic tradition than the subsistence mode of classic big-game hunters such as Folsom around the southern periphery of the Great Plains. Consistent with this and equally revealing are the nature and geographic distribution of Archaic and Clovis sites of various types in the same area. As already noted, Clovis sites do not show the same concordance with the environment favored by large herbivores seen in Folsom sites. This is just part of the distributional story. Relevant to this discussion are kill sites, campsites, chert quarry/workshops, and caches.

Site Distributions

In the early Holocene, a generalized Early Archaic lifeway is indicated for much of the southern plains periphery. The time-diagnostic projectile point forms for this include a series of bifurcate-stemmed types (such as Gower, Hoxie, Jetta, Uvalde). Sites with these and related forms are concentrated along the southern and eastern margin of the Edwards Plateau (Figure 4.14) and are closely tied to an environmental configuration known as the Balcones Canyonlands (Collins 1995; Collins 1998, 2004; Johnson 1991; McKinney 1981). These are deep, well-watered valleys and canyons incised into the plateau with its xeric uplands. The setting is a rich ecotone and afforded these generalized hunter-gatherers with sufficient resources that they never moved toward food production (Collins 1995, 2004; Collins and Mear 1998). This is not an environment well suited to large herbivores as the relief is abrupt and the flora is predominately trees and brush. Clovis sites (Gault, Kincaid, Pavo Real, Spring Lake, Vara Daniel, Wilson-Leonard, and others), too, are concentrated in precisely this same setting (Collins

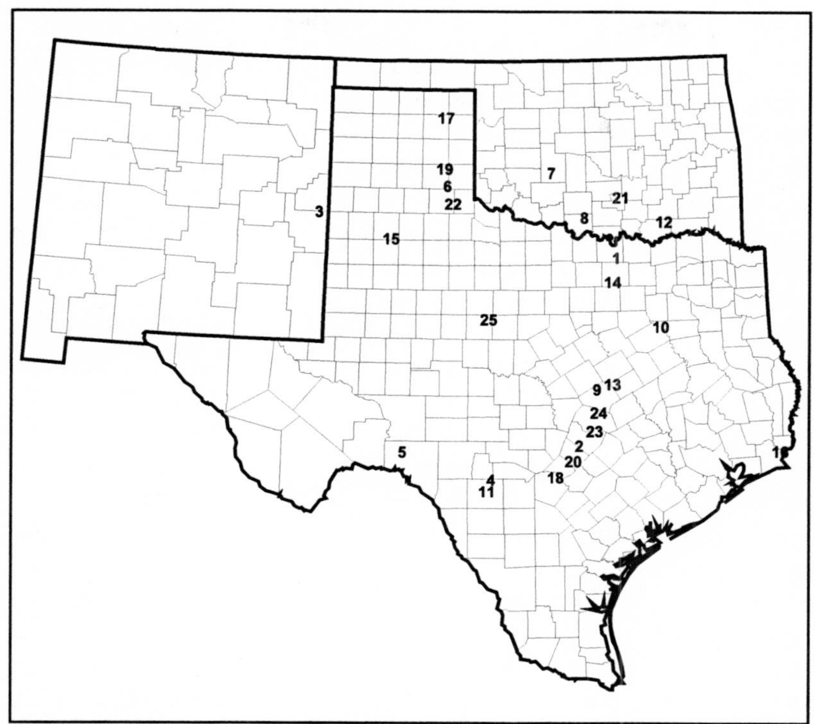

FIGURE 4.14. Distribution of Clovis and Archaic sites mentioned in text. See Table 4.1 for site names and for references.

2002); in fact, at each of these sites extensive Archaic middens overlie the Clovis components. These are the site distributional patterns of generalized hunter-gatherers, not of big-game hunters. Furthermore, environmental evidence indicates that in Clovis and in Early Archaic times, it was drier than at present, and the well-watered valleys may have been particularly favorable as a result (Collins 1995, 2004).

Folsom materials also occur at most of these Clovis sites (Gault, Kincaid, Pavo Real, Spring Lake, and possibly Wilson-Leonard), but in each case the Folsom assemblage differs significantly from the Clovis assemblage. At Gault and Pavo Real, the evidence suggests that these were primarily quarry/workshops in Folsom times; the Clovis material is more numerous, and the assemblages are more diverse (greatly so at Gault); and these sites are not far removed from the open prairies of the Gulf Coastal Plain. Only a single fragmentary Folsom point was recovered at Spring Lake. At Kincaid—also on the margin of the Coastal Plain—it may be that a bison with five Folsom-point-tipped spears in its body escaped its tormentors and died at the site (Collins 1990). Folsom-like materials with remains of bison were found at Wilson-Leonard, which is another of the sites in close proximity to the coastal prairies. No Folsom site in this area is nearly as large and complex as the Clovis components at Gault.

Two other intervals in the regional Archaic sequence offer informative comparisons to Clovis. One of these is the already mentioned Calf Creek/Andice interval (ca. 6000–5500 RCYBP in Texas; Collins 1995, 2004). In central Texas, components of this interval occur in much the same distribution and have some of the same characteristics as do other Archaic sites. Gault is one such site; others include Landslide and Barton. These sites manifest the use of large, stone-paved hearths and diverse tool kits seen at most Archaic sites, differing only by the presence of bison bones and of extremely broad-bladed projectile points. There is at least one bison kill site, Frazier in south-central Oklahoma, attributable to this interval. Frazier is not far from the Clovis mammoth kill site of Domebo. The other interval is that known by its distinctive broad-bladed Montell and Castroville dart points (ca. 2500 RCYBP; Collins 1995, 2004), another brief period of bison presence in the region. Montell and Castroville assemblages occur in most of the major Archaic middens of central Texas, but the points are also found in bison-kill sites. Examples of these kill sites are Bonfire in the Lower Pecos Region of Texas and, in the Texas panhandle, the three sites of Sitter Ranch, Doc Bell, and Twilla. Bonfire also has Paleoindian bison-kill components (Folsom and Plainview), along with what may be a fragmentary Clovis point; also, the three Montell/Castroville bison-kill sites in the Texas panhandle are not far from the Miami Clovis mammoth kill site.

Taking Folsom as the archetypical big-game hunting archaeological manifestation brings out another informative contrast with Clovis and with Archaic manifestations. No Folsom cache sites have been reported. I have taken this to be an expectable trait of far-ranging big-game hunters; have emphasized how this differs from Clovis, where caches are a relatively common site type (e.g., Anzick, Drake, East Wenatchee, Fenn, Keven Davis, Sailor-Helton, and Simon); and have suggested that caching would be more advantageous for foragers who can anticipate returning to a given spot more reliably than can nomadic big-game hunters (Collins 1999b). Caches are also typical kinds of sites throughout much of the Archaic on and near the southern plains periphery (Miller 1993), including the Calf Creek/Andice (Stillman Pit and Lamar sites) and Montell/Castroville (Blue Hole) intervals.

Clovis, Calf Creek/Andice, and Montell/Castroville assemblages exhibit the same concentrations of large, complex sites in and near the Balcones Canyonlands; large herbivore kill sites on the plains and prairies; use of caches; as well as far-flung distributions of their distinctive projectile points. All three of these intervals manifest evidence for a mix of generalized hunting-gathering and big-game hunting subsistence activities; all three include large and relatively broad-bladed projectile points showing extensive resharpening. It is important to reiterate that this overall pattern is distinctly different from that of Folsom, where the primary subsistence activity was big-game hunting. At the more general level, Archaic and Clovis are more alike than Clovis is to the other Paleoindian manifestations where big-game hunting prevails.

Gault is a large, complex, multifunctional Clovis campsite located on the ecotonal edge of the southern Great Plains. It and other Clovis sites preserve faunal evidence of considerable diet breadth and less mobility than are generally ascribed to the Clovis subsistence mode. This evidence differs from that of Folsom, the succeeding Paleoindian interval in much of the plains. The Folsom pattern is one of specialized bison hunting and high mobility.

Archaeologists have long promulgated the interpretation that a fundamental shift in subsistence distinguished Paleoindian from Archaic traditions. In this view, Paleoindians were specialized, nomadic big-game hunters, and Archaic peoples were less mobile, generalized hunters and gatherers. Careful scrutiny of the hunter-gatherer archaeological record on and near the southern periphery of the Great Plains reveals this distinction to be incorrect. Site types, assemblage diversity, and faunal diet breadth throughout the Archaic strongly support the broad generalization that Archaic adaptations were, in fact, based on the hunting and gathering of multiple resources obtained over a fairly limited geographic range. Undoubtedly, these resources were exploited with considerable mobility, but distances traveled were less than in Folsom times, and Archaic mobility probably varied significantly with seasonal or other changes in the resource base. In central Texas, the Archaic lifeway was achieved in part by use of sophisticated stone-lined earth ovens. This Archaic hunting-gathering tradition survived for nearly 9,000 years in spite of significant swings in climate, and it continued throughout prehistory even though populations in all of the surrounding areas moved toward food production over the last two or three millennia of that 9,000 years (Collins 1995, 1998b, 2004).

Bison were generally absent over most of the Archaic span in Texas, but were briefly present ca. 5500 RCYBP and from 3000 to 2000 RCYBP (Collins 1995, 2004; Dillehay 1974). During those two times when bison were present, a change is seen in the subsistence behavior of the Archaic populations, the earlier distinguished by the Calf Creek/Andice point and the later by the Montell/Castroville. In central Texas, little change is noted—large middens with evidence for general hunting and gathering continued, but the addition of bison hunting is evidenced by bison kill sites in the plains or prairie grasslands. There are also caches attributable to the Calf Creek/Andice and Montell/Castroville intervals. This pattern is nearly identical to that seen in Clovis times, and it is distinctly different from the specialized bison-hunting pattern seen in Folsom times.

I would hypothesize that in Clovis, Calf Creek/Andice, and Montell/Castroville times, foragers were based in central Texas or similarly favorable environments and that organized hunting parties at times traveled to outlying regions for big game. In early Clovis times, the big game included mammoth, horse, and bison, whereas in late Clovis times and in the two Archaic intervals, the prey was bison. In this subsistence mode, weapon systems were versatile but lethal and reliable enough for big-game hunting. Caching was an important means of ensuring that stone (and possibly other) materials were available to the hunting parties (and possibly to foraging parties as well). It is likely that in all three of these intervals, plant foods and small to medium-size animals consistently were more important contributors to the diet than was big game.

This mode of subsistence seems to have repeated itself in spite of the fact that much had undoubtedly changed in the region over time. Population numbers had surely increased significantly, and, as a result, the political landscape had become increasingly complex. The use of earth ovens in the Archaic added such staples as wild hyacinth bulbs to the subsistence base, probably significantly increasing the effective carrying capacity of much of the region (Black et al. 1999). These ovens probably also partly explain the abrupt increase in preserved plant food remains at the beginning of the Archaic. The open fireplaces of Clovis times offer far less opportunity for the preservation of charred plant parts than do the Archaic ovens.

I speak here at a very general level of abstraction when suggesting similarities between Clovis and Archaic modes of subsistence. Clovis folk did not employ earth ovens to process bulk foods as did people in Archaic times. Specialized ground stone food-processing tools characteristic of Archaic times are almost absent in Clovis sites (an exception may be the Clovis-age mano at Blackwater Draw [Hester 1972:107]).

In all likelihood, Clovis plant foods were those requiring little or no processing or cooking, such as nuts, berries, and fruits, while Archaic ones included more voluminous amounts of staples requiring considerable processing and/or cooking, such as seeds, geophytes, leaves, roots, and stalks, possibly in response to increasing population pressures. The Archaic subsistence mode may have required a greater divergence in the male-female division of labor over that in Clovis times. What seems not to have changed significantly is a geographic focus on the Balcones Canyonlands ecotone. In Clovis, Calf Creek/Andice, and Montell/Castroville times, this focus remained, but there were also intermittent forays onto the prairies and plains in pursuit of big game.

Evidently, the Clovis subsistence mode postulated here is not unique to the southern plains periphery. The continent-wide distribution of Clovis in a multitude of different environments is a pattern of generalized, not specialized, subsistence (cf. Cannon and Meltzer 2004). The few known large Clovis sites (such as Thunderbird, Carson Conn Short, and possibly El Bajío) may hint at similar exploitation of other environments.

Viewing the bearers of Clovis culture as generalized hunter-gatherers has the further implication that such an adaptation would require more time for people to settle as foragers into diverse habitats across North America. Specialized big-game hunting squares handily with a model of rapid colonization of the continent, but the concept of many generalized adaptations needs to be reconciled with the Clovis First Model. Or, more correctly, it is the model that needs reconciliation with the growing body of evidence that the Clovis record does not represent a highly specialized, nomadic, mammoth-hunting lifeway.

Acknowledgments

The Gault project gratefully acknowledges grants and donations from the Texas Higher Education Coordinating Board, Summerlee Foundation, Houston Endowment, Meadows Foundation, Texas Historical Foundation, and numerous individuals.

Sam Gardner took all of the artifact photographs, drafted the maps, and prepared all of the figures. Marilyn Shoberg provided photomicrographs and supporting data from her microscopic use-wear studies of the Gault lithic artifacts. Comments and suggestions on an earlier draft by David B. Madsen, Boyce Driskell, Renee Walker, and David Anderson significantly improved this chapter, without these individuals assuming any burden of responsibility for its shortcomings.

FIVE

Late Paleoindian Subsistence Strategies in the Western Great Lakes Region

Evidence for Generalized Foraging from Northern Wisconsin

Steven R. Kuehn

Despite a paucity of excavated sites, the Paleoindian occupation of the Great Lakes region has long fascinated archaeologists. Much of what is known, or what we think we know, of Paleoindian lifeways is based on isolated spear points, limited surface scatters and private collections, and comparisons with similar sites across the continent. Examination of Paleoindian subsistence strategies has likewise been hindered by the limited data available, although this situation is beginning to change. In southeastern Wisconsin, for example, the recovery of mammoth and mastodon remains by David Overstreet provides tantalizing clues on one aspect of Early Paleoindian subsistence behavior (Mason 1997; Overstreet 1993, 1998; Overstreet et al. 1993). Chipped stone tools were recovered in association with the Schaefer and Hebior mammoths, and the presence of butchering marks on megafauna elements from several Chesrow Complex sites suggests hunting or scavenging of Pleistocene megafauna in Wisconsin, the first clear evidence of such activity.

By far, however, the great majority of zooarchaeological data in Wisconsin is associated with the Late Paleoindian stage. At present, the database consists of material from five sites: Deadman Slough (47PR46), Sucices (47DG11), Russell Wohlt (47WN718), Kiesow Grove (47WN356), and Wohlt (47WN358). While relatively small in size, the faunal assemblages from these sites provide highly significant information on early foraging strategies in the region.

Environmental Context and Foraging Theory

The available floral, palynological, and fossil beetle evidence indicates that essentially modern floral species were present in the Great Lakes region by 10,000 to 8,000 years ago (Clayton et al. 1992; Davis 1983; Huber 1995; Jacobson et al. 1987; Morgan 1987; Mulholland et al. 1997; Shay 1971; Watts 1983). It can therefore be argued that a mixture of modern and extinct animal taxa were present, an argument supported by paleontological and archaeological evidence from the upper Midwest and northeastern North America (e.g., Brown and Cleland 1968; Graham and Mead 1987). It should be noted, however, that the composition of these animal communities was not identical to that of modern populations. A mosaic of forest communities existed in the region, unlike the more zonal communities that exist currently. A disharmonious mixing of flora and fauna occurred during the early postglacial period, creating communities that lack modern analogs (Cleland et al. 1998; Gaudreau 1988; Graham and Mead 1987; Lundelius et al. 1983; Mulholland et al. 1997; Watts 1983). The terminal Pleistocene and early Holocene inhabitants of the Eastern Woodlands likely had a diverse, rich animal resource base available (e.g., Curran and Dincauze 1977; Custer and Stewart 1990; Dincauze and Mulholland 1977; Jones 1994; Kuehn 1998; Meltzer 1988; Nicholas 1994; Petersen and Putnam 1992; Spiess 1992; Stothers 1996). Early postglacial wetland and glacial lake basin habitats, for example, were relatively rich in resource diversity and biomass (Curran and Dincauze 1977; Nicholas 1988, 1991).

Cultural ecology and foraging theory recognize the difficulty in maintaining a specialized foraging strategy in a mixed forest environment (Meltzer 1988; Meltzer and Smith 1986; Speth 1990; Speth and Spielman 1983). In the western Great Lakes region, no animal species were present in sufficient quantity to meet the energy and nutrient requirements of a specialized economy. Caribou population density, herd size, and migration behavior vary widely based on environmental conditions (Burch 1972; Spiess 1979; Spiess et al. 1985). At present, there is insufficient paleoecological or archaeological data to properly reconstruct late Pleistocene caribou ecology or hunting practices in the western Great Lakes region. The available evidence is inadequate to support arguments of Paleoindian subsistence and settlement behavior based on specialized caribou exploitation. The variety of animal taxa present and mosaic of habitat settings would more readily support a broad-based foraging strategy.

Zooarchaeological Evidence from Five Late Paleoindian Sites

Across northeastern North America, a generalized foraging pattern is indicated by the growing body of late Pleistocene and early Holocene zooarchaeological data (Figure 5.1). In Wisconsin, direct evidence of early forag-

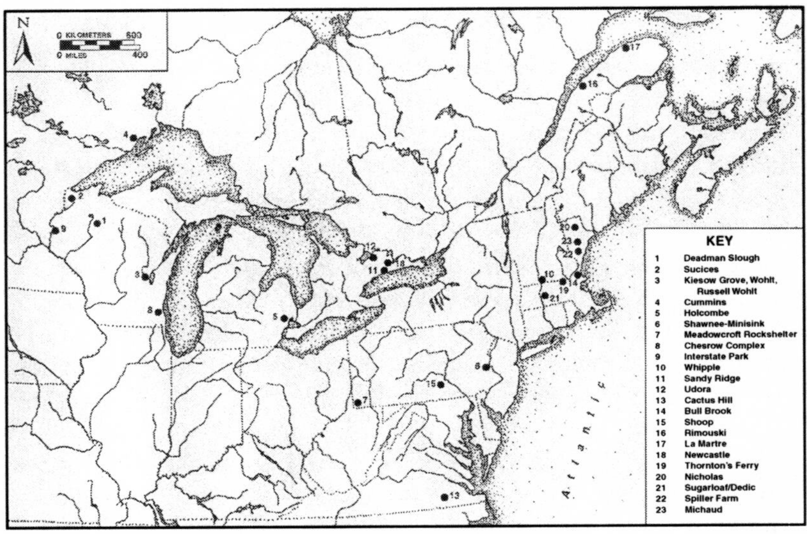

FIGURE 5.1. Late Pleistocene–Early Holocene archaeological sites with subsistence data in northeastern North America (modified from Peterson et al. 2000:114). Courtesy of the Eastern States Archaeological Federation.

ing behavior has been recovered from five Late Paleoindian sites: Sucices, Deadman Slough, Russell Wohlt, Kiesow Grove, and Wohlt (Table 5.1).

Sucices

The Sucices site is situated on a low terrace near the base of an upland slope in far northwestern Wisconsin. Surrounded on three sides by wetlands, the site lies approximately 200 meters west of the St. Croix River. Limited test excavations were conducted at the site in 1983 by the State Historical Society of Wisconsin (Rusch and Penman 1984). Paleoindian artifacts recovered include the base of a chert Plainview point, a Scottsbluff point preform of Hixton silicified sandstone, and a trihedral adze, as well as moderate amounts of lithic debitage and well-preserved faunal material. The majority of bone was obtained from the same excavation units and levels as the diagnostic Paleoindian artifacts.

Excavators recovered 480 pieces of bone at the Sucices site. The assemblage was reanalyzed by the author and is presented in Kuehn (1998). White-tailed deer and beaver were specifically identified, with two individuals of each taxa present. Mammal remains comprise the majority of the assemblage, with large and medium-size animals represented.

TABLE 5.1. Summary of faunal assemblages from five Late Paleoindian sites in Wisconsin.

Taxon		Deadman Sl.		Sucices		Russell Wohlt		Wohlt		Kiesow Gr.		Total	
		NISP	MNI	NISP	MNI	NISP	MNI	NISP	MNI	NISP	MNI	NISP	MNI
Ictaluridae	catfish					1	1					1	1
Fish, indeterminate		2		1		5		31		36		75	
Total Fish		2	0	1	0	6	1	31	0	36	0	76	1
Chrysemys picta	painted turtle			5	1					2	1	7	2
Emydoidea blandingii	Blanding's turtle					1	1					1	1
Apalone sp.	softshell turtle							1	1	2	1	3	2
Emydidae	water/box turtle			15	2	1	1			4	1	20	4
Turtle, indeterminate		247		159		7		28		59		500	
Total Turtles		247	0	179	3	9	2	29	1	67	3	531	9
Anatinae	cf. marsh duck									1	1	1	1
Bird, indeterminate		32				5		4		13		54	
Total Birds		32	0	0	0	5	0	4	0	14	1	55	1
Odocoileus virginianus	white-tailed deer	24	1	108	2	1	1	1	1	1	1	135	6
Cervidae	elk/moose/deer							1		1		2	
Ursus americanus	black bear	1	1									1	1
Erethizon dorsatum	porcupine	2	1									2	1
Castor canadensis	beaver			2	2	2	2	1	1	3	1	8	6
Ondatra zibethicus	muskrat					4	1	2	1	3	1	9	3
Microtus sp.	vole*							1	1			1	1
Large mammal		837		68		30		12		63		1,010	
Medium-large mammal					1				1		2		
Medium mammal		13		18		1		8		9		49	
Small-medium mammal					8		16		38		62		
Small mammal								1		1		2	
Mammal, indeterminate				51				2		23		76	
Total Mammals		877	3	247	4	47	4	45	4	143	3	1,359	18
Mussel, indeterminate*		6										6	
Taxon indeterminate		251		53		59		371		600		1,334	
Total Other		257	0	53	0	59	0	371	0	600	0	1,340	0
Total		1,415	3	480	7	126	7	480	5	860	7	3,361	29

NISP = Number of identified specimens per taxon MNI = Minimum number of individuals per taxon * = Intrusive specimen

Shell fragments of painted and water or box turtle were identified. Indistinct pieces of turtle shell comprise nearly 40 percent of the total assemblage. One fish vertebra tentatively suggests the utilization of fish by Paleoindian foragers.

Deadman Slough

The Deadman Slough site is a multicomponent Late Paleoindian and Middle Woodland site situated on a glacial hill overlooking the confluence of the Flambeau River and Deadman Slough in north-central Wisconsin. A large portion of the site was excavated as part of a highway realignment project in 1991 (Meinholz and Kuehn 1996). The surrounding area is dominated by aquatic settings, including large and small lakes and streams and extensive swamps and wetlands. The archaeological components at the site are horizontally separated, with an essentially intact Late Paleoindian–Early Archaic occupation located in the east-central part of the site, on a landform termed the Main Ridge. Diagnostic artifacts recovered include lanceolate and notched projectile points of Hixton silicified sandstone and ovate, distinctly side-notched chert points. Various adzes and scrapers were recovered, as were numerous large, heat-fractured Hixton bifaces. Similar bifaces were obtained at the Renier site near Green Bay (Mason 1981; Mason and Irwin 1960) and have been associated with Paleoindian ceremonialism in the western Great Lakes region (Buckmaster and Paquette 1988; Dawson 1983; Deller and Ellis 1984; Mason 1981; Mason and Irwin 1960; Meinholz and Kuehn 1995, 1996; Ritzenthaler 1972).

Over 1,400 pieces of bone and shell were recovered from the Late Paleoindian component at the Deadman Slough site. Bone fragments were obtained from pit features, from bone concentration lenses, and throughout the excavated soil horizons (Meinholz and Kuehn 1996). All specimens are heavily calcined or mineralized, suggesting considerable age, and were closely associated with the distribution of Paleoindian artifacts.

Mammal remains are ubiquitous, comprising 63 percent of the total. White-tailed deer and porcupine were specifically identified, along with indistinct large and medium-size mammals. A single black bear canine fragment was obtained from surface contexts, but unfortunately cannot be securely associated with the Paleoindian occupation.

Turtle remains comprise almost 20 percent of the assemblage, with painted and softshell turtle present. Thirty-two long-bone shaft pieces, comparable in size to the bones of migratory waterfowl, also were recovered. Several fish elements and fragments of freshwater mussel shell were obtained, but the condition and context of the specimens suggest that they are recent intrusions.

Lake Poygan Phase

Based on years of intensive survey and testing, James Clark has defined a regional Late Paleoindian manifestation in east-central Wisconsin, the Lake Poygan phase (Clark 1982, 1995). Several dozen sites have been identified in the middle Fox River valley, all located in proximity to extensive wetlands or open waterways. Characteristic artifacts include Scottsbluff and Eden points, trihedral adzes, various bifaces, scrapers, drills, and edge-modified flake tools. Prevalent lithic resources include Hixton and rhyolite, the latter being generally diagnostic for Late Paleoindian sites in this region (e.g., Benchley et al. 1997).

Faunal remains were recovered at three Lake Poygan phase sites, Wohlt, Russell Wohlt, and Kiesow Grove. Final analysis of this material is currently in preparation for publication (Kuehn and Clark n.d.). The Russell Wohlt assemblage, while relatively small with 126 specimens, includes deer, beaver, muskrat, Blanding's turtle, water or box turtle, catfish, and a variety of indistinct mammal, fish, bird, and turtle remains.

The Wohlt and Kiesow Grove assemblages are very similar in composition. Taxa associated with the Paleoindian component at these two sites include deer, beaver, and muskrat; painted, softshell, and water or box turtles; and various-size indeterminate mammals, birds, turtles, and fish. Stratigraphically, the majority of bone from each site was recovered in association with the Late Paleoindian occupation. A Woodland component is present at both sites, and there is the potential for some mixing of faunal material from later occupations. However, the bone from the lower levels, including some obtained from feature contexts, clearly reflects a generalized foraging strategy.

Discussion

The exploitation of a range of animals from a variety of environmental settings contrasts with the classic view of selective, large-mammal hunting behavior often attributed to Paleoindian groups. The resilience of the big-game hunting hypothesis can be attributed in part to the prominent discovery of fluted-point kill sites in the western United States, and the corresponding paucity of zooarchaeological remains in the Great Lakes region. Difficulties in reconstructing the dynamic, postglacial environment of the Northeast further complicate the issue (Cleland et al. 1998:16–17; Dincauze 1988; Kapp 1999; Lepper and Meltzer 1991). Broad-scale paleoenvironmental reconstructions tended to oversimplify ecological conditions and resource availability, as analogous to low resource–bearing, climax boreal forest.

The faunal assemblages from Deadman Slough, Sucices, and the Lake Poygan phase sites indicate that a diverse array of animals, especially aquatic species, were utilized by the early inhabitants of the western Great Lakes region. White-tailed deer and other larger mammals appear to have been a major part of the diet, although smaller mammals such as beaver, muskrat, and porcupine were also utilized. A variety of turtles are represented, as are catfish and other fish and birds. The taxa represented suggest strong utilization of aquatic and wetland habitats, while the deer and porcupine remains indicate exploitation of mixed forest and forest-edge settings as well.

Generalized foraging behavior is similarly reflected in zooarchaeological data from other early postglacial sites in the western Great Lakes region. Calcined deer bone was identified at the Cummins site in Ontario, and blood protein residues on lithic artifacts from the site indicate utilization of bison, cervid, and a variety of small mammals (Julig 1991, 1994:214; Newman and Julig 1990). Several sites with extinct bison remains are present in west-central Wisconsin (Boszhardt et al. 1993), but with one exception, no artifacts have been recovered in association with the faunal remains. In the 1930s, several undiagnostic chipped stone points and a copper awl or pike were collected during salvage operations at the Interstate Park site (Palmer 1954; Pond 1937).

The recovery of caribou bone from the Holcombe site in Michigan (Cleland 1965) suggests utilization of this resource in the western Great Lakes region. Caribou has been identified at northeastern Paleoindian sites such as Whipple, Sandy Ridge, Bull Brook, Shoop (via protein residues), and Udora, among others (Jackson and McKillop 1991; Meltzer 1988:20–21; Spiess et al. 1985; Spiess et al. 1998; Storck and Spiess 1994; Stothers 1996). Various researchers, however, have questioned the abundance and reliability of woodland caribou as a specialized Paleoindian prey resource (Burch 1972; Custer and Stewart 1990; Spiess et al. 1985; Stewart 1994:143–144). Caribou were undoubtedly utilized by postglacial foragers in the Eastern Woodlands, but should be considered as only one of a range of animals utilized.

Additional data from Paleoindian sites such as Shawnee Minisink, Udora, Bull Brook, and Meadowcroft Rockshelter likewise indicate a more broad-based foraging strategy (e.g., Dent 1981; Guilday and Parmalee 1982; McNett ed. 1985; Meltzer and Smith 1986; Parmalee 1968; Storck and Spiess 1994). The recovery of fish bones and hawthorn pits from a hearth at Shawnee Minisink is particularly significant, providing evidence of fish and plant use by early foragers (Dent, this volume). Similar floral data from Maine include a berry seed from feature context at the Michaud site (Spiess et al. 1998:223), and hazelnut, acorn, and unidentified seeds and legumes from the early Holocene Brigham and Sharrow sites (Petersen and Putnam 1992:46).

Immunological analyses of protein residues on stone tools also provide evidence for utilization of a wide array of faunal resources. Recently, protein residue on Clovis artifacts from the Cactus Hill site in Virginia tested positively for elk, deer, rabbit, and bovid (McAvoy and McAvoy 1997:180–181; Newman 1997). Similar data were obtained from Late Paleoindian tools from the Rimouski site (Newman 1994, cited in Chalifoux 1999) and La Martre River valley (Chalifoux 1999) in Quebec, with positive reactions for bear, cervid, rabbit/hare, rodent, trout/salmon (family Salmonidae), and sea lion/seal (order Pinnipedia). A generalized foraging adaptation is suggested, utilizing both coastal (e.g., fish, marine mammals) and interior animals (e.g., caribou, bear, small mammals), and plants, on a seasonal basis. Terminal Pleistocene and early Holocene mammals were exploited by Early Paleoindian peoples in northeastern North America; the available data, however, do not support viewing them as specialized, big-game hunters.

Late Paleoindian Subsistence in Wisconsin

There appears to be a notable association between Paleoindian sites and aquatic habitats. Regional archaeological overviews in Wisconsin note a strong correlation between Paleoindian sites and existing and relic marshes, lakes, and other riparian settings (Boszhardt 1991; Clark 1995; Dudzik 1991; Moore and Willems 1995; Overstreet 1991a, 1991b; Speth 1996; Wendt 1985; Figure 5.2). Extensive wetland and aquatic settings characterize much of northern and eastern Wisconsin and support a wide range of seasonally abundant animal and plant resources (e.g., Benchley et al. 1997:20–21; Goldstein 1987:413–417; Goldstein and Kind 1987:21–25; Martin 1965: 412–417; Novitzki 1979).

A similar pattern of early postglacial exploitation of wetland environments has been noted in the northeastern United States. Wetland settings,

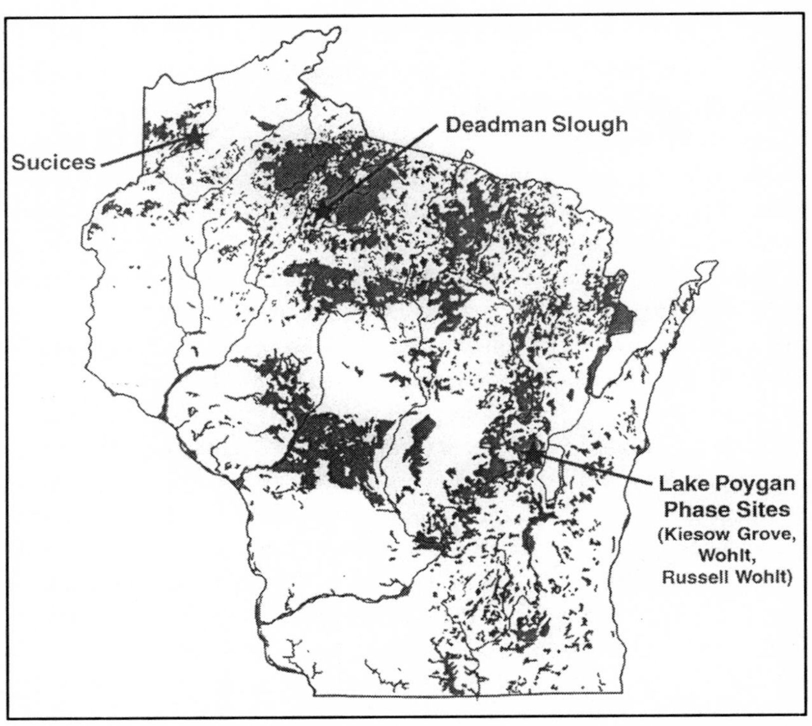

FIGURE 5.2. Location of the Deadman Slough, Sucices, and Lake Poygan phase sites relative to major wetland habitats.

in particular wetland mosaics, were highly significant in terms of resource availability, diversity, and productivity (e.g., Nicholas 1988, 1991, 1994, 1998). This rich resource base would have strongly influenced Paleoindian and Archaic settlement patterns, seasonal mobility, and subsistence practices.

Based on the available zooarchaeological evidence, a preliminary model of Paleoindian subsistence behavior in the western Great Lakes region can be offered. Seasonal exploitation of animal resources most likely reflects patterns noted for later prehistoric foragers and in ethnographic studies (e.g., Custer and Stewart 1990; Keene 1981; Styles 1981; Whelan 1990; Winterhalder 1981, 1983a). For simplicity, the role of plant utilization is not addressed, although the limited evidence available obviously indicates utilization of nuts, fruits, and other floral resources by early foragers.

A generalized adaptive strategy most accurately reflects the year-round subsistence behavior of terminal Pleistocene–early Holocene foragers in the western Great Lakes region. Spring foraging activities centered on spawning fish and returning migratory waterfowl. The trapping of small game and the hunting of large mammals, such as deer, moose, and caribou, were likely also of importance at this time. During the summer months, procurement of wetland and aquatic resources (e.g., turtles and fish) would have supplemented the hunting and trapping of small and large mammals. In autumn and early winter, white-tailed deer and waterfowl would be abundant, with numerous other species in optimum condition for harvesting. During the later winter months, hibernating black bear and yarding deer would serve as dietary staples. Grouse and turkey were also available during the fall and winter season, along with a variety of fur-bearing mammals. While the hunting of deer, moose, bear, and caribou likely played a key role in late Pleistocene and early Holocene foraging strategies, the year-round hunting and trapping of small and medium-size animals were important procurement activities that are often unrecognized in the archaeological record. This model will no doubt undergo revision as new zooarchaeological and paleoethnobotanical data come to light.

The available data strongly indicate that Late Paleoindian groups in the western Great Lakes region employed a generalized foraging strategy. It is plausible that Early Paleoindian foragers utilized a similar strategy. While some animals may have received focused attention during periods of seasonal abundance, a year-round, specialized big-game hunting adaptation is unlikely.

A diverse array of animals were utilized, from a wide variety of environmental settings. In the western Great Lakes region, it is probable that lake, river, and wetland habitats were heavily exploited by early postglacial foragers. Across northeastern North America, zooarchaeological evidence supports a generalized adaptive strategy, beginning with the initial development of essentially modern ecological conditions in the region. The relative abundance and productivity of wetland environments were significant factors influencing Paleoindian subsistence behavior, as well as settlement patterns and group mobility. Future archaeological research at late Pleistocene and early Holocene sites in the Great Lakes and Eastern Woodlands, in conjunction with improved recovery and analytical techniques, will further refine and strengthen the interpretation of Paleoindian subsistence behavior advocated here and add to our overall understanding of Paleoindian lifeways.

Acknowledgments

The figures for this chapter were graciously prepared by Deette Lund. Figure 5.1 is reprinted courtesy of Petersen et al. and the journal *Archaeology of Eastern North America*. Thanks to Jim Clark for permission to utilize data from the Lake Poygan phase sites. I would also like to thank Renee Walker for inviting me to participate in this volume. Any omissions or errors are, of course, my own.

SIX

Hunting in the Late Paleoindian Period

Faunal Remains from Dust Cave, Alabama

Renee B. Walker

As mentioned previously in several chapters of this volume, the "big-game hunting" model has framed ideas about Paleoindian hunting and gathering subsistence adaptations. However, research at many Paleoindian sites has shown that this model is not supported, particularly for Late Paleoindian sites. This research includes sites such as Broken Mammoth in Alaska (Yesner, this volume), Lake Poygan phase sites in Wisconsin (Kuehn, this volume), Shawnee Minisink in Pennsylvania (Dent, this volume), and several sites in Florida (Dunbar and Vojnovski, this volume). Another site that has proved highly valuable in support of broad-spectrum foraging during the Late Paleoindian is Dust Cave in northwest Alabama.

Dust Cave is a multicomponent site with remains of Late Paleoindian, Early Archaic, and Middle Archaic materials. The cave environment has preserved botanical and faunal remains in context with stone tools. Thus, not only does the site date to an early period of prehistory in North America, but it allows for comparisons to later occupations. These comparisons are crucial for understanding changes in lifeways, such as subsistence strategies, in the face of environmental change.

This chapter investigates faunal remains excavated from the Late Paleoindian component at Dust Cave. Faunal analyses focus on the percentage of animal classes present in the Late Paleoindian component. In relation to this, I present an evaluation of bone fragmentation and modification within classes. This will aid assessment of whether a particular animal class is underrepresented due to excessive fragmentation. I also evaluate habitat exploitation and seasonality to determine subsistence and site occupation patterns. Finally, I examine the diversity of the faunal remains in

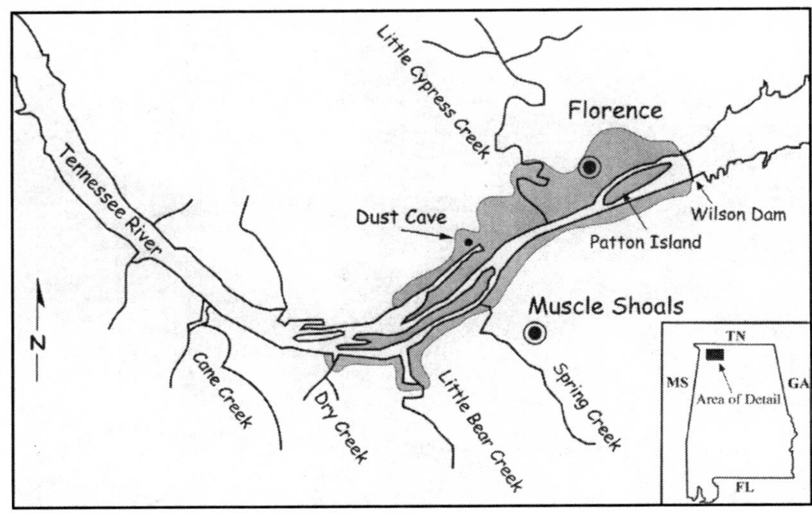

FIGURE 6.1. Location of Dust Cave in Alabama (modified from Walker et al. 2005:85). Courtesy of *Southeastern Archaeology*.

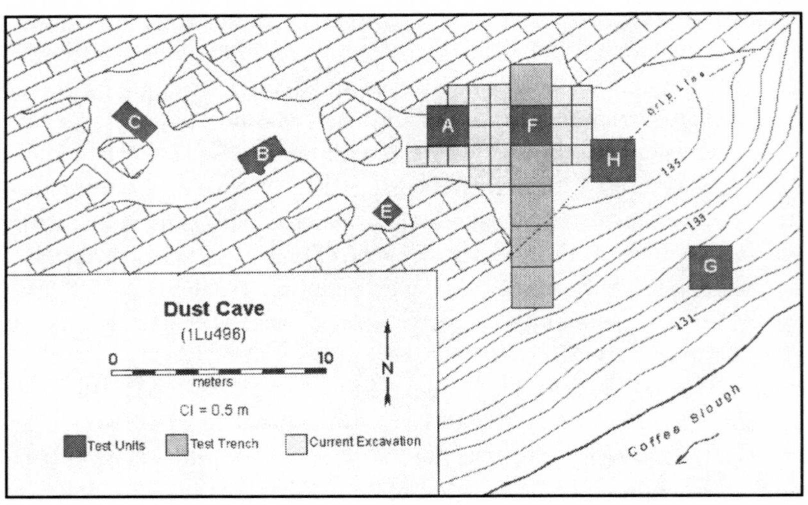

FIGURE 6.2. Location of excavation units at Dust Cave (modified from Walker et al. 2001:172). Courtesy of the *Midcontinental Journal of Archaeology*.

the Late Paleoindian period. Diversity analyses are a valuable assessment tool for understanding if there is a dependence on a particular species. I present the results of this analysis as a guide to framing future assumptions about Late Paleoindian subsistence strategies.

Dust Cave History

The site of Dust Cave is located in northwest Alabama near the Tennessee River section of Pickwick Lake (Figure 6.1). Test excavations were conducted at Dust Cave from 1989 to 1994 by a research team from the University of Alabama Division of Archaeology (Figure 6.2; Goldman-Finn and Driskell 1994). The five years of archaeological test excavations revealed approximately five meters of stratified deposits, with large quantities of faunal, lithic, and botanical remains. Excavations were conducted at Dust Cave as part of a field school project. These excavations focus on deposits to the east and west of the entrance trench.

Geomorphological studies have revealed that Dust Cave was completely filled with sediment from the Tennessee River around 17,000 to 15,000 years ago (Collins et al. 1994; Sherwood 2001). As the level of the Tennessee River decreased, Dust Cave became a conduit for spring water, which flushed out most of the sediments (Collins et al. 1994:50). Following this sediment removal, the Tennessee River periodically inundated the cave with alluvium, evidenced in the sterile silty clays at the rear and base of the cave (Goldberg and Sherwood 1994). Finally, after around 11,000 years ago, the continued downcutting of the river caused the cave spring to dry up, and the cave at this time became suitable for habitation (Sherwood 2001; Sherwood et al. 2004). Thus, Late Paleoindian occupation of the cave probably occurred after 11,000 years ago, and subsequent deposits were primarily due to human activity.

Culture History

Researchers have defined five distinct cultural components for Dust Cave based on projectile point typologies and radiocarbon dates (Driskell 1994). These occupations include: Late Paleoindian, Early Side-Notched, Kirk Stemmed, Eva/Morrow Mountain, and Benton (Figure 6.3). The Late Paleoindian occupation, which is of particular interest to this analysis, has been radiocarbon dated to between 10,500 and 10,000 years ago, or 13,000–11,200 cal BP (Sherwood 2001:420–421; Sherwood et al. 2004). Projectile point types found in the Late Paleoindian component of the site include Dalton, Cumberland, Quad, Hardaway, one fluted point fragment, and three Beaver Lake projectile points (Driskell 1994:28).

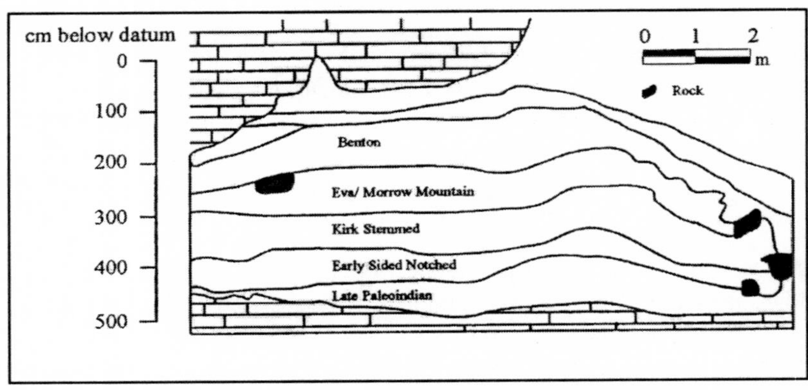

FIGURE 6.3. Cultural components represented at Dust Cave (modified from Walker et al. 2001:172). Courtesy of the *Midcontinental Journal of Archaeology*.

In addition to the identification of projectile point types, lithic analysts evaluated the nondiagnostic stone tools and debitage (Meeks 1994). Most of the material for manufacturing stone tool artifacts was from local Fort Payne chert for both the Late Paleoindian and the later components. A unifacial tool kit is primarily associated with the Late Paleoindian deposits at the site (Meeks 1994:100). These unifaces, or blades, primarily worked bone, wood, and hides (Meeks 1994:96; Walker et al. 2001).

Environment

The present-day environment of Dust Cave is that of cypress swamp along a limestone bluff within Coffee Slough (Goldman-Finn and Driskell 1994). The swampy environment is a result of the inundation of the Tennessee River to form the Pickwick Reservoir. The regional environment during the occupation of Dust Cave was probably highly variable. Late Paleoindian occupation of Dust Cave occurred during the Younger Dryas episode, which lasted from 10,500 to 10,100 BP (Delcourt and Delcourt 1981). This episode was much cooler than the preceding episode and probably prone to temperature fluctuations that may have caused periods of stress for both human and animal populations. Geomorphological research at Dust Cave supports this observation with evidence of "cold climate features" present in the Late Paleoindian deposits, which are probably signs of short-term cold extremes (Sherwood 2001:368). Anderson (2001:156) notes that the Late Paleoindian signified the end of the Clovis period, extinctions of large Pleistocene mammals, and the beginning of regional cultural specialization. If this is the case, animal remains should reflect the regional environmental changes in the Dust Cave area.

The paleobotanical data and mussel fauna recovered from the cave aid understanding of the local environment at the time of the cave's occupation. The paleobotanical data indicates that nuts, particularly from hickory trees, were procured and utilized by people at Dust Cave (Hollenbach, this volume; Gardner 1994; Walker et al. 2001). Diversity of plant species was apparent in the seeds gathered and deposited at the site, including hackberry, persimmon, black gum, poke, and chenopod (Detwiler 2001). Analysis of mussel shells from Dust Cave indicates that people were collecting almost half of their mussel shells from small creeks and rivers, even though the larger Tennessee River also had a supply of mussel fauna (Parmalee 1994:159). Therefore, as suggested by paleobotanical and malacological data, Late Paleoindians at Dust Cave utilized several habitats, including forested uplands, ecotone areas, and backwater creeks, to meet their subsistence needs.

Paleoindian Faunal Remains

The information from the studies of various remains from Dust Cave has provided a substantial context in which to place the Paleoindian faunal subsistence information. A total of 3,216 animal bones from the Late Paleoindian component at Dust Cave were examined (Table 6.1). Excavators recovered these remains from the entrance trench, as well as from units excavated to the east and west of the trench during the 1998 field season. Intrasite comparisons between animal classes illustrated the distributions of animals. An examination of taphonomic factors helped identify signatures resulting from both human and natural causes. In addition, the presence of animals sensitive to particular habitats, such as open, ecotone, and closed, indicated which areas were being exploited during the cave's occupation. A comparison between the numbers of aquatic versus terrestrial species identified habitats utilized by the Dust Cave inhabitants. Animal species, such as waterfowl, allowed identification of the season of site occupation. Additionally, I examine the utilization and mortality of white-tailed deer. Finally, I present estimates of species richness, evenness, and diversity.

Class

The most striking characteristic of the animal class comparison is the extremely high percentage of birds in the Late Paleoindian component (Figure 6.4). Forty percent of the faunal remains were bird. Mammals comprised about

TABLE 6.1. Taxonomic categories represented in the Late Paleoindian component.

	Common Name	NISP	MNI	Wt (g)	Biomass (kg)
Fish					
Applodinotus grunniens	freshwater drum	9	1	13.1	.27
Acipenseridae	possible sturgeon	1	1	0.1	.003
Catostomidae	sucker	30	2	8.4	.18
Centrarchidae	bass/sunfish	1	1	0.1	.003
Ictalurus punctatus	channel catfish	2	1	1.1	.03
Ictaluridae	catfish	2	1	0.2	.006
Moxostoma erythrurum	golden redhorse	5	1	1.0	.026
Moxostoma spp.	redhorse	3	1	0.8	.02
Stizostedion spp.	walleye/sauger	1	1	0.2	.006
Indeterminate fish		112		16.9	.34
SUBTOTAL		166			
Amphibians					
Anura	toad/frog	5		0.9	.02
Rana catesbeiana	bullfrog	2	1	0.2	.006
Rana sp.	frog	6		1.1	.03
Ranidae	indeterminate frog	3		0.3	.009
SUBTOTAL		16			
Reptiles					
Emydidae	pond turtles	5		2.7	.06
Terrapene carolina	eastern box turtle	9	1	7.6	.16
Trionyx spp.	softshelled turtles	1	1	0.3	.009
Testudines	indeterminate turtle	22		16.1	.32
Colubridae	nonvenomous snake	15		3.1	.07
Serpentes	indeterminate snake	1		0.2	.006
SUBTOTAL		53			
Birds					
Anas platyrhynchus	mallard	1	1	1.1	.03
Anas spp.	marsh ducks	11	3	5.9	.13
Anatidae	swans, geese, ducks	5	1	2.1	.05
Anatinae	marsh ducks	4	1	1.6	.04
Anserinae	geese	1	1	1.1	.03
Branta canadensis	Canada goose	1	1	3.7	.09
Branta canadensis cf.	possible Canada goose	1	1	4.4	.10
Chen caerulescens	snow goose	1	1	2.7	.06
Ectopistes migratorius	passenger pigeon	8	4	1.9	.05
Meleagris gallopavo	turkey	2	1	0.4	.01
Accipitridae	indeterminate hawk	2	1	0.4	.01
Colinus virginianus	bobwhite	15	4	2.5	.06
Icteridae	crow/blackbird	1	1	0.2	.006
cf. Emberizidae	sparrow, grosbeak, towhee	1	1	0.1	.003
Passeriformes	indeterminate song birds	2	1	0.2	.006
Quiscula quiscula	common grackle	1	1	0.2	.006
Phasianidae	grouse/pheasant	3	1	3.6	.08
Tympanuchus cupido	greater prairie chicken	7	2	4.1	.10

	Common Name	NISP	MNI	Wt (g)	Biomass (kg)
Birds (cont.)					
Large bird	turkey/goose size	32		27	.51
Medium bird	duck/grouse size	79		29.6	.55
Small bird	pigeon/passerines	29		6.4	.14
Indeterminate bird		1129		244.1	3.70
SUBTOTAL		1336			
Mammals					
Castor canadensis	beaver	2	1	18.8	.37
Ondatra zibethica	muskrat	21	4	24.3	.46
Blarina brevicauda cf.	long-tailed shrew	1	1	0.1	.003
Cricetidae	mice/voles	8	1	0.7	.02
Peromyscus spp.	white-footed mice	2	1	0.2	.006
Microtus spp.	voles	15	4	0.4	.01
Neotoma floridana	wood rat	2	1	0.4	.01
Marmota monax	woodchuck	1	1	1.9	.05
Sylvilagus floridanus	eastern cottontail rabbit	18	2	9.2	.19
Sciurius carolinensis	gray squirrel	10	1	2.2	.05
Sciurius niger	fox squirrel	1	1	0.2	.006
Sorex spp.	shrew	2	1	0.2	.006
Tamias striatus	eastern chipmunk	3	1	0.5	.01
Talpidae	indeterminate mole	1	1	0.1	.003
Scalapus aquaticus	mole	5	1	0.1	.003
Vespertilionidae	indeterminate bat	7	1	0.7	.02
Didelphis marsupialis	opossum	2	1	1.5	.04
Martes pennanti cf.	possible martin	1	1	0.3	.009
Mustela vison	mink	1	1	0.8	.02
Procyon lotor	raccoon	21	3	25.7	.49
Canis cf. *familiaris*	possible domestic dog	1	1	10.5	.22
Canis cf. *latrans*	possible coyote	1	1	16.4	.33
Canis spp.	dog/coyote/wolf	13	1	14	.28
Urocyon cinereoargenteus	gray fox	1	1	0.6	.02
cf. *U. cinereoargenteus*	possible gray fox	1	1	1.2	.03
Vulpes vulpes	red fox	1	1	0.7	.02
Odocoileus virginianus	white-tailed deer	9	1	11.3	.23
Indeterminate mammal		287		69.8	1.2
Large mammal		25		25.3	.48
Medium/large mammal		94		68.3	1.17
Medium mammal		55		23.5	.45
Medium/small mammal		5		1.5	.04
Small mammal		53		10.6	.22
Small/medium mammal		1		0.1	.003
SUBTOTAL		671			
Mammal/bird		1		0.8	.02
Small mammal/bird		21		2.8	.06
Unidentified		952		245.3	3.72
TOTAL		3,216		1,011.4	17.71

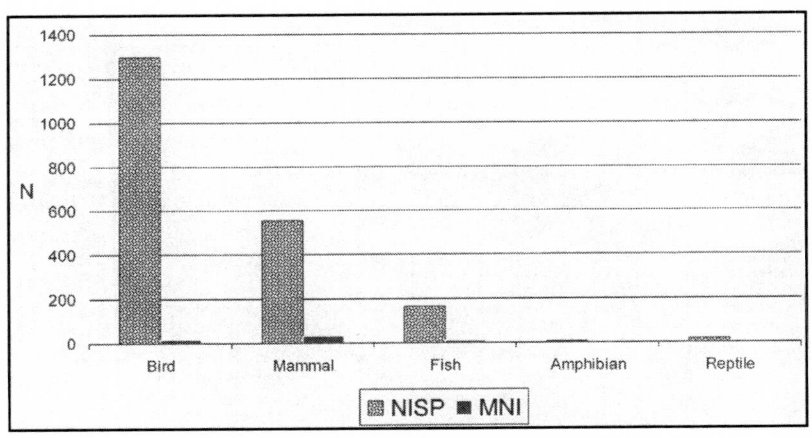

FIGURE 6.4. Animal class represented in component.

17 percent of the assemblage, which is interesting considering that this is usually the most numerous animal class at archaeological sites. Fishes made up 5 percent of the assemblage, reptiles 0.9 percent, amphibians 0.1 percent, and unidentifiable totaled 37 percent.

The bird remains are not only abundant but comprised of a wide variety of species. Waterfowl such as mallards, teals, and snow and Canada geese are present. In addition, I identified birds such as turkey, bobwhite, prairie chicken, passenger pigeon, hawk, grackle, and warbler. However, waterfowl comprised the majority of birds identified from the site.

The importance of waterfowl is clear due to the presence of a cache of Canada goose humeri in the Late Paleoindian occupation of the cave (Walker and Parmalee 2004). This cache consisted of 23 humeri, with a minimum number of individuals (MNI) of 12. Most of the humeri (83 percent) had cutmarks and/or scrape marks on the articular ends. Obviously, this cache was for some particular purpose. It may be that the occupants of the cave cached them for future use in tool manufacture, although researchers have found that in later Native American cultures, bird bones, particularly wing bones, are sometimes associated with human burials (Romanoski 1984). This is not the case at Dust Cave, however. Another interesting aspect of the cache is that several of the specimens were from the "giant" race of Canada geese—*Branta canadensis maxima*—which is only present in northern Canada today.

Taphonomic Factors

I evaluated taphonomic factors such as degree of fragmentation, burning, butchering, and rodent and carnivore gnawing for the Late Paleoindian faunal assemblage. I utilized the degree of fragmentation to explain whether the presence of so many bones identifiable as bird was due to their not being broken open for marrow, as mammal bones often are. Other research has attributed high percentages of fragmentation to the breaking open of mammal long bones to extract highly desirable marrow (Lyman 1994). If more mammal bones are being broken open for marrow, they might not be as easily identified to taxon, whereas unbroken bird bones would be more easily identified. Thus, I examined all the bones to determine if mammal bone fragments were more plentiful in the assemblage.

I categorized bone fragments as mammal or bird according to the curvature of the bone, the thickness of the bone compared to the size of the fragment, and the overall appearance of the bone. Results indicate that a majority of the bone fragments were in an indeterminate-size bird category. A much lower number of bone fragments were identifiable to the mammal-size categories. Obviously, bird bone fragments are more plentiful, and the fewer mammal bone fragments cannot account for a lack of identifiable mammals in the assemblage. It could be, however, that Late Paleoindian people may have deposited the mammal bones (particularly larger mammals like white-tailed deer) outside of the cave and they washed down the talus slope. Because bird bone is smaller, it may have remained in the cave and become part of the excavated deposits. This depositional difference, however, is difficult to assess because the talus contains very little bone due to preservational factors.

In order to determine the degree humans (as opposed to animals) contributed to the animal bone in the cave, I examined the bones for modification. Caves are attractive homes for humans as well as animals, and animals were probably in the cave during the times humans were not. Approximately 70 percent of the Late Paleoindian assemblage exhibited no modification. Human modification of bone in the Late Paleoindian zones at the cave include burned, calcined, and cut marked. Of the bone observed to have modifications, 25 percent was burned, 73 percent was calcined, and 1 percent was cut (Figure 6.5). Only 0.5 percent of the bone was rodent gnawed, and 0.5 percent was carnivore gnawed and ingested. Burned and calcined bones are obvious signs of cooking, with bone becoming dark brown or black at approximately 482 degrees Fahrenheit and bone becoming white or gray (calcined) at approximately 752 degrees Fahrenheit (Bennett 1999). Studies have shown that bone can burn after deposition if a fire or hearth is built above it (Bennett 1999). However, experiments with the Dust Cave sediment suggest that the clayey soils were not conducive to subsurface burn-

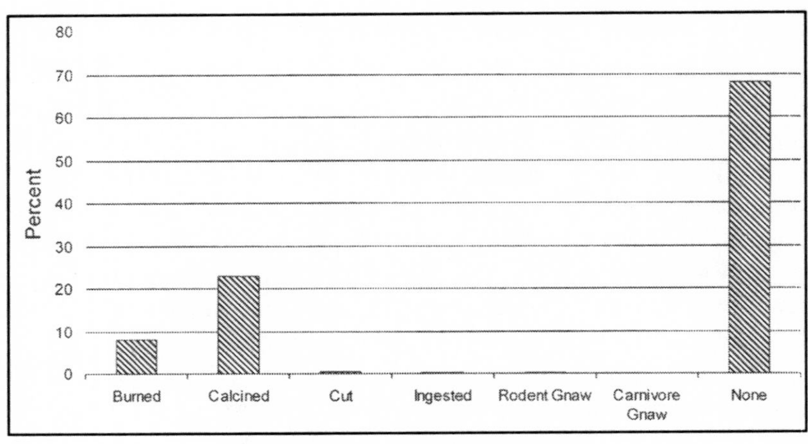

FIGURE 6.5. Percentage of modified bone.

ing of bone. In sum, a higher percentage of rodent- or carnivore-gnawed specimens would be expected if the assemblage accumulated primarily by animals.

Habitat Exploitation

The presence of animals from a variety of habitats in the Late Paleoindian assemblage at Dust Cave obviously indicates that habitat and prey selection were very complicated (Walker et al. 2001). Several of these species are particularly conducive to understanding the environment during Late Paleoindian occupation. For example, Late Paleoindian people utilized an open, or grassland, habitat given the presence of bobwhite and prairie chicken remains, which together with others comprised 35 percent of the identified species (Figure 6.6) (Walker 1998, 2000). Prairie chickens are gone from the area today and only exist in tall, undisturbed prairies (Bull and Farrand 1995). Two of the prairie chicken bones examined in this analysis had distinct cutmarks. Additionally, closed habitat species represent the most diverse group of animals in the assemblage and comprise 40 percent of the identified species. Finally, approximately 25 percent of the species present in the Late Paleoindian assemblage, such as white-tailed deer, rabbit, passenger pigeon, and grackle, preferred ecotone habitats (Bull and Farrand 1995; Whitaker 1992).

A slightly higher selection of aquatic species, such as waterfowl, muskrat, swamp rabbit, and pond turtles, was the pattern in the Late Paleoindian component. This changed to a dependence on terrestrial animals, such

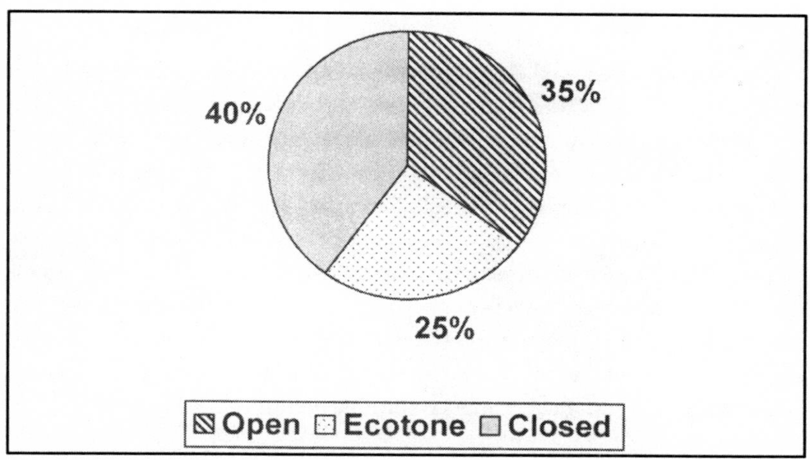

FIGURE 6.6. Percentage of open, closed, and ecotone species represented (modified from Walker et al. 2001:182). Courtesy of the *Midcontinental Journal of Archaeology*.

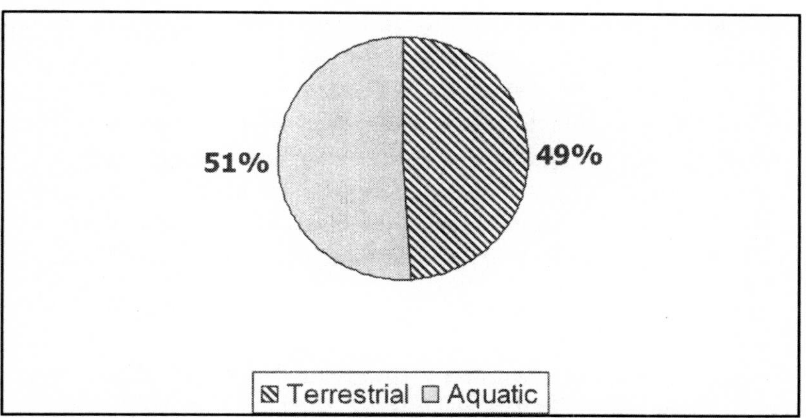

FIGURE 6.7. Comparison of aquatic versus terrestrial species by component.

as white-tailed deer, turkey, squirrels, and box turtle, in later occupations (Figure 6.7). In the Late Paleoindian period, 51 percent of the resources were aquatic, and 49 percent were terrestrial (Walker 1998).

Excavators recovered no extinct Pleistocene species in the levels occupied by humans. The only species of this type recovered from the site, including *Canis dirus* (dire wolf) and *Castroides* (giant beaver), were from sediments flushed down to the cave through sink holes on the top of the bluff (Parmalee, personal communication 1998; Sherwood 2001:200). The presence of "giant" Canada geese in the Late Paleoindian period has also been tentatively documented, which would be the only faunal indicator of colder climate at the site (Walker and Parmalee 2004). Geomorphological data indicate "extreme seasonal cold" was probably the norm at this time (Sherwood 2001:213).

The slightly higher number of aquatic species, combined with the presence of waterfowl, is probably due to the wetter conditions that existed at the end of the Ice Age. The animal and plant species, combined with geomorphological data, indicate that by the time of the cave's occupation, climate was well into the warmer conditions typical of the Holocene.

Season

The presence of passenger pigeon in the assemblage aids in the identification of site seasonality. This now-extinct bird would only have been present in the Southeast during the fall and winter, after which it would have traveled north for nesting (Schorger 1973). Other birds, such as geese, would have passed through this area on their way south during the early fall and then again on their way north during the late spring. In particular, the two species of geese identified in the assemblage, snow goose (*Chen caerulescencs*) and Canada goose (*Branta canadensis*), would have been present in the middle Tennessee River area from late September to November (Bull and Farrand 1995). Some populations of Canada geese may have wintered in the region, as they do today, but they may have also wintered along the Gulf Coast.

White-tailed Deer Utilization and Mortality

The amount of white-tailed deer recovered from the site varied between the five occupations, indicating possible differences in deer utilization. Although white-tailed deer were from all levels of the cave's deposits, the interesting aspect of the white-tailed deer assemblage is that very few, only nine specimens, representing an MNI of 1, came from the Late Paleoindian component of the cave. Most of the white-tailed deer were from the Early and Middle Archaic occupations. Again, this may indicate either less emphasis on white-tailed deer as a primary food resource or deposition of deer bone outside of the cave during the Late Paleoindian period.

Crown height analysis of the deer tooth assemblage determined that a total of 84 percent of the individuals were in the subadult age category, 16 percent fell into the prime-adult category, and there were no aged adults identified (Beauchamp 1993; Walker 1998, 2000). This type of mortality profile has at least two explanations. First, a seasonal occupation during the fall would furnish an abundance of subadult deer (that is, deer from 6- or 18-month-age cohorts). Second, the hunting techniques of the Dust Cave occupants, such as flushing them into nets, could have been more favorable to acquiring groups of deer, which would contain more subadults (Beauchamp 1993; Hudson 1991). It may be that a combination of these two factors—fall hunting of larger groups of deer—resulted in the subadult-dominated profile.

Assemblage Diversity

Analysis of assemblage diversity is a considerable tool for determining whether groups used focal or diffuse economies (Grayson 1984:131; Reitz and Wing 1999). Measures of richness, diversity and equitability are valuable tools for recognizing the regional diversity of animal populations and the means of human exploitation of these populations (Reitz and Wing 1999:102). Taxonomic richness measures the number of taxa in an assemblage and compares assemblages based on these numbers (Grayson 1984:132; Reitz and Wing 1999:102). Generally, species richness relates to climate and habitat complexity, with greater richness equal to greater habitat complexity, and lower richness equal to less complex habitats (Reitz and Wing 1999:104). Diversity is the measure of heterogeneity of an assemblage. The Shannon-Weaver function (or Shannon-Wiener) is often used in ecology studies to estimate diversity (Reitz and Wing 1999:105). This function is:

$$H' = -\sum_{i=1}^{s} (p_i)(\text{Log}p_i)$$

where H' is the information content of the sample, s is the number of taxonomic categories, p_i is the relative abundance within the sample, and log p_i is the natural log of relative abundance. Equitability is a measurement that estimates the distribution of the sample between taxa. For example, one faunal assemblage may be very rich, but have only a few taxa well represented. This would be a less equitable assemblage. Equitability is:

$$V' = H'/\text{Log}S$$

V' is the equitability of a sample, where H' is divided by the log of the number of species in a community (Reitz and Wing 1999:105).

The Late Paleoindian assemblage is very rich, with more than 61 different taxa represented (Table 6.2). Diversity is also very high, with an estimate of

TABLE 6.2. Assemblage diversity for the Dust Cave Late Paleoindian faunal remains.

Richness	Diversity	Equability
61	H' = 4.65	V' = 1.13
High	High	Even

4.65. The equitability of the sample (V' = 1.13) indicates the number of specimens in the taxonomic categories were evenly distributed. In comparison to the assemblages from other components at the site, the Late Paleoindian is the most rich and had the highest evenness value. However, assemblage diversity is "tightly correlated" with sample size (Grayson 1984:131) and may be a reflection of intercomponent variation rather than greater richness and evenness.

Discussion

In considering the role Dust Cave plays in guiding interpretations of Late Paleoindian subsistence strategies, the uniqueness of the Dust Cave assemblage is of importance. To this end, a comparison between the faunal remains from Dust Cave and sites of similar antiquity with preserved faunal assemblages is necessary. The Dust Cave faunal assemblage is comparable to assemblages from sites such as Graham Cave (Logan 1952; McMillan and Klippel 1981) and Rodgers Shelter in Missouri (McMillan 1976); Modoc Rock Shelter in Illinois (Fowler 1959; Parmalee 1959; Styles et al. 1983); and Russell Cave (Griffin 1974; Weigel et al. 1974), Stanfield-Worley Bluff Shelter (Parmalee 1962), and Smith Bottom Cave in Alabama (Snyder and Parmalee 1991). All of these sites have deposits dating to around or before 10,000 BP (Walker 1998, 2000).

Comparisons of percentages of white-tailed deer recovered from the sites indicate that Dust Cave had the lowest percentage of deer, while Modoc Rock Shelter had the highest (Table 6.3). In addition, Dust Cave had the highest number of aquatic species during the Late Paleoindian period. All six of the comparison sites had a lower number of aquatic species that showed an increase through time to the Middle Archaic period, while Dust Cave has the opposite trend. Finally, Dust Cave had the highest number of bird remains represented when compared to the other sites.

Thus, when compared to other sites of similar occupation times, Dust Cave is somewhat atypical. However, all of the sites are rather unique,

TABLE 6.3. Comparisons between Dust Cave fauna and other early sites with faunal assemblages.

Site	Major Class Represented	Utilization of Whitetail Deer	Utilization of Aquatic Resources
Dust Cave	bird	low	high
Graham Cave	mammal	low	low
Rodgers Shelter	mammal	low	low
Modoc Rock Shelter	fish	high	low
Russell Cave	mammal	high	high
Stanfield–Worley Bluff Shelter	mammal	high	high
Smith Bottom Cave	mammal	low	low

suggesting that the Late Paleoindian period does represent the regional specialization that Anderson (2001) advocates as characteristic of terminal Pleistocene adaptations. In this sense, it is difficult to use results of subsistence studies from one Late Paleoindian site as a model for interpreting the patterns of another. It may be that the approach of modeling is not sufficient to explain the diversity and regional aspects of cultural adaptations during the terminal Pleistocene.

In conclusion, it is evident that the analysis of the Dust Cave fauna supports a view of Paleoindians as generalists who were specially adapted to a particular region (Anderson 1996:32). This is clear through the following observations:

1. The presence of so many birds in a faunal assemblage is not generally expected of a Paleoindian component, even a Late Paleoindian occupation. In addition, the lack of identifiable mammal bones is not due to fragmentation of long bones for marrow; their relative scarcity may be explained by the discard of larger mammal bones outside of the cave.
2. There is also a relatively small percentage of the assemblage modified by animals. This significantly decreases the possibility the assemblage accumulated due to the activities of nonhuman predators or rodents.
3. The Dust Cave inhabitants exploited many different habitats that provided them with a large variety of animal species. A riverine

habitat provided fish, waterfowl, and turtles. The woodland and ecotone habitats provided many small and medium-size mammals and birds. A nearby grassland habitat supplied many animals, including bobwhites and prairie chickens.

4. Seasonality data suggests that the primary season of occupation was the fall and early winter months, indicated by the presence of passenger pigeons, ducks, and geese in the assemblage.

5. White-tailed deer remains were less common in the Late Paleoindian assemblage than in the later occupation of the site, and of these, most of the deer were subadults.

6. The diversity analysis of the Dust Cave assemblage suggests that the Paleoindian assemblage is greater in terms of richness, diversity, and evenness than any of the later components at the site.

7. Comparisons between Dust Cave and six other early sites with faunal remains indicate the uniqueness of adaptations during the Late Paleoindian period.

The information provided by the zooarchaeological analysis of a well-dated and preserved Late Paleoindian deposit certainly alters preconceived ideas about Paleoindian subsistence. The data provided by this analysis suggests that Late Paleoindians at Dust Cave placed more importance on birds and small to medium-size mammals within a wide variety of habitats. Also significant is the relative distinctiveness of the Dust Cave faunal remains in Late Paleoindian contexts, which represents regional adaptations. Dust Cave's ideal location between riverine and upland habitats provided ample resources for the Late Paleoindian occupants to exploit. If this is the case, modeling Late Paleoindian subsistence strategies in relation to other Late Paleoindian sites would be problematic if the sites are from different regions and habitats. However, as other chapters in this volume attest, more and more Late Paleoindian sites with this general foraging pattern are being documented. Regional modeling may be possible as we accumulate more data on this particular problem. Thus, the Dust Cave faunal assemblage provides additional insight into the much more diverse and complex subsistence strategy of Late Paleoindian hunter-gatherers.

Acknowledgments

I wish to acknowledge all of the people with whom I have worked at Dust Cave; this research was truly a cooperative effort. Most important, I would like to thank Boyce Driskell for being so steadfast and dedicated to the Dust Cave project. I would also like to thank fellow Dust Cave teaching assistants Scott Meeks, Kandi Hollenbach, Asa Randall, Nick Richardson, and Lara Homsey. I would especially like to acknowledge the support of fellow University of Tennessee at Knoxville graduate Sarah Sherwood. Finally, none of this research would have been possible without the support of my family.

SEVEN

Seed Collecting and Fishing at the Shawnee Minisink Paleoindian Site

Everyday Life in the Late Pleistocene

Richard J. Dent

The Shawnee Minisink site is located at the confluence of the Delaware River and Brodhead Creek within what is known as the Upper Delaware Valley of northeastern Pennsylvania. Archaeological deposits at the site extend to a depth of about 10 feet below the surface of a second terrace of the nearby Delaware River. The site was discovered by a local avocational archaeologist, Donald Kline of Mt. Bethel, Pennsylvania. American University carried out further excavations at the site over a four-year period of the mid to late 1970s. The National Geographic Society and the National Science Foundation sponsored those investigations.

Excavations at Shawnee Minisink revealed a column of buried and well-stratified living surfaces. Based on diagnostic artifacts and a suite of radiocarbon assays, the basal component of Shawnee Minisink is securely assigned to the Paleoindian period, ca. 10,900 BP. Chronologically later components are assigned to the Transitional (Late Paleoindian), Archaic (Early and Late), and Woodland (Early to Late) periods. This chapter focuses on the site's Paleoindian component.

The Paleoindian component is buried about 10 feet under the present ground surface at the site, and associated remains are sealed within a layer of gently deposited loess. That component is completely sealed and separated from the Transitional (Late Paleoindian) component above by up to 3 feet of alluvially deposited and culturally sterile sand. There are arguably few Paleoindian components currently available for study that have been subject to less postdepositional disturbance.

Buried soil yielding the Paleoindian artifacts is classified as silt loam. The nature of that soil indicates that this was a loess (silty loam) deposit (see Foss 1977) laid down by winds transporting glacially derived materials into the Upper Delaware Valley ca. 10,900 years ago. The boundaries of the stratum are therefore not perfectly horizontal in profile, instead presenting a gently undulating surface with both high and low areas. In the course of excavating this stratum, we were able to expose the former contours of the Paleoindian living surface at the site.

Given the unique nature of the stratum yielding Paleoindian artifacts at the site, it is reasonable to argue that very little postdepositional disturbance of those artifacts occurred. Artifacts and features were gently covered by loess and suffered no hydraulic displacement typical of alluvially deposited soils. All artifacts, both formal tool types and associated debitage, were recovered as a thin deposit on the undulating living surface. Most features encountered in the Paleoindian stratum appeared to have represented chipping clusters associated with tool manufacturing. Three hearths or firefloors were discovered during the course of excavations. These appeared as shallow depressions with reddish, fire-hardened surfaces. Concentrations of charcoal flecks were also noted in the immediate proximity of these features, and all yielded diagnostic Paleoindian artifacts either within or immediately around feature boundaries.

The integrity of the Paleoindian deposit at Shawnee Minisink is likewise secure in terms of the potential introduction of later cultural materials from stratigraphically superior deposits. Next earliest archaeological deposits at the site are separated from the Paleoindian layers by at least three feet of sediments. Those overlying sediments are culturally sterile and thus effectively seal the Paleoindian stratum. It should also be noted that none of the Late Paleoindian or Early Archaic peoples as represented in overlying strata are known to have excavated subterranean pits. Transport of later artifacts down to lower levels therefore does not seem to have been very possible. In short, the Paleoindian component at Shawnee Minisink would seem to represent a remarkably intact, undisturbed archaeological deposit.

Chronology of the Paleoindian component at Shawnee Minisink is as secure as possible given its extreme age, and Shawnee Minisink is certainly one of the most securely dated Paleoindian sites in eastern North America. All radiocarbon assays discussed below are cited as RCYBP, and no calibration functions have been applied. Calendar interpretation of all radiocarbon dates from the Paleoindian era is currently under some scrutiny (Fiedel 1999b), and calibration formulas for the late Pleistocene are therefore likely to change in the near future.

During the course of excavations, over 55,000 artifacts were recovered from an area of about 3,900 square feet, estimated to represent about one-quarter of the total site. A substantial portion of this assemblage was recovered from the site's Paleoindian component. In addition to diagnostic Paleoindian tool types and associated lithic debris, a significant number of carbonized seed remains and small amounts of calcined fish bone were also collected. Many of these floral and faunal remains were recovered from within the confines of a Paleoindian hearth or fire-floor area encountered during excavation. At the time of their recovery, this data represented some of the first evidence to suggest the complete breadth of Paleoindian subsistence patterns in eastern North America.

Yet the subsistence evidence from Shawnee Minisink, carbonized plant seeds and fish bone, appeared to contradict the theories of most archaeologists at that time. During the era of the site's excavation, and for a long time afterward, archaeologists labored under the shadow of the so-called big-game hunting model of Paleoindian subsistence patterns. That subsistence model was a direct import from western North America. Watching Paleoindian artifacts being recovered west of the Mississippi River in direct association with the remains of Pleistocene megafauna made a definite impact on eastern archaeologists. Unfortunately, similar associations between Paleoindians and extinct proboscideans continued to remain elusive in eastern North America.

Two responses to the big-game hunting model should be considered here (from Dent 1995:105). One camp charged ahead in the belief that absence of evidence was ultimately not evidence of absence, and thus continued to lump all Paleoindians into a universal pancontinental big-game hunting tradition (e.g., see Dragoo 1976; Funk 1978; Stoltman 1978). As Mason has commented (1981:98), more than a few continued to insist that the onetime connection between Paleoindians and megafauna in the East was ultimately more than platonic. Others retreated into what might be called a wait-and-see posture. One such prehistorian, in a state of frustration, went so far as to lament that the hard evidence indicated that eastern Paleoindians "ate nothing and lived primarily as isolated individuals" (Brose 1978:729).

All of this had a direct impact on archaeologists' take on the subsistence data being reported from the Shawnee Minisink site. Few could realistically challenge the integrity of the association given the secure radiocarbon assays, the nature of the deposit, and its direct association with diagnostic artifacts of the Paleoindian era. The site had also been excavated in a manner that well surpassed almost all standard field methods of the era. Nevertheless, the great hunters of the late Pleistocene still seemed nowhere in sight given the food remains that were recovered. And many archaeologists found themselves reluctant to spend much time considering any Paleoindian site that did not hint of the chase for mastodon, or at the very least yield a caribou bone or two. Most therefore ultimately simply chose to ignore the site, treating it as an outright anomaly in the larger universe of data. Only a very few lonely voices (e.g., Dincauze 1981; Meltzer 1988) eventually appeared ready to consider a more diverse subsistence base for eastern Paleoindians.

Such a perspective is now fortunately beginning to change. Archaeologists have grown impatient in their wait for the discovery of a secure kill site unequivocally linking Paleoindians in eastern North America with now-extinct late Pleistocene megafauna. In addition, some other more recently excavated Paleoindian sites have yielded good evidence for the hunting of various herding (Spiess et al. 1985) and other small-game animal species (Storck and Spiess 1994; Walker 2000), along with the gathering of available plant resources (Detwiler 2000). With the arrival of these new data, Shawnee Minisink seems less and less the subsistence anomaly that many once viewed it to be. We are now at a point where many archaeologists appear open to the possibility that Paleoindians in eastern North America followed a more unique subsistence pattern effectively attuned to a broad spectrum of locally available animal and plant resources. Paleoindians in eastern North American may have been global in their maintenance of a remarkable tool tradition that was spread across much of the New World and that may have even had its roots in northern Europe or Asia. But there is now growing evidence that these same Paleoindians acted much more locally in adapting to the subsistence resources of the moment.

In the paragraphs below I want to look back at the evidence from the Shawnee Minisink site that is supportive of this newly emerging belief that Paleoindians followed a truly diverse range of subsistence practices in eastern North America. To do this, I first offer a description of the site, its excavation, and the data we recovered from the Paleoindian component. I then turn to a discussion of the implications of the floral and faunal remains recovered from Shawnee Minisink on our understanding of Paleoindian adaptations in the Upper Delaware Valley and beyond.

Setting

The Upper Delaware Valley is defined as the immediate environs of the Delaware River as it flows about 36 miles from Port Jervis, New York, to Delaware Water Gap, Pennsylvania. New York State is situated at the top of the Upper Delaware Valley, and the Delaware River forms the boundary between Pennsylvania and New Jersey as it flows southward through the valley. Most of the valley lies within the ridge and valley physiographic province. The Kittatinny Ridge on the New Jersey side of the river rises to a height of about 1,500 feet above mean sea level (amsl). Some discontinuous ridges stand between it and the Allegheny Front on the Pennsylvania side to the west. Those landforms are broadly known as the Pocono Mountains. The Shawnee Minisink site on the valley floor is itself situated about 370 feet amsl.

The known geologic history of the region stretches over 600 million years. It was during the Pleistocene epoch, however, that the Upper Delaware Valley took on most of its present form. Glacial ice invaded the valley two or three times, with the last glacial advance being of particular importance. The Wisconsin glacial intrusion reached this location by about 20,000 to 18,000 years ago and scoured the valley to a depth of 150 to 249 feet below the present surface (Epstein 1969:7). This advance ground to a halt about four miles past the valley's southern boundary. Deglaciation of the Upper Delaware Valley began with downmelt and retreat about 15,000 years ago (Crowl and Stuckenrath 1977:219). Outwash gravels from the retreating glacier were subsequently carried in and deposited on the valley floor. The Delaware River and its tributaries then deposited alluvial terraces on this base. These alluvial terraces also encapsulate the remains of various archaeological cultures over the past 11,000 years.

The Shawnee Minisink site is elevated 21 feet above the nearby Delaware River and Brodhead Creek. The location offers a southern exposure and is protected by elevated terrain just to the north. This location is also rather strategic in that most human and animal travelers through the Upper Delaware Valley would have moved past the site when heading to or from the Delaware Water Gap. That geologic feature provides unrestricted access both into and out of the southern end of the valley. The nearby Brodhead Creek is in turn the first major corridor to and from the western reaches of the Upper Delaware Valley and beyond.

The lower first terrace formation underlying the site consists primarily of outwash gravel deposited after the retreat of the Wisconsin glacial intrusion into the Upper Delaware Valley. An alluvial second terrace formation rests on this base. At the Shawnee Minisink location, slightly more than 16 feet of sediments have accumulated over this foundation in the last 14,000–15,000 years. The upper 10 feet of that accumulation yields an archaeological column that stretches from Paleoindian to Late Woodland times. A glacial-era kame terrace is also located a short distance north of the site. Primary quarry deposits of black chert outcrop on a ridge behind the site, and this and other suitable rock can also be collected from the valley's floodplains and streambeds. The entire region is generally rich in high-quality siliceous lithic materials.

Today the Upper Delaware Valley offers a generally temperate climate. It ecologically falls within Shelford's (1963:18) temperate deciduous or oak-deer-maple biome, more particularly what he refers to as the oak-chestnut region. Climax fauna includes deer, turkey, bear, and elk. About 58 other species of mammals are also known to have inhabited the valley before extinction or extirpation. Amphibian and avifauna communities comprise another 69 known species, and about 53 species of resident or diadromous fishes are believed to inhabit the region's river and streams.

Paleoenvironment

A significant effort was made concurrent with the program of excavations at Shawnee Minisink to reconstruct the ecological context of the Upper Delaware Valley during the late Pleistocene. Numerous sources of data were available in that regard (see Dent 1979, 1985), including pollen cores, soil profiles, phytoliths, and even some micro- and macrofaunal remains. For example, 19 different pollen suites of the appropriate age are available from the Upper Delaware Valley or situated nearby. More site-specific data included terrestrial gastropod remains and phytoliths.

Paleoindians entered the Upper Delaware Valley as the terminal preboreal forest that had established itself sometime after glacial retreat was transitioning into a true boreal association. In this case, an earlier spruce-fir and pine association was giving way to a pine-birch forest. Both associations manifested themselves as very dense coniferous forests with a corresponding low biotic carrying capacity. Such boreal associations feign monotony over both time and space (Winterhalder 1983b:9). In reality, however, boreal forests are actually complex and relatively dynamic mosaics consisting of many different small habitats, or what have been labeled patches. These patches, usually very dispersed, are created by local edaphic conditions as well as by an internal rhythm of disturbance and succession endemic to the ecosystem itself (Winterhalder 1983b:32). The Shawnee Minisink site location is a good example of one such patch.

During the Paleoindian occupation of the Shawnee Minisink site, the habitation area was situated in an open floodplain meadow approximately 300 feet back from the Delaware River and its tributary, Brodhead Creek.

Seed types recovered in the Paleoindian stratum are generally from plants that enjoy open habitat. Terrestrial gastropod remains recovered from this same deposit indicate damp, often wet conditions at the site. Phytolith analysis (Greenan 1985:36) substantiates the presence of significant stands of grasses around the site.

Various statistical models were employed to generate specific climatic variables. All such models are typically based on the logical assumption that climate controls vegetation, and that one can predict the nature of past climatic regimes based on percentages of certain plant pollens. These models are essentially transfer functions that look at the modern relationship between pollen deposition and climate and then extrapolate that back into the more distant past. For the Paleoindian period in the Upper Delaware Valley, the mean July temperature is thought to have been approximately 70 degrees Fahrenheit, some 6 degrees cooler than today. Snowfall during winter is reconstructed at 17 inches per year more than in the present, and overall yearly precipitation registers close to twice what it is today. These same models predict increased duration of southern air masses during the summer months. It appears that the Paleoindian occupation of Shawnee Minisink was a late summer event. A possible verification of dominant southern air may be evident around the one hearth or fire-floor at the site that had significant areas of its borders exposed. Artifacts cluster around this feature's eastern, western, and southern edges, but not at its northern edge. This may register the fact that the predominant air flow was from the south to the north, thus blowing fumes, heat, and sparks in that direction.

During the course of excavations, four radiocarbon assays were run on collected charcoal. The U.S. Geological Survey Radiocarbon Laboratory in Reston, Virginia, processed all four samples. Two of these assays were thought at the time to best date the Paleoindian component of the site to ca. 10,500 BP (Table 7.1). Both were run on collected wood charcoal, one from a hearth or fire-floor exposed in the southwest portion of the site, and the other from a similar feature in the northwest portion of the site.

Two additional radiocarbon assays were attempted on a single sample of charcoal-stained soil from the southeast quadrant of the site. The sample had to be heavily diluted and produced two very different dates, both with large sigmas (see Table 7.1). Given the nature of the original sample and the large sigmas, both resulting dates are viewed as equivocal.

With advances in the radiocarbon dating technique, I recently decided to submit curated charred seed fragments for assay. Two samples of car-

TABLE 7.1. Radiocarbon assays run on Paleoindian component at the Shawnee Minisink site.

Assay	Laboratory Number	Comment
10,590±300 RCYBP	W-2994	assay run on wood charcoal collected from hearth exposed in southwest portion of excavated area; sample in direct association with floral and faunal remains as well Paleoindian artifacts
10,750±600 RCYBP	W-3134	assay run on wood charcoal collected from hearth exposed in northwest portion of excavated area; sample in direct association with Paleoindian artifacts
9310±1000 RCYBP	W-3388	assay run on diluted sample of charcoal stained soil recovered from southeast portion of site; equivocal
11,050±1000 RCYBP	W-3391	assay run on alkali fraction of above charcoal stained soil; also equivocal
10,940±90 RCYBP	Beta-101935	Accelerator Mass Spectrometry radiocarbon assay; sample run on charred seed from hearth in southwest portion of excavated area; seed in direct association with other floral and faunal remains and Paleoindian artifacts
10,900±40 RCYBP	Beta-127162	Accelerator Mass Spectrometry radiocarbon assay; sample run on charred seed from hearth in southwest portion of excavated area; seed in direct association with other floral and faunal remains and Paleoindian artifacts

bonized hawthorn plum seeds (*Crataegus* sp.), originally collected from the hearth or fire-floor in the southwest portion of the excavation grid, were submitted for radiocarbon assay using the Accelerator Mass Spectrometry (AMS) method. Both were processed and counted by Beta Analytic, Inc. in Miami, Florida (see Table 7.1). The resulting new AMS dates are quite consistent in age, ca. 10,900 BP. In addition, both samples produced dates with remarkably small sigmas. While both new AMS dates are generally consistent with most of the original assays run in the 1970s, the new dates do point to a slightly earlier period of Paleoindian occupation at the Shawnee Minisink site.

The hearth or fire-floor from which these carbonized seeds were collected also contained both calcined fish bones and diagnostic Paleoindian artifacts and associated debitage. Black chert end scrapers typical of the Paleoindian occupation of the site are the majority tool type recovered from within and around this feature. The southeastern edge of the hearth or fire-floor is approximately 23 linear feet from the fluted biface recovered at the site.

Paleoindian Tool Assemblage

The American University's excavations at Shawnee Minisink exposed 3,000 square feet of the Paleoindian artifact-bearing stratum. All artifacts encountered at the site, both recognizable tool types and individual debitage flakes, were mapped in exact provenience. We collected both horizontal and vertical coordinates on over 55,000 individual artifacts during our investigation of the site. Charles McNett (1985a:21–31) has offered a complete description of this procedure. For the time, and even by the standards of today, it is not unreasonable to argue that Shawnee Minisink was excavated with an uncommon and high degree of precision. We estimate that 95 percent of all artifacts were recorded *in situ*. The remaining artifacts, almost always minute retouch flakes, were retrieved through screening of all soil matrix.

McNett (ed. 1985:83–120) has published a complete description of all the artifact assemblages recovered at Shawnee Minisink. Sydney Marshall (1981, 1985) has published a technological analysis of a large sample of the Paleoindian artifacts recovered at the site, and Pam Rule and June Evans (1985) have looked closely at the collection of Paleoindian end scrapers. Evans (1978, 1985) examined the technological transition evident between the Paleoindian and transitional Late Paleoindian components at Shawnee Minisink. All of these studies offer detailed analyses of the Paleoindian technological tradition as expressed at this site. Here I would just briefly like to describe the Paleoindian assemblage recovered through our excavation.

Artifacts recovered from the Paleoindian stratum of the site include a complete fluted biface of somewhat grainy Onondoga chert, along with end scrapers (n = 126), side scrapers (n = 23), multiple-edged scrapers (n = 2), flake knives (n = 4), generalized bifaces (n = 9), spokeshaves (n = 2), utilized flakes (n = 158), discoidal cores (n = 7), tabular cores (n = 5), and hammerstones (n = 10). Figure 7.1 presents a sample of the tool types recovered. Enormous amounts of debitage were also recovered during the course of excavation. Marshall's analysis (1985:170) reveals that about 91 percent of the artifact assemblage was manufactured from locally available black chert. The remaining objects were made from gray chert, argillite, or jasper. She argues (Marshall 1985:195) that some tool manufacturing and considerable tool use and rejuvenation were taking place at the site during the Paleoindian occupation. Given the generalized nature of the Paleoindian tool kit, we suspect that a wide range of activities focusing on local resource procurement and processing were taking place along with this manufacturing and tool rejuvenation.

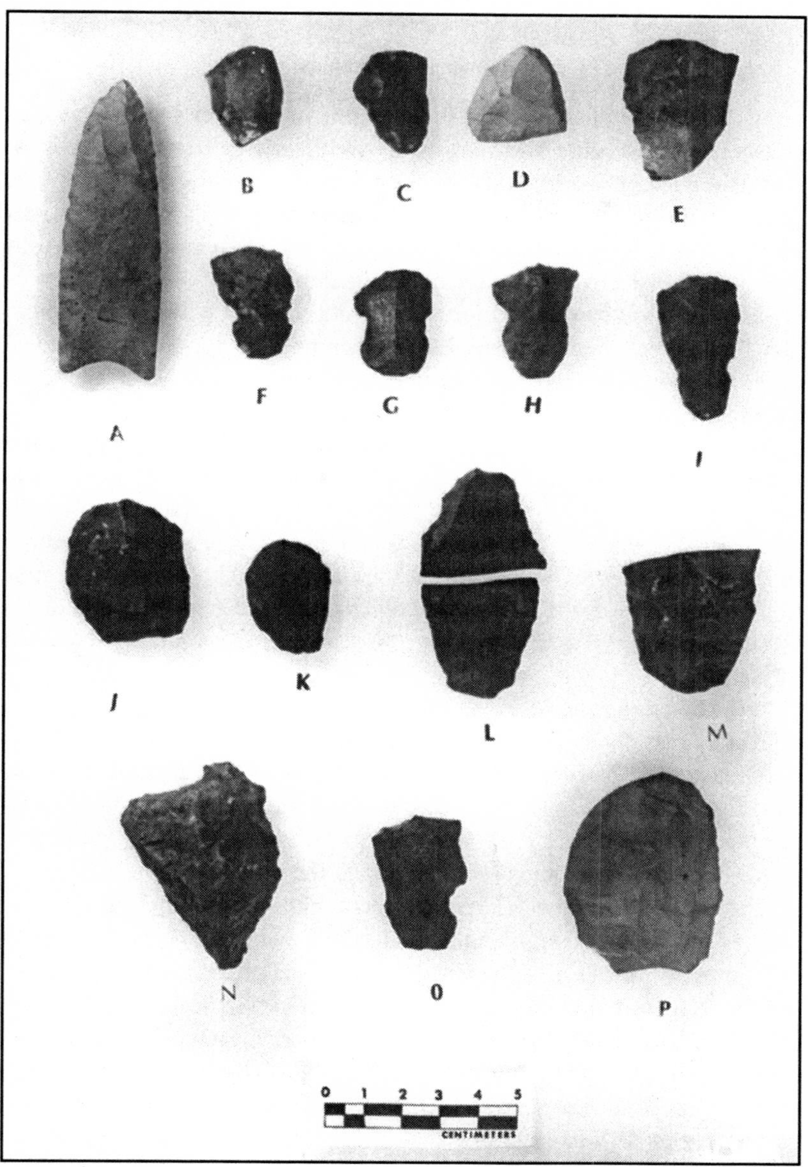

FIGURE 7.1. Sample of artifacts from Paleoindian component at Shawnee Minisink: a, fluted projectile point; b–e, end scrapers, f–i; notched end scrapers, j–k, full scrapers; l–m, snapped-flake scrapers; n, multiedge scraper; o. spokeshave; p, flake knife.

Subsistence Remains

Excavation at the Shawnee Minisink site was undertaken with the goal of recovering all possible information on prehistoric subsistence practices. Our field strategy directly reflected the processual paradigm of that era. A variation of Struever's (1968) water-separation or floatation technique was employed in a systematic fashion during the entire four seasons of excavation. Arbitrary 3-inch levels were maintained during the course of excavating each 10-by-10-foot excavation unit at the site. From within each such 3-inch level a 2.15-cubic-foot sample of soil matrix was consistently subjected to the flotation procedure. That sample represented about 10 percent of the total matrix within any given arbitrary level.

Any features encountered during excavation were likewise subject to the same procedure. If possible, the same size sample of matrix noted above was processed from each feature. If the feature's size precluded a sample of that size, all available feature matrix was floated. Given the careful nature of the general excavation protocol at the site, it was also possible at times to directly recover some subsistence remains. If such remains were noted, all surrounding soil matrix was water screened through fine-mesh screen or floated.

In the flotation procedure, the sample of soil matrix was poured slowly, a little at a time, into a standard galvanized bucket, the bottom of which had been replaced by 1/16-inch mesh screen. This bucket, half immersed in a larger container of water, was gently rotated in alternating clockwise and counterclockwise directions, allowing the soil matrix to escape. On lifting the bucket gently out of the water and then replacing it, the various materials caught in the screen would become free and proceed to settle at different rates.

The light fraction containing floral debris, fine bone, and the like would remain momentarily near the surface (because of differential porosity) and was quickly removed with a small strainer. Less-porous material, such as minute lithic flakes, pottery, and other denser material, would then be trapped and removed from the screen on the bottom of the flotation bucket. Each fraction, the light and the heavy, would then be placed in a lined container and allowed to air dry.

Material recovered during this flotation procedure was then transferred to the field laboratory to be bagged and cataloged. After the field season these samples were individually picked or sorted for carbonized seeds, nutshells, charcoal, small faunal remains, and the like. Over the course of four seasons of excavation, 1,287 flotation samples were processed. All seeds were identified by Charles Gunn, chief curator of the U.S. Department of Agriculture National Seed Herbarium, Plant Taxonomy Laboratory, in Beltsville, Maryland.

Ten distinct types of seeds were recovered from the levels and features yielding Paleoindian artifacts at Shawnee Minisink. All seeds reported from the Paleoindian component were carbonized. Taxa and numbers of seed specimens identified in direct association with the Paleoindian occupation at the site include acalypha (*Acalypha virginica*; n = 13), amaranth (*Amaranthus* sp.; n = 1), blackberry (*Rubus* sp.; n = 15), buckbean (*Menyanthes trifoliata* L.; n = 2), chenopod (*Chenopodium* sp.; n = 23), grape (*Vitis* sp.; n = 3), hackberry (*Celtis* sp.; n = 1), hawthorn plum (*Crataegus* sp.; n = 15), smartweed (*Polygonum* sp.; n = 2), and winter cress (*Barbarea orthoceras*; n = 1). A number of these seed types are interpreted as direct evidence of Paleoindian subsistence practices, given either their quantity, context of discovery, or potential dietary benefits. Others are seen as more problematic and may be viewed as inclusions from the era of occupation, but not necessarily items of consumer choice.

Given the context of recovery and potential human dietary value, there is little doubt that hackberry, blackberry, hawthorn plum, and grape were being consumed by the Paleoindian inhabitants of the site. Representatives of each type were recovered in a carbonized state within the Paleoindian stratum of the site. Numerous examples of carbonized hawthorn plum seeds were recovered from within the matrix of a feature (Figure 7.2). That feature represented a hearth or fire-floor in the Paleoindian stratum at the southwest portion of the excavation grid. The fire-reddened matrix of that feature yielded diagnostic Paleoindian artifacts, calcined fish bone fragments, and the hawthorn plum seeds whose fragments were recently radiocarbon dated. I can suggest no more secure context between subsistence remains, diagnostic Paleoindian artifacts, and multiple consistent radiocarbon dates at any Paleoindian site in North America.

Several plant species have perhaps the greatest potential nutritional value to humans. Fruits encasing hawthorn plum, blackberry, grape, and hackberry are high in carbohydrates. The pulp of these would likewise be important in terms of supplying essential vitamins and other trace elements. Hawthorn plum is in particular high in vitamin C. In addition, some of these same species have now been recovered in other similar early archaeological contexts. For example, Kandace Detwiler (2000:4; Hollenbach, this volume) has recently reported hackberry and grape from Dust Cave in Alabama. The Late Paleoindian component at that site is dated to ca. 10,500–10,000 years ago. Hackberry likewise appears to be an item of con-

FIGURE 7.2. Sample of Paleoindian floral and faunal remains from hearth in direct association with three radiocarbon assays (ca. 11,000 BP) and diagnostic artifacts. Fish bone fragment is visible in top right quadrant, and hawthorn plum seeds are visible throughout sample (crescent-shaped objects).

sumer choice in early levels of Meadowcroft Rockshelter in Pennsylvania (see Adovasio et al. 1998:55).

Other species of seeds recovered are more problematic in terms of arguing for a direct connection to Paleoindian subsistence practices. This is a result of lack of precedence for their use this early in time or the fact that quantities were minor. In the case of Shawnee Minisink, I would place the remains of acalypha, amaranth, buckbean, chenopod, smartweed, and winter cress in such a category. It is always a possibility that some seeds recovered on any given site may have become carbonized through various cultural or natural processes, but not necessarily consumed by site occupants. This is particularly true of seeds that are not recovered in the context of features or in association with particular artifacts that suggest human exploitation. On the other hand, some of the seeds noted above could well represent what Detwiler (2000:4) refers to as commensal species in her analysis of the seeds from Dust Cave. They might be from plants whose greens but perhaps not seeds were consumed. But even with these caveats, it is important to note that later in prehistory, humans intensively harvested the six seed taxa discussed above.

Several fragments of calcined fish bone (see Figure 7.2) were recovered from the same hearth or fire-floor as the majority of the carbonized hawthorn plum seeds. As noted previously, that feature was directly associated with diagnostic Paleoindian artifacts and the hawthorn plum seeds that produced the recent AMS radiocarbon dates for the earliest component at Shawnee Minisink. At the time of recovery, curators in the Smithsonian's Department of Vertebrate Zoology, Division of Fishes, at the National Museum of Natural History identified the calcined bone fragments as fish. Based only on the small calcined fragments of whole bone, however, they were reluctant to suggest exact species.

Nonetheless, these bone fragments remain some of the earliest evidence for fishing in North America. This early evidence of fishing by Paleoindians at Shawnee Minisink has now been duplicated in another similar component. Renee Walker (2000:73–74) has reported the recovery of fish bone in association with a Late Paleoindian component at Dust Cave in Alabama. At this site, she reports (Walker 2000:76) that 9 percent of the identifiable remains were from various species of fishes, and that aquatic resources in general were a favorite of site occupants 10,500 to 10,000 years ago. The faunal data from Dust Cave represents a remarkable new discovery. It furthermore helps to substantiate the fact that fish were quite possibly an important item of consumer choice during the Paleoindian era in North America.

Meaning

The fact that Paleoindians in eastern North America exploited plant resources along with small game and aquatic species now seems established. Sites such as Shawnee Minisink, Dust Cave, and a few others offer direct evidence of such subsistence patterns. In fact, this small suite of sites offers the only evidence on the matter of regional Paleoindian foodways. Other similar sites will hopefully be excavated in the future. At this point, it appears that the most relevant question should ask exactly how large a role such nonlarge-mammal subsistence resources played in the everyday life of Paleoindians in eastern North America. Based on evidence available from the Shawnee Minisink site, I would like to suggest some possible answers to that question.

It appears likely that sites such as Shawnee Minisink represent the beginning of the so-called broad-spectrum revolution (Cohen 1989:21) in human subsistence patterns for eastern North America. The shift to this lifeway is probably an artifact of changing environmental circumstances beginning ca. 11,000 years ago. The rich grasslands of the late Pleistocene, with their large land fauna, did not linger long after glacial retreat. I doubt that Paleoindians in the Upper Delaware Valley ever saw the megafauna of that earlier era. In that regard, the remains of a good number of mastodons have been pulled from the peat bogs near or just north of the Shawnee Minisink site. One such creature was excavated less than three miles away from the site. Its remains, however, were radiocarbon dated 1,000 years previous to the occupation of Shawnee Minisink. Timing may be everything regarding the hope that some still hold for the linkage between Paleoindians and megafauna in eastern North America. Broad-spectrum subsistence systems were instead the response by Paleoindians to local environment in eastern North America.

As part of a broad-spectrum subsistence system, the Shawnee Minisink site no doubt represented one element of a larger settlement pattern. Seed remains recovered there indicate a late summer/autumn season of occupation. I would suggest the site's occupants represented a small group of foragers (Binford 1980:5–10) who arrived to exploit a patch in the larger boreal forest then blanketing the Upper Delaware Valley. They came to gather plant foods, fish, and both rejuvenate old tools and manufacture a new stone tool assemblage. This location must have been strategic for such activities given its location on the floodplain between the confluence of the Delaware River and Brodhead Creek as well as its nearness to substantial deposits of high-grade cherts. The nature of this settlement location appears reflected in the unique tool assemblage recovered during excavation of the site. That assemblage contained only one fluted biface, but large numbers of end scrapers, utilized flakes, and various other unifacial tools.

Finally, based on common ethnographically based assumptions concerning gender roles in prehistory, the seeds recovered at Shawnee Minisink perhaps bring women's activities into better resolution (see Driskell and Walker, this volume, for discussion). The extension of such gender-linked activities into the late Pleistocene, however, is of course tenuous. But the seeds from Shawnee Minisink may indeed be directly linked to women's activities. Women might likewise have been responsible for fish remains recovered at the site. Women could have also been involved in at least some stone tool modification and use at Shawnee Minisink, given the high ratio of modified and utilized flakes within the assemblage.

Acknowledgments

Don Kline, of Mt. Bethel, Pennsylvania, discovered the Shawnee Minisink site. He recovered the first seeds and the fish bone from the site and extended an invitation for American University to continue his work. Nothing would have been possible without his help. Charles W. McNett Jr. was the principal investigator at the site and invited me to excavate there for three field seasons. Russ Handsman originally introduced me to the site. June Evans and Sydney Marshall worked with me at Shawnee Minisink and continue as my friends and valued colleagues. Special thanks to the multitude of field school students and others like me who were fortunate enough to learn archaeology in the Upper Delaware Valley.

EIGHT

Gathering in the Late Paleoindian Period

Archaeobotanical Remains from Dust Cave, Alabama

Kandace D. Hollenbach

There are a number of models regarding settlement and subsistence strategies during the late Pleistocene/early Holocene transition in the southeastern United States. Each has a particular emphasis: subsistence strategies (e.g., Meltzer and Smith 1986), orientation and organization of territories (e.g., Anderson 1996; Morse 1997), and patterns of mobility, including the scheduling of group aggregations (e.g., Anderson 1996; Walthall 1998b), seasonal shifts in group mobility (e.g., Cable 1996; Walthall 1998a, 1998b), and the influence of raw materials on mobility (e.g., Daniel 2001; Goodyear 1983).

While these models differ in their details, they share the premise that Paleoindian and Early Archaic societies were organized into mobile bands of hunter-gatherers. Such an assumption is not necessarily problematic, especially given an archaeological record consisting of chipped stone tools (many of which are curated), a lack of pottery, no substantial architecture, and the absence of domesticated plants. More troubling is the seemingly innocuous description of these peoples as hunter-gatherers: hunters first and secondarily gatherers. The hunting component of subsistence has been emphasized since the early twentieth century, when archaeologists initiated discussions of early Native Americans (Gero 1995). This focus on hunting is partly due to the nature of the evidence: southeastern Paleoindian and Early Archaic sites, especially in open-air locations, largely consist of isolated projectile points or scatters of stone tools and debitage. Faunal remains may be present, but plant materials are rarely recovered. Subsequently, current models rely heavily on environmental reconstructions and regional distributions of sites (in particular, stone tool finds) as support for their arguments about subsistence and settlement strategies. Because of this lopsided dataset, the models tend to focus on the influence of hunting and quarrying activities on subsistence and settlement decisions. Plant foods are mentioned in passing—surely people ate nuts and berries that they gathered somewhere along the way. The activities associated with plant food use have largely been deemed beyond archaeological detection, other than the occasional find of a nutting stone or pestle.

Here I would like to demonstrate that the available data on Paleoindian and Early Archaic plant resources can open new avenues for models of settlement and subsistence strategies during this time period. Each plant item (indeed, every artifact) articulates with the world surrounding it (Heidegger 1971, 1977). As part of "being," every "thing" engages with various aspects of the world, including the landscape, the plants and animals that occupy that landscape, seasonality and climate, people and forces beyond the control or predictive powers of people, and perhaps including contingency as well as the supernatural. We can trace these connections between a plant taxon and its surrounding world so as to begin to perceive that world from the perspective of that plant. By considering the different aspects of the world that the activity labeled "gathering" engages (Heidegger 1971, 1977), we can gain a greater understanding of how "gathering" structured Late Paleoindian lifeways.

In this chapter I examine the botanical assemblage from the Late Paleoindian component at Dust Cave, one of a handful of sites in the Southeast at which plant remains dating to this period have been preserved. Following Heidegger (1971, 1977), I explore the strands of the world of "gathering" with which the hickory nut, the dominant plant taxon recovered from the cave and at most prehorticultural southeastern sites, is interconnected. Using the information gleaned from a consideration of the manner in which hickory nuts are embedded in a gathering/hunting lifestyle, I offer a broad interpretation of the Late Paleoindian occupation at Dust Cave, as well as some suggestions for the expansion of settlement/subsistence models beyond their current emphasis on hunting.

Dust Cave, Alabama

As discussed in chapter 6, Dust Cave is located in the northwest corner of Alabama, on the backwaters of the Tennessee River (see Figure 6.1). Diagnostic stone tools and radiocarbon dates have provided a comprehensive culture history for the site (see Figure 6.3), which dates between 10,500 and 5,200 BP. Preservation of organic material within the cave is remarkable (Driskell 1994, 1996; Walker et al. 1999; Walker et al. 2001).

Faunal remains indicate that the inhabitants of the cave exploited a wide variety of resources, from terrestrial and aquatic, open, closed, and ecotone habitats (Walker 1998; Walker et al. 1999; Walker et al. 2001). Rather than focusing on deer, hunters apparently brought back a large proportion of waterfowl and small and medium-size mammals (Walker 1998, 2000). The plant assemblage at the site is dominated by nut mast, in particular hickory (Gardner 1994; Walker et al. 1999). Wild fruits, such as grapes and hackberries, and possibly greens from chenopod and poke likely supplemented the diet (Walker et al. 1999; Walker et al. 2001).

Dust Cave appears to have been used as an autumn/early winter campsite during the Late Paleoindian period (Driskell 1996; Walker 1998; Walker et al. 1999). Circular, shallow, basin-shaped features filled with charcoal and ash, as well as flecks of charcoal dispersed throughout the zones, indicate that numerous fires were built within the cave (Driskell 1996; Walker et al. 1999). The seasonal use of the cave is implied by the plant and faunal data, particularly deer mandibles and migratory waterfowl (Walker 1998, 2000). Dust Cave appears to have been a stopover point during Late Paleoindian peoples' seasonal round, perhaps on their way to the uplands for autumn and winter, and on their return to the floodplain for the spring and summer (Walthall 1998a, 1998b). This stop would have allowed them to take advantage of the numerous resources in the cave's immediate vicinity.

Botanical Assemblage

The plant analysis presented here is based on 15 floatation samples from the Late Paleoindian component of Dust Cave. These samples were excavated in 1993 from Test Unit F, located in the entrance trench of the cave (see Figure 6.2). Eleven of the samples were excavated in natural and arbitrary 5-centimeter levels within a 50-by-50-centimeter column (Table 8.1). The remaining four samples represent features (Table 8.2), two of which were excavated in Test Unit F, and two of which derive from the unit directly south of Test Unit F. Feature 37 was described in the field as a pocket of burned sediment and ash, while the other three are charcoal pits. All are roughly oval in shape.

The samples were processed in the field using a modified Shell Mound Archaeological Project (SMAP) machine. The heavy fraction mesh size was 1 millimeter; the light fraction was captured in fine mesh with approximately 0.3-millimeter openings. The heavy fractions were refloated in the laboratory to remove remaining sediment. Exceptions include samples from

TABLE 8.1. Results of botanical analysis of column samples from Late Paleoindian contexts at Dust Cave (modified from Walker et al. 2001:175). Taxa are listed as count/weight (g). Courtesy of *Midcontinental Journal of Archaeology*.

Level	32	33	34	34	35	36	37	38	39	40	40
Top Depth	430	435	440	440	445	450	455	460	465	470	475
Bottom Depth*	435	440	445	445	450	455	460	465	470	475	bedrock
Zone	T1	T1a	T1a	T1	T1	T1	T1	U	U2	U2	U2
Volume	10 L	6 L	6 L	13 L	14 L	14 L	9 L	10 L	8 L	13 L	12 L
Taxon											
Acorn (*Quercus alba*)		1/negl.			1/negl.				1/negl.		
Beech family (Fagaceae)									1/negl.		
Black walnut (*Juglans nigra*)	1/ 0.03g			1/ 0.01g				39/ 0.93g			
Chenopod** (*Chenopodium* sp.)	1										1
Grape(?) (*Vitis* sp.)	1/ 0.01g										
Hackberry**(*Celtis occidentalis*)	15/ 0.25g	25/ 0.26g	43/ 0.36g	6/ 0.05g			1/negl.	2/negl.	13/ 0.23g	3/ 0.02g	1/negl.
Hazelnut (*Corylus americana*)					1/ 0.01g						
Hickory (*Carya* sp.)	10/ 0.05g	1/negl.	2/negl.	11/ 0.06g	107/ 1.32g	17/ 0.10g	37/ 0.28g	93/ 0.92g	4/ 0.02g	4/ 0.02g	4/ 0.03g
Pokeweed(?)** (*Phytolacca americana*)				2			1			1	
Stargrass (*Hypoxis hirsuta*)								1			
Wood	0.16g	0.01g	0.02g	0.08g	0.13g	0.07g	0.03g	0.10g	0.04g	0.01g	0.01g
Pine pitch		0.02g		0.04g			0.01g	0.03g	0.03g		0.01g
Bark/pine cone							4/ negl.				
Unidentified seed**	1			1		1			1	2	1
Unidentified	20/ 0.07g	15/negl.	20/ 0.10g	9/ 0.01g	1/negl.	4/negl.	5/ 0.01g	2/negl.			
Total Plant Weight	0.57g	0.29g	0.48g	0.25g	1.46g	0.17g	0.33g	1.98g	0.32g	0.05g	0.05g

* Depth is listed in centimeters below datum. ** Estimated seed counts are given.

TABLE 8.2. Results of analysis of feature samples from the Late Paleoindian contexts at Dust Cave. Taxa are listed as count/weight (g).

Level/Feature	**Fea 37**	**Fea 99**	**Fea 116**	**Fea 118**
Unit	N62W64 (TU F)	N62W64 (TU F)	N60W64	N60W64
Depth below datum	425–433 cm	457–459 cm	419–425 cm	455–460 cm
Maximum depth	8 cm	2 cm	6 cm	5 cm
Maximum dimensions	65 x 25 cm	20 x 15 cm	33 x 32 cm	38 x 34 cm
Volume floated	0.8 L	1 L	1 L	2 L
Taxon				
Acorn (*Quercus alba*)		8/negl.	5/negl.	
Black gum(?)				
(*Nyssa sylvatica*)				1/negl.
Black walnut (*Juglans nigra*)				5/ 0.14g
Chenopod* (*Chenopodium* sp.)	1	1		
Grape(?) (*Vitis* sp.)	1			
Hackberry*				
(*Celtis occidentalis*)	2/negl.	3/ 0.03g	3/ negl.	
Hickory (*Carya* sp.)	1/negl.	22/ 0.20g	4/ 0.03g	39/ 0.37g
Pokeweed(?)*				
(*Phytolacca americana*)	1	1		
Wood	0.01g	0.06g	0.22g	0.01g
Pine pitch	negl.	0.02g	negl.	negl.
Bark/pine cone				
Unidentified seed*		2	1	2
Unidentified	7/negl.			
Total Plant Weight	0.01g	0.31g	0.25g	0.52g

* Estimated seed counts are given.

Features 37 and 99, which were processed entirely by hand in the laboratory, and the sample from Feature 118, which was not refloated.

Analysis was performed with the aid of a stereoscopic microscope under 10 to 40 power magnification. Materials greater than 2.00 millimeters were sorted into categories, including bone, shell, lithic debitage, and carbonized plant taxa; each category was subsequently counted and weighed. Materials less than 2.00 millimeters were scanned for seeds, as well as plant taxa that may not have been present in the greater-than-2.00-millimeters portion of the sample. These items were counted but not weighed. However, acorn shell was removed down to the 0.71-millimeter size grade in order to mitigate preservation and recovery biases. Uncarbonized plant materials found in the samples were assumed to be modern contaminants and are not considered here. Identifications were made with reference to the comparative collection at the Ethnobotany Laboratory of the University of North Carolina–Chapel Hill, as well as Martin and Barkley's (1961) *Seed Identification Manual*.

As indicated in Table 8.1, the samples are dominated by nutshell, primarily hickory. While walnut shell was recovered from several samples, 39 of the 46 fragments, nearly 85 percent, come from a single sample (Level 38) within the column. Only 16 fragments of acorn shell and cap were identified. A single fragment of hazel nutshell was also found.

The majority of the seeds recovered from the site are charred hackberry seed fragments. Other seeds identified include wild chenopod, stargrass, possible grape, and a possible black gum seed fragment. In addition, numerous seed coat fragments, probably pokeweed, were identified in the samples. While hackberries and grapes, and possibly wild chenopod seeds, were probably consumed by the inhabitants of the cave, the remaining seed taxa present are likely commensal species. However, the spring leaves of chenopods and pokeweed may have been eaten as greens (Medsger 1966; Peterson 1997).

All of the nuts, fruits, and seeds in the assemblage are available in the late summer or autumn (Table 8.3). The nuts ripen and fall from September through November, although hazelnuts mature somewhat earlier. Grapes and hackberries are available in the late summer and fall. While the weedy plant taxa flower during the late spring and summer, their seeds ripen in autumn. This data supports the faunal evidence, indicating an autumn occupation of the cave (Walker 1998; Walker et al. 1999; Walker et al. 2001). However, the possibility of storage should not be dismissed. While the occupants of Dust Cave, similar to other Late Paleoindian and Dalton peoples in the Eastern Woodlands, do not appear to have employed subterranean storage strategies, nuts could have been stored by other means, such as baskets. In addition, plant foods that would have been consumed in the spring and summer, such as greens and flowers, are not typically preserved in botanical assemblages. In short, the plant remains cannot be used to exclude occupation during seasons other than late summer and autumn.

When comparing the plant remains recovered from the features (see Table 8.2), it is not surprising that Feature 37, an ash pit, has the least amount of nutshell and a negligible amount of wood charcoal. The large amount of nutshell relative to wood in Features 99 and 118 demonstrates the importance of mast resources to the inhabitants of Dust Cave. The amount of hickory is particularly significant. It comprises 65 percent of the plant weight from Feature 99 and 71 percent of the plant weight from Feature 118. While hickory nutshell was probably used secondarily as a fuel source (Lopinot 1984), the occupants of the cave undoubtedly collected hickory nuts as a foodstuff.

TABLE 8.3. Seasonality of nuts and seeds recovered from Late Paleoindian contexts at Dust Cave.

Taxon	Mar	Apr	May	June	July	Aug	Sept	Oct	Nov
Hickory (*Carya* sp.)							X	X	X
Black walnut (*Juglans nigra*)							X	X	X
Acorn (*Quercus* sp.)							X	X	X
Black gum (*Nyssa sylvatica*)							X	X	X
Hazelnut (*Corylus americana*)				X	X	X			
Hackberry (*Celtis occidentalis*)							X	X	
Grape (*Vitis* sp.)						X	X	X	X
Chenopod (*Chenopodium* sp.)						X	X	X	
Stargrass* (*Hypoxis hirsuta*)	X	X	X	X	X	X	X	X	
Pokeweed (*Phytolacca americana*)						X	X	X	

* Data on stargrass reflects flowering period of the plant.

Exploring Hickory Nuts

As evidenced by the data presented above, hickory nuts are an important component of the diet at Dust Cave. Because of their significance, not only during the Late Paleoindian period at Dust Cave but also throughout prehistory in the greater Southeast, it is useful to explore the implications that the use of hickory nuts holds for hunting-and-gathering lifeways. Following Heidegger's (1971) treatment of "things" as objects that engage the world around them, I examine the hickory nut and investigate the strands that extend from it to the world of "gathering." After discussing the characteristics and habits of hickory trees, I touch on their relations with the landscape and climate. I then discuss the numerous ways in which people interact with the trees and nuts, and conclude by briefly considering how forces beyond the control of people, the supernatural as well as contingencies, may be drawn into the world of the hickory.

A logical point of entry into the world of the hickory nut is the nut itself. It is highly nutritive and a good source of calories, particularly calories derived from fat (Gardner 1997; McCarthy and Matthews 1984). Its high fat content must have made it attractive to foraging peoples. Bodily stores of fat are particularly important to groups that must rely on hunting during the winter and early spring, when game is lean, until plant resources become available again in the spring (Gardner 1997). While bodily stores could have been stocked by eating one's fill of nuts during autumn, hickory nuts come neatly packaged and are stored easily in the shell. If stored, they could have provided a source of fat throughout the lean season.

Not only are hickory nuts an appealing food item, they are also relatively abundant in the Southeast, and hickory trees are highly productive. Paul Gardner (1997:163) uses data from commercial hickory groves and U.S. Department of Agriculture studies of the nutritional composition of hickory nuts to calculate that only seven trees are needed to provide enough calories to feed one person for a year, given a yield of 42 pounds of edible nutmeat per tree and a daily energy requirement of 2,200 kilocalories. As Gardner (1997:164) warns, estimates of yields derived from commercial stands are undoubtedly higher than those that would be obtained from natural stands. Nonetheless, when the distributions of hickory trees in the Late Paleoindian landscape are considered, it is apparent that nut mast harvests would have been plentiful.

Hickories were probably common in forests of the Tennessee River valley during Late Paleoindian times. By around 10,000 years ago, oak-hickory deciduous forests were well established, having replaced the spruce-pine forests that had dominated the region 2,500 years earlier (Delcourt and Delcourt 1981). Preferring moist valley soils and upland slopes (Little 1980), hickory trees are well suited to the undulating topography of northern Alabama, and likely grew in groves along and above the bluff in which Dust Cave is situated.

While hickory nuts may have littered Paleoindian forest floors during autumn, they would not have remained there long in significant quantities. A number of woodland animals, including squirrels, chipmunks, deer, and turkeys, also eat hickory nuts. If the nuts remain on the ground long enough, they will be attacked by molds. This competition would have limited the length of time during which the nuts could be harvested (Gardner 1997; Talalay et al. 1984).

Temporal aspects of the availability of hickory nuts are just as important as spatial considerations. As mentioned above, hickory nuts ripen during the fall, largely between September and November. But as we have seen, animal and microbial activity shortens that window of availability to several weeks during the year, not months. On a slightly larger temporal scale, hickory trees, as well as walnuts and oaks, only yield appreciable harvests every two to three years (Gardner 1997; Petruso and Wickens 1984; Schopmeyer 1974; Talalay et al. 1984). Simultaneously productive stands therefore may be widely spaced across the landscape (Stafford 1991). Yearly fluctuations in climate also affect harvests. A particularly hard spring negatively impacts the yield of mast-producing trees (Gardner 1997). So in addition to the properties and distribution of nut-bearing trees and the activities of animals, one must also be aware of cyclical variability in and the effect of climate on nut harvests.

People are entwined with hickory nuts through a variety of activities. Prior to the collection, processing, consumption, and disposal of nuts (and their subsequent recovery, analysis, and interpretation), people may have affected the growth of nuts through some degree of landscape management. Both historic and ethnographic evidence exists for the use of fire by hunting-and-gathering groups, for everything from chasing game to improving plant growth to creating an aesthetically pleasing landscape (Fowler 1996; Lewis 1980; Mellars 1976). A number of groups, including Native Americans of Canada and the northern plains, the northwestern United States, and California, often set fires during the spring and/or fall (Lewis 1980, 1982). In order to successfully control fires, these people called upon an intimate familiarity with wind and weather conditions, moisture content of ground cover, the response of different plants to fire, and the manner in which fire travels over particular landforms (Heinselman 1973; Lewis 1980). As fires tend to clear forests of underbrush and young saplings that cannot withstand the trauma, remaining trees have access to more space in which to spread their branches. This would have benefited gatherers, as the productivity of hickories, oaks, and walnuts increases as their crown areas increase (Hammett 1992). Groves may also have been actively thinned and pruned by people to the same effect. The removal of ground cover by fire also would have facilitated the gathering of wild food resources such as nuts, as they could be more easily seen and reached (Hammett 1992).

The collection of hickory nuts involved more than simply picking them up off the forest floor as one walked along. Minimally, gatherers must have used a container of some sort, whether a basket, bag, or large skin, to carry the nuts. Beyond this rather simple "tool kit," knowledge of the landscape and fruiting behaviors of hickories is required. One needs to know not only where hickory groves are located but also which ones are productive in a particular year and when their harvests are at their prime for collecting. These spatial and temporal demands suggest that the exploitation of nut mast requires monitoring, planning, and scheduling on the part of foragers (Stafford 1991), in addition to honing a vast array of practical and discursive knowledge of hickory ecology.

Gatherers may have employed different strategies in their collection of nuts. These may have ranged from opportunistic strategies, where any nuts that are encountered are gathered, to logistical strategies, in which only certain species are targeted (Stafford 1991). Involving when, where, and how, decisions regarding the gathering of nuts are far from simple.

Decisions as to who gathered also must have been made. Ethnographic and historic sources indicate that in hunting-and-gathering societies, women perform the majority of tasks related to the gathering and processing of plant foods (Kelly 1995). If the carbonized nutshells found at sites such as Dust Cave represent more than the remains of a snack for hungry hunters, then it is likely that women were involved in their collection. This does not preclude the involvement of men, however. Among indigenous California groups, men aided women and children in collecting ripened acorns, a key food item, before animals such as deer and squirrels could get to them (Jackson 1991). Like most hunting-and-gathering societies in temperate climates, Late Paleoindian peoples in the Southeast probably relied more heavily on predictable plant foods for their diet than less easily acquired animal resources (Walthall 1998a). As such, we might expect both women and men to participate in gathering, although perhaps to differing degrees.

Once collected, hickory nuts must be processed. Experimental studies indicate that the most efficient technique for processing hickory nuts is to pound them into small fragments, and then place them in boiling water. The nutmeats and oil float to the top and are easily skimmed off. Otherwise, the nutmeats are tightly enmeshed in their shells, making it extremely time-consuming, and not energetically worthwhile, to pick the meats from the shell (Talalay et al. 1984). The boiling method presumes that people used hot rocks and a container for water, such as a skin pouch or a pit lined with skins, prior to the availability of stone bowls and ceramic pots. Alternatively, people may have processed hickory nuts by what Gardner (1997) terms "snarfing and spitting," a method by which one extracts nutmeats simply by putting broken hickory nuts—nutmeat, shell and all—into one's mouth, eating the nutmeat, and spitting out the shell. Gardner suspects that this method may be even more efficient that the boiling technique, even though hickory nuts are processed in bulk using the latter (Gardner 1997). No matter which method was employed, at least two stones would have been required to smash open the hard shell, one to use as a hammer and the other as an anvil.

The manner in which the nuts were consumed is a topic for speculation. If the "snarfing and spitting" method was employed, then the nuts themselves presumably would have been eaten. If the nuts were extracted by boiling, however, the resulting nutmeats and oil could have been used as ingredients in larger dishes, such as stews. Regardless of the processing method, hickory nuts were probably available to and eaten by all members of the group.

Another topic of interest is whether the nuts were consumed immediately or stored for a period of time. Because they are easily stored in the shell, hickory nuts can be kept for months, especially if parched to ward off insects and mold. This requires a storage technology, whether in the form of portable baskets or bags, or decidedly stationary storage pits. One could also store the oil derived from the nuts in skin bags, but this runs the risk of the liquid turning rancid. If the nuts were not stored, Late Paleoindians may have feasted on the nuts during autumn, filling their fat stores for the coming lean months.

Once the nuts served their dietary purpose, the remaining nutshells were probably burned in fires. Due to their high oil content, the shells burn hot and give off little smoke (Lopinot 1984). The use of hickory nutshell as a fuel source would have been secondary to the nuts' importance as a food item, as the nutshells do not burn so well that one would collect hickory nuts for this purpose alone (Lopinot 1984). In this light, it is not surprising that hickory nutshell is one of the predominant plant remains recovered from southeastern sites, as burning the nutshells was likely purposeful, rather than merely accidental.

Ultimately, the activities involved in collecting and processing hickory nuts may have long-term impacts on the human body. If rough terrain, such as valley slopes, is covered to reach the groves, gatherers may be accidentally injured or may develop arthritis in joints (Smith 1996). The repeated bending or crouching to pick nuts off the forest floor may result in pathologies to the lower back and knees. Similarly, repetitious pounding of nuts may give rise to arthritis in the elbow (Smith 1996). Dental wear can also indicate the consumption of hard materials, such as fragments of shell that were impossible to separate from nutmeats (Powell and Steele 1994). Thus, human involvement with hickory nuts may even be inscribed on the body and could be investigated further through skeletal analyses.

A brief consideration of the interaction between hickories and the supernatural, although speculative, is an important exercise, as the supernatural world likely played an important role in Paleoindian peoples' lives. Historic and ethnographic hunting-and-gathering groups perceive their environment, including their prey, in terms other than the Western dichotomy of nature versus culture. Instead, the plants, animals, and landscape that surround them embody personae, metaphors, and meanings that draw the natural world into culture, rather than setting it apart from culture (Bird-David 1993; Descola 1994). It is not too farfetched to grant that Late Paleoindian peoples lived in a world in which nonhumans were endowed with agency, a world that included a supernatural or cosmological aspect.

Similar to the supernatural, in that they are beyond the direct control of people, are sets of contingencies. These contingencies are particularly relevant to the interaction between archaeologists, Paleoindian peoples, and hickory nuts. Why did a group choose to build a fire at this site in the past? What were the chances that the nutshells that they spit or threw into the fire did not burn completely to ash? How did archaeologists find this site in the present? Why and how did excavation proceed? What chain of events brought these samples to be studied and lead to this research? The contingencies behind the answers to these questions are beyond any one person's control, and yet brought innumerous people, animals, equipment, and locales into contact with hickory nuts.

This last point highlights the incomplete nature of this sketch of the world engaged by the hickory nut. I have barely hinted at the articulations of the past and the present, which range from using studies of present-day plant and animal communities to reconstruct past environments to the archaeologist troweling away the centuries encased in dirt. As well, each of the different aspects of the hickory nut's world is interconnected in innumerable ways, so that to speak of one demands reference to one, if not all, of the others (Heidegger 1971, 1977).

Gathering at Dust Cave

While this compilation of the different aspects of a hunting-and-gathering lifestyle with which hickory nuts articulate is admittedly incomplete, it does provide an avenue for understanding the significance of the botanical remains at Dust Cave. The hickory nuts recovered from the Late Paleoindian component at Dust Cave can inform us about more than the fact that they were consumed, or at least burned, by the occupants of the site.

The first topic to address is: who ate the nuts recovered at Dust Cave? The fragments of nutshell could have been procured by a hunting party, a group of men, perhaps accompanied by at least one woman, who stayed one or several nights at the cave. They may have been supplied with nuts from the stores of their group prior to setting out, or they may have gathered them as they waited for or pursued their prey, or on their way back after an unsuccessful day of hunting.

Alternatively, the nutshells could have been byproducts of a family group who used the cave while harvesting nuts from the surrounding area. The large quantities of hickory nutshell in relation to other plant materials found in the features examined, as well as in the column samples, speak to a relatively intensive use of nuts. If harvesting-and-processing activities were indeed intense, then we might expect women to have been present at the cave, and likely their children with them. This scenario is supported by the burial remains from later components at the site (Hogue 1994). The composition of such a group, as well as the range of activities performed by them, is presumably much different from and much broader than those of a hunting party. The wide variety of tasks indicated by the use-wear analysis of stone tools seems to support an argument that Dust Cave served as more than an overnight camping spot (Walker et al. 1999; Walker et al. 2001). It may have served as a residential camp for a family who timed their arrival at the site to coincide with the ripening of hickory nuts, a season also marked by the ripening of other nut species and fruits, as well as the hunting of many animals.

If one of the main activities performed by the occupants of Dust Cave was the gathering of mast harvests, we can see a whole range of decisions surrounding their use of the site. Should the groves be managed to increase productivity? Should the forest floor be set on fire to remove underbrush so that the nuts can be more easily seen? Which groves are productive this year, and when will the peak of harvest fall? Who should be sent out to collect the nuts; that is, is the harvest period significantly limited so that the labor of the entire group—men, women, and children—is required? Should all nuts be collected, or should gathering efforts focus on hickory nuts? Should the nuts be processed and eaten immediately or stored for future use? Who should process the nuts, and which method should they employ? How should the shells be discarded?

Most of these questions cannot be answered using the archaeological record alone. For example, management efforts are difficult to detect, and even more so the gender of those involved in any of the activities. But some of these decisions do have material correlates. Certainly the choice of tools used to collect and process nuts can be recognized. Baskets or skin bags must have been used to transport as well as possibly store the nuts, as no storage pits have been found at Dust Cave. While baskets and bags have not been preserved at the site, impressions of textiles on pieces of clay recovered from the Archaic levels at Dust Cave hint at some of the items that could have been used for collection and storage (Detwiler field notes 1999, 2000). Items used for processing may include large pieces of limestone with decidedly concave surfaces, which are also associated with the Archaic periods and have been interpreted as nutting stones (Detwiler field notes 1999, 2000). In addition, three pestles have been found within the Middle Archaic deposits (Scott C. Meeks, personal communication 2000). The lack of such artifacts in the Late Paleoindian component may be explained by lower intensity of occupation and concomitant lower artifact density during this period. Alternatively, the Archaic period tools may reflect an increased focus on mast resources during later periods, requiring more specialized tools that may have been left at the site for seasonal use. Or we may simply be unable to recognize tools used for nut processing in the Late Paleoindian period.

The strategy of nut collection may also be reflected in the archaeological record. Stafford (1991) argues that if an opportunistic strategy is employed, the botanical assemblage will contain a relatively diverse array of nut species. If the assemblage is largely limited to a single species, a logistical strategy may be inferred. Using Stafford's (1991) criteria, one might suggest that hickory nuts were the targets of focal harvesting activities, as so few nutshells from other taxa were recovered. However, the dominance of hickory nuts in the samples may reflect their properties relative to those of other nuts rather than peoples' preference. Compared to acorns, hickory nuts have a high preservation potential: their dense shells survive fires much more readily than the thin shells of acorns (Lopinot 1984). While walnuts are solitary trees, hickories grow in groves. Hickory nuts are simply available for collection in larger concentrations in a given area than walnuts. These complicating factors must be kept in mind when evaluating the relative quantities of different nut taxa.

The most elusive question is that regarding the spiritual, supernatural, and/or cosmological interactions between the occupants of the cave and their surrounding environment. Rather than speculate further about these relations, suffice it to say that Late Paleoindian peoples possessed an intimate knowledge of the landscape in which they lived, as well as the habits and interactions of the plants, animals, and climate in that region.

In sum, the botanical remains from Dust Cave inform us not only about subsistence and the seasonal occupation of the site but also about the strategies and practices underlying the cave's use. Late Paleoindian peoples, perhaps in family groups, appear to have occupied Dust Cave during autumn, not only to exploit animals that feed on mast, such as deer, turkeys, and a variety of small and medium-size mammals, but also to harvest mast resources themselves. The abundance of hickory nutshell recovered suggests that the collection of this resource, which to some extent is spatially and temporally limited, may have been a significant undertaking of the cave's inhabitants. Thus, nut mast exploitation may well have been an impetus for Dust Cave's autumn occupation.

Toward Gathering in the Southeast

By exploring the world with which the hickory nut articulates and engages, we gain a broader understanding of the decisions and activities involved in a gathering lifestyle such as that pursued by the Late Paleoindians living at Dust Cave. The hunter-gatherer tool kit contained more than baskets, nutting stones, and chipped stone tools: a mental map of the landscape, a knowledge of the behaviors and responses of plants and animals, and an understanding of climatic effects were also necessary. The decision to gather plant foods was deliberate, not an afterthought of unsuccessful hunters. Scheduling of gathering activities surely played at least as large a role in mobility decisions as did those connected with hunting and quarrying. This much we have gleaned by focusing on a single taxon of the assemblage, and much more could be gained by considering each nut, fruit, and seed in turn.

These aspects of gathering need to be incorporated into regional models of Late Paleoindian lifeways. Revised models would emphasize the role of plants in the diet and in mobility decisions, recognizing the fact that the oft-hypothesized seasonal rounds are responses, by both people and animals, to plant availability. They would bring women's influences on the movement of the group to the foreground. Bands may have been tethered to groves as well as quarries. Groups may have aggregated not only to exchange mates or raw materials and share information about the availability of deer, but also to discuss the location of productive tree stands.

Far too often gathering is simply assumed—certainly people ate nuts and berries. But by relegating gathering to a "given," the tasks, tools, and knowledge wielded by gatherers (likely women) are overlooked. The gathering component of the hunting-and-gathering equation needs to be more thoroughly explored, lest we neglect the activities of half of the population and gloss over a significant portion of the subsistence base and the social and technical networks developed for its appropriation.

Acknowledgments

I would like to thank Renee Walker for inviting me to participate in this volume on Paleoindian subsistence, as well as for her comments on this and previous versions of this chapter. I especially thank Boyce Driskell for giving me the opportunity to return time and again to Dust Cave and analyze the plant remains, and for his consistent support. Many thanks are also due my other colleagues at the site—Asa Randall, Scott Meeks, Sarah Sherwood, Lara Homsey, and Nick Richardson—for their assistance and insight. Special thanks also to the field school students and volunteers, especially the Copelands, for all of their hard work. I am very grateful to Margaret Scarry, Peter Whitridge, Mintcy Maxham, Amber VanDerwarker, and Greg Wilson for their very helpful comments on many versions of this chapter. I acknowledge the National Science Foundation for its financial support during the writing of this chapter.

NINE

Revising the Paleoindian Environmental Picture in Northeastern North America

Lucinda McWeeney

Reevaluation of our modern mind-set is critical to understanding some of the archaeological biases toward how we once viewed the early people in North America and their environmental setting. Recent paleoecological studies, oxygen and carbon isotope analyses, and temperature extrapolations from the Greenland ice core annular layers have helped to refine our views on global climate change and its expression in eastern North America. Calibration of radiocarbon dates (Stuiver and Reimer 1993) and refinement of dating methods using Accelerator Mass Spectrometry (AMS) (Gove 1994) and Optimal Scintillation Luminescence (OSL) have enhanced our ability to distinguish cultural stratification in deeply buried sites (Goodyear 2000; McAvoy et al. 2000).

This chapter presents some of the methods employed to examine post-glacial vegetation changes, followed by the results correlated with human settlements from Maine to Virginia. Often the *in situ* Paleoindian imprint on the late Pleistocene landscape appears ephemeral. However, the incorporation of advanced paleobotanical techniques for identifying plant macrofossils, pollen, phytoliths, and diatoms increases our ability to view the prehistoric environment. The results provide a greater understanding of rates of plant migration, presence on the landscape, and plant selection by people. Understanding the fluctuations in plant regimes during major climatic reversals is a critical factor to include in our evaluation of Paleoindian settlement patterns and lifeways.

As temperatures changed between 11,200 and 10,000 BP—colder, warmer, colder—the vegetation and animals available would have influenced Paleoindian migration routes. By discussing the results of recent charcoal and seed analyses from archaeological sites in the Northeast, along with pollen and macrofossil identifications from sediment cores recovered from lakes and swamps located close to the cultural sites, a better picture will be provided regarding how climate and environmental change impacted the late Pleistocene settlers.

In the last few decades, our views have changed about the first humans entering New England by crossing tundra environments (see McWeeney 1996b) following the megafauna such as mammoths, mastodons, and bison. For a long time, an absence of preserved plant remains (more a function of excavation techniques) found in Paleoindian context led archaeologists to hypothesize a lifestyle based on hunting, with gathering taking second place. Clearly, we need to remind ourselves that our ancestors were gathering plants and scavenging meat from the beginning. Evolution to modern *Homo sapiens sapiens* included peoples' ability to manufacture a variety of tools, including implements for hide working, sewing, spinning, and weaving (Adovasio et al. 1998; Soffer et al. 1998; Soffer et al. 2000); thus, activities probably were not all big-game hunting during the Upper Paleolithic. For example, the use of plants and birds is depicted in European cave paintings and on carved bone, ivory, and horn (Fiedel, this volume; Leroi-Gourhan 1981). Archaeological evidence records a diverse use of plants (Tyldesley and Bahn 1983) and demonstrates that plants played a role in early human lifeways.

It is important to credit these Upper Paleolithic economic and technological strengths to those who settled North America (Hall 2000; Heite 1998; Jodry 1999a). Adaptation to new environments was not an impediment to survival in the New World. People knew their plants and animals and clearly knew how to test new food resources for safe eating; thus, it would not take them long to acclimate to a new environment. However, dealing with the late Pleistocene, postglacial fluctuating climate and seasonal extremes when humans entered North America must have proved challenging as people traveled across the continent.

Current methods of investigation along with the results from macro- and microfossil plant analyses for several northeastern and mid-Atlantic Paleoindian period sites will be presented in this chapter, along with reference to palynological studies that enhance the body of knowledge gained from the selected archaeological sites. The locations include the Neal Garrison site near York, Maine; Bull Brook in Ipswich, Massachusetts; the Israel River Complex in northern New Hampshire; Pequot Cedar Swamp near Ledyard, Connecticut; Templeton on the Shepaug River in Washington,

Connecticut; Sheridan Cave in north-central Ohio; and Cactus Hill in southeastern Virginia. Each site required more than one paleobotanical approach to determine the prehistoric vegetation (see map on page xv).

Methods

Archaeologists have long relied upon palynological studies for environmental reconstruction. Today, several additional archaeobotanical techniques include working with residue analyses from stone tools, ceramics, and structural components, along with processing archaeological and wetland sediment for phytoliths, starches, and diatoms (McWeeney 1994; Pearsall 2000; Piperno 1988). Even more details can be obtained through analysis of preserved human and other animal coprolites, which can provide specific information as to past diets and seasonality (Cummings 1990; Reinhard and Bryant 1992; Schoenwetter 1998).

The introduction of water and/or chemical flotation treatments for archaeological sediments opened a vast store of information to archaeologists (Pearsall 2000; Struever 1968; Watson 1976). Flotation allows the light fraction of organics such as charcoal, seeds, small bone, hair (see Bonnichsen et al. 1999), and fish scales to rise to the surface of the water and to be recovered in fine mesh for drying and sorting (Pearsall 2000) prior to analysis by experts. Microscopic identification of the organic remains now flourishes in the archaeological sciences.

Currently, researchers have proclaimed that there was potential for Paleoindians to exploit abundant wetland resources in New England (McWeeney 1994; Nicholas 1996). In fact, Nicholas (1996) went as far as to measure the distance between Paleoindian sites and associated wetlands in northwestern Connecticut. He (Nicholas 1988, 1996) noted the ideal setting of Paleoindian loci between wetlands and the uplands, where they could exploit diverse environmental zones (McWeeney 1994, 1997a). My analysis of plant macrofossils from archaeological sites and proximally located wetlands produced significant documentation for the actual availability of specific wetland and terrestrial plants for people living in northeastern North America more than 10,000 years ago (McWeeney 1994, 1997a, 1997b). Perry's (Perry and McBride n.d.) use of the scanning electron microscope to document charred aquatic resources by people living around Pequot Cedar Swamp expands our knowledge and confirms what we should have known all along, that the use of aquatic plants by Paleoindians was well incorporated into their lifeways since Paleolithic times.

Absolute Dating

With the introduction of radiocarbon dating, the bulk of recovered charred and uncharred organic remains were converted to carbon atoms for dates. However, in the past several decades new attitudes and innovative methods (Taylor et al. 1992) such as AMS dating, which requires only 25 milligrams per sample, have increased our ability to establish site chronology (Gove 1992). Better dates along with improved recovery techniques for botanical remains make it possible to revise our prior interpretations of the Paleoindian environment. A recently introduced dating method for quartz and feldspar grains using OSL has further spurred our ability to provide absolute dates useful in bracketing cultural living floors at archaeological sites.

Phytoliths

The use of phytolith analysis in archaeology has taken significant strides in the past decades (Pearsall 2000; Piperno 1988). Used in relation to late Pleistocene environments and human settlement of the New World, it adds even greater significance to the value of these micron-size silica casts of plant cells. In order to determine stratigraphic integrity for the pre-Clovis component at the Cactus Hill "dune" site, I employed a method first used in Great Britain (Powers-Jones et al. 1989), where the quantification of phytoliths, based on weight, increased evidence on when humans occupied the site. In addition, Powers-Jones and her research team (1989:27) discovered through their Outer Hebrides Islands research that "there is no effective differentiation between areas of dune which supports non-ruminant grazed vegetation and areas of woodland, shrub, or herb cover, or even between unvegetated, mobile sand, and the 'natural' vegetated deposits, despite the abundance of phytoliths in the superjacent vegetation and an apparent lack of erosion or disturbance of the accumulating vegetated sediment surfaces."

Based on this evidence, the Nottoway River Survey (NRS) team selected a 0.25-meter sediment column unit to be excavated in 2.5-centimeter increments from the area along the ridgeline at Cactus Hill. The sediments were processed following methods established by Mulholland (1989) and Zhao and Pearsall (1998). The working hypothesis was that the phytoliths would increase in levels occupied by humans compared to the noncultural strata. Phosphate analyses coupled with the phytoliths contributed a second human indicator to the equation. Thus, parallel fluctuations in quantity of phytoliths and phosphates would suggest varying periods of human occupation.

In the absence of obvious organic remains, new avenues for obtaining an absolute chronology exist by dating the trapped carbon found in phytoliths (Mulholland 1989; Wilding 1967). Special processing is required to eliminate extraneous surface carbon. Depending on the environmental setting and preservation conditions, it is estimated that approximately one kilo of sediment has the potential to provide enough phytoliths with carbon for an AMS date. The availability of phytoliths and the quantity of sediment needed for a date will vary. However, for sites that do not have preserved charcoal or bone, the potential for dating phytoliths is worth exploring.

Diatoms

Diatoms, single-celled algae with silica exoskeletons, play a significant role in sourcing clays used in ceramics and interpreting changing sea level, paleolimnological changes, and site taphonomy. Used in conjunction with wetland sediment cores, determining fluctuations in water levels adjacent to archaeological sites is also possible (McWeeney 1997a). Examination of the diatoms from Pequot Cedar Swamp showed that fragments of species associated with muddy or slimy conditions were present at an apparent break in the sedimentary record. This oxidation and mechanical breakdown of the organisms confirmed a sediment hiatus between 11,200 and 10,100 BP.

Pollen

Archaeologists have long relied on pollen interpretations to re-create the environmental scene for the first settlers in the New World. However, wind-blown pollen that ends up in the rigidly selected coring site is biased against plants pollinated by other means and oxidative phases in the environmental record. Variation in preservation factors, sampling in broad time scales, or modeling based on a few selected dominant taxa often resulted in gaps that archaeologists would like to see filled for their particular area. Extrapolating from one pollen diagram from a state or region to formulate interpretations for an archaeological site located several kilometers away will not inform us as to what environmental variables may have attracted people to select a particular site for living. Good science requires us to stay up to date with the literature in several ecological fields if we are to accurately interpret the prehistoric environment. For instance, it has taken archaeologists a long time to recognize what a few palynologists admitted in 1979 (Amundson and Wright 1979), that during the late Pleistocene years, from Maine to Minnesota, deciduous trees were growing on the landscape.

With this knowledge, we can re-create the picture of what the first settlers witnessed when they migrated into the Northeast.

Starches

A breakthrough in the hunter versus gatherer emphasis occurred at the 1999 meeting of the Society for American Archaeology. As a graduate student, Melissa Darby amazed the media and Paleoindian specialists by passing around prepared slices of wapato (Darby 1999), the aquatic plant tubers from *Saggitaria latifolia*. Her presentation of ethnographic and nutritional evidence for the use of wapato strongly supported her hypothesis that the early Americans most likely collected tubers from ponds and swamps during the fall and winter. However, she lacked the preserved tuberous parenchyma, starch grains, or other plant parts from a Paleoindian context to prove the use of wapato 11,000 years ago. But a lack of preservation does not indicate that Paleoindians neglected available wetland resources. Humans had full knowledge of valuable plant resources in their environment before they arrived here. As Dincauze (2000:43) acknowledged, "Paleoindian exploration of the region was comparable to a moon walk, or settling island in the Pacific, relying entirely on one's own ingenuity." Starch analyses are employed internationally by archaeologists to discover further evidence of prehistoric diet and origins of agriculture in tropical environments where other organic remains have deteriorated beyond recovery (Pearsall 2000).

Ice Cores and Isotopes

Recently published documentation for global and regional paleoclimatic data obtained from the Greenland Ice Core Project (GISP) demonstrate the widespread impact of the Younger Dryas cooling oscillation. Between 11,000 and 10,000 BP, evidence from the Greenland ice cores has alerted us to the abrupt climate changes that occurred during the late Pleistocene and early Holocene (Taylor et al. 1993). Oxygen isotope analyses parallel these results, reinforcing the authenticity of temperature fluctuations during our period of focus. A study in southern Ontario (Yu and Eicher 1998) demonstrates in one example, using multiple lines of evidence, the extent to which the cooling during the Younger Dryas spread beyond the region of impetus in the North Atlantic Ocean. The ratio of Oxygen 18 to Oxygen 16 represents a proxy for changing temperature: a decrease in the ratio reflects a decrease in temperature. The isotope analysis (Yu and Eicher 1998) indicates a warming trend around 12,500 BP, a period known as the Bølling/

Allerød period in Europe. Significantly, the warming climate between approximately 12,300 to 11,200 BP established temperate climatic conditions in postglacial New England. However, the Killarney Oscillation, a cold thrust at 11,200 BP, first recognized in Nova Scotia (Levesque et al. 1993), refocuses our attention on how swiftly the climate can change. In addition, a major drop in temperature occurred by 10,920 BP, followed by a slight rise during the middle of the millennium. However, the climate remained much colder than recorded prior to 11,200 BP, and the colder temperatures lasted until there was a dramatic rise in temperature around 10,000 BP, signifying the beginning of the Holocene.

Sites and Associated Wetlands

Neal Garrison Site

Discovered on a pipeline survey (Kellogg and Simons 2000), the Neal Garrison site is located in southwestern Maine in the modern conifer-hardwood forest region (Braun 1950). Artifacts reflecting a Paleoindian occupation include stone tools made from Munsungun Lake cherts (Spiess et al. 1998), including a channel flake, a graver, and side scrapers, many of which came from Feature 2. Excavating the feature in discrete levels for flotation purposes made it possible to recover charcoal and seeds. A control column from a unit devoid of artifacts was excavated for comparison purposes.

Charcoal analyses produced oak and conifer charcoal, along with abundant uncharred modern seeds and fungi. Radiometric dating by AMS produced a date of ca. 9,000 BP, at a minimum, 1,000 years too young for what is regarded to be appropriate for Paleoindian sites. The ligninized conifer charcoal may include spruce and pine; however, the deteriorated condition of the charcoal made that difficult to ascertain.

Based on pollen data, spruce trees reached Maine between 13,000 and 12,000 BP (Davis and Jacobson 1985) and had spread into northern New Hampshire by 11,000 BP (Spear et al. 1994) and Debert in Nova Scotia by 10,600 BP (McDonald 1968). The possibility of pine is a different matter. Red, jack, and white pine grow in Maine today, but red and jack pine were probably the first pines to grow in northern New England following the glacier. Based on the pollen, white pine probably arrived in coastal Maine around 10,000 years ago (Davis and Jacobson 1985). According to Gaudreau and Webb (1985), the 5 percent isopol indicates the local presence of oak trees, suggesting oak, probably northern red oak, arrived in coastal Maine as early as 11,400 years ago (Davis and Jacobson 1985:353–361), just before the Killarney Oscillation (Levesque et al. 1993) and possibly before the entrance of the first humans.

Unfortunately, the restricted area of excavation within the pipeline corridor inhibited further sampling of additional areas of Paleoindian habitation. If future impact threatened the location, then additional charred botanical remains could become available for dating and verification of a late Pleistocene occupation.

Jefferson Site

A series of paleobotanical techniques are being employed for the plant remains recovered in Jefferson, New Hampshire, for the Israel River Paleoindian Complex. Surveys and site excavations directed by Richard Boisvert (1999, 2001), New Hampshire's deputy state archaeologist, indicate that the Paleoindian components are uninterrupted by younger occupations. That is a rare occurrence in New England. In addition, spectacular-looking stone tools made from Munsungun-like chert and banded rhyolites define the cultures inhabiting the northern terraces above the east-west-trending Israel River. A complete fluted point was recovered from the Jefferson IV site.

In 1998, a program of column sampling was undertaken at each locus, removing 25-by-25-centimeter units in 2.5-centimeter increments for flotation. Spruce and Canadian hemlock (*Taxus canadensis*) charcoal have been identified from two of the loci; however, the AMS dates places their presence around 8,000 radiocarbon years ago, suggesting a fire of natural origin. As a major contributor to the archaeobotanical assemblage, a charred water lily seed (*Nymphaea odorata*) found in a feature from one locus strongly suggests that the inhabitants were collecting this wetland plant for processing back at the campsite, away from the water. Ethnographic studies indicate roasted water lily seeds could be consumed, and the floral disk and seeds could be ground to make flour for roasting patties in the smoldering coals (McWeeney 2001). The water lily plant may be used medicinally, and small amounts of the tubers may be digested without suffering toxic repercussions.

Sediment cores recovered from Cherry Pond, Martin Meadow Pond, and York Pond are being analyzed to gain a greater understanding of the postglacial environment in the Israel River drainage. High-resolution sampling techniques at one-centimeter increments already provide macrofossils, pollen, and phytolith evidence from these cores. Evidence of insect exoskeltons proliferated in the varved sediments that were deposited as the glacier remained close to the ice and till dammed Lake Israel. Soon after the glacier pulled back, the lake drained, leaving Cherry Pond as the only extant open-water basin, while the Israel River flowed east to west in the valley. Small fragments of spruce and ericaceous berry plants (*Vaccinium* sp.) appeared on the land shortly after the glacier withdrew. Water milfoil (*Myriophyllum* sp.) dominated the aquatic plant remains in the basal organic level and was soon joined by pondweed (*Potamogeton* sp.). The insects and both aquatic plants are well known as food for waterfowl. The insects may have initially attracted the birds to the pond, and the waterfowl would deposit seeds either from their gullet or from trapped seeds dropping off their feathers and feet. The pondweeds also would have attracted ungulates to the site, and as they lowered their heads to grab at the submerged plants they may have easily been captured by humans. Even without faunal remains, the plants provide irrefutable evidence for migrating birds arriving at Cherry Pond more than 11,000 BP (13,000 cal BP). The presence of ice would not have impeded the migration of birds to the north country since many modern species travel to the Arctic today (Elfhick 1995). The arrival of plant and animal life to the postglacial lake provided abundant biodiversity for human exploitation.

The relationship between plants and birds opens a whole new venue for peopling the Northeast (Dincauze 2000) and awakens the possibility of connections between the Israel River Paleoindian Complex with the Bull Brook sites in coastal Massachusetts. The location of Bull Brook close to the coast 11,000 radiocarbon years ago, and just south of the mouth of the Merrimac River, needs further examination. The area known as Plum Island, a famous location for migrating fowl to stop and breed today, is also very close to Bull Brook. It's reasonable to presume there may be a link between settlement at Bull Brook and hunting/gathering birds in prehistory. The Merrimac Valley flyway would have presented a northward route between the mountains and the shore, drawing people inland and northward through the valleys seeking cryptocrystalline lithics and food.

Bull Brook Sites

Located in northeastern Massachusetts, the Bull Brook sites in Ipswich remain the best-known Paleoindian sites in New England. Absolute dating of the charcoal recovered from the salvage excavations during the sand-mining process produced dates ca. 9,000 BP, similar to the radiometric dates from the Neal Garrison site in Maine and the Nevers site in New Hampshire (Grimes et al. 1982). More recently dated white pine charcoal found in the archived site collections at the Salem Peabody Museum also returned a ca. 9000 BP date (Curran, personal communication 1999). Because of the lack of charred remains to identify, other means were necessary to obtain a paleoenvironmental record. Sediment coring was determined to be the best approach for recovering late Pleistocene plant remains close to the Bull Brook sites. Byron Stone of the U.S. Geological Survey (USGS), who mapped the surficial geology of the Ipswich quadrangle for the USGS, recommended that a core be taken from a north-draining river. In that scenario, the river would have swamped its headwaters during postglacial uplift. Therefore, the headwater of Bull Brook, in Willowdale State Forest, was selected to recover late Pleistocene plant remains (McWeeney 1994).

Located in the modern conifer hardwood forest region (Braun 1950), Willowdale Swamp is part of the Massachusetts state forest system, presenting an ideal setting to look for the preservation of late Pleistocene plant remains. Preservation of the macrofossil record began approximately 11,800 years ago (McWeeney 1994). At that time, the coast was several kilometers to the east. Curran (1994) describes the Bull Brook I site as a central base camp from which local inhabitants dispersed for collecting food and other resources (McWeeney 1994:108). Based on the more than 200 fluted points discovered during the sand-mining operations, the Bull Brook site is considered to be the largest Paleoindian site in New England to date.

Identification of aquatic plants that grew in the headwaters of Bull Brook over 11,000 years ago indicate the basin was initially populated by waterfowl bringing and discharging remnants of previous meals into the recently deglaciated area. The proximity of Bull Brook to Plum Island and the mouth of the Merrimack River suggests that wildfowl migrations along the Atlantic flyway may have played a role in human settlement selection and repeated visits to Bull Brook.

Pollen cores from Black Pond, southwest of Bull Brook (Sneddon and Kaplan 1987), and from Bull Brook indicate the presence of oak, hornbeam, and small amounts of ash, elm, and hazelnut, along with representatives of the walnut family mixed with the spruce, fir, and larch. The conifer presence is reinforced by the presence of needles. Abundant grasses and sedges project an image of meadows, wetlands, and open woodlands where the early settlers chose to set up camp. Herbaceous plants such as cattail, mint, and horehound, which do not grow in the modern boreal forest, grew at Bull Brook close to 12,000 BP, indicating a warmer climatic regime than the tundra or open spruce forest originally interpreted from previous data. Burned spruce needles from the Willowdale core suggest that a natural fire may have opened the site up to colonization by new species. If the fire was widespread, it may have created massive edge effects, encouraging the grazing of animals and attracting humans to the site. A drop in water level during the Younger Dryas at Bull Brook, similar to that at Pequot between 11,200 and 10,000 BP, is inferred based on a decline in the preservation of pollen and macrofossils (McWeeney 1994). Cold and deteriorating environmental conditions appear to have been widespread in southern New England.

Pequot Cedar Swamp

In the mid-1980s, the Mashantucket Pequot Tribal Nation and Kevin McBride initiated an extensive environmental reconstruction project in the Great Swamp as part of their archaeological survey of the oldest Native American reservation in the United States. At the site known as the Pequot Cedar Swamp, several sediment cores were recovered from the north, south, and east sides of the basin, which enabled us to interpret the last 15,000 years of vegetation changes (McWeeney 1994). Archaeological surveys around the swamp produced evidence of numerous sites, beginning with a Late Paleoindian site (Jones 2000) and spanning Early Archaic pit houses (Forrest 2000), numerous Middle Archaic occupations, and Late Archaic through contact period sites, all of which provided charred plant remains to complement the anaerobically preserved vegetation. Another Late Paleoindian site, the Hidden Creek site, is located in a hollow just below the ridge, above the southeast side of the basin (Jones 2000). Analysis of the charred remains from the survey excavations clearly demonstrates the prehistoric cultural use of wetland plants.

The plant macrofossil investigations at Pequot Cedar Swamp followed earlier geological and palynological research (Thorson and Webb 1991; Webb 1992). The initial pollen analysis encountered several difficulties due to lack of recognition of some taxa as well as large sampling intervals. By identifying the plant macrofossils, it was possible to expand our knowledge of what was growing locally in and around the basin. Because macrofossils do not travel far from their source, they provide a significant documentation of plants that may not be represented by the pollen.

The results from Pequot Cedar Swamp cores (McWeeney 1994) demonstrate that this part of Connecticut was vegetated with tundra or arctic/alpine-type plants by 15,210 BP (18,000 cal BP), establishing a minimum time for deglaciation in southeastern Connecticut. Similar tundra plant assemblages from several other sites in Connecticut dating between 14,100 and 13,540 BP (16,930 and 16,220 cal BP) have been identified (McWeeney 1991; Miller 1994; Stone and Ashley 1992).

Following the Bøllling/Allerød period, vegetation growing in and around the basin began to be preserved under anaerobic and alkaline conditions. Pondweeds, algae, and cattail seeds were preserved. Cattail is well recognized as providing multiple resources for humans besides the food value obtained from the tubers harvested in the spring. The stalks and leaves were woven into mats for ground cover and wall insulation of the wigwams, and the seed heads were used for insulation in clothing. *Vaccinium* berry–producing plants such a bilberry grew near the basin, as did sedges and ferns, presenting more available food and medicinal resources. Water lily seeds were AMS dated to 10,050 BP and 8890 BP, indicating the presence of an open-water pond fringed by a marsh with sedges and cattails at the end of the Younger Dryas cold period. The pollen from Pequot Swamp indicates the local presence of hazelnut shrubs during the eleventh millennium BP. Jones (2000) reported an AMS date of 10,260±70 on the hazelnut shell from the Hidden Creek Late Paleoindian site. In addition, charred hazelnut shells proliferated at the Sandy Hill site (Forrest 2000), located several meters from the east side of the swamp, suggesting that hazelnut played an important role in the local prehistoric diet. Charred remains of aquatic plants such as cattail, bulrush, and arrowhead found at both the Hidden Creek and Sandy Hill sites between 10,200 and 8,500 BP provide hard proof for the prehistoric exploitation of wetland plants (Perry n.d.). The charred remains of oak and pine from fuel wood indicate their selection from the available terrestrial vegetation.

Based on the macrofossil remains recovered at the south end of Pequot Swamp, the tundra plants rapidly disappeared and trees sprang up on the landscape by 12,030 radiocarbon years BP. Most significant, white pine (*Pinus strobus*) needles were preserved along with the first spruce (*Picea* sp.), larch (*Larix laricina*), and fir (*Abies balsamea*) needles (McWeeney 1994, 1997a). The presence of white pine needles indicates warming temperatures, documenting the local landscape changes during the Bøllling/Allerød period. The temperature restrictions for the survival of white pine furthermore supports the actual presence of temperate deciduous trees whose pollen had been reported for the late-glacial period pollen diagrams across northeastern North America (Gaudreau and Webb 1985).

Willimantic Kettle

Sediments from a postglacial kettle hole in Willimantic, Connecticut (Thorson, personal communication 1990), received dates that fall before the Younger Dryas at 11,470 BP (13,454 cal BP) and close to the end of the interval at 10,440 BP (12,350 cal BP). The plant macrofossils demonstrate a much richer biodiversity prior to the Younger Dryas, with spruce, willow, and brambles (raspberries) growing on the land; marsh species such as cattail and sedges fringed an open-water pond supporting aquatic pondweeds and water lilies. However, based on the macrofossils, during the Younger Dryas there was a loss of boreal trees and emergence of a leather leaf bog filled with grasses and sedges. This type of landscape alteration clearly impacted the potential vegetation available for human inhabitants and the prey they hunted.

Templeton Paleoindian Site

Currently, the oldest radiocarbon date for a Late Paleoindian site in Connecticut comes from the Templeton site (6LF21). Located along the Shepaug River and Mallory Brook, the site contained diagnostic artifacts such as fluted points, gravers, and scrapers, along with charcoal radiocarbon dated to 10,200 years ago (10,190±300 W-3931, published by Moeller [1980] and an AMS date of 10,215±90 AA-7160 from McWeeney [1994]). Moeller's (1980) publication detailed the initial excavation of the site along with the significant discovery and subsequent identification of charcoal from the red oak subgenus (*Quercus* sp. in the Erythrobolanus) and possibly juniper or cedar from the cedar family (Cupressaceae) (identification by Bruce Hoadley [1990]). In the late 1980s, Templeton was the only Paleoindian site in New England to have charred remains available for analyses. Excavation of 1/8th of each unit in three-centimeter increments for flotation (Moeller 1980, 1984) made this remarkable recovery possible. Botanical, faunal, and lithic materials contributed to the Paleoindian assemblage. The debitage and plant remains recovered at Templeton made it possible to determine living floors and to have charcoal for identification purposes (McWeeney 1994; Moeller 1980, 1984). Combining the plant macrofossil assemblage and pollen reports, paleoenvironmental reconstructions can be inferred with some accuracy (McWeeney 2002).

As detailed previously, climatic warming around 12,000 BP made it possible for deciduous trees such as oak, hornbeam (*Ostrya/Carpinus*), elm (*Ulmus* sp.), maple (*Acer* sp.), and ash (*Fraxinus* sp.) to grow during the late Pleistocene in southern New England. The pollen has been documented in sediment cores as far west as Minnesota (Amundson and Wright 1979; Gaudreau 1988). In southern New England, the deciduous tree pollen, except for birch (*Betula papyrifera*), disappears from the sediments between approximately 11,000 and 10,000 radiocarbon years ago, corresponding to the Younger Dryas cold interval (Gaudreau 1988; Peteet et al. 1993). This disappearance may be due to a loss of those trees or, at the very least, an inability to pollinate due to the colder temperatures. In the absence of deciduous trees, an increase in grass pollen marks the eleventh millennium BP, suggesting open meadows probably proliferated across the landscape along with spruce (*Picea* sp.) and larch (*Larix laricina*) growing around the wetlands.

In order to further document the reentrance of deciduous trees into Connecticut, permission was gained from the American Indian Archaeological Institute to identify the 1980 charcoal assemblage from 6LF21, renamed the Templeton site. New taxa identified from the Paleoindian strata include white pine (*Pinus strobus*), a component of the northern conifer forest (Burns and Honkala 1990), aspen (*Populus tremuloides*), and oak from the white oak subgenus (*Leucobalanus*). Today, white pine has a broad growth range, extending from southern Canada south through the Appalachian Mountains into northern Georgia. According to the Roger's Lake, Connecticut, pollen record frequently cited by regional archaeologists, white pine pollen dominated in coastal southern New England during Zone B between 8100 and 7900 BP (Davis 1969:418). However, at Mohawk Pond in northwestern Connecticut, Belmont Pond in New York, and Duck Pond in Massachusetts, pine pollen peaked around 10,000 years ago (see synopsis in Gaudreau 1988). Moreover, as mentioned earlier, white pine needles recovered at Pequot Cedar Swamp and Durham Meadows demonstrate pine grew locally in Connecticut as early as 12,000 years ago (McWeeney 1994). Previously, it was believed that jack pine (*Pinus banksiana*) was the primary source for the late Pleistocene pine pollen.

The charcoal identified from the Paleoindian component at the Templeton site—white and red oaks, aspen, the Cupressaceae, (possibly eastern red cedar), and white pine—suggests a transitional forest between the boreal and central hardwood forest, similar to what grows there today. By extrapolation from silviculture studies (Burns and Honkala 1990; Eyre 1980), other plant community associates could have included hazelnut shrubs (*Corylus cornuta*, *C. americana*), mountain maple (*Acer spicatum*), alder (*Alnus rugosa*), willow (*Salix* sp.), brambles/blackberries (*Rubus* sp.), and gooseberries (*Ribes* sp.).

White pine is often called "old-field pine" due to its propensity to settle in abandoned pastures. Therefore, it may represent the early stages of succession along the Shepaug River following the Younger Dryas. The combination of white pine, the Cupressaceae charcoal, and the aspen suggests an open meadow in the process of being colonized by several pioneering species over 10,000 years ago. In this hypothesized reconstruction, when the climate ameliorated, one would expect white pine, eastern red cedar, aspen, and birch to enter the gaps in the forests. These species can survive on dry, nutrient-poor substrates, while many other taxa cannot. The abundant pine and birch pollen, along with oak, white pine, and aspen charcoal, distributed across southern New England suggests that a rapid infilling of clearings occurred.

Wildfires during the millennium-long cold/dry interval contributed to the environmental deterioration generated by a thousand years of cold temperature extremes postulated for the Younger Dryas (Peteet et al. 1993). An increase in fire frequency is recorded by the charcoal found in the regional pollen cores (McWeeney 1996a) during the warm/dry climate caused by the peak in solar insolation following the Younger Dryas (Kutzbach and Guetter 1986). Birch and aspen trees are well recognized as pioneering species that colonize land soon after a fire (Cwynar 1978; Heinselman 1973). This propensity may account for the flood of birch pollen during the tenth millennium BP. The decrease in pine, birch, and aspen during the following millennium would naturally follow as deciduous trees such as elm (*Ulmus* sp.), maple (*Acer* sp.), sycamore (*Platanus occidentalis*), and hickory (*Carya* sp.) joined the community and eventually overshadowed the shade-intolerant pine, birch, and aspen. This is exactly what was seen in the Templeton charcoal record.

The oak charcoal from the Paleoindian strata provides strong evidence that deciduous trees, along with cedar, aspen, white pine, and Canadian hemlock, existed close to the Templeton site, creating a biome where open areas met the woodland, forming an edge effect. Along that edge of woodlands and meadows, hazelnut shrubs could have grown locally, suggested by the late Pleistocene regional pollen. Wild cherry (*Prunus serotina*) would fit easily into that community, as would hawthorn (*Crataegus* sp.) and raspberries (*Rubus* sp.). These taxa are insect pollinated and rarely appear in pollen reports. Clearly, the Templeton site held as much potential for a diverse fuel and food supply as that preserved over 10,000 to 11,000 radiocarbon years ago at Shawnee Minisink along the Delaware River in Pennsylvania (Dent, this volume; McNett ed. 1985:67, table 5.2) and Dust Cave, Alabama (Detwiler 2000; Hollenbach, this volume), where species such as charred hawthorn, raspberry, and grape (*Vitis* sp.) seeds were found in the Paleoindian component.

Whipple Site

Paleoindians migrated into the Northeast and left abundant cultural remains at the Whipple site in southern New Hampshire, between the Connecticut River on the west and the Ashchulot River in Swanzey. Comparisons between the fluted points recovered at Bull Brook and points found at the Whipple site (Curran 1984) correspond to ca. 11,000 BP (12,800 cal BP). The limited charcoal collected was identified as willow or poplar and softwood, indicating coniferous taxa. The pollen evidence from the basal organic zone in Swanzey bog (Richard et al. 1989) provides concrete evidence for the presence of conifers such as spruce, balsam fir, pine (*Pinus sp.*), cedar family (Cupressaceae), possibly northern white cedar (*Thuja occidentalis*), or juniper (*Juniperous* sp.). Minor amounts of deciduous tree pollen from maple (*Acer* sp.), oak (*Quercus* sp.), elm (*Ulmus* sp.), walnut family (Juglandaceae), ash (*Fraxinus nigra*), hornbeam (*Ostrya/Carpinus*), and aspen (*Populus tremuloides*) assert the concept of temperate environmental conditions in southern New Hampshire during the late Pleistocene. Unfortunately, the pollen core was not radiocarbon dated, and a future coring project appears to be necessary to pinpoint the vegetation changes at Whipple.

Sheridan Cave

The initial discovery of Sheridan Cave in the Indian Trails complex of karst caves in north-central Ohio created excitement over the spectacular Pleistocene faunal assemblage. Preservation in the cave included bones from fish, amphibians, reptiles, giant beaver, peccary, short-faced bear, stag moose, and caribou, just to name a few (Wisner 1998).

Tankersley and Redman (1999a, 1999b; Tankersley 1999) explain that the faunal material indicates potential exploitation of several different environments around the cave by the Paleoindians, who also found shelter there. A Paleoindian bone projectile point found at the site, very similar to one in the Upper Paleolithic Salutrean tool kits in Iberia, also shares similar characteristics with bone points from several other North American Paleoindian sites (Tankersely 1999).

Rhythmite formations deep inside the cave and below the Paleoindian strata were examined for diatoms, to help understand the sedimentary deposition. However, the discovery of a silicified pine wood tracheid, or phytolith, suggested that some of the prehuman occupation sediments were washed in from outside of the cave, 30 feet below the modern surface. The pine appears to be jack pine, with a modern-day southern boundary north of Lake Erie. Pollen reports for nearby water bodies such as Neville Marsh indicate that jack pine would have been in north-central Ohio during the late Pleistocene (Shane and Anderson 1991). Some of the charcoal that I analyzed from the cave suggests it arrived by water transport. With dates bracketing 11,000 BP, the presence of charred willow or poplar, possibly aspen, oak, and hornbeam, not only reflects the immediate impact of the Younger Dryas cooling at the site but also the early presence of oak in northern Ohio. These taxa allow us to expand on the paleoenvironmental picture to envision an open woodland with a mix of conifer and temperate deciduous taxa outside of the cave, where a mixture of faunal remains indicate a wetland and terrestrial environs. A date of 11,400 BP obtained on ash wood found in a bog in northern Ohio (Gramly 1993) further validates the deciduous species present at least prior to Paleoindian habitation in the region.

Cactus Hill Site

The Cactus Hill site is located 40 miles south of Richmond, Virginia, along the Nottoway River. A date of 15,070 BP (18,000 cal BP) on white pine charcoal brought the Cactus Hill site to the forefront of media attention for its potential pre-Clovis human occupation level. Excavations by the Nottoway River Survey team found a hearth feature three inches below the level containing Paleoindian fluted points, where southern hard pine charcoal had been dated to 10,920 BP (McWeeney 1997b).

White pine does not grow near the site today and provides some early documentation to the changing environment south of the glaciated region. The temperature range for white pine indicated a climatic amelioration to -6 degrees Celsius in the winter and revises our image of a dark spruce or jack pine forest encompassing the south, similar to what we discovered at Pequot Cedar Swamp at 12,000 BP. McAvoy (McAvoy and McAvoy 1997) recently received notice of a 15,000 BP date on oak charcoal from the Williamson site. Once again, the presence of white pine suggests the opportunity for local representation of temperate deciduous taxa, and I can confirm that oak grew in a similar environ. Ash and hornbeam are clearly represented in minor amounts by pollen. As mentioned earlier, the working hypothesis for establishing human association with the 15,070 BP date at Cactus Hill proposed that the phytolith quantities would increase by orders of magnitude in the cultural strata. If the quantity of phytoliths and phosphates varied through time, it would establish overall stratigraphic integrity despite knowing bioturbation must have occurred to some degree. Phytolith quantity was based on actual weight of recovered material. The results of the initial investigation showed that the phytoliths increased in the levels with cultural artifacts and declined in nonoccupied levels.

The phosphate analyses for each of these levels provided additional lines of evidence, especially when mapped along with the quantity of cultural material based on the weight of the lithics. The phosphates increased in strata associated with stone tools, in support of the human presence. The correlation of the phytoliths, phosphates, and lithics produces demonstrable stratigraphic integrity and goes a long way toward establishing human presence prior to the fluted point level at 10,920 BP. Ongoing research involves processing sediments for phytoliths and phosphates from an off-site column and a second on-site column. The addition of OSL dating already confirms stratigraphic integrity, and more samples will be dated in correlation with the on-site column. Soil micromorphology and macrosoil analyses (McAvoy, personal communication 2003) currently indicate human-modified sediments from this portion of the Cactus Hill site as well as a buried A horizon below the pre-Clovis level.

The data from these sites allows us to interpret the paleoenvironmental changes that took place at the end of the Pleistocene. Initially, after the glacier withdrew from southern New England before 15,000 BP (18,000 cal BP), a tundralike environment dominated the vegetation for nearly 4,000 years (McWeeney 1994). Arctic/alpine plants such as dwarf birch (*Betula michauxii* or *nana*), dwarf willow (*Salix herbacea*), driads (*Dryas intergrifolia*), and bilberry (*Vaccinium uliginosum*) blanketed the landscape. During the next 2,000 years, several environmental changes occurred. The temperature warmed, and the first conifer and deciduous trees appeared between 12,500 and 12,000 BP (14,500 and 14,000 cal BP), when spruce, larch, fir, and white pine colonized the land along with temperate deciduous species such as oak, hornbeam, ash, and red maple.

Postglacial lakes and ponds either drained or began to fill in by natural vegetative succession. Swamps and bogs developed, yielding a diverse assemblage of aquatic and moist-adapted vegetation. Temperate-adapted animals probably inhabited southern New England at this time (McWeeney 1994). All of this occurred while the Paleoindians were migrating across the Northeast. However, by 11,000 BP (13,000 cal BP) numerous climatic indicators point to colder winters and hotter summers. During the interlude known as the Younger Dryas episode, 11,000 to 10,200 (12,800 to 11,800 cal BP), a climatic change of global proportions enveloped the region with a decrease in temperature of 3 to 4 degrees Celsius or more (suggested by

Peteet et al. 1993). The dominant impact experienced by humans, other animals, and plant life alike was a period of cold so severe it may have forced many animals, such as white-tailed deer, out of the region. Fluctuations midway through the Younger Dryas indicated by the GISP may correlate with periods when humans could have temporarily expanded their settlement pattern into northern New England and Nova Scotia, only to withdraw until the climatic amelioration documented by the white oak charcoal from the Templeton site at around 10,200 BP (11,600 cal BP).

The results from this synthesis of plant data from several archaeological sites have illuminated the necessity of recovering plant remains from Paleoindian sites. By anticipating the need for flotation and systematically collecting column samples from each unit, whether or not we see a feature, we will expand the environmental picture for the late Pleistocene. Examination of the charred remains before AMS dating will provide valuable information, which documents precisely what vegetation was growing near a site at a specific time. Identifying plant remains to genus and species level will help establish postglacial rates of vegetation migration and changes in growth ranges that document climatic fluctuations for the last 18,000 years. Examination of the organics prior to dating also allows us to rule out contamination by making sure the sample is fully carbonized (which is important if you want a good date), because elimination of root material is critical to defining the temporal aspect of the site. In the absence of charred organics or bone, it is possible to obtain a date from phytoliths or by using OSL techniques. Employing more than one dating method ensures more reliable chronologies. As science and technology improve, we will be able to expand our knowledge of the past and continue to calculate the environmental variable in cultural patterns such as those occurring at the end of the Pleistocene.

TEN

Early Floridians and Late Megamammals

Some Technological and Dietary Evidence from Four North Florida Paleoindian Sites

James S. Dunbar and Pamela K. Vojnovski

Some of the most informative Paleoindian sites in North America are places where late Pleistocene peoples lived—their habitation or campsites. In general, Paleoindian campsites provide a more complete picture of lifeways because they reflect the shared, day-to-day activities of the men, women, and children rather than the out-of-camp, often gender-, age-, and/or task-specific activities. For example, a greater diversity of information has been obtained from the Lindenmeier, Colorado (Wilmsen and Roberts 1978), and Hanson, Wyoming (Frison and Bradley 1980), campsites compared to the view gained from Folsom-age bison kill sites.

In addition, habitation sites promise to provide a more complete picture of paleo-nutrition because specialized sites such as the kill-butcher locations of large Pleistocene animals (e.g., mastodons) are often biased toward a single species. Conversely, sites of small animal captures are more likely to be archaeologically invisible. Therefore, specialized animal procurement sites may exclude a significant portion of a culture's overall diet. Depending on carcass size and cultural practice, all or part of the bones from collectively shared prey animals are likely to have been brought back to the campsite. However, a problem that has impeded the greater potential for interpreting Paleoindian campsites east of the Mississippi River has been poor organic preservation. The occurrence of bone is typically nonexistent at open-terrain campsites. In Florida, for example, the Harney Flats site (8HI507) (Daniel and Wisenbaker 1987) represents a major base camp with lithic artifacts but no organic preservation. There are exceptions, however, and eastern Paleoindian sites located in karst caves, wetlands, or inundated locations often have surviving faunal and sometimes botanical remains.

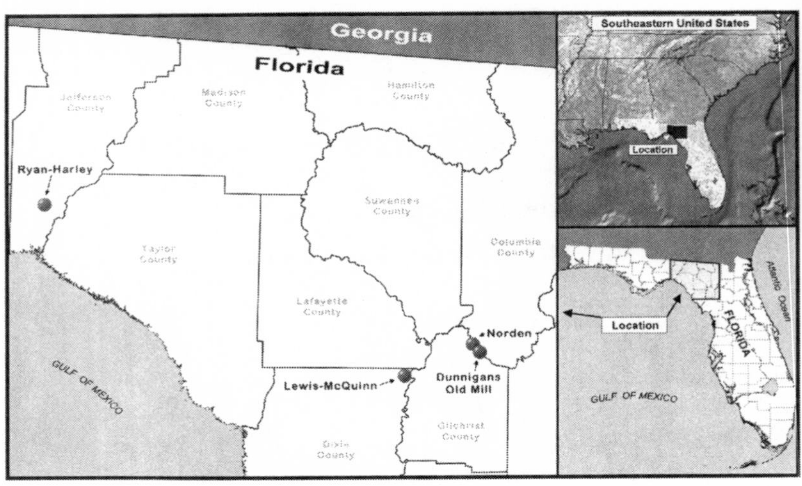

FIGURE 10.1. Location map showing the positions of the Ryan-Harley, Norden, Dunnigans Old Mill, and Lewis-McQuinn sites, North Florida.

There have been a handful of Paleoindian and Early Archaic cave (and sinkhole) sites investigated in the eastern United States. These include Dust Cave (Walker 1998) in northwestern Alabama, Modoc Rock Shelter in Illinois (Styles et al. 1983), Meadowcroft Rockshelter (Advasio et al. 1984; Advasio et al. 1999) in Pennsylvania, Stanfield-Worley Bluff Shelter (DeJarnette et al. 1962) in Alabama, Cutler Ridge (Carr 1987) near Miami, Florida, and Sheridan Cave (Tankersley et al. 1997; Tankersley and Redmond 2000) in Ohio, among others.

Open-terrain Paleoindian campsites with bone preservation, while elusive, have now been identified in submerged and wetland river basin settings in the Wacissa, Suwannee, and Santa Fe river basins in North Florida. In general, the karst river basins of Florida have long been recognized as an excellent source of late Pleistocene faunal material. As a result of archaeological investigations, four open-terrain Paleoindian campsites are now known in Florida, and will be the focus of this chapter. They are the Ryan-Harley site (8JE1004) in the Wacissa River basin, the Dunnigans Old Mill (8GI24) and Norden (8GI40) sites in the Santa Fe River basin, and the Lewis-McQuinn site (8DI112) in the Suwannee River basin (Figure 10.1). These sites, coupled with sites such as Dust Cave (Walker 1998, 2000) and Meadowcroft Rockshelter (Advasio et al. 1984; Advasio et al. 1999), provide evidence that Paleoindians in the eastern United States had a more varied diet, with some sites indicative of a more generalized subsistence pattern and others more focused on mammals for subsistence. The reliance of certain cultural groups on wetland resources is well documented in Florida; however, it has never before been traced to a Paleoindian context.

Along with faunal remains, these sites have also produced stone tools and lithic debitage and, in three out of the four sites, bone tools. Because these sites also offer the opportunity to clarify aspects about the tools and toolmaking debris that are associated with megafauna remains, we consider both the fauna and artifact assemblages. It is a threefold approach, taking into account the implications of the faunal and artifact assemblages in a comparative way. We not only compare the assemblages between sites, we also consider the implications of the faunal assemblage not necessarily reflected in the artifact assemblage as well as the implications reflected in both.

Ryan-Harley

The Ryan-Harley site is the first stratified Suwannee point site in the southeastern United States that meets two crucial tests of archaeological significance (Figure 10.2). First, the Suwannee point level of the site has survived uncontaminated by other cultural deposits; second, the bones of extinct and extant species have been preserved in association with numerous stone artifacts. The analysis of cultural and faunal remains (Dunbar et al. 2005) and the site's stratigraphy (Balsillie et al. 2006) are reported elsewhere. It is our intent to use the Ryan-Harley site as a baseline to compare its faunal and cultural remains to the Norden and Dunnigans Old Mill sites located in the lower Santa Fe River basin and the Lewis-McQuinn site in the lower Suwannee River basin (Figure 10.3).

The Ryan-Harley site is located in and along a relatively recently formed, low-energy, braided channel of the Wacissa River. Here the floodplain of the river is about 5 kilometers wide, and the difference in elevation between the low-river stage and the surrounding wetlands rarely exceeds about 0.5 meter. As a result, the Ryan-Harley site is located in the middle of a heavily vegetated swamp forest. A larger part of the site extends under the riverbank for an undetermined distance.

Norden

The Norden site encompasses a large area with many horizontally separated components that extend from the sandhill uplands into the Santa Fe River

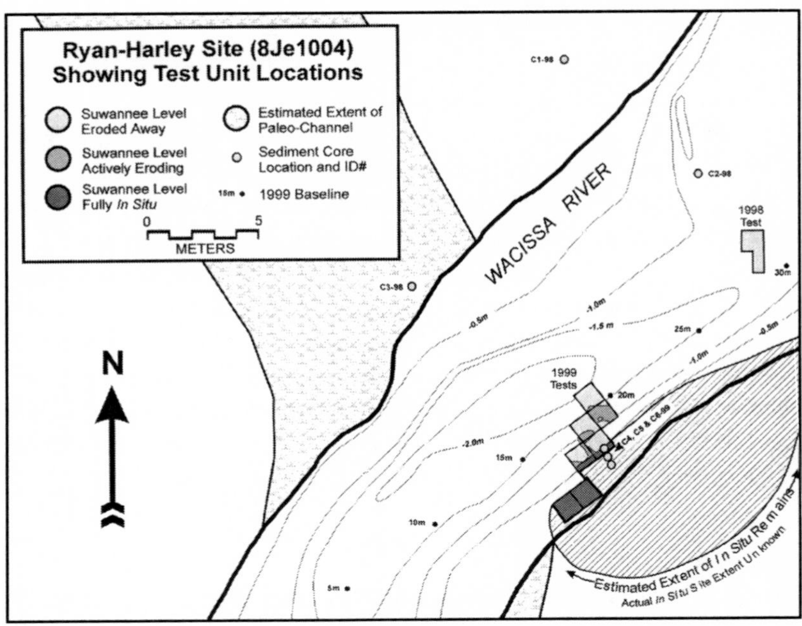

FIGURE 10.2. Ryan-Harley site test units and the estimated extent of the Paleo-channel and undisturbed site.

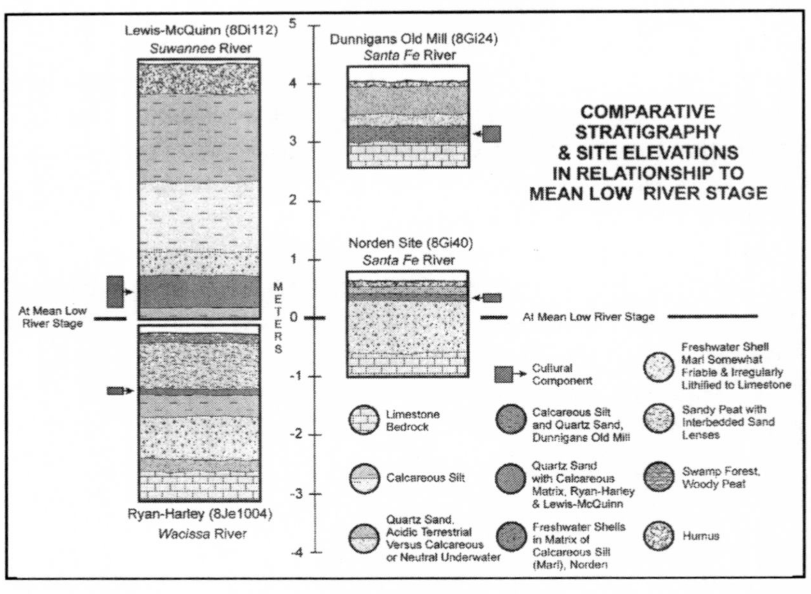

FIGURE 10.3. Stratigraphic profiles of the Ryan-Harley, Norden, Dunnigans Old Mill, and Lewis-McQuinn sites, North Florida.

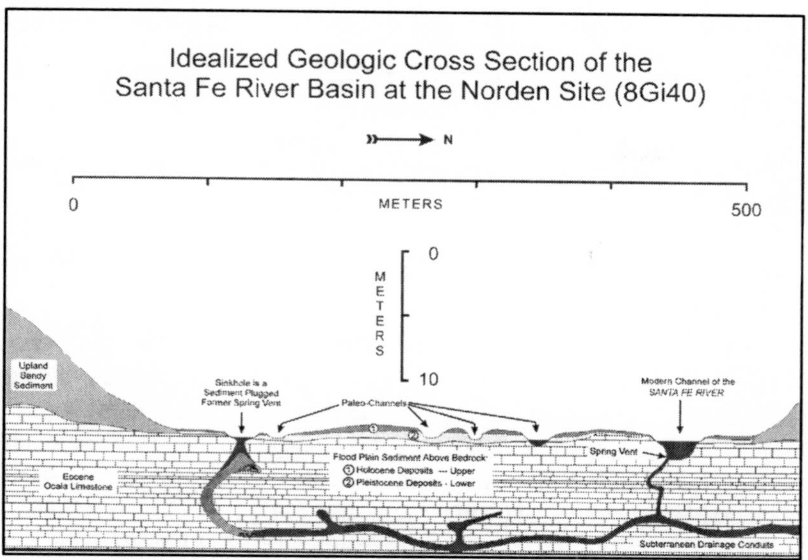

FIGURE 10.4. Norden site geologic cross section.

floodplain, and from there into the river. For this chapter, we consider only one of the components, which is distinct and encompasses no more than about 800 square meters, probably much less (Figure 10.4). This is a small subarea of the Norden site, with in-place remains buried in the floodplain and stratigraphically deflated remains in the adjacent river channel. A total of 936 stone artifacts were collected from this area, with most representing surface finds in the deflated river channel section. Two test units placed in the floodplain yielded 40 stone artifacts and 43 bone fragments, confirming the site's buried expression. In this chapter, we will refer to this component as the Norden site, but the actual site boundaries are much larger and encompass multiple cultural components ranging in age from Paleoindian to Mississippian.

Dunnigans Old Mill

Clarence J. Simpson originally discovered the Dunnigans Old Mill site when he surface collected the proximal, hafting ends of two waisted Suwannee points from the Santa Fe River and another specimen from the adjacent uplands. Subsequently, river-diver Ben Waller reported collecting two additional Suwannee points from the river. The Dunnigans Old Mill site is located above, below, and in the largest white water rapids on the Santa

TABLE 10.1. Faunal specimens discarded from the Dunnigans Old Mill site.

	Test I		Test II		Test III	
Condition	Discarded	Retained	Discarded	Retained	Discarded	Retained
Mineralized	115	25	57	29	66	34
Calcined	10	29	0	16	2	8
Gnawed	0	0	0	1	0	0

Fe River as well as overlooking that section of swift water on the river's southern bank. Many finds have been made on the down-current side of the rapids, where the current velocity becomes dispersed. Faunal remains are typically well preserved in underwater settings, and at Dunnigans Old Mill surface finds of llama, *Mammut americanum*, *Mammuthus columbi*, and *Equus* sp. have been documented (Dunbar 1991:200–201).

The results of placing three test units on top of a bluff overlooking the river produced faunal remains, including *Equus* sp. and possibly *Bison antiquus* in association with lithic artifacts. Shortly after the tests were completed, recovered specimens were cleaned and examined. Many of the bone specimens were in very poor condition and were discarded as unidentifiable fragments (Table 10.1).

Had the bone not survived in the terra rossa–like sediment at Dunnigans Old Mill, the scarcity of lithic artifacts at the site would likely have been judged to be archaeologically insignificant. Due to the scarcity of stone tools, the fauna and bone tools will be primarily considered.

Lewis-McQuinn

The Lewis-McQuinn site is located on the margins of the lower Suwannee River, where part of the site is buried under river levee deposits (Figure 10.5). Here the floodplain is wide and karstified in places. Some of the exposed limestone sinks and caves expel groundwater as springs, while others are nonflowing. The closest-known active spring is located about 350 meters from the site.

The Lewis-McQuinn site was initially discovered and surface collected by river-divers Chris Lewis and Rusty McQuinn. Both reported finding lanceolate points in and along the river, and Lewis provided an unfluted Clovis-like base and a Bolen side-notched point for the Bureau of Archaeological Research (BAR) collections (BAR Accessions 92A.63.0.1 Clovis-like and 92A.63.0.2 Bolen).

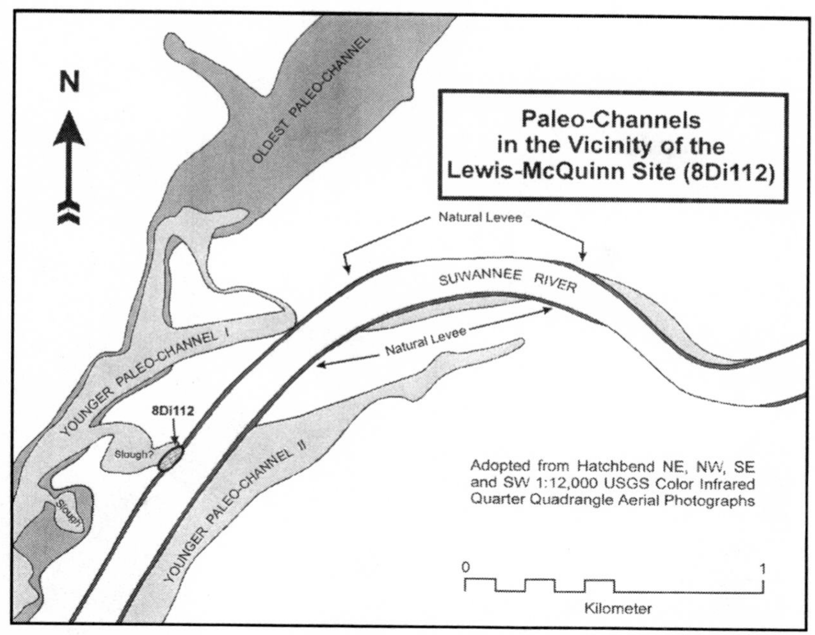

FIGURE 10.5. Lewis-McQuinn Paleo-channels.

Chronology

All four of these karst river basin sites have components that are placed relatively in time as Middle Paleoindian or earlier based on the *in situ* occurrence of Pleistocene megafaunal remains. This is in contrast to the complete absence of Pleistocene fauna in Late Paleoindian contexts at sites such as Dust Cave in Alabama, or in Early Archaic contexts at sites such as Page-Ladson (Dunbar et al. 1989; Carter and Dunbar 2006), Little Salt Springs (Dietrich and Gifford 1996), and Cutler Ridge (Carr 1987) in Florida. Furthermore, the occurrence of waisted Suwannee points at the Ryan-Harley (*in situ* and displaced; Figure 10.6) and Norden (displaced; Figure 10.7) sites and an unfluted lanceolate point base at Lewis McQuinn (displaced) support a Middle to Early Paleoindian temporal context. None of the four sites has been radiometrically dated. In the southeastern United States, the Early Paleoindian is estimated to be the period of initial human occupation lasting until ca. 10,900 BP, the Middle Paleoindian from ca. 10,900 to ca. 10,500 BP, and the Late Paleoindian from ca. 10,500 to ca. 10,000 BP (Anderson et al. 1996; Goodyear 1999).

Attempts to acquire radiocarbon dates from six bone samples at the Ryan-Harley site failed because the bone was too mineralized. Attempts to

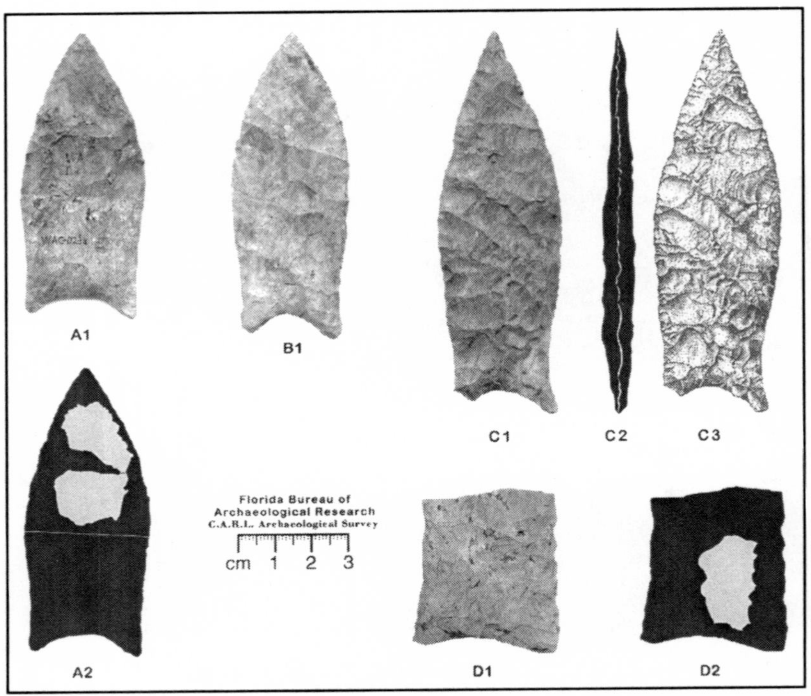

FIGURE 10.6. Ryan-Harley site Suwannee points and preform.

radiometrically date the other sites have not been attempted, in part because the only available specimens are bones that also appear mineralized, and because investigations at the other sites have been less intensive. Bone specimens from the Norden and Lewis-McQuinn sites are not as well preserved compared to specimens from the Ryan-Harley site. In general, the bone from Dunnigans Old Mill was the least well preserved, and 238 bone specimens were discarded prior to accessioning because they represented deteriorated, unidentifiable fragments.

Due to the lack of organic datable material, we are left to date these sites by relative means. The Ryan-Harley site is judged to be on the earlier end of the Middle Paleoindian time frame, which would place it closer in time to the onset of the Younger Dryas. This evaluation is based on the assumption that Suwannee points are post Clovis, not its contemporary, and that there are a sufficient number of Clovis and Clovis-like traits present in the Suwannee tool kit from the Ryan-Harley site. The Norden site is the other waisted Suwannee site among the four being considered. The notched, expanding-stem, auriculate-based point from the Norden site (see Figure

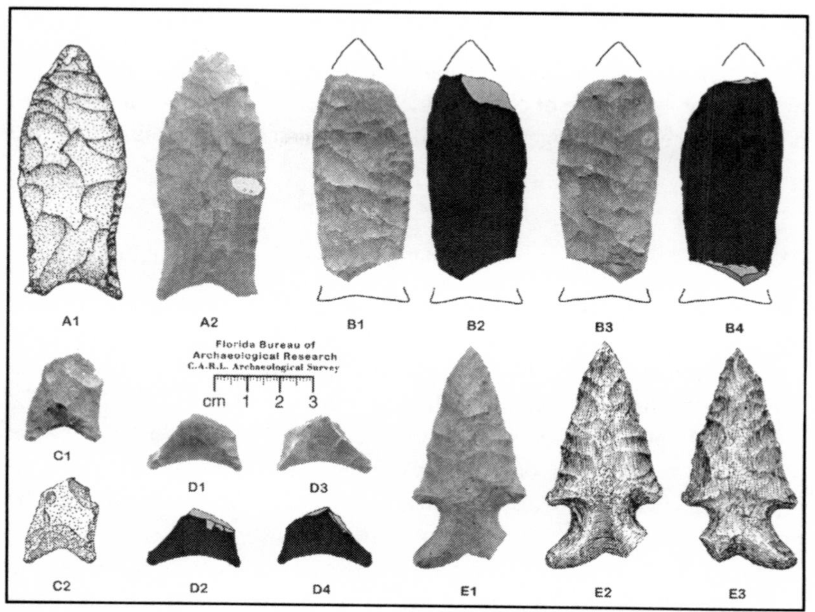

FIGURE 10.7. Norden site projectile points.

10.7) shares some traits with Suwannee points. Therefore, the Norden site might be indicative of a transitional late Middle Paleoindian occupation mostly dominated by Suwannee tools, but also having a few tools indicative of the developing Late Paleoindian continuum. If this is true, the Norden site is significant because it will have produced evidence of some of the latest known Pleistocene megafauna in context. The Norden site may contain evidence of the beginnings of a changing hunting strategy from a Pleistocene to Holocene faunal reliance. If the Norden site represents a late Middle Paleoindian occupation, it most likely dates to the latter part of the Younger Dryas cold phase prior to ca. 10,400 BP.

Placing the Lewis-McQuinn and Dunnigans Old Mill sites in chronological context is much more a matter of speculation. At the Lewis-McQuinn site, several lanceolate points were found in displaced context, and the deepest artifact-bearing level of that site has produced Pleistocene faunal remains and lithic artifacts. The Lewis-McQuinn paleo point base most closely resembles an unfluted Clovis or parallel-sided Suwannee-like point. The Dunnigans Old Mill site is even more equivocal. Other than a graver similar to those found elsewhere in Paleoindian context, there were no lithic artifacts suggestive of age. In fact, this site is remarkable for its lack of lithic artifacts versus its abundance of bone. One nondiagnostic bone point was recovered but was not suggestive of chronological placement. However, the presence of Pleistocene fauna suggests a Middle Paleoindian or earlier time range.

Faunal Analysis

Ryan-Harley Fauna

The faunal sample from Ryan-Harley was collected from seven 1-by-1-meter test units. Artifacts were piece plotted in place or were recovered from a water-screen with a 1/8-inch mesh. All of the samples were recovered from a single stratum that represents the Suwannee point level. Therefore, for quantitative purposes, all of the samples were combined to form a total sample for the site. The faunal remains from Ryan-Harley have been reported elsewhere (Dunbar et al. 2005), and only a brief overview will be presented here.

The Ryan-Harley site has been the subject of the most intensive testing of the four sites being considered and has the best-preserved faunal material of the four. The site has produced a total of 368 bone fragments collectively weighing 871.0 grams from *in situ* deposits. The taxa recovered are shown in Table 10.2. By weight, reptiles contributed the most, accounting for 48.53 percent of the total in-place deposit. They were followed closely by mammals, which accounted for 44.07 percent. Unidentified vertebrates contributed 4.35 percent, with fish contributing 2.15 percent, birds contributing 0.7 percent, and amphibians contributing 0.15 percent. The majority of the species represent wetland or mixed wetland and upland habitats. By weight, wetland resources account for 51.72 percent of the faunal assemblage, followed by mixed resources with 48.13 percent. Upland resources, represented by a single gopher tortoise, account for 0.15 percent of the total. The large number of wetland species may be an indication that the site's inhabitants utilized most extensively the catchment areas closest to the site. Based on the *in situ* faunal remains, the environmental picture that emerges is that of a shallow, freshwater stream, or perhaps pond, as a permanent, nearby water source (Dunbar et al. 2005).

One of the more interesting aspects of the Ryan-Harley faunal assemblage is the inclusion of the American mink (*Mustela vison*). The remains of at least two individuals were recovered from the in-place deposits, and additional specimens of mink are known to be included in the out-of-place deposits. However, because the analysis of the out-of-place deposits is incomplete, the total minimum number of individuals (MNI) for this species at the site

TABLE 10.2. Taxa recovered from the Ryan-Harley site in-place deposits.

Class	Taxon	Name	NISP	MNI	Weight (gms)
Fish	*Lepisosteus* spp.	gars	3	1	0.4
	Amia calva	bowfin	6	2	2.5
	Ictaluridae	bullhead catfishes	2	2	2.6
	Lepomis microlophus	redear sunfish	1	1	1.8
	Micropterus salmoides	largemouth bass	5	1	4.3
	Centrarchidae	sunfishes	1	-	0.3
	UID Osteichthyes	unidentified bony fishes	20	-	6.7
	Subtotal		38	7	18.6
Amphibian	*Siren lacertian*	greater siren	1	1	0.1
	Amphiuma sp.	amphiumas	3	1	1.2
	Anura	frogs and toads	1	1	0.1
	UID Amphibia	unidentified amphibian	1	-	0.1
	Subtotal		6	3	1.5
Reptile	*Apalone ferox*	softshell turtle	2	1	10.2
	Kinosternidae	mud and musk turtles	19	2	11.0
	Trachemys scripta	slider	26	1	127.3
	Emydidae	subaquatic turtles	7	-	39.3
	Gopherus polyphemus	gopher tortoise	1	1	1.3
	UID Testudines	unidentified turtles	45	-	80.6
	cf. Testudines	probable turtle	1	-	10.7
	Colubridae	harmless snakes	1	1	0.2
	Agkistrodon piscivorus	cottonmouth	1	1	0.4
	Viperidae	pit vipers	3	-	3.3
	UID Serpentes	unidentified snakes	1	-	0.6
	Alligator mississippiensis	American alligator	13	1	87.7
	cf. *Alligator mississippiensis*	probable American alligator	2	-	5.3
	UID large Reptilia	unidentified large reptile	7	-	35.9
	UID Reptilia	unidentified reptile	1	-	5.2
	Subtotal		130	8	419.0
Bird	UID small Aves	unidentified small birds	7	1	2.0
	UID medium Aves	unidentified medium birds	3	1	1.5
	UID medium/large Aves	unidentified medium/large birds	8	1	2.6
	Subtotal		18	3	6.1
Mammal	*Procyon lotor*	raccoon	4	2	9.1
	cf. *Procyon lotor*	probable raccoon	1	-	0.5
	Mustela vison	American mink	1	1	1.0
	Ondatra zibethicus	marsh muskrat	5	2	7.9
	Sylvilagus spp.	rabbits	3	1	5.9
	cf. Leporidae	probable rabbit	1	-	0.9
	UID Rodentia	unidentified rodent	1	-	0.1
	Odocoileus virginianus	white-tailed deer	34	2	206.2
	cf. *Odocoileus virginianus*	probable white-tailed deer	36	-	74.3
	Equus sp.	Pleistocene horse	1	1	15.2
	Tapirus veroensis	tapir	6	1	4.9
	UID small Mammalia	unidentified small mammals	6	-	2.5
	UID small/medium Mammalia	unidentified small/ medium mammals	2	-	0.1
	UID medium Mammalia	unidentified medium mammal	7	-	14.7
	UID medium/large Mammalia	unidentified medium/ large mammals	4	-	6.6
	UID large Mammalia	unidentified large mammals	7	-	12.8
	UID Mammalia	unidentified mammals	12	-	17.8
	Subtotal		131	10	380.5
Vertebrate	UID Vertebrata	unidentified vertebrates	44	-	37.6
	Subtotal		44	-	37.6
	Site Total		367	31	863.3

is still unknown. Kurtén and Anderson note that mink are uncommon in Pleistocene faunas (1980:151). They also note that these solitary and nocturnal animals are the American furriery industry's most valuable furbearers. Mink are aquatic and den along stream banks, where they feed on crayfish, fish, frogs, birds, muskrats, and the like (Kurtén and Anderson 1980:151).

For interpretive purposes, we are left with two possibilities: either the mink remains are part of a natural deposit or, conversely, they are part of the cultural deposit. If the mink remains are considered to be part of the natural deposit, it is also possible that some of the other species such as fish, young turtles, amphibians, birds, and muskrats might also represent the remains of captured prey animals prior to the predator's death. However, as Whitaker (1992:579) points out, mink "eat on the spot or carry prey by the neck to their dens, where any surplus is cached. They den in protected places near water, often in a muskrat burrow, an abandoned beaver den, or hollow log, or they may dig their own den in the streambank; all dens are temporary, as minks move frequently." In addition, Rattner et al. (n.d.) indicate that male mink can weigh up to twice as much as females. Due to their size, female mink have difficulty hunting large prey such as muskrats and rabbits, and as a result are more limited in their diet. Mink are generally solitary, with association occurring mostly between the female and her young. Males move frequently within their range of 1.8 to 5 kilometers. Today, mink have a typical population density of 0.01 to 0.10 mink per hectare (Rattner et al. n.d.).

The possibility that mink and potential prey animal bones were deposited as a result of a natural accumulation by mink that eventually also died on site seems unlikely. The mink and other faunal remains from the Ryan-Harley site were found within a seven-square-meter test area. Because mink are solitary and do not stay in one place, and because the males are the most mobile and take the large prey animals, it is difficult to attribute the bone assemblage to mink predation. On the contrary, the mink remains as well as the other animal bones appear to have accumulated as a result of human activity within the seven square meters excavated at the Ryan-Harley site. This is particularly true since the archaeological signature at this site is so clear and includes other, much larger fauna. We are not discounting the possibility that part of the faunal remains from Ryan-Harley may be of commensal or of natural occurrence. Rather, we believe that much of the faunal remains, regardless of animal size, accumulated as a result of cultural deposition.

If the mink remains are considered part of the cultural deposit, an interesting possibility is revealed. Mink, muskrats, and rabbits are primarily nocturnal, being active at dusk, nighttime, and around dawn (Whitaker 1992:509–511, 578–579). Thus, the best time to successfully capture these creatures is at night when they are most likely to be active. A possible capture technique could have been the placement of unattended traps along the water's edge before dark, followed by a check of the traps the next day. Mink, for example, can be lured into traps baited with dead birds and other prey. However, this certainly does not sound like the type of Paleoindian hunting technique we are accustomed to reading about or, in this case, have we found evidence of in the Ryan-Harley artifact suite. Trapping devices may have been made from wood, sinew, fiber, and cordage, all things that rarely survive in the archaeological record. Thus, our evidence comes from the fauna and their nocturnal habits.

But why go to all of the trouble to capture such small animals? Today both mink and muskrat are prized for their furs, and muskrat for its meat. Rabbits also provide good fur. After the Younger Dryas episode began about 11,000 BP, the northern latitudes in both Europe and North America were plunged back into glacial maximum–like cold conditions (Björck et al. 1996; Lotter et al. 2000). To what degree these cold conditions were experienced at latitudes as far south as northern Florida at latitude 30° N is uncertain. However, the signature of the Younger Dryas episode is seen in tropical deep ocean sediments as far south as the Cariaco Basin at latitude 10°40' N, a location off the northern coast of Venezuela (Hughen et al. 1996). Therefore, fur might have been needed for clothing during the cold phase of the Younger Dryas. Today, mink pelts are highly valued as high-priced adornment, but it is more likely, if used in the prehistoric past, that they were used for practical reasons, such as clothing to keep an infant both warm and comfortable. It is also possible that rabbit pelts could have served a similar function. Likewise, the "durability and waterproof qualities of muskrat fur are considered extremely valuable, and it is of great importance to the fur trade" (Hughen et al. 1996). The same qualities recognized in these fur-bearing animals today may have also been important to the Paleoindians. At least one rabbit, two muskrats, and two mink were recovered from the seven-square-meter area tested, and there are probably more individuals represented in the out-of-place deposits that have not been quantified.

Norden

The Norden site is similar to the Ryan-Harley site in that it has produced waisted Suwannee points and a similar stone tool kit. Based on the concentration and variety of lithic tools, as well as the relative abundance of faunal remains that were recovered from two small test units, we believe the Norden site assemblage is indicative of a campsite. Our primary consideration of the Norden site faunal remains is limited to the specimens recovered from the test units conducted in the floodplain. In addition, elements of *Mammut americanum* (mastodon), *Equus* sp. (horse), *Bison* sp. (buffalo), and *Hesperotestudo crassiscutata* (giant tortoise), along with the remains of numerous extant vertebrates, came from the deflated part of the site, and the fragmentary remains of a *Mammuthus columbi* (mammoth) were found about 200 meters downstream from the site in the river channel.

The faunal remains examined from the Norden site were recovered from a single 0.50-meter sondage excavated in November 1975 and a 10-centimeter core-size test in 1992. Because sediment from the tests was not screened, the faunal remains recovered from the tests are biased toward medium-size and large bone fragments. Forty-three bone fragments, collectively weighing 189.8 grams, were examined and separated to the lowest possible taxon. At least five individuals (MNI = 5) are present in the assemblage. The remains consisted of an unidentified bird, an unidentified ungulate that was most likely either a horse (*Equus* sp.) or bison (*Bison* sp.), a white-tailed deer (*Odocoileus virginianus*), a river otter (*Lutra canadensis*), unidentified medium-size and large mammals, a cooter or slider (*Pseudemys*/*Trachemys* spp.), and unidentified vertebrates (Table 10.3). Two of the deer long-bone fragments may be green fractured. The medium-size mammal bone fragment appears to have a cutmark on it. One of the species present in the Norden assemblage is river otter (*Lutra canadensis*), an important fur-bearing animal.

The Norden site is the most biased of the four due to the extremely small sample size and limited testing of the in-place component without screening. Nevertheless, all of the faunal specimens, along with 40 lithic artifacts, came from the two test units, which suggests the undisturbed part of this site has good archaeological potential. Because of the small sample size, the faunal remains from this site cannot be characterized as either generalized or specialized foraging. Therefore, the Norden site fauna only tentatively bear a resemblance to the mixed mammalian faunal assemblage recovered from the Dunnigans Old Mill site.

Dunnigans Old Mill

The faunal specimens and artifacts from the Dunnigans Old Mill site were recovered from a 6.5-square-meter test area. The artifacts removed from

TABLE 10.3. Summary of taxa recovered from the Norden site.

Taxon	Common Name	Element	Count	Weight (gms)	MNI	Habitat
Pseudemys/ Trachemys spp.	cooter/slider	unidentified carapace fragments	2	2.0	1	W
Aves	medium bird	long-bone shaft fragment	1	1.1	1	M
Lutra canadensis	river otter	distal humerus fragment	1	2.0	1	W
Lutra canadensis	river otter	proximal femur fragment	1	2.6	0	W
Odocoileus virginianus	white-tailed deer	long-bone shaft fragment	3	2.9	1	M
Ungulata	ungulate	long-bone shaft fragments	8	163.3	1	M
Unidentified medium Mammalia	medium mammal	long-bone shaft fragment	1	2.0	0	M
Unidentified large Mammalia	large mammal	unidentified fragments	7	9.8	0	M
Unidentified vertebrata	vertebrate	long-bone shaft fragments	4	0.7	0	X
Unidentified vertebrata	vertebrate	unidentified fragments	15	3.4	0	X
Total			43	189.8	5	

Key: U = upland, M = Mixed wetland and upland, W = wetland, X = unknown

the test units were piece plotted, but the soil was not sieved. Therefore, the assemblage is heavily biased toward larger specimens. A total of 267 bone fragments, collectively weighing 891.2 grams, were recovered from the site (Table 10.4). Unidentified large mammals dominate the Dunnigans Old Mill assemblage. Large mammals include Pleistocene horse (*Equus* sp.) and bison (*Bison antiquus*). Some small and medium-size mammals are also present, but not in large numbers. Turtles (mostly unidentified) and alligator occur in the assemblage, but are relatively rare. Bird and fish remains are very rare in the assemblage. The scarcity of aquatic and avian faunal remains may reflect an actual preference for large mammals, or may be a result of the lack of screening. The majority of large-mammal remains in the assemblage belong to very large mammals, specifically bison-size and larger. The majority of species present in the assemblage inhabit mixed upland and wetland habitats. Most of the bone could not be identified beyond the class level due to the extremely poor state of preservation of the faunal remains recovered from the site (see Table 10.4).

The small sample size may represent the remains of a short-term camp occupied by a small group of people. The low counts of lithic material versus high counts of bone may also reflect a short occupation period. Nevertheless, the mixture of the small mammals with the large extinct forms and the inclusion of reptiles, birds, and fish are not reflective of the idealized big-game hunting paradigm. Although this site is most heavily

TABLE 10.4. Summary of taxa recovered from the Dunnigans Old Mill site.

Taxon	Common Name	Element	Count	Weight (gms)	MNI	Habitat
Osteichtyes	bony fish	dentary? fragment	1	0.7	1	W
cf. *Trachemys scripta*	probable slider	unidentified carapace fragments	3	3.2	1	W
Pseudemys/Trachemys spp.	cooter/slider	unidentified carapace fragments	2	9.5	0	W
cf. *Pseudemys/ Trachemys* spp.	possible cooter/ slider	unidentified carapace fragment	1	1.3	0	W
Testudines	turtles	marginal	1	1.6	0	M
Testudines	turtles	neural	1	6.6	0	M
Testudines	turtles	unidentified plastron fragment	3	15.7	0	M
Testudines	turtles	unidentified carapace fragment	1	3.3	0	M
Testudines	turtles	carapace fragment?	1	6.9	0	M
Testudines	turtles	carapace or plastron fragments	6	21.3	0	M
Testudines	turtles	plastron fragments?	2	2.7	0	M
Testudines	turtles	unidentified fragments	12	16.9	0	M
Alligator mississippiensis	American alligator	dermal scutes	2	5.2	1	W
Alligator mississippiensis	American alligator	unidentified fragment	1	12.3	0	W
Reptilia	large reptile	unidentified fragment	1	14.2	0	W
Aves	small bird	long-bone shaft fragment	1	0.3	1	M
Odocoileus virginianus	white-tailed deer	LF petrosal	1	3.0	1	M
cf. *Odocoileus virginianus*	probable white-tailed deer	long-bone shaft fragments	2	1.8	0	M
Bison antiquus	bison	proximal and medial phalanges	2	59.8	1	U
Equus sp.	Pleistocene horse	lower cheek tooth	1	1.5	1	M
Equus sp.	Pleistocene horse	unidentified tooth fragment	1	1.7	0	M
cf. *Equus* sp.	possible Pleistocene horse	possible tooth enamel fragment	1	0.1	0	M
Mammalia	large mammal	auditory bulla?	1	3.9	0	M
Mammalia	large mammal	tooth? fragment	1	0.5	0	M
Mammalia	large mammal	distal femur fragment	1	11.0	0	M
Mammalia	large mammal	long-bone shaft fragments	27	143.6	0	M
Mammalia	large mammal	possible long-bone fragment	1	3.7	0	M
Mammalia	large mammal	unidentified long-bone fragment	1	23.4	0	M
Mammalia	large mammal	unidentified fragments	50	258.9	0	M
Mammalia	large mammal	long-bone shaft fragment?	1	7.5	0	M
Mammalia	large mammal	long-bone or rib fragment	1	30.8	0	M
Mammalia	large mammal	rib fragment?	1	31.5	0	M
Mammalia	large mammal	possible proximal femur or humerus fragment	1	13.8	0	M
Mammalia	large mammal	unidentified cranial	1	5.0	0	M
Mammalia	probable large mammal	cancellous bone, unidentified fragment	1	3.4	0	X
Mammalia	probable large mammal	unidentified fragment	1	1.1	0	X
Mammalia	large mammal?	unidentified fragments	4	10.9	0	X
Mammalia	medium/large mammal	long-bone shaft fragments	8	4.1	0	M
Mammalia	medium mammal	long-bone shaft fragments	3	0.8	1	M
Mammalia	probable small mammal	long-bone shaft fragment	1	0.3	1	M
Mammalia	mammal	unidentified fragments	3	0.3	0	M
Mammalia?	mammal?	unidentified fragment	1	0.2	0	X
Unidentified vertebrata	unidentified vertebrate	cancellous tissue	1	2.3	0	X
Unidentified vertebrata	unidentified vertebrate	possible long-bone fragments	3	0.1	0	X
Unidentified vertebrata	unidentified vertebrates	unidentified fragments	107	144.5	0	X
Total			267	891.2	9	

Key: U = Upland, M = Mixed Wetland and Upland, W = Wetland, X = Unknown

TABLE 10.5. Summary of taxa recovered from the Lewis-McQuinn site, Level 1.

Taxon	Common name	Element	Count	Weight (gms)	MNI	Habitat
Amia calva	bowfin	vertebra	1	1.0	1	W
Lepisosteus spp.	gars	vertebra	1	0.1	1	W
Lepisosteus spp.	gars	unidentified cranial fragments	9	4.0	0	W
Micropterus salmoides	largemouth bass	vertebra	1	0.3	1	W
Osteichthyes	bony fishes	vertebrae	15	3.2	0	W
Osteichthyes	bony fishes	unidentified fragments	8	2.0	0	W
cf. Osteichthyes	probable bony fishes	unidentified fragment	1	0.1	0	W
Siren lacertina	greater siren	vertebra	1	0.2	1	W
Anura	frogs and toads	vertebrae	2	0.3	1	W
Kinosternidae	mud and musk turtles	carapace fragments	17	2.9	1	W
Testudines	turtles	unidentified carapace fragments	10	7.1	1	M
Testudines	turtles	unidentified plastron fragments	2	1.5	0	M
Testudines	turtles	unidentified carapace 23 or plastron fragments	4.9	0	M	
Testudines	turtles	marginals	2	0.3	0	M
Testudines	turtles	unidentified fragments	45	30.7	0	M
Colubridae	harmless snakes	vertebra	1	0.1	1	M
Aves	small birds	coracoid fragments	3	0.4	1	M
Aves	small birds	proximal humerus fragment	1	0.5	0	M
Aves	small birds	long-bone shaft fragments	13	2.1	0	M
Aves	small birds	unidentified long-bone fragments	2	1.0	0	M
Aves	small/medium birds	long-bone shaft fragments	8	1.2	0	M
Aves	small/medium birds	vertebrae	2	0.4	0	M
Aves	birds	long-bone shaft fragment	1	0.8	0	M
Didelphis virginiana	opossum	vertebra	1	0.7	1	M
Sylvilagus sp.	rabbits	maxilla fragment with teeth	1	0.6	1	M
Sylvilagus sp.	rabbits	proximal femur fragment	1	0.6	0	M
Odocoileus virginianus	white-tailed deer	unidentified tooth fragment	1	0.9	1	M
Odocoileus virginianus	white-tailed deer	long-bone shaft fragments	2	1.2	0	M
Mammalia	small mammal	metatarsal	1	0.1	0	M
Mammalia	medium mammal	LF calcaneus	1	0.1	1	M
Mammalia	medium mammal	proximal humerus fragment	1	2.1	0	M
Mammalia	medium mammal	distal humerus fragment	1	4.7	0	M
Mammalia	medium mammal	long-bone shaft fragments	7	0.8	0	M
Mammalia	large mammal	unidentified fragment	1	153.5	0	M
Vertebrata	unidentified vertebrates	unidentified fragments	264	52.3	0	X
Vertebrata	unidentified vertebrate	unidentified tooth fragments	2	0.1	0	X
Unionidae	freshwater mussels	umbo and partial shell	1	1.6	1	W
Gastropoda	unidentified univalve	apex, partial body, whorl	1	0.5	1	W
Invertebrata	invertebrate	body fragments	1	0.2	0	W
Total			456	285.1	15	

Key: U = Upland, M = Mixed Wetland and Upland, W = Wetland, X = Unknown biased toward very large mammals, it is clear that they were not the sole source of food.

Lewis-McQuinn

The faunal remains from the Lewis-McQuinn site discussed in this chapter were recovered from three one-square-meter test units. The soil removed from these units was water-sieved through 1/8-inch screen. All of the remains were taken from Level 1 of these units. A total of 453 vertebrate fragments and three invertebrate fragments were recovered, which collectively weighed 285.1 grams (Table 10.5). At least 15 individuals are represented in this assemblage.

By weight, the largest contributors to the site's faunal assemblage were mammals, with 165.3 grams, or about 58 percent of the total, followed by unidentified vertebrates, with 52.4 grams, or about 18 percent of the total. These were followed by reptiles, with 47.5 grams, or about 17 percent of the total; fish, with 10.7 grams, or about 4 percent of the total; birds, with 6.4 grams, or about 2 percent of the total; invertebrates, with 2.3 grams, or about 1 percent of the total; and amphibians, with 0.5 gram, or about 0.2 percent of the total. By weight, mixed wetland and upland resources were the most important to the site's inhabitants, contributing 216.3 grams, or about 76 percent of the total, followed by unknown resources with 52.4 grams, or about 18 percent of the total. Wetland resources contributed 16.4 grams, or about 6 percent of the total (see Table 10.5). Together, wetland and mixed resources account for about 82 percent of the assemblage for Level 1. This is similar to the percentages for the Ryan-Harley site, where wetland and mixed resources dominated the assemblage and accounted for nearly 100 percent of the examined remains. Based on these numbers, it is clear that wetland resources were important to the economies of the Suwannee point makers. Again, as in the case of Ryan-Harley, the site's inhabitants utilized the catchment areas closest to the site. From the faunal perspective, the Ryan-Harley and Lewis-McQuinn sites are more similar to each other than to the Norden and Dunnigans Old Mill sites. One of the species present in the Lewis-McQuinn assemblage is the rabbit (Leporidae), an important fur-bearing animal.

Lithic Analysis

This analysis of stone artifacts primarily includes a comparison of debitage and tools from the Ryan-Harley and Norden sites. Both sites are Middle

TABLE 10.6. Lithic artifact size distribution at the Lewis-McQuinn site.

Size	0-1 cm	1-2 cms	2-3 cms	3-4 cms	4-5 cms	5-6 cms	Total
Count	12	50	8	5	0	1	76
Percent	16	65	11	7	0	1	100

Paleoindian, Suwannee point sites. The Lewis-McQuinn site produced few stone tools for analysis but provides a debitage assemblage for comparative purposes (Table 10.6). The age of the Lewis-McQuinn Paleoindian level is uncertain but appears to represent either a Middle or Early Paleoindian time frame. Lithic artifacts from the Dunnigans Old Mill site represent an insignificant sample of lithic specimens for comparative purposes and are not considered here.

Both the *in situ* as well as the displaced artifacts from the Norden site are considered because they appear to be distinctly Paleoindian. This assumption is supported by the recovery of a similar but smaller sample collected in context from two test units. Also, there is little evidence of contamination by younger artifacts in the deflated part of the Norden site that was surface collected. The only post-Paleoindian artifacts collected were one Early Archaic and two Middle Archaic stemmed points. Although there may be other, perhaps less diagnostic, post-Paleoindian artifacts from the surface collection at the Norden site, we believe there has been minimal contamination. Elsewhere, within the larger upland boundaries of the Norden site, Early and Middle Archaic biface and uniface artifacts are common, and the signature of Paleoindian diagnostics, although present, is diffuse.

Lithic artifacts were present but scarce at Dunnigans Old Mill. The only stone tools recovered from the excavation units were a fragment of hammerstone and a graver spur on a flake (the graver spur is now missing from the collection). All other specimens were debitage.

Biface Tools

A fluted Suwannee preform and an earlier-stage lanceolate paleo-preform were recovered from context at the Ryan-Harley site, along with a preform tip and a biface fragment (Table 10.7). All other Suwannee points and preforms were surface collected within the area of concentrated Suwannee tools. This area was directly adjacent to or on the eroding surface of the Suwannee point level. One of the surface collected points was found in two pieces and refitted together. The refitted point was collected in the vicinity of,

TABLE 10.7. In situ versus surface-collected bifaces (Norden [8Gi40] and Ryan-Harley sites [8Je1004] all accessions).

Bifaces	Gi40 GS Count	Gi40 GS %	Gi40 Count*	Gi40 %*	Je1004 Count*	Je1004 %*	Je1004 GS Count	Je1004 GS %
Waisted Suwannees	4	13%	0	0%	0	0%	3	30%
Suwannee preform (fluted)	0	0%	0	0%	1	20%	0	0%
Notched auriculate base point	1	3%	0	0%	0	0%	0	0%
Greenbriar side notched	1	3%	0	0%	0	0%	0	0%
Bolen beveled	0	0%	0	0%	0	0%	1	10%
Kirk serrated	1	3%	0	0%	0	0%	1	10%
Archaic stemmed	2	6%	0	0%	0	0%	0	0%
Misc. bifaces	7	23%	0	0%	1	20%	0	0%
Lanceolate Paleo-preforms	9	29%	0	0%	1	20%	2	20%
Preform distals	4	13%	0	0%	2	40%	3	30%
Rounded base preforms	1	3%	0	0%	0	0%	0	0%
Dalton adze	1	3%	0	0%	0	0%	0	0%
Total	31	100%	0	100%	5	100%	10	100%

* in situ

if not in, either Test Unit 6 or 7 prior to site testing. The other two Suwannee points, along with the ivory shaft fragment and most of the lanceolate-paleo preforms, were collected from the Test 6–7 area to an area about 10 meters upstream, where most of the Suwannee component had already been deflated by river current. Both of the Early Archaic Bolen Beveled and Kirk Serrated points were surface collected from the deeper water downstream from the test units in a paleo-channel. The Kirk point appeared to be dislodged from channel-fill deposits above the Bolen while a naturally cut bank was being trimmed for profile sketching. The Bolen point was recovered from the interface between the paleo-channel's older channel-cut and younger channel-fill deposits.

No bifaces were collected *in situ* from the Norden site testing. However, the Norden site produced four waisted Suwannee points and nine lanceolate paleo-preforms from displaced contexts, along with the other bifaces listed in Table 10.7.

The Ryan-Harley site seems to differ from the Norden site primarily in having a much greater percentage of bifaces. When analysis data was compiled for the Ryan-Harley assemblage of lithic artifacts, C. Andrew Hemmings astutely observed there was an unusually high number of bifaces and bifacial reduction debitage recovered from the site. If the percentages of three stone tool categories (bifaces, unifaces, and hammerstone–core-abrader)

TABLE 10.8. Occurrence of stone tool categories, general surface and in situ combined (Norden and Ryan-Harley all accessions).

Category of Tool*	Gi40 Count	Gi40 %	Je1004 Count	Je1004 %
Unifaces	340	91%	37	71%
Paleo bifaces	13	3%	10	19%
Hammer-core-abrader	22	6%	5	10%
Total	375	100%	52	100%

* Does not include undiagnostic preforms and notched and stemmed points from displaced contexts.

are calculated for each site and used to evaluate the differences between the samples, it appears that Hemmings is correct (Table 10.8). The Norden site included about 3 percent bifaces versus 19 percent bifaces for the Ryan-Harley site. Conversely, looking at all debitage with striking platforms, the Norden site yielded 22 percent of the bifacial-thinning ground-platform flakes, while the Ryan-Harley site yielded only 7 percent of the total from the sites. The Lewis-McQuinn site produced 32 percent of the bifacial-thinning ground-platform flakes, which is more in line with the totals from the Norden site. A possible reason for these differences will be discussed in more detail in the section on debitage.

The assemblage of bifaces from the Ryan-Harley site suggests there was a considerable amount of biface manufacturing taking place at least within the area tested. The waisted Suwannee points from the site are complete specimens, even though one was recovered in two pieces that refit. Although possible, the broken specimen from Ryan-Harley does not appear to have failed due to postmanufacture use. Thus, there are no identifiable projectile fragments from Ryan-Harley suggesting failure due to use, and only one of the waisted Suwannee points appears to have been resharpened after manufacture.

On the other hand, the Norden site yielded preforms at various stages of manufacture, finished points, and at least two fragmentary waisted Suwannee points displaying heavy impact damage resulting from their use as projectile points. The severity of the impact damage on the Norden site specimens is remarkably similar to the type of heavy damage often found on waisted Clovis specimens from Florida (Dunbar and Hemmings 2004). Similar impact damage to a waisted Clovis point is also evident on the specimen recovered from the bison kill area of the Murray Springs site in

TABLE 10.9. In situ versus surface-collected uniface tools (Norden, Ryan-Harley, and Lewis-McQuinn all accessions).

Uniface Tools	**Gi40 Count***	**Gi40 %***	**Gi40 GS Count**	**Gi40 GS %**	**Je1004 Count***	**Je1004 %***	**Je1004 GS Count**	**Je1004 GS %**	**Di112 Count***	**Di112 %***	**Di112 GS Count**	**Di112 GS %**
End scraper	1	25%	35	10%	1	6%	0	0%	1	20%	0	0%
Turtleback scrapers, small	0	0%	34	10%	3	18%	2	10%	0	0%	0	0%
Small rectangular scrapers	0	0%	2	1%	0	0%	0	0%	0	0%	0	0%
Oval scrapers	0	0%	6	2%	3	18%	2	10%	0	0%	1	50%
Scrapers	0	0%	37	11%	1	6%	7	35%	1	20%	0	0%
Thumbnail scrapers	0	0%	10	3%	1	6%	0	0%	0	0%	0	0%
Beveled-edged scrapers	0	0%	3	1%	0	0%	0	0%	0	0%	0	0%
Hendrix scraper	0	0%	0	0%	0	0%	0	0%	0	0%	1	50%
Large scraper-choppers	0	0%	2	1%	0	0%	1	5%	0	0%	0	0%
Small gravers (w/ 23 spurs)	2	50%	19	6%	0	0%	0	0%	1	20%	0	0%
Large Gravers	0	0%	3	1%	0	0%	0	0%	0	0%	0	0%
Spokeshaves on random flakes	0	0%	5	1%	0	0%	0	0%	1	20%	0	0%
Beaked tools	0	0%	2	1%	0	0%	0	0%	0	0%	0	0%
Wedge-shaped tools	0	0%	2	1%	0	0%	2	10%	0	0%	0	0%
Worked-utilized blades	0	0%	6	2%	1	6%	1	5%	0	0%	0	0%
Utilized flakes	1	25%	170	51%	7	41%	5	25%	1	20%	0	0%
Total	4	100.0%	336	100.0%	17	100%	20	100%	5	100%	2	100%

* in situ

Arizona (Haynes 1982:387, figure 3). If similarities such as the occurrence of heavy impact fractures represent permissible evidence, then the Norden site waisted Suwannee points add to the notion that they are genetically related to waisted Clovis.

Uniface Tools

A total of 384 uniface tools were collected from the Norden, Ryan-Harley, and Lewis-McQuinn sites (Table 10.9). Most of the uniface tools were surface-collected specimens (93 percent). The Norden site not only produced most of the specimens (88 percent), it also produced the majority of surface-collected finds (87 percent) compared to the other two sites. Four uniface tools have been recovered from context at the Norden site, which accounts for only 1 percent of the uniface tools recovered from the site. The small number of uniface tools recovered from context at the Norden site is directly related to the lack of substantial subsurface testing at the site. The combined area of both test units at the Norden site was less than three-quarters of a square meter, but yielded a total of 83 bone and lithic specimens. Conversely, about half the specimens from the Ryan-Harley site were recovered from context within a seven-square-meter test area.

Uniface tools that commonly occur include end scrapers on blade-shaped flakes and flakes, both medium-size and small ovate scrapers (turtlebacks), scrapers of various configurations, and utilized flakes and blade-shaped flakes. Gravers have not been accounted for at the Ryan-Harley site but have been recovered in context from the other three sites. Spokeshaves on random flakes are similarly present at the Norden and Lewis-McQuinn sites, but none have been recovered from Ryan-Harley. The Norden site has produced an assemblage of uniface tools that for now are unique to that site. The most notable of these are beveled-edge scrapers that are beveled on one side or, in one instance, opposite-beveled. The beveled scrapers are made on flakes or flake fragments that have a relatively uniform thickness of about 1 centimeter (Figure 10.8). Other interesting tools include the small rectangular scrapers, which may be some type of variation of the turtleback scraper, and the beaked tools (see Figure 10.8).

Debitage

The Norden site produced the highest counts of debitage (n = 596), followed by Ryan-Harley (n = 174) and Lewis-McQuinn (n = 76). Four methods of platform preparation were identified on the inventory of complete and proximal

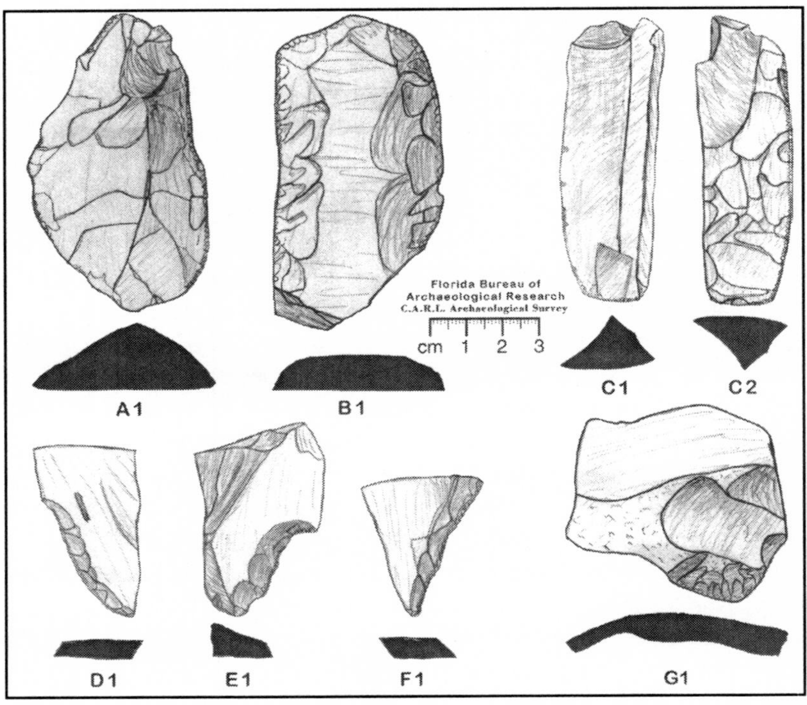

FIGURE 10.8. Selected uniface tools from the Norden site.

end debitage recovered from each site. The debitage from the Ryan-Harley and Lewis-McQuinn sites was recovered *in situ*, while most of the platform debitage from the Norden site was from displaced context but within the area of concentrated Paleoindian tools. Admittedly, the number of platform flakes from Lewis-McQuinn is small. Recognized platform types include:

- No platform preparation—where no attempt was made to alter the striking surface of the material being knapped;
- Back-flaked platform—where the platform was prepared by small back-flake removals that were done either toward or away from the direction of the subsequent flake detachment;
- Back-flaked and ground platform—where the platform was prepared first by back flaking and then ground by an abrader, and;
- Ground platform—where the method of platform preparation was by grinding with an abrader, and there was no evidence of prior back-flaking.

The percentages of the different platform types are fairly uniform for the Norden and Lewis-McQuinn sites (Table 10.10). The Ryan-Harley site differs considerably, especially in having the lowest occurrence of ground-platform flakes versus highest percentage of back-flaked platforms. It is likely that there is a mechanical reason for these differences related to the quality of lithic resources available in the Santa Fe–Suwannee area versus the Aucilla-Wacissa area. The Norden site is located in the heart of the old land-pebble phosphate district of Florida. Here, geologists were quick to realize that the phosphate beds were also a source of residual Eocene and Oligocene chert. Today, these chert-bearing sediments are included under the Hawthorne Group (Scott et al. 2001), but were formerly referred to as the Alachua Formation (Puri et al. 1967; Vernon 1951). Vernon (1951:191–192) offers a good description of the chert:

> Silicified limestone and flint boulders occur in many of the abandoned phosphate pits in Citrus and Levy counties and occur in all degrees of consolidation from a very porous and friable silicified coquina of foraminifers to dense, crystalline, completely silicified, flint boulders. The silicified limestone is yellow to brown and the flint may be yellow, white and light blue. These boulders are a nuisance in mining phosphate as they are intimately mixed in the ore and must be eliminated, often a selective job of hand picking.

The chert-bearing sediment of the Hawthorne Group is mapped in the Norden site area (Puri et al. 1967), and phosphate and silicified phosphate nodules, along with a variety of chert grades, have been recovered from the site. The sometimes good to excellent quality microcrystalline chert, associated with the so-called Alachua Formation and now subsumed in the Hawthorne Group, was a significant and sought-after prehistoric resource. This chert resource can be found in the Santa Fe River basin and the surrounding karst lowlands. Of particular interest are ovoid and round nodules of Suwannee Limestone formation chert (hereafter referred to as Suwannee chert) that are of good knapping quality. The chert tends to be both homogenous and fine grained. The Lewis-McQuinn site in the lower Suwannee River basin is also located in the area of Hawthorne Group chert outcrops. Ryan-Harley and other sites in the Wacissa and Aucilla river basins are considerably west of any chert-bearing Hawthorne Group outcrops. Nevertheless, the Aucilla-Wacissa area is located in one of the state's major prehistoric quarry areas, where plentiful Suwannee chert is avail-

TABLE 10.10. Comparison of striking platform preparation.

Site	No Platform Preparation		Back-Flaked Platform		Back-Flaked and Ground Platform		Ground Platform	
Norden	55	19%	120	41%	53	18%	66	22%
Ryan-Harley	17	23%	37	50%	15	20%	5	7%
Lewis-McQuinn	5	18%	9	32%	5	18%	9	32%

able (Upchurch et al. 1982). The primary difference between the Santa Fe–Suwannee and Aucilla-Wacissa chert appears to be one of knapping quality. Bifaces of vitreous, fine-grained chert are more likely to have been ground in preparation for bifacial thinning, in contrast to those of medium- or varied-grained chert, which were more likely to be back flaked for bifacial thinning. It is also possible that complete or partial platform failures obscure evidence of grinding more frequently on medium- or varied-grained chert than on homogenous, fine-grained chert.

The Suwannee chert in the Aucilla-Wacissa area tends to have concretionary bands that vary in grain size but are otherwise homogenous, or that are riddled with voids and unincorporated fossil inclusions. This is not to say that fine-grained chert does not exist in the Aucilla-Wacissa basins, but that it is less common. In the Santa Fe–Suwannee area, nodules of dense, vitreous to semivitreous, black, gray-blue, and light gray chert are not uncommon, and one outcrop location near High Springs is known to modern flint knappers as a place to go for black "flint" (Patton, personal communication 1999).

Claude VanOrder, one of Florida's finest present-day knappers, was given five large flakes or blanks of Wacissa Cannonball chert. His challenge was to manufacture replica waisted Clovis points in order to conduct utilization experiments. Because Paleoindians did not pretreat the blanks by thermal alteration, he was asked to knap the pieces from unaltered chert. Three of the five production blanks failed due to breakage, but the two that were successfully finished eventually proved to be tough and resistant to breakage.

It is possible that the structure of the stone in the Aucilla-Wacissa area represented a greater challenge to the Paleoindian peoples attempting to bifacially reduce blanks to points. Certainly the scarcity of ground platform flakes versus the abundance of back-flaked platform flakes from the Ryan-Harley site is almost the inverse of similar debitage counts from the Norden and Lewis-McQuinn sites. The proposed difference in workability of the chert from the Aucilla and Wacissa river area versus the fine-grained

TABLE 10.11. Stone artifacts by lithographic grade of the chert.

Type of Lithic Artifact	Grade I	Grade II	Grade III
Hammerstones	0	3	3
Abraders	0	0	2
Cores	2	3	2
Lanceolate preforms	2	6	0
Rounded base preforms	1	1	0
Distal ends	4	0	0
Misc. bifaces	2	3	0
Suwannee	4	0	0
Dalton-like adze	0	1	0
Turtleback scrapers	17	15	0
Ovate scrapers	3	3	0
Thumbnail scrapers	5	4	0
Scrapers/random flakes	5	21	2
End scrapers	11	15	0
Beveled-edged scrapers	2	1	0
Spokeshaves	1	4	0
Small gravers	8	10	0
Large gravers	0	2	0
Wedge-shaped tools	0	2	0
Utilized flakes	56	58	3
Worked-utilized blades	2	4	0
Beaked tools	0	2	0
Debitage	198	212	16
Total	**323**	**370**	**28**

chert from the Santa Fe and lower Suwannee river area is a likely scenario. This scenario bears further testing but is also supported by data from the Norden site, where most of the lanceolate paleo-preform failures occur on inferior-grade chert (Table 10.11).

Bone Artifacts

The most interesting bone tool from the Ryan-Harley site is a fragment of ivory shaft or foreshaft recovered from eroded context, adjacent to the in-

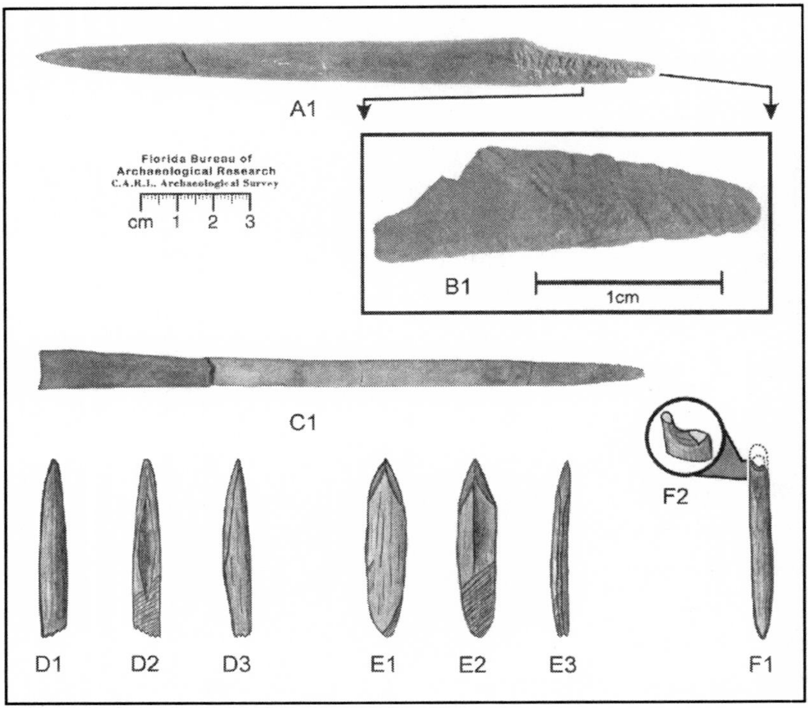

FIGURE 10.9. Bone and ivory tools.

place component (Figure 10.9). It is quite possible that it originated from the Suwannee point component. Although the ivory shaft fragment was recovered from displaced context and might represent Clovis, there is no identifiable Clovis component at the site, and the stratigraphy suggests that the site area had been inundated prior to the Suwannee occupation (Hemmings 2004; Balsillie et al. 2006). In addition, the ivory shaft fragment was collected inside the concentrated area of surface-collected Suwannee tools directly adjacent to the *in situ* remains.

In Florida, the typical Paleoindian shafts, foreshafts, or rods, as they have been referred to interchangeably, are made of ivory (Dunbar and Webb 1996:340), although elsewhere in North America they are just as likely to be made of thick-walled bone (Lahren and Bonnichsen 1974:147–150). The typical ivory shaft is almost perfectly round in cross section, tapers to a point on the distal end, and has been obliquely truncated and basally roughened on the proximal end to facilitate hafting. The terms "proximal" and "distal" may be somewhat misused in this case because there are at least two hypotheses about the use of shafts as part of Paleoindian weaponry. Some researchers believe the shafts were used as osseous projectile points, with the pointed end used as the impacting projectile tip (Guthrie 1983:273–294). Other researchers believe they were used as spear foreshafts, with the pointed end fit into a socket on the end of the spear shaft, while the obliquely truncated, hafting end held a Clovis point as the impacting projectile tip (Tankersley 1994a, 1994b; Lahren and Bonnichsen 1974).

At the Norden site, small bone pins or points were recovered that are similar to the Ryan-Harley site ivory shaft, in that the hafting end was obliquely truncated to form the hafting platform or bevel (see Figure 10.9). The hafting platforms on the smaller bone specimens from the Norden site as well as the larger ivory specimen from the Ryan-Harley site are basally roughened to facilitate hafting. However, the Norden site bone pins were manufactured from deer-size long-bone elements, which is a characteristic of bone tool assemblages after the late Pleistocene megafauna died out. After the megafauna extinction, the thick-walled bone necessary for large-size bone tool production was no longer available. Besides bone pins, the Norden site also yielded an eyed bone needle indicative of some type of sewing technology. Obliquely truncated, basally roughened bone pins as well as eyed bone needles have also been recovered in Early Archaic context in Florida at the Page-Ladson site in the Aucilla River (Dunbar et al. 1989) and at the Warm Mineral Springs site near Venice, Florida (Cockrell and Murphy 1978). In addition, bone needles are known to occur in Paleoindian context elsewhere in North America (Gramley 1992:39). Although not necessarily diagnostic, the dual occurrence of artifacts such as eyed bone needles and common artifact attributes such as the same type of hafting platform in both the Paleoindian and Early Archaic bone tool assemblages represents yet another indication of in-place cultural development and continuity.

A bone projectile point recovered in four pieces came from the Dunnigans Old Mill test units (see Figure 10.9). Three of the pieces were touching one another, and the breaks between them appear to have resulted from post-depositional, old bone breakage. The fourth proximal end piece was recovered from another test unit. This fragment fits onto the proximal-most end of the other three, and, pieced together, all four form a complete artifact. The break on the proximal end appears to have resulted from a longitudinal, green bone fracture and indicates failure due to a thrusting or head-on impact. The green bone fracture at the proximal end suggests the point functioned as a projectile or stabbing weapon. The bone point is unlike the "typical" osseous shaft or foreshaft in that it was manufactured from deer-size long bone and not from megafauna-size bone or ivory. The Dunnigans Old Mill bone point is also unlike the bone pins and eyed bone needle recovered from the Norden site (see Figure 10.9).

In many respects, the Dunnigans Old Mill bone point resembles a single-pointed type on one end and a blunt-ended type on the other end, similar to those found on younger sites. There are only so many ways one can fashion a bone point or pin when using the splinter-groove technique, and, as a result, there are seldom any distinguishing morphological features. Perhaps the one unusual feature of the Dunnigans Old Mill specimen is how the point was finished. Once the bone splinter had been burin cut and removed from the long bone, a point was fashioned on one end while the other end was left flat. The point was honed down on its dorsal and ventral surfaces but not along its laterals, thereby leaving part of the original burin cuts intact. In contrast, a sample of 923 Archaic or later bipointed and single-pointed bone pins recovered from the Little River Rapids site (8JE603) had been honed smooth around their circumferences (Willis 1988:467). This latter type of finishing seldom leaves any traces of the original burin cuts. This difference in manufacture finishing prior to utilization may or may not prove to be indicative of a Paleoindian origin, but is worthy of note.

Discussion

The general faunal evidence from the Ryan-Harley and Lewis McQuinn sites indicates that wetland resources, including fish, turtles, alligators, and birds, were perhaps as heavily relied upon as mammals as sources of food. However, the evidence from the Dunnigans Old Mill site and possibly the Norden site may reflect Paleoindian camps dominated by mixed large-mammal remains. This latter conclusion remains uncertain, however, due to the extreme biases inherent in the samples thus far collected from the two sites.

The Late Paleoindian Dust Cave site in Alabama (Walker 1998) produced surprisingly large numbers of migratory birds, along with mammals, reptiles, fish, and amphibians. At Modoc Rock Shelter in Missouri (Styles et al. 1983), small mammals dominated the faunal assemblage during the Early Archaic, with the subsequent increase in the utilization of fish. The use of fine screening in both cases helped to clarify the diversity in the assemblages. At Ryan-Harley, mammals and reptiles dominate the assemblage, although fish and birds are present in significant quantities. The testing accomplished at Ryan-Harley was aimed at salvaging that part of the Suwannee-age site component threatened by river current down cutting. This effort utilized a surface screen with a 1/8-inch mesh. Such a large screen mesh may have skewed the counts of the small fauna present, particularly fish. An additional soil sample collected after the initial salvage effort confirms this; however, additional testing is needed to clarify the results.

Pleistocene muskrat, tapir, and horse remains were recovered from context at the Ryan-Harley site. In addition, the ivory shaft fragment recovered from displaced context is from a mastodon. The remains of other species that were recovered from displaced context at Ryan-Harley include giant tortoise, *Paramylodon* (sloth), and giant armadillo. The mastodon and giant armadillo remains were particularly convincing as candidates probably originating from the Suwannee component because they were recovered within the concentration of displaced Suwannee artifacts (Dunbar et al. 2005). At the Norden site, minimal testing has yielded ungulate and other large-mammal bone most likely representing horse and/or bison. At the Dunnigans Old Mill site, both bison and horse are represented, along with many other unidentifiable specimens of large-mammal bone. At Lewis-McQuinn, a long-bone fragment of proboscidean or comparable very large mammal was recovered in context from Level 1.

Perhaps the most important implication of the fauna assemblages is that both the Ryan-Harley site and the Norden site have yielded Pleistocene species that appear to have survived beyond the Younger Dryas boundary ca. 11,000 BP. This means there was no devastation of Pleistocene species prior to the onset of the Younger Dryas in the southeastern United States (Dunbar et al. 2005) as there was in the desert Southwest (Fiedel 1999b; Haynes et al. 1999; Haynes 2006). Consequently, there may be reason for the waisted Suwannee to reflect a greater continuity between it and waisted Clovis than a comparison of the Clovis to Folsom sequence out west.

Another important aspect of the fauna assemblage is the diversity of small and medium-size wetland animal species. The data presented here is preliminary in the sense that none of the sites has been extensively tested; however, many of the species represented reflect a range of different-size fauna from a variety of habitats. All of the sites have yielded the remains of reptiles, especially turtles as well as birds and mammals, notably deer. Three of the sites have yielded the remains of fish and two of the sites the remains of American alligator. Although large mammals appear to dominate the Dunnigans Old Mill assemblage, preservation and the lack of screening may have biased that sample. Certainly fish, reptiles, and birds are present, and the impact-fractured bone point suggests a possible capture method. The small bone pins from the Norden site may represent barbs or points. Small fauna from the Norden site included the remains of a turtle, medium-size bird, and river otter, none of which were likely to have been taken by the hunting tackle associated with waisted Suwannee points. The turtle may have been captured by hand, but the other small animals were likely captured by another technique involving some type of lighter hunting tackle that included bone points made from deer-size long bone.

In *The Foraging Spectrum* (1995), Robert Kelly cautions archaeologists not to expect or to make one-to-one correlations between living hunter-gatherer societies and those of the distant past. We do not attempt to do so here; rather, we provide an example of the diversity in hunting tackle used by modern Hadza males of Tanzania, East Africa. The Hadza are among the last big-game hunting, hunter-gather cultures of the world. Hadza males use bows and arrows for hunting. Big-game hunting is accomplished with the use of poison on metal-tipped arrowheads. For medium-size game, smaller, nonpoison metal arrowheads are used. Finally, for birds, hyrax, and other small game, the Hadza use a variety of nonpoison wooden arrowheads with barbs and occasional harpoon heads, which detach to slow the animal (Woodburn 1970:17–31). The argument here is that there is no reason to believe that the American Paleoindians were myopic about animal capture methods. Certainly, both the fauna and the artifact assemblages of at least the Middle Paleoindian waisted Suwannee point makers indicate multiple capture methods and technology.

Smaller, fur-bearing animals were recovered from the Ryan-Harley, Norden, and Lewis-McQuinn sites. The Norden site yielded the remains of the diurnal river otter. However, the other two sites yielded the remains of nocturnal furbearers. Although there is no evidence in the artifact record for trap-setting technology as a means of small-animal capture, the evidence presented here suggests the possibility is likely. In addition, if trap setting took place, it is likely to have become archaeologically invisible. However, because at least five fur-bearing, nocturnal animals were recovered from the small areas tested at the Ryan-Harley site, these animals seem to have somehow been important. By present American standards, mink does not seem like it would be a prized protein source. Not only is there a small amount of meat, but mink also emit "a fetid discharge from the anal glands, which is at least as malodorous as a skunk's, although it does not carry as far" (Whitaker 1992:579). Muskrats, although edible, should be prepared carefully. In the wild game preparation section, the *Woman's Day Encyclopedia of Cookery #5* includes some of the following steps for the preparation of "Maryland Muskrat" (Tighe 1966:769):

1. Carefully remove the musk sacks without breaking them and the two kernels along the back.

2. Cure by hanging cleaned carcass in air for several days.

3. Parboil for two hours in brine-water with cut onions and bay leaf.

4. Then bake in oven with other ingredients until tender.

Thus, at least two of the small fur-bearing animals likely took extra care in processing, assuming their meat was used as a source of protein. If not too ethnocentric, the difficulty with food preparation might provide evidence of a different primary use, which brings us back to the idea of fur pelts. Finally, the eyed bone needle from the Norden site further suggests that Paleoindians had the means to stitch hides with cordage for clothing and blankets or, possibly, the production of entanglement netting for traps.

The Ryan-Harley and Norden sites produced superb samples of Suwannee-age bone and stone tools. Because of the similarities of tool kits, both sites are assumed to be Middle Paleoindian, with the Ryan-Harley site more likely to be on the early end and the Norden site more likely to be on the later end of that time frame. The artifact assemblages from Ryan-Harley and Norden are similar, even though most of the sample from the Norden site came from displaced contexts in the river adjacent to the *in situ* component. Both collections include waisted Suwannee points. Those from the Ryan-Harley site include overshot flaking and fluting, while those from the Norden site may be associated with an early notched point having Suwannee-like traits and a solitary Dalton-like adze.

The lithic assemblage from the Ryan-Harley site and most of the lithics from the Norden site include a proliferation of unifacial tools that are distinctly different from the subsequent Late Paleoindian Dalton-Hardaway-Greenbriar as well as Early Archaic Bolen–Big Sandy projectile point makers. Whereas uniface triangular and notched forms designed for basal hafting as well as Dalton-like adzes occur with frequency in the Late Paleoindian and Early Archaic period (Goodyear 1974; Purdy 1981), they appear only to show up rarely at the Norden site. There are also some traits of the waisted Suwannee point, including occasional fluting, overshot flaking, impact fracture patterns from use, and hafting area attributes, that are waisted Clovis-like. Waisted Suwannee and Clovis points often display heavy impact fractures. An impact-fractured waisted Clovis point was recovered from the bison kill area at Murray Springs, Arizona; its tip was recovered over 100 meters away at the hunter's camp (Haynes 1982). The skull cap with horn cores and other elements of a *Bison antiquus* dating to ca. 11,000 BP was recovered from the Wacissa River a little less than nine kilometers north of the Ryan-Harley site. The most interesting feature of this find was an impact-fractured projectile point tip lodged in the frontal bone between the horn cores (Webb et al. 1984:384–392). The Ryan-Harley, Norden, and Dunnigans Old Mill sites have produced in-place ungulate remains. The Ryan-Harley site yielded a fluted Suwannee preform from the Suwannee component as well as three waisted Suwannee points in the area of concentrated Suwannee artifacts deflated by recent river action. Likewise, the Norden site has produced a concentration of waisted Suwannee points and lanceolate preforms, and previous recoveries at Dunnigans Old Mill also included Suwannee points from displaced context. The evidence is rather compelling that large game was being taken, but it was not the only game to be exploited.

In some ways, the Suwannee uniface tools are most similar to the waisted Clovis assemblage. The Suwannee assemblage includes a variety of well-made oval, round, and oblong scrapers; thick-nosed end scrapers; gravers of various sizes; conical blade-flake cores; thumbnail scrapers; burins; wedges; beveled flake tools; and a variety of carefully retouched flake tools.

The contrast between the exploitation of mammals for subsistence versus the exploitation of diversified terrestrial and wetland faunas is significant and may indicate technological adaptability and flexibility dependent on the species and resources available in the area settled as well as the season and the need for certain animal by-products, such as furs, skins, bone for tools, and so forth; or that some sites are chronologically separated and therefore reflect an evolutionary continuum of adaptations to late glacial climate and habitat change; or that cultural diversification had already taken place by the Early or Middle Paleoindian time frame and that differentiation of cultural groups had taken place in such a way that they coexisted in time and perhaps space but exploited different food sources.

Whichever scenario best explains the assemblage of faunal remains at these sites, all of the sites have mixed assemblages, albeit to different degrees. At Dunnigans Old Mill and perhaps Norden, the fauna appears to be dominated by large mammals. These mammal-dominated sites appear to represent activities that are focused more toward specialized foraging. At Ryan-Harley, the activities appear to be more generalized, as fish, reptiles, and birds figure prominently along with large and small mammals, including extinct late Pleistocene species. The analysis of the Level 1 fauna from the Lewis-McQuinn site also shows more of a generalized pattern. Perhaps a conservative view of this data would place all of the sites into a Middle Paleoindian context because none of them fit a big-game-hunting-only paradigm. That is to say, sites like Dunnigans Old Mill and Norden have too many smaller mammals, and still more diverse sites like Ryan-Harley and Lewis-McQuinn include animals that walked, swam, crawled, or flew. The faunal assemblages suggest a greater technological diversity than is readily apparent from the surviving artifact assemblages or that has been generally attributed to known Paleoindian occupations of Suwannee, Clovis, or beyond.

Another important aspect of the faunal assemblages from all of the sites is that all include extinct Pleistocene species. Continuing with the concept of a conservative view, the standard suggesting when and where Pleistocene megamammals became extinct, like the big-game hunting paradigm, originated from research focused on the desert Southwest. Most recently, the extinction date for mammoths and other Pleistocene species has been set during the later Allerød between ca. 11,500 to ca. 11,000 BP. In the desert Southwest, this is the time of the Clovis drought (Haynes et al. 1999). Thus, by the onset of the Younger Dryas at ca. 11,000 BP, Pleistocene megafauna is believed to have already become extinct in the Southwest (Fiedel 1999b; Haynes 2006).

The evidence from Florida is that no such drought affected the Southeast until the end of the Younger Dryas at ca. 10,000 BP, but that drying conditions began at ca. 10,400 BP during the warm (glacial recession) phase of the Younger Dryas (Dunbar 2002; Dunbar 2006a,b,c). Thus, our view is that all of the Florida sites date no later than the cold phase of the Younger Dryas between ca. 11,000 and ca. 10,400 BP and that the Dunnigans Old Mill and Lewis-McQuinn sites may or may not date before the onset of the Younger Dryas. The apparent significance is that Pleistocene megafauna survived beyond the Allerød boundary into the Younger Dryas in the southeastern United States, and that Suwannee point makers, who we believe to be post-Clovis offspring, not only relied on megamammals but various other species as well. The need for furs and other necessities appear to have made this essential.

Based on the faunal assemblages from the Ryan-Harley, Norden, Lewis-McQuinn, and Dunnigans Old Mill sites, the notion that Paleoindian peoples in Florida were solely devoted to big-game hunting of megamammals is not correct. Nor is it correct that Paleoindian peoples were solely focused on medium-size and small, mostly modern (extant) game; rather, they had varied hunting strategies that included large, medium-size, and small animals. The faunal assemblage also includes nocturnal fur-bearing animals, which suggests that Paleoindians utilized alternative means of capture, such as traps or snares, even though the artifactual evidence for either technique has not been found or preserved. Finally, the Paleoindian stone tool technology appears to reflect a degree of flexibility between areas of lithic materials of differing quality.

We leave unresolved the question as to whether the Dunnigans Old Mill and Lewis-McQuinn sites represent the Middle or Early Paleoindian time frame but suggest that the Ryan-Harley and Norden sites do. Therefore, for the first time in the extreme southeastern United States, there are several Paleoindian sites that share a potential to provide additional and more persuasive research data.

ELEVEN

Ethnography, Analogy, and the Reconstruction of Paleoindian Lifeways

Asa R. Randall and Kandace D. Hollenbach

Interpretation of the material record left behind by Paleoindian peoples living in North America is difficult at best. Subsistence remains are rarely recovered, organic tools have long since disappeared, and low population densities leave only scatters of artifacts. Those materials that are recovered present their own difficulties as we try to understand how Paleoindians made, used, and discarded them. Archaeologists have long recognized that there are no direct analogues for late Pleistocene foragers (Wilmsen 1970). The reasons for this are clear: no ethnographically documented group has shared similar environments, technological traditions, or demographic parameters with these early hunter-gatherers.

Rather than being hampered by the inadequacies of an imperfect record, archaeologists have the capabilities to more fully address the diversity in hunter-gatherer lifeways, given the time depth of the archaeological record. This diversity is clearly reflected in the essays presented in this volume. While the theme of generalized subsistence strategies recurs throughout this book, so does reference to exploitation of local resources. These local resources are found in settings ranging from the icy corridors of Beringia to karstic northwestern Florida. Certainly these essays demonstrate that there was nothing monolithic or essentialist about Paleoindian lifeways.

In this chapter, we would like to discuss the merits of ethnographic analogy in the study of early hunter-gatherer peoples. First, we outline the two major types of analogies used by archaeologists: direct historical analogies and general comparative analogies. We then look at several approaches to documenting the diversity of hunter-gatherers and how they employ ethnographic analogies. These include middle-range theory, evolutionary ecology, and so-called revisionist perspectives. Finally, we close with some suggestions regarding how these approaches might aid us in pushing our interpretations beyond subsistence strategies and adaptations to understandings of the relationships between Paleoindian peoples and their use of the landscape.

Archaeological Analogy

Analogies are comprised of several distinct elements. These include the two sides of the analogy, the source analogue and the subject analogue. Information about the source is used to infer information about the subject. To validate such inferences, comparisons are made between the source and subject, including comparisons of their similarities, differences, and areas in which their likeness is unknown. Analogies are successful when it can be shown that the commonalities observed between the source and subject can be extended to these unknown contexts (Wylie 1985:93–94). In archaeological analogies, the source is commonly an ethnographically or historically documented group, and the subject the archaeologically described group. (The term "group" is used here to refer to the subject of either ethnographic or archaeological study. As this use of "subject" is confusing in tandem with the "subject side" of analogies, "group" will be used instead.) There are two common types of analogies, and the difference between them lies in how the similarities between the source and subject groups are drawn.

In direct historical analogies, similarities are described in terms of cultural continuity between the source and subject groups (Wylie 1985:70). This continuity is primarily illustrated with material culture, but may also include "geographic origin" (Lyman and O'Brien 2001:312). The reasoning behind the analogy is that because there is continuity between the source and subject in use of material culture, and often also in use of locale, there will be similar continuity in the behaviors associated with that material culture, and perhaps in social structures as well. Archaeologists can then work back from the ethnographically or historically known to the archaeologically unknown. The analogy is further validated by an underlying argument of "descent with modification" (Lyman and O'Brien 2001). The archaeological subject is held to be the predecessor of the ethnographic source, whether described in cultural, ethnic, or genetic terms (Lyman and O'Brien 2001; Wylie 1985:70). The argument follows, then, that the cultural traits of the ethnographic group were passed down from their archaeological predecessors, allowing for some change through time (Lyman and O'Brien 2001).

Direct historic analogues cannot always be found, however, and such analogies are difficult to apply past the late prehistoric periods, when material cultures and subsistence bases are markedly different from those of historic groups. In these cases, general comparative analogies must be used. In these analogies, source and subject groups are linked by use of similar subsistence strategies, often in comparable ecological settings (Lyman and O'Brien 2001:325–326; Wylie 1985:71). Use of similar artifacts in similar subsistence and perhaps environmental frameworks is extended to infer similar behaviors among the source and subject groups.

General comparative analogies can be further distinguished along a continuum, ranging from formal to relational analogies. In formal analogies, lists of attributes are simply compared between the source and subject groups; further similarities between the two are inferred because they share some number of cultural traits (Wylie 1985:94). The strength of these analogies lies primarily in the number of similarities that the source and subject share. They can be further strengthened by increasing the number and range of sources used.

On the other end of the spectrum, relations among these traits, not simply their presence or absence, are considered. These relations may be contingent, functional, or causal. "At their strongest, relational comparisons involve a demonstration that there are similarities between source and subject with respect to the causal mechanisms, processes, or factors that determine the presence and interrelationships of (at least some of) their manifest properties" (Wylie 1985:95). Thus, if functional or causal relations hold between certain artifact sets and an associated set of behaviors observed among source groups, then such behaviors may be inferred among subject groups who display similar artifact categories.

Perspectives on Hunter-Gatherer Analogues

Recognizing that direct historic analogues are not available for the vast majority of the prehistoric record, archaeologists commonly use general comparative analogies in their studies of hunter-gatherer groups. These are typically employed within the framework of middle-range theory. However, perspectives from anthropological studies of hunter-gatherers, particularly from evolutionary ecology and "revisionist" analyses, show particular promise for elucidating lifeways of Paleoindian hunter-gatherers.

Given the diversity of hunter-gatherers, both in the past and present, it is worthwhile to briefly consider who exactly hunter-gatherers are. Is there something inherent in food procurement strategies that links behavioral responses? What is the linkage, if any, between environment, social structure, and technological practice? The literature on ethnographically documented hunter-gatherers reveals that archaeologists are not the only scholars who have struggled with understanding the diversity of hunter-gatherer lifeways. Hunter-gatherers have been viewed as evolutionary throwbacks (Lee and Daly 1999), primitive communists (Lee 1988), optimal foragers (Hames and Vickers 1982), and resisters of dominant traditions (Sassaman 2001).

Lee and Daly (1999:3–5) have noted several core features that most hunter-gatherers are supposed to exhibit: they are organized into small bands related by kinship; they are egalitarian; they are typically mobile and often have periods of dispersion and aggregation; they have common property; and sharing and generalized reciprocity is a central tenet of intergroup and interpersonal interaction. Kelly (1995) notes, however, that there are significant variations on this theme. While hunter-gatherer studies have long been of interest to anthropology (Barnard 1999; Kelly 1995; Lee 1992), it has only been in the last several decades that attempts at documenting this diversity have come to the forefront.

Ethnographic studies are of prime importance in forcing archaeologists to recognize the multitude of sources of variation in the archaeological record. In particular, the full range of human variation, from technological practice to identity maintenance and meaning making, is writ large in ethnographic fieldwork. It is important, then, to recognize not only how analogical reasoning is organized within interpretive frameworks but also how the diversity of hunter-gatherer lifeways can be brought to bear on the Paleoindian residues. Below we discuss how three perspectives—middle-range theory, evolutionary ecology, and "revisionist" analyses—employ analogy and address diversity, and we suggest ways these perspectives can be used to elucidate the Paleoindian hunter-gatherer record.

Middle-Range Theory

The main thrust of middle-range theory is to bridge the gap between the static archaeological record and the dynamic behaviors that produced that record (Binford 1980; Johnson 1999). Archaeologists develop bridging arguments by observing how artifacts and/or assemblages are made, modified, discarded, and disturbed in the present. Attributes of these artifacts and assemblages that can be directly related to the observed behaviors are identified, and then searched for in the archaeological subject. A functional comparative analogy is thus drawn: if the source and subject artifacts share similar attributes, and these attributes were a function of the behaviors that produced them in the source, then these attributes were likely produced by similar behaviors in the archaeological subject.

While source materials can include ethnographies and historical accounts, sociocultural anthropologists and historians have often focused on nonmaterial aspects of culture. Accordingly, archaeologists often perform their own ethnographic (or ethnoarchaeological) fieldwork or develop controlled experiments to serve as sources for comparison (Gumerman and Phillips 1978).

Ethnoarchaeological research has been key to developing functional relations between artifacts and behaviors (e.g., Gamble and Boismier 1991). Binford's observations of Inuit peoples (e.g., Binford 1978a, 1978b, 1979) and Australian aborigines (e.g., Binford 1986) are among the most well known of these studies. From these, Binford developed useful source material, including relationships between group mobility and the caching and curation of tools and resources (Binford 1979, 1980); how animals are butchered and now various elements of carcasses are selected for transport to base camps for sharing (Binford 1978b); and how stone is acquired and ultimately manufactured into tools (Binford 1986). Ethnoarchaeology is a vibrant area of research, covering a vast array of topics, including how space is used within closed areas such as rock shelters (Gorecki 1991); how plant foods are collected and processed (Jackson 1991; Fritz et al. 2001); and how sites are abandoned (Stevenson 1982, 1985). The activities of living groups, and the material results of these activities, are thus mined for interpretive insight that may be applied to the archaeological record.

Experimental archaeology tends to concentrate not on how particular artifacts or spaces are used by particular groups but instead on processes related to use of a tool, resource, or space that hold constant under particular physical conditions. Examples include the production of cutmarks on bone and examination of the resulting effects on both the bone and the tool used (Reitz and Wing 1999); the use of stone tools on different materials in order to identify wear patterns and polishes (Keeley 1980); the processing of nuts or seeds to determine the by-products and evaluate the efficiency of various techniques (Munson 1984); and the replication of trampling in order to observe its effects on the movement and modification of artifacts (Flenniken and Haggarty 1979; McBrearty et al. 1998). Similar to ethnoarchaeological observations, archaeological experiments describe characteristics of the artifact record as functions of behaviors involved in the manufacture, use, discard, and disturbance of assemblages.

Paleoindian researchers typically employ middle-range theory in two manners. The first is to describe how particular artifacts or assemblages were made or used. For example, through microwear analysis, the manner(s) in which stone or bone tools were used, and the materials upon which they were used, can be determined (e.g., Walker et al. 2001). At the assemblage level, the spatial distribution of artifacts and debitage can be used to delineate activity areas at a site (e.g., Goodyear 1974).

The second manner in which Paleoindian researchers commonly use middle-range theory is to determine where a particular archaeological group falls on Binford's (1980) forager/collector continuum. This continuum distinguishes between peoples who move their residences to be near resources (foragers) and those who move resources to their residences (collectors), neatly wrapping subsistence strategies, settlement systems, and mobility patterns into a single measure. At the assemblage level, whether tools are curated or expedient can be related to collecting and foraging, respectively (e.g., Meltzer and Smith 1986). Level of curation can be coupled with the diversity of tools recovered to suggest whether a site is a base camp or a resource extraction site (e.g., Gardner 1983; Morse 1975). Similar analyses can be performed at the regional scale by comparing assemblages from various sites and thus forming a model of regional lifeways described in terms of foraging and/or collecting strategies (e.g., Cable 1996).

At all levels of analysis, middle-range theory addresses how artifact assemblages are formed, placing them in a behavioral context. The ultimate goal of middle-range theory is to develop these analogies into a set of generalizations that aid archaeological interpretation. The strength of middle-range theory is its focus on functional relations between material culture and the actions and activities that create it. The theory has several weaknesses, however. First, it suffers from the equifinality that plagues most archaeological interpretations; multiple behaviors can lead to the same artifact assemblage. Second, novel situations and processes that cannot be replicated or observed in the present lie beyond the reach of middle-range theory. This can be problematic, given claims that there are no modern analogues for late Pleistocene environments. Third, while middle-range theory can describe how artifacts, assemblages, and sites were created and used, it cannot explain why (Bettinger 1991; Broughton and O'Connell 1999). For such answers, we turn to our remaining two perspectives on hunter-gatherer research.

Evolutionary Ecology

In contrast to middle-range theory's focus on functional relations between artifacts and behaviors, evolutionary ecology searches for causal relations between people and their surroundings, largely by viewing behaviors as evolutionarily adaptive within a particular ecological context (Winterhalder and Smith 1992:3). Both middle-range theory and evolutionary ecology derive from observations of living hunting-and-gathering peoples. Evolutionary ecologists are concerned, however, not with how material culture is formed from these behaviors but with the decisions people made that led to these behaviors. Archaeologists are further interested in the material outcomes of these decisions.

In attempting to ascertain the decisions that individuals make when faced with particular environmental parameters, evolutionary ecologists make two key assumptions. First, they assume that individuals make rational choices within a set of conditions, constraints, preferences, and beliefs (Smith and Winterhalder 1992:45). Using these rational choices, individuals attempt to optimize their performance to achieve some goal. This typically involves either maximizing net returns on energy investments or minimizing risk due to variations in resource structure over time (Smith 1988; Smith and Winterhalder 1992:51), but may also include minimizing time spent in economic pursuits in order to maximize time for social or extracurricular interests (Kelly 1995). Second, evolutionary ecologists assume that selective pressures exist on individual work-effort returns, such that individuals are expected to choose adaptive strategies that maximize their reproductive fitness or their ability to produce viable offspring (Smith and Winterhalder 1992).

The goal of evolutionary ecology is to express these decisions in the form of mathematical models to be used as heuristic devices. As such, models simplify complex processes in order to better define the problem, understand the data, test that understanding, and make further predictions (Winterhalder and Smith 1992:13). Models of adaptive strategies typically take the form of cost-benefit analyses using microeconomic models and detailed studies of available resources (Hames and Vickers 1982; Hawkes et al. 1982), as well as game theory analyses to understand the dynamics of interactions between two or more interested parties (Smith 1988).

In developing useful analogies, then, archaeologists do not look for similarities in the functional attributes of artifacts or assemblages, but instead for similarities in the decisions faced by the source and subject individuals. An important consequence of focusing on decisions, and distilling those decisions into heuristic models, is that it is not necessary for the source and subject groups to share identical environments; the various parameters of the models take into account particular ecological settings. The models are then used to explain aspects of the observed archaeological record.

For Paleoindian researchers, several working theories within evolutionary ecology are useful, both at the site and regional levels, particularly in tackling economic issues. Optimal foraging theory addresses the food items that an individual should hunt or gather, given a particular set of resources and their distribution on the landscape (e.g., Meltzer and Smith 1986; Stiner et al. 2000). Central-place foraging theory concerns the placement of camps and movement between them, with respect to the distribution and seasonal availability of resources (e.g., Bettinger et al. 1997; Cashdan 1992; Zeanah 2000). Other issues include population growth (e.g., Belovsky 1988), group migration (e.g., Kelly and Todd 1988), and demographic trends (Surovell 2000), all of which have been used to address the peopling of the New World. Potential topics that deal directly with social dynamics include sharing (Winterhalder 1990, 1996) and division of labor both by gender and age (Hawkes et al. 1995; Kelly 1995; Panter-Brick 2002; Walker et al. 2002).

While heuristic models make it possible to employ these analogies in environmental settings that lack modern equivalents, such as the late Pleistocene, these models often require detailed environmental data that is difficult to obtain for the Paleoindian period. This demonstrates the need for more fine-grained ecological analyses, such as McWeeney's (this volume) site-based environmental reconstruction in the Northeast. It also pushes archaeologists to be creative with assemblages and landscape data that are currently available (e.g., Anderson and Gillam 2000; Gillam 2002). Despite this weakness, evolutionary ecology highlights salient relationships between foragers and their environment that are useful in developing our understanding, particularly of the economic pursuits, of early hunter-gatherers. With its focus on causal relationships, it is also capable of explaining, rather than simply describing, dynamic processes (Bettinger 1991; Broughton and O'Connell 1999). Furthermore, an evolutionary ecology approach urges us to envision the Paleoindian record as the result of actions and decisions made by individuals.

Alternative Perspectives

Where evolutionary ecology and middle-range theory focus particularly on forager behavior as evolutionarily adaptive (and have made significant inroads within Paleoindian studies), there exists a broad range of literature that to date has found limited exposure within Paleoindian studies. This literature departs from evolutionary ecology and middle-range theory by foregrounding history and social processes, and by approaching hunting and gathering as a distinct way of being that is political and dynamic. Hunting and gathering is not simply what people do, but is a sociality that is always historically situated and forms the basis for identity, cosmology, interaction, mobility, and subsistence practices. A number of important issues are generated that potentially undermine many of the favored assumptions of archaeologists working with hunter-gatherers. It is not our intent here to review all of this literature, as recent syntheses and discussions can be found in Ames (2004), Lee and Daly (1999), and Panter-Brick et al. (2001). Instead, we focus on two main trends that have implications for analogy and Paleo-studies. These approaches can be loosely divided into two camps: "revisionist" or "historicist" perspectives (Ames 2004; Shott 1992), and studies that loosely fit under a blanket of agency or landscape theory and focus on hunter-gatherer technology, mobility, and worldviews.

The historicist perspective stands as a direct critique and rebuttal of evolutionary or behavioral approaches (Ames 2004). The central premise is that hunter-gatherers are not isolated entities, and that their practices today cannot be decoupled from their histories of interaction with nonforaging societies. A consideration of archaeological, ethnographic, and historic data indicates that all ethnographically documented foragers have histories of contact with nonforagers (Layton 2001; Spielmann and Eder 1994). Denbow (1984) suggests that the adaptations of the San and other foragers of the Kalahari are actually the result of at least 1,500 years of interaction with pastoralists. Grinker (1994) has documented the effects of a long history of interdependence between the Lese horticulturalists and Efe foragers. Like the foragers of the Kalahari, the Lese and Efe have been involved in European trade and subjected to economic and physical oppression by state society. As Grinker has documented (1994:130–133), Lese-Efe interactions involve not only economic transactions; the economic categories of "forager" and "farmer" are also encompassing ethnic categories. Hunter-gatherer identity, as it is composed of in daily practice, ritual, and social interaction, is understood in tandem with nonforagers.

The implications of this are that the oft-cited essentialist features of hunter-gatherer existence (i.e., egalitarian relations, flexibility in kinship, sharing, frequent mobility) which often find their way into Paleoindian studies, do not result from purely economic decisions and are not an original evolutionary condition that is timeless (Layton 2001; Rowley-Conwy 2001), but are politically motivated and historically contingent. For example, Woodburn (1988) has argued that modern hunter-gatherer adaptations are more the result of encapsulation and oppression from more powerful societies. Ingold (1999) maintains that they do not represent similar adaptations to environmental parameters, but instead represent an antistructure, or to use Woodburn's (1988:63) term, an "oppositional solidarity," in which the structure of interpersonal relations is built not on dominance, but on trust. Such societies are characterized by resistant traditions (Sassaman 2001) that are employed to maintain an autonomy in the face of "others." This perspective requires that we truly consider the political situatedness of foraging societies. Some suggest that these approaches focus too much on external causation (Lee 1992; Solway and Lee 1990). That is, hunter-gatherer social reproduction and transformation are also products of internal contradictions within these societies. Tensions and unequal power relationships are always present between age sets, kin, genders, and economic partners (Kelly 1995). Taken from either perspective, change within either internal or external relationships drives both stability and change.

These observations have several clear implications for how we proceed with analogy. On one side, the historical critique casts doubt on the use of ethnographic data (Shott 1992), and in its most extreme indicates that hunter-gatherers can only be understood within the context of their particular social histories, and not within a comparative framework. However, as Layton notes (2001), there are many similarities between the social histories of modern foraging groups to suggest that similar processes can occur within hunter-gatherer societies in the past. As a start, we can move past this by first considering that even in "egalitarian" societies, there are contradictions that exist. In this way, modern foraging societies might be used as direct analogues, for example, to suggest the specific kinds of conflict that may lead to group fissioning. In the case of Paleoindian foragers, perhaps one the greatest points of interest is the kinds of compromises that must have been made to maintain group stability in the face of low population densities. That is, what kind of social relationships were necessary to maintain within-group cohesion, and what kinds of interaction would be necessary to reproduce social relationships without transforming them? This last point is particularly important given the potential for shifts in subsistence patterns, mobility strategies, and the social relationships inherent in these configurations.

Just as the historicist position provides a framework for exploring

Paleoindian social dynamics, we must also consider how traditional social practices occurred within a historically situated cultural milieu. That is, drawing on practice and landscape approaches, it can be said that behavior is situated in a world that is socially meaningful (Morphy 1995; Tilley 1994). How people act, what kinds of behaviors they engage in, the kinds of potentialities they see, and the problems they encounter are both informed by and further inform their worldview. Importantly, it is not possible to parse out different aspects of social behavior (e.g., technology, mobility, ecological knowledge, social dynamics, or cosmology), as each of these aspects is coimplicated in social process. Moreover, there is a very important historical dimension, as preceding and current events have a bearing on how practices are reproduced through human action (Sahlins 1985). From this perspective, it is necessary to consider how engagement with the material and nonmaterial world affects the process of social reproduction and history making.

Unfortunately, from the perspective of analogy, all meaning is historically contingent, and thus recovering specific meanings of practices, artifacts, or other traditions are beyond our abilities. We can move past this by first accepting that foragers inhabited a world that was meaningful to them, and that it was the ways in which the world was interpreted that were most important. As an example of forager worldview, Fowler and Turner (1999:424) have noted

> The natural world and all of its complexities hold special meaning for indigenous hunting and gathering peoples; this is reflected in various aspects of their traditional ecological knowledge. Particularly important is the sense of place and purpose communicated by the oral tradition, and the cumulative wisdom derived from knowledge of complex ecological relationships, and by the day-to-day interaction with the things of these places. People are as much a part of the natural world as any other organism.

This position is echoed by Ingold (1994), who suggests that forager worldviews involve an extension of social ties between human and nonhuman actions, which can influence how and why foragers make particular decisions. Similarly, Bird-David (1988) suggests that hunter-gatherer relations are structured in such a way that hunter-gatherers can maximize their extraction of both social and environmental resources. Not only do these perspectives force us to problematize the context of interaction between individuals, but we must also investigate how practices such as technological choice, as well as landscape use, speak to forager worldview.

An Example from the Middle Tennessee River Valley

In order to demonstrate how these different perspectives can be articulated, we provide an example of Paleoindian lifeways drawn from the Middle Tennessee River Valley in northern Alabama. The focus of the discussion is on those archaeological patterns with the most robust datasets: site selection, tool types and distributions, and subsistence remains. We first offer a general overview, and then examine these patterns from multiple perspectives.

In this section of the Tennessee Valley, the river cuts a rather narrow floodplain through the karstic Highland Rim and winds its way toward the Fall Line Hills of the Coastal Plain near the Alabama-Mississippi border. An important geologic attribute of the region is the presence of abundant primary and secondary deposits of cryptocrystalline cherts. In particular, dense deposits of blue/gray Fort Payne chert are found in the Pickwick Basin near Muscle Shoals, and similarly dense outcrops and deposits of Bangor chert occur in the vicinity of Huntsville in the Wheeler Basin.

Fine-grained environmental reconstructions have yet to be compiled for the southeastern United States, but existing studies indicate that between 12,000 and 10,000 years ago, the Pleistocene spruce-pine boreal forest-parkland in this region was being replaced by mesic hardwood forests dominated by oak and hickory (Delcourt and Delcourt 1985). River hydrology during the Pleistocene is characterized by instability, particularly incision and flooding, especially during the Younger Dryas episode (ca. 12,900–11,600 cal BP) (Meeks 2001).

Several sites in the region have provided important evidence for the Paleoindian period, particularly Dust Cave (Driskell 1994, 1996; Sherwood et al. 2004; Walker et al. 2001), Stanfield-Worley Bluff Shelter (DeJarnette et al. 1962; Parmalee 1962), and the Quad site (Cambron and Hulse 1960). The Paleoindian period is traditionally divided into three subperiods based on corresponding changes in hafted biface morphology: Early (13,500–12,900 cal BP), characterized by Clovis; Middle (12,900–12,000 cal BP), characterized by Cumberland, Quad, and Beaver Lake; and Late (12,000–11,200 cal BP), characterized by Dalton and Hardaway side-notched forms (Anderson et al. 1996; Sherwood et al. 2004). This division is somewhat arbitrary, with the potential for chronological overlap between types likely (Anderson et al. 1996:14).

There are three major patterns in the chipped stone tool assemblages in the region: continuity in tool types, relatively high frequencies of tools, and a focus on high-quality raw materials. The most striking pattern is the sheer density of chipped stone tools. Two counties in the western section of the valley (Colbert and Lauderdale) have produced over 1,000 fluted hafted bifaces (both Early and Middle periods combined) (Futato 1996). With the exception of excavated examples at Belle Mina (Ensor 1992), Dust Cave, and Stanfield-Worley, the majority are found in surface or near-surface concentrations at sites such as the Quad locality. At Quad, Hulse and Wright (1989) report finding 184 fluted forms and over 9,000 unifaces and stage bifaces. A similar locality probably exists submerged or under alluvium near Muscle Shoals in the Pickwick Basin (Futato 1996). The reason for such density of chipped stone tools at these localities—due to repeated single occupancy of locales (Hubbert 1989) or aggregation of groups (Wilmsen 1970)—is the subject of some debate. One factor contributing to the density of finds is the local availability of high-quality raw material. Based on anecdotal accounts and some absolute frequency data (Ensor 1992; Futato 1983), the vast majority of tools are made out of blue/gray Fort Payne chert, with examples occurring outside of the source area in high frequencies.

There is apparent continuity in tool types. Hafted bifaces occur in significant frequencies, yet many assemblages are dominated by a unifacial tool kit (Meeks 1994; Randall 2001; Soday 1954). Many of the types of tools found here have analogues elsewhere, such as the tear-dropped end scraper, thumbnail scraper, and prepared-core-derived blades (Meeks 1994). While there is clear continuity in one sense, there are some major technological changes. The most obvious are changes in hafted biface design, with a trend toward more elongated and narrower fluted forms such as Cumberland, and the later reduction or loss in fluting altogether in Beaver Lake, Quad, and Dalton. These changes clearly signal shifts in hafting strategies commensurate with potential differences in hunting strategies. There are changes in the unifacial technology as well. Unfortunately, with the exception of Dust Cave, there is limited evidence for change through time prior to the onset of the Holocene. The blades, which appear to have been reduced from prepared cores, differ from "classic" Clovis blade technology in that the platforms are quite thick (Collins 1999b). Whether this represents a change from earlier Clovis technologies or whether Clovis entered this part of the country with a changed reduction strategy is unknown.

Excavation of rock shelters with Late Paleoindian components within the region have contributed greatly to our understanding of early subsistence practices. Faunal remains from Stanfield-Worley Bluff Shelter indicate that white-tailed deer were a major food source, but squirrels and raccoons may have been targeted prey as well. Other small mammals and turkeys are also represented in the assemblage (Parmalee 1962). At Dust Cave, however, deer are relatively infrequent from the Late Paleoindian levels. Instead, birds, particularly waterfowl, represent the majority of the zooarchaeological remains, followed by small mammals, especially aquatic and closed habitat species, and fish (Walker 1998, this volume; Walker et al. 2001).

Plant remains from the region also derive primarily from rock shelter deposits. Late Paleoindian samples from Dust Cave, Stanfield-Worley, LaGrange, and Rollins Bluff Shelter indicate that nut mast was an important gathered resource. Hickory nuts appear to be a dietary mainstay, but acorns, black walnuts, and hazelnuts were regularly eaten as well. Fruits such as grapes, persimmons, and sumac are also represented in the assemblages, as were weedy seeds, particularly chenopod. The regular occurrence of the seeds suggests that by Late Paleoindian times, foragers had already established a relationship with these eventual cultigens (Detwiler 2001; Hollenbach, this volume, 2004).

Analyses of data from the Alabama State Site Files show distinct patterns of site use through time (Meeks 2001). Early and Middle Paleoindian sites occur most frequently in upland settings, near sinks, while Late Paleoindian sites are more prevalent in floodplains. When time span is taken into account, Quad sites are the least numerous but are the largest in size (even when multicomponent sites are excluded), suggesting that people frequently reoccupied the same site, that group sizes may have been larger, and/or that aggregation sites may have been more important during the Quad period. These Quad sites are often reoccupied during the Late Paleoindian period, which also witnesses a rise in the frequency of sites that may be linked to an increasing population. Meeks (2001) suggests that these trends may be related to the Younger Dryas climatic event, which likely increased economic risk due to colder temperatures during the Middle Paleoindian, and the subsequent amelioration of these conditions in later Late Paleoindian times.

The Paleoindian record in this region has figured into several regional models of settlement and mobility. Because of the density of projectile points, the Middle Tennessee Valley figures prominently in Anderson's (1991) model of Paleoindian settlement systems in the Southeast. Noting high densities along a number of river systems, Anderson argues that while the earliest settlers may have initially moved across the landscape in a "technology-oriented" fashion, focusing on hunting game (Kelly and Todd 1988), these groups settled into resource-rich habitats such as the Tennessee Valley and soon became "place oriented." River valleys thus became "staging areas" and aggregation loci, which groups moved out of as population increased and returned to for exchange of information, mates, and goods. Regional traditions emerged during the Middle Paleoindian, as groups became loosely tethered to certain ranges, and continued to develop as population further increased in the Late Paleoindian and Early Archaic periods.

The numerous rock shelters located in the area also appear in Walthall's (1998b) discussion of rock shelter use during the Dalton period in the Eastern Woodlands. He suggests that Dalton groups aggregated in the major river valleys in the fall, and, as winter approached, dispersed into the uplands, where rock shelters are located, to hunt deer. During the course of these seasonal rounds, rock shelters may have been visited briefly by hunting parties or served as residential bases for family groups. This upland/lowland settlement dichotomy has been further suggested by Futato (1996) and Hubbert (1989) for the Middle and Late Paleoindian periods.

From a Middle-Range Theory Perspective

In making sense of the archaeological data from the Middle Tennessee Valley, middle-range theory provides some valuable avenues for interpretation. Much information can be gained from the stone tools themselves. Assuming that procurement is embedded in settlement mobility, the range of mobility may be determined from the distance to raw material sources. Analyses from Dust Cave indicate that settlement range was relatively restricted by the Late Paleoindian period (Randall 2001). Tools in various stages of manufacture, use, and reuse, as well as the debitage, indicate not only how tools were made and used, but also which steps occurred at particular sites. Analyses of use-wear patterns and edge polish suggest the functions that particular tool types performed and also the materials on which they were used. Such studies indicate that, at least by Late Paleoindian times, people used hafted bifaces both as projectiles and knives, and primarily on animal hides (Walker et al. 2001). The high level of curation and meticulous work involved in tool production suggest that the hunters who used them targeted specific prey of considerable size and dietary importance.

It is notable, then, that there is not dietary evidence that indicates a focal hunting strategy. Instead, southeastern Paleoindians appear more likely to have employed a generalized subsistence strategy (Meltzer and Smith 1986). This is evident at least by the Late Paleoindian period, for which faunal and botanical remains do reflect the inclusion of smaller game, as well as nuts and other wild plant foods, in the diet (Walker et al. 2001).

Beyond indicating the foods people ate, organic remains provide information about the season of occupation of the sites, which aids in the reconstruction of seasonal rounds. This task is made easier due to the presumed lack of food storage by Paleoindian peoples. For example, the numerous rock shelters in the Middle Tennessee Valley appear to be occupied during the fall and early winter, and perhaps in late summer, as suggested by nut mast, ripening berries, and the timing of the deer rutting season and shedding of antlers (Hollenbach 2004; Walker et al. 2001). Organic materials may also suggest the catchment area of a site's occupants, or the distance that people traveled to obtain foods to bring back to a campsite, if sufficient information about the local ecology is available.

By combining stone tool and organic data, further details about site use can be determined. The range of plant and animal foods, as well as the diversity of tool types, may indicate differences in site use, perhaps making it possible to distinguish between special-purpose sites, base camps, and aggregation sites. Weaving site information in with seasonality data and mobility patterns as suggested by stone procurement for tools and by catchment areas, a settlement system and seasonal rounds can be sketched.

Shifts through time are somewhat more difficult to explain. Trends in site use may be related to climatic changes: it is perhaps not surprising that few sites are located in the valley floodplains prior to stabilization of the river during Late Paleoindian times. Similarly, increases in site numbers during the Late Paleoindian period are presumably related to increases in population, assuming that the number of people per campsite remains the same. However, changes in tool forms and types are more difficult to address. Fluting technology slowly disappears from knappers' repertoires, although the primary prey of southeastern Paleoindian hunters does not seem to change. Even if Early and Middle Paleoindians relied more substantially on deer than did Late Paleoindians, there is no evidence for significant differences between Late Paleoindian and Early Archaic foodstuffs in the Middle Tennessee Valley (Detwiler 2001; Hollenbach 2004; Walker 1998). Yet the last vestiges of fluting, as well as blade technology, disappear from the Early Archaic tool kit. Lacking significant changes in diet and climate (Meeks 2001), middle-range theory has difficulty addressing this cultural shift.

From an Evolutionary Ecology Perspective

Rather than pulling as much information as possible out of particular artifacts, evolutionary ecology pulls together suites of data to address particular questions. These questions typically derive from the various working theories within evolutionary ecology, including optimal foraging theory, central place foraging theory, and sharing as a form of risk reduction.

Optimal foraging theory, while a hallmark of evolutionary ecology, is difficult to employ for the Paleoindian period. This theory contends that the salient variables in a forager's decision to pursue a particular prey include the energy content of that prey, the search time to find it, and the handling time to down and process it. Detailed information is required, however, not only of local ecological conditions but also of people's dietary patterns. While Late Paleoindian organic remains have been studied in detail, comparable data do not exist for the earlier Paleoindian periods. Thus, although the decision to no longer make fluted bifaces may be approached by optimal foraging theory—that the benefits of fluted bifaces in terms of downing and processing particular prey no longer outweigh the costs of making and maintaining these tools—we lack data to suggest that diet changed in such a fashion as to require shifts in the tool kit. The loss of blades in the tool kit by the Early Archaic period can be addressed in this manner, although the existing data suggest that there was no corresponding dietary change. This hints at the possibility that noneconomic factors are involved in the decline of formal blade technology.

Settlement systems may be approached by central place foraging theory, which maintains that campsites should be located to minimize travel time to and transport costs from resource patches (Orians and Pearson 1979; Zeanah 2000). In general, foragers will travel farther for resources with high energy returns, such as deer, than for lower energy resources, like nuts and fruits (Orians and Pearson 1979). If resources can be reliably mapped on the local landscape, the travel and transport costs associated with these resources can be calculated. It is possible, then, to determine whether people were moving from one campsite to the next in order to take advantage of particular resources. In this manner, a settlement system and seasonal rounds can be modeled.

Risk reduction (Kelly 1995; Smith and Winterhalder 1992) may be used to address patterns in site use through time. Early and Middle Paleoindian peoples may have placed their sites away from the less stable floodplain environment, where foodstuffs, as well as the suitability of campsites, may have been less predictable. Furthermore, the larger sites noted during the Quad period, including aggregation sites, may also reflect risk-reduction strategies. Bands may have been larger in size and/or aggregated more frequently in order to share foods, raw materials, and perhaps most important, valuable information about the rapidly changing landscape.

As mentioned above, although evolutionary ecology provides a framework to examine dynamic processes such as the peopling of the New World and shifts in dietary patterns, the models that evolutionary ecology employs frequently require somewhat rigorous datasets, which are often not available in Paleoindian research. Returning to the central place foraging theory example, it is relatively easy to map lithic resources on a landscape, but biotic resources have shifted significantly over the past 10,000 years, not only in place but also in kind. Thus, evolutionary ecology requires some creative use of the available data.

From Alternative Perspectives

Just as evolutionary ecology requires detailed datasets, historicist or landscape approaches require a detailed understanding of context, as it permeates society, subsistence, technology, and settlement. While we are far from having a clear understanding of many facets of Paleoindian traditions, the broad synchronic and diachronic patterns in the Middle Tennessee Valley are more than adequate starting points. Several observations in particular present an opening: changing settlement patterns, stable subsistence practices, and technological conservatism. One of the more intriguing issues surrounds the arrival of groups into a landscape free of human actors, and the subsequent historical trajectories of these populations. Subsistence, settlement, and technological studies have demonstrated that early Paleoindians did this, and did it well. What is required is a shift in our own view on what these patterns mean.

Landscape studies have shown that humans entering new landscapes (populated or not) carry with them structures of reference based on prior learning and experience (Morphy 1993; Taçon 1999). This entails not only what to eat, and where to camp, but the recognition of resources as useful and significant. Although conservative, mobile populations also incorporate recent places and events (and nonevents) into their histories (Santos-Granero 1998). The result is that people never enter unknown territory, as places, things, and other people are already meaningful in some way. How individuals and groups engage landscape (both human and nonhuman) is predicated on perceptions of how such places exist.

When viewed from the traditional perspective of base camps and logistical stations, the landscapes of Paleoindians, which were clearly formed and informed through their own experiences, are both decontextualized and dehistoricised. Instead, these places need to be understood as a process whereby movement between sites, and the relationships forged between foragers and animals, informed the Paleoindian worldview. For example, the lack of early Paleoindian rock shelter use stands in stark contrast to the apparent widespread use of rock shelters by at least Dalton times, if not earlier. That these places meant something beyond "habitation site" or "extraction camp" is evidenced by the lack of occupation in them. The practice of avoiding or "excluding" spaces has been documented ethnographically (Munn 1996). There are other potential factors as well, including the potential for some cavities near floodplains to be sediment filled or otherwise obscured (Sherwood 2001). Teasing these multiple factors apart will prove difficult, but assessing the earliest context of use can potentially provide a frame of reference for earlier and later perspectives.

Just as we see emergent settlement strategies, there is a striking conservatism in Paleoindian technology and raw material selection. A major feature in the Middle Tennessee Valley is the almost exclusive use of specific cryptocrystalline raw materials, a pattern that is not deviated from until the early Holocene (Randall 2001). Traditionally, the occurrence of quality raw materials outside of their source range is taken as reflecting planning and reduction strategies. However, raw materials are potentially a way of linking people with distant places and, by extension, with different people (Gould 1985; Morphy 1995). Whether raw material formed a basis of interaction among the earliest populations is unknown, but the continued use of these resources, in tandem with the repeated deposition of artifacts made of these varieties at potential aggregation loci such as the Quad site, indicates that we need to look harder at the contexts of raw material procurement and dispersal on the landscape.

Similarly, many of the features of Paleoindian lithic technology are better explained in terms of history and social reproduction than energetics. In particular, blades continued to be used throughout the late Pleistocene and are seemingly anachronistic given what we know of subsistence practices in comparison with the early Holocene. Ethnographic studies of technological choice indicate that the selection of technologies is only partially mediated by efficiency (Lemonnier 1992, 1993). That is, it is insufficient to simply state that technology was adaptive (Burnham 1973). The ethnographic literature is replete with examples of technological form and function being affected by knowledge sets between individuals, age sets, or genders (Grimm 2000; Larick 1985). Technological practice, including transmission of techniques and methods, is one way in which society is reproduced. Unfortunately, we do not yet understand the contexts in which this technology played, outside the realm of pure function. It is likely that blades and blade production were important components of identity, either of hunters, hide processors, or blade producers in general. Moreover, it is possible that the knowledge of such tool production was in some way controlled, if only between age sets.

One possible line of inference is the idea of a hunter-gatherer "narrative technology" (Ridington 1999). Narrative technology is essentially a discourse between technological knowledge, information on the ecological system, and a culturally defined relationship between human and nonhuman actors. Clearly, it does not leave material traces in the way that archaeologists typically view technology. Narrative technology exists beyond the actual artifacts produced. It is technology as embedded in social practice and environmental constraints. The point is that we need to reframe our inquiry in terms of how this knowledge was reproduced, and how it allowed societies or individuals to maintain social ties. Decisions to move (i.e., mobility strategies) may be just as motivated, if not more so, by a need to exchange information as a need to acquire specific resources.

Melding Perspectives

Having visited these three sets of perspectives on analogy and interpretation of the Paleoindian period, the question that arises is which of these best serves us in understanding early foraging lifeways in the Middle Tennessee Valley or elsewhere. On the one hand, we could retreat from the marked differences between the three perspectives. Middle-range theory focuses on the connection between behavior and function in the archaeological record, while evolutionary ecology and revisionist perspectives emphasize different causal factors for the diversity observed among hunter-gatherer groups. Evolutionary ecology demonstrates that foraging behaviors are evolutionarily adaptive responses to environmental parameters. Alternative approaches, however, highlight diversity as the result of different histories and patterns of social practice and reproduction, and take issue with the fact that contingencies of time and space are overlooked by general comparative analogies.

On the other hand, it would be much more productive to meld these approaches, taking advantage of the strengths of each. Middle-range theory pushes us to extract as much behavioral information as possible from artifacts and assemblages. Evolutionary ecology encourages us to look at the decision processes behind those behaviors. Revisionist approaches urge us to contextualize these processes with histories and social practices. Each perspective adds a dimension to the larger picture of hunter-gatherer lifeways.

The conservatism of Paleoindian lithic technology in the Middle Tennessee Valley best exemplifies the benefits of melding these perspectives. Detailed studies of Late Paleoindian stone tools from the region, including typologies, sourcing of raw materials, and microwear analyses, indicate that much effort was invested in obtaining high-quality materials for making these highly wrought uniface blades and projectile points. This specialized and highly curated tool kit suggests intensive focus on larger prey, such as deer. However, analyses of organic remains indicate that these groups practiced a generalized subsistence strategy, and may have relied as much upon waterfowl and smaller mammals, as well as nuts and fruits, as they did upon deer. Evolutionary ecology provides models to further investigate whether the costs of manufacturing such a tool kit outweigh the benefits of tool performance in taking smaller prey. Revisionist perspectives note that whether or not the costs are justified in economic terms, these blades and projectile points have meaning beyond their function, relating to the identities of the toolmakers and users, perhaps linking them with other people and places. In concert, these various perspectives should enrich our understanding of why these tools were made and used, not just how.

Implications for Analogies in the Paleoindian Period

In sum, analogies are not merely useful but essential to the interpretation of the archaeological record. Because we must use them, our only recourse is to develop analogies that are useful and robust. As mentioned above, Wylie (1985) instructs us that analogies that rely on causal relations between cultural attributes and their correlated behaviors or consequences are most useful to archaeologists. She further suggests that these analogies can be strengthened by work both on the subject and source side (Wylie 1985).

On the source side of the analogy, we need to expand the perspectives with which we approach these causal relations. Evolutionary ecologists direct our attention to the importance of decisions made by individuals, giving purpose and intent to otherwise functional relations. We thus find ourselves concerned not just with mobility, but asking under what conditions people move or leave camps. Questions regarding subsistence strategies involve not only what they ate and when but also why they changed their food choices and how they decided on the size and composition of work groups.

Historicists further suggest that we move beyond the effect of the physical environment on these decisions and place greater importance on socially and historically contingent parameters. Thus, considerations for moving or leaving camp include not only the local resource structure but also the arrangement of and relationships with other groups, beings, and features on the landscape. Subsistence strategies may consider not only the biological needs of people but also social relations among people, and between people, plants, and animals.

On the subject side, we need to improve our understanding of the archaeological variables involved so that we can evaluate whether these causal relations hold in the past. Middle-range theory's detailed treatment of artifacts and assemblages is particularly instructive in this regard. Its emphasis on deriving as much information as possible from a single artifact must be extended to include better integration of various artifact classes; for example, stone tool data must be understood within the context of available faunal and botanical remains. These artifact categories should also be explored at varying scales, from site through regional levels.

In addition, ecological and physical settings must be better documented, and at a scale useful to understanding the occupation of sites or regions. This includes the development of environmental reconstructions at a much finer scale, employing pollen cores, microfaunal analyses, and micromorphological studies. Like Gillam's (2002) study of the impact of slope aspect on site location, we need to consider the effect of local physical variables on the use of various landscapes.

The focus of employing ethnographic analogy thus becomes not finding a source group that exploits an environment similar to the archaeological group being studied, but instead finding groups that are faced with similar decisions. Our concern should then be defining the conditions and contingencies in which these decisions are made, detailing the variables that impact these decisions. These conditions, contingencies, and variables are not only environmental or biological in nature but also cultural and social.

Ultimately, we should be able to triangulate between these ethnographically derived decisions, the nature of the archaeological record, and the structure of the immediate physical and social landscape, thus constructing models of Paleoindian lifeways that are informed by all three sets of data (Winterhalder, personal communication 2002). In this way, Paleoindians may be viewed as people with settlement and mobility strategies related to their relationships with other beings, resources, and places on the landscape.

Acknowledgments

We would like to thank Renee Walker and Boyce Driskell for inviting us to write this chapter, for their suggestions and insight, and for their patience. In addition, we would like to thank our anonymous reviewer for valuable comments, and acknowledge Bruce Winterhalder for his suggestion to triangulate between the ethnographic record, archaeological data, and environmental setting. Ken Sassaman provided much food for thought in his hunter-gatherer seminar at the University of Florida.

TWELVE

Making Sense of Paleoindian Subsistence Strategies

Boyce N. Driskell and Renee B. Walker

From the earliest discoveries of the ancient makers of fluted points, professional and avocational archaeologists alike conjured quite romantic images of these "first" Americans as highly proficient and mobile hunters of the large, now-extinct mammals of the Late Pleistocene. The evidence was indeed compelling. Clovis projectile points were found across the North American continent; production techniques and form were quite similar across this broad area, suggesting regular interaction of Clovis peoples or rapid colonization of the continent, or both. The Clovis tool kit was dominated by tools associated with hunting or meat and hide processing, or tools to make these tools. Prominent in the inventory of these early people were stone tools from quite distant source areas, supporting the notion of long-distance travel. And fluted projectile points found conspicuously in direct association with remains of large Pleistocene animals provided direct evidence of hunting practices by these early Americans. Recently, this line of explanation has been popularized as the high-technology forager model (Kelly and Todd 1988; see also the introduction to this volume).

Were Clovis peoples and other fluted point makers the highly mobile, megafaunal predators implied by these observations? What about successor peoples of the terminal Pleistocene? As the reader will have seen in previous chapters, new evidence from across North America hints at answers that are a bit surprising. The following sections discuss the new bits and pieces of the puzzle, which range from information on diet to new evidence on the extent or range of movement of these early Americans.

Diet

Chapters in this volume report findings of a wide variety of plant and animal specimens recovered from the Paleoindian archaeological record. Questions of taphonomy aside, many of these plants and animals were a part of the Paleoindian diet.

While Clovis megafauna kill sites are rare when compared to the mounting numbers of other Paleoindian site types (Kornfeld, chapter 3; Meltzer 1993a), these now-extinct mammals were obviously the prey of some Paleoindians. Frison (1993:244–246) has experimentally demonstrated the potential of a properly rendered Clovis projectile to penetrate the hide of a fully grown elephant, but questions mount as to the importance of these animals to the diet, particularly to Clovis peoples of the eastern United States, where kill sites are rare.

Yesner (chapter 2) argues that Beringians increasingly employed a broad-spectrum strategy as large mammals became less reliably procured. He believes that rapid climatic change in eastern Beringia during the Late Pleistocene caused extinction of many elements of the Rancholabrean fauna by ca, 12,000 BP. He argues that broad-spectrum subsistence strategies would have been required by early Beringians to compensate for the loss of these large animals. Indeed, faunal data cited by Yesner (mostly from the Broken Mammoth site in interior Alaska) supports this contention, with evidence for utilization of some large game (bison and wapiti), but substantial utilization of small game (particularly hares and ground squirrels), birds (waterfowl and ptarmigan), and salmonid fish. Yesner concludes that subsistence strategies focused on large game to the extent profitable, but as these herd animals became less predictable during the terminal Pleistocene, subsistence activities shifted rapidly to emphasize exploitation of a large number of smaller animal resources, especially waterfowl.

Arguing mostly from the ecotonal setting of the Gault site and other southern plains Clovis sites, Collins (chapter 4) contends that while Clovis peoples in this area were involved in megafaunal predation, plant and small to medium-size animal resources were probably more important contributors to the diet than large Pleistocene mammals. Similarly, Kornfeld (chapter 3) cites examples of recovered bone from sites in the western plains and mountain region suggesting utilization of small to medium-size animals in Paleoindian diets, particularly on a seasonal basis.

McWeeney (chapter 9), who surveys the paleontological record for the northeastern United States and contrasts it with archaeological and macrofloral remains from the area, concludes that postglacial plant migration northward occurred earlier than usually proposed, with the presence of temperate deciduous trees such as oak, ash, and hornbeam in some areas before the arrival of early Paleoindian peoples. Under these conditions, the Northeast would have supported a much larger group of economic species than originally imagined.

Undoubtedly, Paleoindian peoples were quick to take advantage of this increasing diversity of resources, as suggested by Dent's essay (chapter 7), which draws attention to the recovery of a significant number of charred seeds and some calcined fish bone from a hearth deposit within the Paleoindian deposits of the Shawnee Minisink site (northeastern Pennsylvania) excavated in the 1970s. Even though the context seemed secure and artifact associations and a radiocarbon date confirmed its antiquity, most archaeologists at the time were skeptical that these remains represented anything more than a curious anomaly in the subsistence record of Paleoindian hunters. However, these remains make much better sense in the light of McWeeney's interpretations and in the company of new finds reported in this volume and elsewhere suggesting the importance of gathering in the subsistence strategies of many early Americans.

In contrast, peninsular Florida may have been a late refuge for large Pleistocene mammals. Dunbar and Vojnovski (chapter 10) recount limited excavations at four Florida sites where faunal remains, mixed with some ivory and other megafauna, suggest a varied diet for Paleoindian peoples of Florida. Assemblages vary from site to site, indicating either somewhat varied subsistence patterns, different exploitative settings, or different seasons of exploitation. Alternatively, these differences may simply be the result of sampling error from the limited excavations. Also, the temporal range of these assemblages is poorly understood.

Walker (chapter 6) reports results of analysis of thousands of animal bones from a Middle to Late Paleoindian (Quad/Beaver Lake) context at Dust Cave in northwestern Alabama. Excavations at the site produced a large amount of well-preserved faunal remains from small and medium-size animals, but relatively few deer or other large-mammal remains. Studies of the remains indicate that most of the "hunting" activities at the site were focused on small game and waterfowl, which is in marked contrast to an expected reliance on white-tailed deer. Aquatic species were abundant in the collections, suggesting heavy reliance on this habitat.

In a companion chapter (chapter 8), Hollenbach presents results of an analysis of some of the botanical materials from the Paleoindian component at Dust Cave. Several nut species and several seed species were exploited.

The prevalence of hickory nutshell at the site suggests that mast collection may have been a significant impetus for the seasonal occupation of the site. Heavy dependence on these mast crops, originally thought to become important much later in hunter-gatherer prehistory in the mid-South, may have been a seasonal focus of Paleoindian subsistence in this region, and some hunting activities were probably embedded in this seasonal collection activity (Hollenbach 2005).

Reporting on five little-known Paleoindian sites from Wisconsin, Kuehn (chapter 5) concludes that early inhabitants of the western Great Lakes region also exploited a wide variety of local fauna from a variety of environmental settings. Like subsistence strategies suggested by data from Dust Cave, aquatic species exploitation, particularly of waterfowl, was apparently a focus of subsistence activities.

There is little doubt that aquatic resources, and therefore aquatic environs (wetlands), were important to Paleoindians. In the second chapter of this volume, Fiedel cites faunal data from Alaska suggesting that birds, particularly waterfowl, were more important than generally recognized in Paleoindian subsistence as well as Paleoindian ideology.

Technology

Until recently, arguments about the nature of Paleoindian subsistence were supported mostly through evidence from stone tools and the most durable of bone, antler, and ivory specimens; however, the floral and faunal remains discussed in this volume and elsewhere in the recent Paleoindian literature often are testimony to procurement technologies utilizing very simple strategies not requiring tools, or requiring implements made only from perishable materials (baskets, bags, lines, hooks, nets, traps, harpoons, digging sticks, etc.).

Even though fiber artifacts are generally not preserved in most areas of North America, a few examples have been found that suggest that basketry containers, mats, sandals, and cordage were important to Paleoindian peoples and that this set of fiber technologies "were part and parcel of the armamentarium of the first colonists to the New World" (Adovasio et al. 2001:211). Basketry-impressed fired-clay hearth fragments at Dust Cave (Freeman 2003) testify to the presence of basketry (most likely, matting) in the material inventory of the Southeast by Middle Paleoindian times. Other Pleistocene-age basketry specimens include a plaited container fragment from the Miller Complex at Meadowcroft (Andrews and Adovasio 1996), perhaps a Pleistocene-age plaited mat or burden basket from a salt dome in Louisiana (Wilson 1889; Andrews and Adovasio 1996:34), and perhaps an impression of a twined specimen from the Hiscock site in New York (Adovasio et al. 2001:208).

The Sheep Mountain net (Kornfeld, chapter 3), a 9,000-year-old artifact of juniper fiber cordage found near Cody, Wyoming, is a rare example of a no doubt rich Paleoindian material culture in plant fiber cordage. Bola stones or net sinkers from the Allen site (Kornfeld, chapter 3) also are artifacts relating possibly to composite tools involving fiber technology. Cordage recovered from Danger Cave (Jennings 1957) and other sites in the western United States may be remnants of knotted netting (Adovasio et al. 2001:209). Recently, it has been pointed out that net hunting is unlike taking individual animals with projectiles in that it is often practiced as a communal activity involving men, women, and children, and may be associated with mass harvests (Adovasio et al. 2001:212–213) or other communal collecting activities.

Technologies producing tools and other artifacts from perishable materials such as wood or bone are poorly attested directly in the artifactual record, although a few apparently early bone and antler artifacts have survived, such as the quizzical ivory shafts from Florida sinkholes and rivers. Dust Cave (Goldman-Finn and Walker 1994) produced a number of bone tools and ornaments from Middle and Late Paleoindian contexts. Other perishables of bone or wood may be inferred from more durable parts of composite tools like projectile points, and microscopic use-wear analyses suggest that many stone tools were used to cut, incise, scrape, saw, and otherwise shape bone and wood implements.

Fishing was no doubt an important activity of Paleoindian peoples, as implied by large percentages of fish remains recovered and analyzed from some sites; however, little is known about the techniques of procurement. Fish could have been caught using a variety of methods leaving no archaeological signature. Similarly, other aquatic resources that figure prominently in many of the studies reported in this volume may have been collected, snared, or trapped in ways that leave no archaeological evidence. A bone fishhook found at Dust Cave testifies to line fishing very early (ca. 9,000 BP) in the Archaic Stage of the Middle Tennessee River Valley (Goldman-Finn and Walker 1994:113).

Regardless of the intriguing clues to richness of material culture rendered in perishable materials, technologies utilizing stone tools are the best understood because of the ubiquitous occurrence of stone tools in the archaeological record. A few simple ground stone tools (Kornfeld, chapter 3) such as hammerstones, anvils, and grinding slabs are now known from Paleoindian contexts, suggesting that processing of plant materials was of considerable importance. However, the chipped stone inventory from Paleoindian sites monopolizes site inventories and garners the most attention. This inventory includes a variety of artifact and tool types, most seemingly related to hunting or processing the products of the hunt. Inventories include technologically simple or expedient tools such as sharp flakes and blades or retouched flakes and blades, as well as shaped unifacial and bifacial tools. Of six retouched flakes from the Late Paleoindian component from Dust Cave that were analyzed for microwear, three were used to cut meat, and two exhibited bone or antler polish (Walker et al. 2001:186). Two "spokeshaves" from Dust Cave exhibited wood polish on the working edge, while two artifacts with "graver" spurs exhibited bone or antler polish in one case and an undifferentiated hard material in the other.

Blades, while not part of all Clovis and derivative Paleoindian technologies (Collins 1999b), were important tools in some areas of the continent, and in some regions such as the Tennessee Valley, prismatic blades were produced well into the early Holocene. Blades from the Gault site (Collins, chapter 4), modified and unmodified, were found to have been used for multiple cutting tasks such as butchering and hide working, but also a well-developed silica gloss from cutting grasses was found on some blades and flakes. Were the Clovis people of Gault cutting grasses for bedding, basketry, mats, or seed harvest? All of the Late Paleoindian blades inspected by Scott Meeks from Dust Cave (Walker et al. 2001:187) functioned as knives used in butchering activities. In addition, unifacial end and side scrapers (n = 7) analyzed for use wear from Dust Cave were primarily used to scrape hide, although one exhibited use on hard material. Two simple, unifacially worked tools from the Wilson-Leonard site in central Texas were trimmed in such a way that protruding, tapered areas exhibiting bone or antler polish may have been from a bone- or antler-socketed handle (Driskell 1998:739).

Bifaces were an important component of all Paleoindian inventories. It is assumed that most were intended as preforms for projectile points. Bifaces that are too crude to be considered Clovis preforms have been observed in Clovis sites but are not very common (Collins 1999b); their function is not known, although chopping/cleaving seems likely. Collins and his research team have recognized wear patterns on thin unifaces and thin bifaces from the Gault site that suggest use on soft materials, wear consistent with butchering. At Dust Cave, of four thinned bifaces examined for microwear, two were used as butchering tools (Walker et al. 2001:186–187). A hafted "drill" was actually used as a leather or hide perforator.

Gouges are a prominent category of Paleoindian bifaces that seem to have been primarily woodworking tools. A crude biface from Dust Cave was used to adze or plane wood (Walker et al. 2001:187). Small chipped stone adzes from the Gault site also seem to be woodworking tools (Collins, chapter 4). Morse (1998:195–196) has identified similar woodworking tools in Dalton assemblages from Arkansas.

Chipped stone projectile points tipped spearlike weapons for all Paleoindian groups. Fluted Clovis projectile points (Wormington 1957), the earliest of the projectile point styles from the Paleoindian stage in North America, were produced across the continent. Regional fluted variants developed during the Middle Paleoindian. Late Paleoindian derivatives were also regionally separate, but oftentimes unfluted (see introduction to this volume).

Paleoindian groups may have used different types of spears. Collins (chapter 4) interprets the sparsity of impact fractures on Clovis points to suggest use as a tip for a thrusting spear (lance), where strong impacts from bone could be avoided by the user. Collins also reports that Clovis points often exhibit use-wear traces consistent with use as knives in butchering. Dalton points from Arkansas (Morse 1998:195) seem to have also functioned as butchering tools. Three Beaver Lake projectile points from Dust Cave that were examined for use wear exhibited no evidence for use as knives. Rather, all three exhibited impact fractures (Walker et al. 2001:187), indicating that these artifacts functioned primarily as propelled (javelin or atlatl dart) projectile tips.

In slightly altered or derivative form, Clovis-style hunting tools (prominently lanceolate projectile points) were produced for a hundred generations. How do we account for this long continuity? Apparently, the Clovis tool kit continued to satisfy needs for the hunt. Perhaps part of the reason has to do with the usual conservative nature of traditional cultures, resisting change, including change to the style if not the function of their tools or tool kits. But if the explanation was this simple, why were there changes to the tool kit that occurred during the early Holocene?

As Randall and Hollenbach (chapter 11) have made clear, modern (ethnographically known) hunting-gathering analogues may not adequately model aspects of North American hunting-gathering societies of the terminal Pleistocene; however, it is difficult to avoid the assumption that men hunted and women, elders, and uninitiated children collected, more or less. Even so, direct evidence for engendering sets of behaviors associated with these two strategies of forager subsistence, collecting and hunting, will be unlikely in the near future.

As men's tools, the hunting tool kit, or certain artifacts in the tool kit such as the spear (with finely crafted projectile point), served as a status symbol of manhood. When combined with the possible ritual associated with the hunt, and weapons of the hunt, long-term stylistic stability would be more expectable.

Mobility and Settlement

How mobile were Paleoindians? What circumstances or resources influenced decisions about movements, siting, and site tenure? The high-technology forager model (Kelly and Todd 1988) portrays Clovis peoples as highly mobile bands of foragers focusing subsistence strategies and decision making on large mammals. Similarity of Clovis stone tools across North America and long-distance transport of tool stone support this model of mobility.

The Paleoindian tool kit, particularly the Clovis projectile point, is quite similar across the continent, suggesting social interaction that would seemingly be made possible only by widely roving bands of foragers. On the other hand, uniformity of Clovis projectile points may be more apparent than real (Meltzer 1993a; Deller and Ellis 1988), with regional (or intraregional) differences expressed in fluting method (Justice 1987), base configuration (Morrow and Morrow 1999), and resharpening.

Some Clovis points are made of material originating a long distance from the location of discovery (Tankersley 1991). This trait is often used to support theories about rapid, sustained, or long-distance movement of Clovis people. While long-distance movement of high-quality lithic material is a remarkable trait of Clovis peoples, distances vary by area or region. Meltzer (1993a) notes that there appears to be a different scale of mobility in the northern (300 kilometers) and southern plains (30 kilometers). Long-distance movement of lithic resources is also less commonly observed in the southeastern United States, possibly due to the availability of good-quality tool stone in many areas.

Kornfeld (chapter 3) points out that while exotic materials in Paleoindian assemblages in the western United States are notable, the vast majority of tools and debitage recovered are made of stone from nearby sources. Also, it is yet unclear as to whether chert transport distance may be a factor of single moves or possibly the result of a number of discrete moves (Meltzer 1993a).

Also cited in support of the high mobility of Clovis peoples is the lack of evidence for site improvements like storage facilities, which would be less likely where people used a site for short duration and had no plans to return. Apparently as a general rule, Clovis peoples did not employ storage facilities such as pits or crypts, although Clovis peoples may have practiced cold weather meat caching at the Sheaman site (Frison 1982). Caches of stone artifacts are reported in the literature (Collins 1999b:173–177), including the recent find at East Wenatchee in Washington State, which gained national exposure. These behaviors suggest that Clovis people sometimes planned to return to certain sites. Kornfeld (chapter 3) describes possible storage pits from a Late Paleoindian context at the Medicine Lodge Creek site.

In chapter 3, Kornfeld makes a strong argument for substantial campsites (base camps) in the western United States with tenure necessary to justify features such as hearths, domestic structure bases, and possibly storage pits. He interprets some of the Paleoindian finds in this area as travel camps and others as base camps. Base camps such as the Hell's Gap and Ray Long sites exhibit hearth and activity areas, possible storage facilities, and possible domestic structural remains. Clovis sites in the eastern United States are also primarily residential sites (base camp–like) or quarry/workshops, or both (Dincauze 1993b). Also, Collins's (chapter 4) analysis of tool function from the Gault site of central Texas suggests activities consistent with base camps.

Much of the evidence reported in this volume can be interpreted to suggest that Paleoindians carefully sited their settlements to be able to exploit nearby resources and oftentimes closely juxtaposed contrasting habitats. Kornfeld (chapter 3) sees evidence for winter hunting of large game in the western United States, with off-season siting in other areas. Certainly, several authors have mentioned siting at strategic overlooks. Collins (chapter 4) sees Clovis peoples in the southern plains tethered to ecotone sites like Gault, where water, stone, and biotic resources could be found in close proximity.

At Dust Cave, siting was indeed important. Located in a limestone bluff line punctuated by steep-sloped ravines, the site is just below a relic prairie with sinkhole lakes to the northwest and looks out on a several-thousand-acre floodplain drained by a series of small, sluggish, spring-fed streams emptying into the Tennessee River to the southeast.

This volume stresses that the economy of Clovis peoples is presently poorly understood. The extent to which Clovis peoples at any time focused hunting efforts on megafauna is not so clear; they may simply have opportunistically pursued these animals or scavenged weak, dying, or recently dead animals. In Meltzer's (1993a) opinion, the fact that a few highly visible "kill" sites were discovered early has unduly influenced our view of Clovis people as primarily big-game hunters. Although less visible in the archaeological record, small animals, and presumably other collectables, figured prominently in Paleoindian subsistence activities. Perhaps the Clovis peoples utilizing the Gault site in central Texas provide a better example of Clovis economy than the high-technology forager model (Kelly and Todd 1988). In spite of the similarities in Clovis artifacts, it is yet not clear that these early Paleoindians applied similar subsistence strategies across the continent. The likelihood of their doing so seems remote.

On the other hand, some North American Paleoindian cultures derivative from Clovis peoples conformed to the conventional high-technology forager model of mobile hunters; these specialized economies sometimes arose as the result of specific factors of resource availability:

> I think that the evidence is overwhelming that Folsom, probably Cody, and possibly Plainview points were made and used by specialized bison hunters—virtually single-species adaptations, at least in the case of Folsom. Folsom sites are all in, or on the edge of, grasslands; all have bison remains; the pattern to come to light in recent years is short-term campsites close to kill sites (e.g., Cattle Guard); only Lindenmeier seems large and complex enough to be considered anything more than a temporary campsite, and it may be a palimpsest of brief camping events; the tool kit epitomizes mobility; weaponry is specialized for big game, etc. And, I think that the lack of Folsom cache sites is an important clue. It's all about the bison! (Collins, personal communication 2003)

With the exception of Folsom and similar bison hunters of the plains, subsistence was seemingly based on exploitation of a wide variety of collectable resources. Settlement patterns remain problematical until more Paleoindian sites are investigated in each region, but by Middle to Late Paleoindian times, regional tethering, strategic resource siting, and seasonality were likely important aspects of the settlement system.

The importance of collecting as a subsistence strategy probably varied from group to group, from site to site, and from season to season. However, this volume illustrates that this strategy should not be underestimated in spite of the prominence of durable stone hunting paraphernalia. In many if not most Paleoindian societies, collection strategies including canvassing, trapping, and netting were adequate to support dietary needs, particularly in the more hospitable climates of North America.

Future interpretations of Paleoindian subsistence systems must adopt more sophisticated, complex models of subsistence strategies, which include the interaction of these modes of production. That is, in addition to strict dietary needs, the organization of work, settlement, and mobility may be influenced by emphases placed on these modes of subsistence. What were the ways in which one mode facilitated, or was coordinated with, the other, and how was overall subsistence strategy operationalized on a daily, seasonal, and annual basis?

The chapters in this volume are a testament to recent insights provided mostly by new data generated from the recovery of faunal and floral remains from unusual contexts. By this we mean that much of the new data is from protected contexts found in unusual circumstances (dry deposits, cave deposits, wet deposits, etc.) that have preserved fragile, otherwise perishable remains. Zooarchaeologists and archaeological botanists have developed an impressive set of interpretative tools for the reconstruction of archaeological economies, but interest in the faunal and floral remains from early hunter-gatherer sites is quite recent, and results are still rudimentary and regionally fragmented.

The numbers of these finds will increase as we spend more time looking for them. Recovery has improved, and will continue to do so, because of application of fine-screening and flotation techniques, microscopic examination of soil constituents, and archaeological chemistry of residues of various kinds. Fine-grained paleoenvironmental reconstructions will increasingly provide localized environmental backdrops for our interpretations.

Gary Haynes (2002b:208–215) points out that archaeologists who study Paleoindians have not yet agreed on a definition of subsistence "specialization," a circumstance arising partly from failure to articulate and apply formal theory toward understanding Paleoindian lifeways. Even though Paleoindians existed in a world like none recorded ethnographically, Randall and Hollenbach (chapter 11) emphasize that sophisticated modeling of forager decision making can be formulated and tested for fit with the archaeological and environmental data within our regions of interest.

In conclusion, have we made much sense of Paleoindian subsistence? The answer is a resounding no. In fact, we seem to be in that middle phase of the development of explanation, where the evidence appears to make less sense than it once did. At present, juxtaposed with bits and pieces of the puzzle long known are new bits that seemingly are contradictory. We are still below the critical mass of evidence necessary for regional syntheses of Paleoindian lifeways in most areas of North America.

With new data, and improving methodologies and new technologies to examine this data, the future of North American Paleoindian subsistence studies indeed looks bright and exciting. While mammoth kill sites still whet our archaeological imaginations, we have spread our interests to less spectacular finds, which paradoxically may actually shed more light on Paleoindian adaptations.

BIBLIOGRAPHY

Abbott, M. B., B. P. Finney, M. E. Edwards, and K. R. Kelts

2000 Lake-Level Reconstruction and Paleohydrology of Birch Lake, Central Alaska, Based on Seismic Reflection Curves and Core Transects. *Quaternary Research* 53(2): 154–166.

Ackerman, R. E.

1992 Earliest Stone Industries on the North Pacific Coast of North America. *Arctic Anthropology* 29(2): 18–27.

Adovasio, J. M.

1993 The Ones That Will Not Go Away: A Biased View of Pre-Clovis Populations in the New World. In *From Kostenki to Clovis: Upper Paleolithic–Paleo-Indian Adaptations*, ed. O. Soffer and N. D. Praslov, 199–218. New York: Plenum Press.

Adovasio, J. M., A. T. Boldurian, and R. C. Carlisle

1998 Who Are Those Guys? Some Biased Thoughts on the Initial Peopling of the New World. In *Americans before Columbus: Ice-Age Origins*, ed. R. C. Carlisle, 45–62. Ethnology Monographs No. 12. Pittsburgh: Department of Anthropology, University of Pittsburgh.

Adovasio, J. M., J. Donahue, and R. C. Carlisle

1984 Meadowcroft Rockshelter and the Pleistocene/Holocene Transition in Southwest Pennsylvania. In *Contributions in Quaternary Vertebrate Paleontology: A Volume in Memorial to John E. Guilday*, ed. H. H. Genoways and M. R. Dawson, 347–369. Special Publication No. 8. Pittsburgh: Carnegie Museum of Natural History.

Adovasio, J. M., D. C. Hyland, and O. Soffer

2001 Perishable Technology and Early Human Populations in the New World. In *On Being First: Cultural Innovation and Environmental Consequences of First Peopling*, ed. J. Gillespie, S. Tupakka, and C. de Mille, 201–221. Proceedings of the 31st Annual Chacmool Conference. Calgary: Archaeological Association of the University of Calgary.

Adovasio, J. M., D. Pedler, J. Donahue, and R. Stuckenrath

1999 No Vestige of a Beginning nor Prospect for an End: Two Decades of Debate on Meadowcroft Rockshelter. In *Ice Age People of North America: Environments, Origins, and Adaptations*, ed. R. Bonnichsen and K. L. Turnmire, 416–431. Corvallis: Oregon State University Press.

Adovasio, J. M., O. Soffer, and B. Klima

1996 Upper Paleolithic Fibre Technology: Interlaced Woven Finds from Pavlov I, Czech Republic, c. 26,000 Years Ago. *Antiquity* 70:526–534.

2000 Paleolithic Fiber Technology: Data from Pavlov I, Czech Republic, ca. 27,000 BP. Paper presented at the 60th Annual Meeting of the Society for American Archaeology, Minneapolis.

Agenbroad, L. D.

1978 *The Hudson-Meng Site: An Alberta Bison Kill in the Nebraska High Plains.* Washington DC: University of America Press.

Ager, T. A.

1975 *Late Quaternary Environmental History of the Tanana Valley, Alaska.* Report No. 54. Columbus: Institute of Polar Studies, Ohio State University.

Ager, T. A., and L. Brubaker

1985 Quaternary Palynology and Vegetational History of Alaska. In *Pollen Records of Late-Quaternary North American Sediments*, ed. Vaughn M. Bryant Jr. and Ralph G. Holloway, 353–384. Dallas: American Association of Stratigraphic Palynologists.

Agogino, G. A., and E. Galloway

1965 The Sister's Hill Site: A Hell Gap Site in North-Central Wyoming. *Plains Anthropologist* 10:190–195.

Allen, R. R.

1967 *Studies on the Paleo-Indian Era of Florida.* Gainesville: Department of Anthropology, University of Florida.

Ames, K. M.

2004 Supposing Hunter-Gatherer Variability. *American Antiquity* 69:364–374.

Amick, D.

1998 Folsom Site. In *Archaeology of Prehistoric Native America: An Encyclopedia*, ed. G. Gibbon, 282–284. New York: Garland.

Amundson, D. C., and H. E. Wright Jr.

1979 Forest Changes in Minnesota at the End of the Pleistocene. *Ecological Monographs* 49(1): 1–16.

Anderson, D. G.

1990 The Paleoindian Colonization of Eastern North America: A View from the Southeastern United States. In *Early Paleoindian Economies of Eastern North America*, ed. K. B. Tankersley and B. L. Isaac, 163–216. Research in Economic Anthropology, Supplement 5. Greenwich CT: JAI Press.

1991 Examining Prehistoric Settlement Distribution in Eastern North America. *Archaeology of Eastern North America* 19:1–22.

1993 Recent Advances in Paleoindian and Archaic Period Research in the Southeastern United States. *Archaeology of Eastern North America* 23:145–176.

1996 Models of Paleoindian and Early Archaic Settlement in the Lower Southeast. In *The Paleoindian and Early Archaic Southeast*, ed. D. G. Anderson and K. E. Sassaman, 29–57. Tuscaloosa: University of Alabama Press.

2001 Climate and Culture Change in Prehistoric and Early Historic Eastern North America. *Archaeology of Eastern North America* 29:143–186.

Anderson, D. G., and C. Gillam

2000 Paleoindian Colonization of the Americas: Implications from an Examination of Physiography, Demography, and Artifact Distribution. *American Antiquity* 65:43–66.

Anderson, D. G., R. J. Ledbetter, and L. O'Steen.

1990 *Paleoindian Period Archaeology of Georgia*. Georgia Archaeological Research Design Paper No. 6, Laboratory of Archaeology Series Report No. 28. Athens: University of Georgia.

Anderson, D. G., L. O'Steen, and K. E. Sassaman

1996 Environmental and Chronological Considerations. In *The Paleoindian and Early Archaic Southeast*, ed. D. G. Anderson and K. E. Sassaman, 3–15. Tuscaloosa: University of Alabama Press.

Anderson, D. G., and K. E. Sassaman, eds.

1996 *The Paleoindian and Early Archaic Southeast*. Tuscaloosa: University of Alabama Press.

Andrews, R. L., and J. M. Adovasio

1996 The Origins of Fiber Perishables Production East of the Rockies. In *A Most Indispensable Art: Native Fiber Industries from Eastern North America*, ed. J. B. Peterson, 30–49. Knoxville: University of Tennessee Press.

Anonymous

1999 Bird Bones Indicate Possible Human Presence in Ice Age Yukon. Canadian Museum of Nature News, Extra! Extra! April 20, 1999. http://www.nature.ca/English/extra.htm.

Arima, E. Y.

1984 Caribou Eskimo. In *Handbook of North American Indians*, W. C. Sturtevant, gen. ed. Vol. 5, *Arctic*, ed. D. Damas, 397–414. Washington DC: Smithsonian Institution Press.

Baker, B. W.

1998 Vertebrate Faunal Remains from the 1/4-Inch and 1/8-Inch Screens. In *Wilson-Leonard: An 11,000-Year Archeological Record of Hunter-Gatherers in Central Texas*. Vol. 5, *Special Studies*, ed. M. B. Collins, 1463–1509. Studies in Archeology 31, Texas Archeological Research Laboratory, University of Texas at Austin and Archeology Studies Program, Report 10, Environmental Affairs Division, Texas Department of Transportation.

Balsille, J. H., G. H. Means, and J. S. Dunbar

2006 The Ryan/Harley Site: Sedimentology of an Inundated Paleoindian Site in North Florida. *Geoarchaeology* 21(4): 363–391.

Bamforth, D. B.

1985 The Technological Organization of Paleo-Indian Small-Group Bison Hunting on the Llano Estacado. *Plains Anthropologist* 30:243–258.

1988 *Ecology and Human Organization on the Great Plains*. New York: Plenum Press.

1991 Population Dispersion and Paleoindian Technology at the Allen Site. In *Raw Material Economies among Prehistoric Hunter-Gatherers*, ed. A. Montet-White and S. Holen, 359–374. Publications in Anthropology No. 19. Lawrence: University of Kansas.

2002 The Paleoindian Occupation of the *Medicine Creek Drainage, Southwestern Nebraska*. In *Medicine Creek: Seventy Years of Archaeological Investigations*, ed. D. C. Roper, 54–83. Tuscaloosa: University of Alabama Press.

Bamforth, D. B., ed.

In press *The Allen Site: A Paleoindian Campsite in Southwestern Nebraska*. Albuquerque: University of New Mexico Press.

Barnard, A.

1999 Images of Hunters and Gatherers in European Social Thought. In *The Cambridge Encyclopedia of Hunters and Gatherers*, ed. R. B. Lee and R. Daly, 375–383. Cambridge: Cambridge University Press.

Barrett, J. C.

1994 *Fragments from Antiquity: An Archaeology of Social Life in Britain, 2900–1200* BC. Oxford: Blackwell.

Bartlett, R.

1994 The Calf Creek Component at the Stilman Pit Site (34MR71) and Its Relation to Calf Creek Caching Strategy. *Bulletin of the Oklahoma Anthropological Society* 40:69–90.

Beauchamp, R.

1993 White-tailed Deer Crown Height Measurements and Mortality Profiles for the Hayes Site, Middle Tennessee. Master's thesis, University of Tennessee, Knoxville.

Beaudoin, A. B.

1998 Bison, Birds, and Bulrushes: Early Holocene Macroremains at the Fletcher Site (DJOW-1), Alberta, and Implications for Plains Landscape and Climate. Paper presented at the annual meeting of the Geological Society of America, Toronto.

Belovsky, G. E.

1998 An Optimal Foraging-Based Model of Hunter-Gatherer Population Dynamics. *Journal of Anthropological Archaeology* 7:329–372.

Benchley, E. D., B. Nansel, C. A. Dobbs, S. M. Thurston Myster, and B. H. O'Connell

1991 Paleoindian Study Unit: Region 6, Western Wisconsin. *Wisconsin Archeologist* 72:155–200.

1997 *Archeology and Bioarcheology of the Northern Woodlands*. Arkansas Archeological Survey Research Series No. 52. Fayetteville: Arkansas Archeological Survey.

Benedict, J. B.

1992 Along the Great Divide: Paleoindian Archaeology of the High Colorado Front Range. In *Ice Age Hunters of the Rockies*, ed. D. J. Stanford and J. S. Day, 343–359. Niwot: University of Colorado Press.

Bennett, J. L.

1999 Thermal Alteration of Bone. *Journal of Archaeological Science* 26:1–8.

Bettinger, R. L.

1991 *Hunter-Gatherers: Archaeological and Evolutionary Theory*. New York: Plenum Press.

Bettinger, R. L., R. Malhi, and H. McCarthy

1997 Central Place Models of Acorn and Mussel Processing. *Journal of Archaeological Science* 24:887–899.

Bettison, C. A.

1985 An Experimental Approach to Sickle Sheen Deposition and Archaeological Interpretation. *Lithic Technology* 14(1): 26–32.

Bigelow, N .H., J. E. Beget, and W. R. Powers

1990 Latest Pleistocene Increase in Wind Intensity Recorded in Aeolian Sediments from Central Alaska. *Quaternary Research* 34:160–168.

Binford, L. R.

1978a Dimensional Analysis of Behavior and Site Structure: Learning from an Eskimo Hunting Stand. *American Antiquity* 43:330–361.

1978b *Nunamiut Ethnoarchaeology*. Academic Press, New York.

1979 Organization and Formation Processes: Looking at Curated Technologies. *Journal of Anthropological Research* 35:255–273.

1980 Willow Smoke and Dog's Tails: Hunter-Gatherer Settlement Systems and Archaeological Site Formation. *American Antiquity* 45:4–20.

1986 An Alyawara Day: Making Men's Knives and Beyond. *American Antiquity* 51:547–562.

Bird-David, N. H.

1988 Hunter-Gatherers and Other People: A Re-examination. In *Hunters and Gatherers. Vol. 1, History, Evolution and Social Change*, ed. T. Ingold, D. Riches, and J. Woodburn, 17–30. Washington DC: Berg.

1993 Tribal Metaphorization of Human-Nature Relatedness: A Comparative Analysis. In *Environmentalism: The View from Anthropology*, ed. K. Milton, 112–125. New York: Routledge.

Bird Studies Canada

n.d. Migration Routes of Satellite Tracked Tundra Swans. http://www.bsc-eoc.org/swans/allswans.html.

Björck, S., B. Kromer, S. Johnsen, O. Bennike, D. Hammarlund, G. Lemdahi, G. Possnert, T. L. Rassmussen, B. Wohlfarth, C. Uffe Hammer, and M. Spunk.

1996 Synchronized Terrestrial-Atmospheric Deglacial Records Around the North Atlantic. *Science* 274:1155–1160.

Black, S. L., W. L. Ellis, D. G. Creel, and G. T. Goode

1999 *Hot Rock Cooking on the Greater Edwards Plateau: Four Burned Rock Midden Sites in West Central Texas*. Studies in Archeology 22, Texas Archeological Research Laboratory, University of Texas at Austin and Archeology Studies Program Report 2, Environmental Affairs Division, Texas Department of Transportation.

Bobrowsky, P. T., and B. Ball

1989 The Theory and Mechanics of Ecological Diversity in Archaeology. In *Quantifying Diversity in Archaeology*, ed. R. D. Leonard and G. T. Jones, 4–10. Cambridge: Cambridge University Press.

Boisvert, R. A.

1999 Paleoindian Occupation of the White Mountains, New Hampshire. *Geographie physique et Quaternaire* 53(1): 159–174.

2001 Paleoindian of Northern New England in an Environmental Context: The Israel River Complex, Jefferson, New Hampshire. Paper presented at the 66th Annual Meeting of the Society for American Archaeology, New Orleans.

Boldurian A. T., and J. Cotter

1999 *Clovis Revisited: New Perspectives on Paleoindian Adaptations from Blackwater Draw, New Mexico*. Philadelphia: University Museum, University of Pennsylvania.

Bonnichsen, R., L. Hodges, W. Ream, K. G. Field, D. L. Kirner, K. Selsor, and R. E. Taylor

2001 Methods for the Study of Ancient Hair: Radiocarbon Dates and Gene Sequences from Individual Hairs. *Journal of Archaeological Science* 28:775–785.

Borrero, L. A., and N. V. Franco

1997 Early Patagonian Hunter-Gatherers: Subsistence and Technology. *Journal of Anthropological Research* 53(2): 219–239.

Boszhardt, R. F.

1991 Paleoindian Study Unit: Region 6, Western Wisconsin. *Wisconsin Archeologist* 72:155–200.

Boszhardt, R. F., J. L. Theler, and D. G. Wilder
1993 *Megafauna of Wisconsin*. University of Wisconsin–La Crosse, Reports of Investigations No. 161. Mississippi Valley Archaeology Center, La Crosse WI.

Bradley, B. A.
1982 Lithic Technology. In *The Agate Basin Site*, ed. G. C. Frison and D. J. Stanford, 181–208. New York: Academic Press.

Braun, L.
1950 *Deciduous Forests of Eastern North America*. Philadelphia: Blakson.

Breitburg, E., J. B. Broster, A. L. Reesman, R. G. Stearns
1996 The Coats-Hines Site: Tennessee's First Paleoindian-Mastodon Association. *Current Research in the Pleistocene* 13:6–7.

Brennan, L. A.
1982 A Compilation of Fluted Points of Eastern North America by Count and Distribution: An AENA Project. *Archaeology of Eastern North America* 10:27–46.

Breternitz, D. A., A. C. Swedlund, and D. C. Anderson
1971 An Early Burial from Gordon Creek, Colorado. *American Antiquity* 36:170–182.

Brightman, R. A.
1993 *Grateful Prey: Rock Cree Human-Animal Relationships*. Los Angeles: University of California Press.

Brink, J., and R. Dawe
1989 *Final Report of the 1985 and 1986 Field Season at Head-Smashed-In Buffalo Jump, Alberta*. Archaeological Survey of Alberta, Manuscript Series No. 16. Edmonton: Alberta Culture and Multiculturalism.

Brose, D. S.
1978 Comments on Stoltman's "Temporal Models in Prehistory." *Current Anthropology* 19:729–731.

Broster, J. B., and M. R. Norton
1993 The Carson-Conn-Short Site (40BN190): An Extensive Clovis Habitation in Benton County, Tennessee. *Current Research in the Pleistocene* 10:3–4.

Broughton, J. M., and J. F. O'Connell
1999 On Evolutionary Ecology, Selectionist Archaeology, and Behavioral Ecology. *American Antiquity* 64:153–165.

Brown, J., and C. E. Cleland
1968 The Late Glacial and Early Postglacial Faunal Resources in Midwestern Biomes Newly Opened to Human Adaptation. In *The Quaternary of Illinois*, ed. R. E. Bergstrom, 114–122. Special Publication No. 14. Urbana: College of Agriculture, University of Illinois.

Bryant, V. M., Jr.
1998 Pre-Clovis. In *Archaeology of Prehistoric Native America: An Encyclopedia*, ed. G. Gibbon, 682–683. New York: Garland.

Buckmaster, M. M., and J. R. Paquette
1988 The Gorto Site: Preliminary Report on a Late Paleoindian Site in Marquette County, Michigan. *Wisconsin Archeologist* 69:88–112.

Bull, J., and J. Farrand Jr.
1995 *The Audubon Society Field Guide to North American Birds*. New York: Alfred A. Knopf.

Bullen, R. P.
1975 *A Guide to the Identification of Florida Projectile Points*. Gainesville FL: Kendall Books.

Burch, E. S.
1972 The Caribou/Wild Reindeer as a Human Resource. *American Antiquity* 37:339–368.

Burnham, P.
1973 The Explanatory Value of the Concept of Adaptation in Studies of Culture Change. In *The Explanation of Culture Change: Models in Prehistory*, ed. C. Renfrew, 93–103. Pittsburgh: University of Pittsburgh Press.

Burns, R. M., and B. H. Honkala
1990 *Silvics of North America*. Vol. 1, *Conifers*. U.S. Department of Agriculture Forest Service Handbook 654. Washington DC: U.S. Department of Agriculture.

Butler, B. R.
1963 An Early Man Site at Big Camas Prairie, South-Central Idaho. *Tebiwa* 6(1): 22–33.
1964 A Recent Early Man Find in Southeastern Idaho. *Tebiwa* 7(1): 39–40.

Byers, D. A.
2001 The Hell Gap Site Locality II Agate Basin Faunal Assemblage. Master's thesis, University of Wyoming.

Cable, J. S.
1996 Haw River Revisited: Implications for Modeling Terminal Late Glacial and Early Holocene Hunter-Gatherer Settlement Systems in the Southeast. In *The Paleoindian and Early Archaic Southeast*, ed. D. G. Anderson and K. E. Sassaman, 107–148. Tuscaloosa: University of Alabama Press.
1998 Review of *Archaeology of the Mid-Holocene Southeast*, edited by K. E. Sassaman and D. G. Anderson. *American Antiquity* 63:184–185.

Caldwell, J. R.
1958 *Trend and Tradition in the Prehistory of the Eastern United States*. American Anthropological Association, Memoir No. 88.

Callahan, E.
1979 The Basics of Biface Knapping in the Eastern Fluted Point Tradition: A Manual for Flintknappers and Lithic Analysts. *Archaeology of Eastern North America* 7(1): 1–180.

Cambron, J. W., and D. C. Hulse
1960 An Excavation on the Quad Site. *Tennessee Archaeologist* 16(1): 14–26.

Cannon, M. D., and D. J. Meltzer
2004 Early Paleoindian Foraging: Examining the Faunal Evidence for Large Mammal Specialization and Regional Variability in Prey Choice. *Quaternary Science Reviews* 23:1955–1987.

Carlson, R. L.
1998 Coastal British Columbia in the Light of North Pacific Maritime Adaptations. *Arctic Anthropology* 35(1): 23–35.

Carr, R. S.
1987 Early Man in South Florida. *Archaeology* (Nov./Dec.): 62–63.

Carter, B.C., and J.S. Dunbar
2006 Early Archaic Archaeology, Chapter 18, *First Floridians and Last Mastodons: The Page-Ladson Site on the Aucilla River*, ed. S.D. Webb, pp. 493–516. Dordrect, the Netherlands: Springer.

Cashdan, E.
1992 Spatial Organization and Habitat Use. In *Evolutionary Ecology and Human Behavior*, ed. E. A. Smith and B. Winterhalder, 237–266. Hawthorne NY: Aldine de Gruyter.

Cassells, S. E.
1997 *The Archaeology of Colorado*. Boulder CO: Johnson Books.

Cattelain, P.
1997 Hunting during the Upper Paleolithic: Bow, Spearthrower, or Both? In *Projectile Technology*, ed. H. Knecht, 213–240. New York: Plenum Press.

Chalifoux, E.
1999 Late Paleoindian Occupation in a Coastal Environment: A Perspective from La Martre (Gaspé Peninsula). *Northeast Anthropology* 57:69–79.

Christenson, A. L.
1986 Reconstructing Prehistoric Projectiles from Their Stone Points. *Journal of the Society of Archer-Antiquaries* 29:21–27.

Cinq-Mars, J.
1979 Blue Fish Cave I: A Late Pleistocene Eastern Beringian Cave Deposit in the Northern Yukon. *Canadian Journal of Archaeology* 3:1–32.

Cinq-Mars, J., and R. E. Morlan

1999 Bluefish Caves and Old Crow Basin: A New Rapport. In *Ice Age People of North America: Environments, Origins, and Adaptations*, ed. R. Bonnichsen and K. L. Turnmire, 200–212. Corvallis: Oregon State University Press.

Claggett, S. R., and J. S. Cable, assemblers

1982 *The Haw River Sites: Archaeological Investigations at Two Stratified Sites in the North Carolina Piedmont*. Report R-2386. Jackson MI: Commonwealth Associates.

Clark, J. A.

1982 Some Early and Late Paleo-Indian Points from Winnebago County. *Wisconsin Archeologist* 63:117–127.

1995 The Lake Poygan Phase: A Late Paleoindian Manifestation in East Central Wisconsin. Paper presented at the 40th Midwest Archaeological Conference, South Beloit IL.

Clarke, D. L.

1968 *Analytical Archaeology*. London: Methuen.

Clarke, W. E.

1965 *Relation of Ground-Water Inflow and of Bank and Channel Storage to Streamflow Pickup in the Santa Fe River, Florida*. Geological Survey Professional Papers, Hydrologic Studies.

Clastres, P.

1998 *Chronicle of the Guayaki*. New York: Zone Books.

Clayton, L., J. W. Attig, D. M. Mickelson, and M. D. Johnson

1992 *Glaciation of Wisconsin*. Education Series No. 36. Madison WI: Geological and Natural History Survey.

Cleland, C. E.

1965 Barren Ground Caribou (*Rangifer articus*) from an Early Man Site in Southwestern Michigan. *American Antiquity* 30:350–351.

Cleland, C. E., M. B. Holman, and J. A. Holman

1998 The Mason-Quimby Line Revisited. *Wisconsin Archeologist* 79:8–27.

Cockrell, W. A., and L. Murphy

1978 Pleistocene Man in Florida. *Archaeology of Eastern North America* 6:1–12.

Cohen, M. N.

1989 *Health and the Rise of Civilization*. New Haven CT: Yale University Press.

Collins, M. B.

1968 A Note on Broad Corner-Notched Projectile Points Used in Bison Hunting in Western Texas. *Bull-Roarer* 3(2):13–14.

1971 A Review of Llano Estacado Archaeology and Ethnohistory. *Plains Anthropologist* 16:85–104.

1990 The Archeological Sequence at Kincaid Rockshelter, Uvalde County, Texas. *Transactions of the Twenty-fifth Regional Archeological Symposium for Southeastern New Mexico and Western Texas*, 25–33. Midland TX: Midland Archeological Society.

1995 Forty Years of Archeology in Central Texas. *Bulletin of the Texas Archeological Society* 66:361–400.

1998a Interpreting the Clovis Artifacts from the Gault Site. TARL *Research Notes* 6(1): 4–12.

1998b The Place of Wilson-Leonard in Southern Plains Prehistory. In *Wilson-Leonard: An 11,000-Year Archeological Record of Hunter-Gatherers in Central Texas*. Vol. 1, *Introduction, Background, and Synthesis*, ed. M. B. Collins, 277–291. Studies in Archeology 31, Texas Archeological Research Laboratory, University of Texas at Austin and Archeology Studies Program, Report 10, Environmental Affairs Division, Texas Department of Transportation.

1999a Clovis and Folsom Lithic Technology on and near the Southern Plains: Similar Ends, Different Means. In *Folsom Lithic Technology*, ed. D. S. Amick, 12–38. Ann Arbor MI: International Monographs in Prehistory, Archaeological Series 12.

1999b *Clovis Blade Technology: A Comparative Study of the Keven Davis Cache, Texas*. Austin: University of Texas Press.

2002 The Gault Site, Texas, and Clovis Research. *Athena Review* 3(2): 31–41, 100–101.

2004 Archeology in Central Texas. In *The Prehistory of Texas*, ed. T. K. Perttula, 101–126. College Station: Texas A&M University Press.

Collins, M. B., ed.

1998 *Wilson-Leonard: An 11,000-Year Archeological Record of Hunter-Gatherers in Central Texas*. 5 vols. Studies in Archeology 31, Texas Archeological Research Laboratory, University of Texas at Austin and Archeology Studies Program, Report 10, Environmental Affairs Division, Texas Department of Transportation.

Collins, M. B., M. D. Blum, R. A. Rickliss, and S. Valastro

1990 Quaternary Geology and Prehistory of the Vera Daniels Site, Travis County, Texas. *Current Research in the Pleistocene* 7:8–10.

Collins, M. B., and C. B. Bousman, organizers

1995 Rethinking Paleoindian Subsistence on the Southern Plains. Symposium organized for the 60th Annual Meeting of the Society for American Archaeology, Minneapolis.

Collins, M. B., and K. M. Brown

2000 The Gault Gisement. *Current Archaeology in Texas* 2(1): 8–11.

Collins, M. B., G. L. Evans, T. N. Campbell, M. C. Winans, and C. E. Mear

1989 Clovis Occupation at Kincaid Shelter, Texas. *Current Research in the Pleistocene* 10:10–11.

Collins, M. B., W. A. Gose, and S. Shaw

1994 Preliminary Geomorphological Findings at Dust and Nearby Caves. *Journal of Alabama Archaeology* 40(1–2): 35–56.

Collins, M. B., T. R. Hester, and P. J. Headrick

1992 Engraved Cobbles from the Gault Site, Central Texas. *Current Research in the Pleistocene* 9:3–4.

Collins, M. B., D. B. Hudler, and S. L. Black

2003 *Pavo Real (41bx52): A Paleoindian and Archaic Camp and Workshop on the Balcones Escarpment, South-Central Texas.* Studies in Archeology 41, Texas Archeological Research Laboratory, University of Texas at Austin and Archeological Studies Program, Report 50, Environmental Affairs Division, Texas Department of Transportation.

Collins, M. B., and J. C. Lohse

2004 The Nature of Clovis Blades and Blade Cores. In *Entering America: Northeast Asia and Beringia before the Last Glacial Maximum*, ed. D. B. Madsen, 159–183. Salt Lake City: University of Utah Press.

Collins, M. B., and C. E. Mear

1998 The Site and Its Setting. In *Wilson-Leonard: An 11,000-Year Archeological Record of Hunter-Gatherers in Central Texas.* Vol. 1, *Introduction, Background, and Synthesis*, ed. M. B. Collins, 5–32. Studies in Archeology 31, Texas Archeological Research Laboratory, University of Texas at Austin and Archeology Studies Program, Report 10, Environmental Affairs Division, Texas Department of Transportation.

Cook, H.

1927 Definite Evidence of Human Artifacts in the American Pleistocene. *Science* 62:459–460.

Count, E. W.

1935 The Earth-Diver: An Attempt at an Asiatic-American Correlation. Ph.D. diss., University of California.

Crook, W. W., and R. K. Harris

1957 Hearths and Artifacts of Early Man near Lewisville, Texas, and Associated Faunal Material. *Bulletin of the Texas Archeological Society* 28:7–97.

Crowl, G. H., and R. Stuckenrath

1977 Geologic Setting of the Shawnee Minisink Paleoindian Site. In *Amerinds and Their Paleoenvironments in Northeastern North America*, ed. W. S. Newman and B. Salwen, 218–222. Annals of the New York Academy of Sciences 288. New York: Academy of Sciences.

Cummings, L. S.

1990 Coprolites from Medieval Christian Nubia: An Interpretation of Diet and Nutritional Stress. Ph.D. diss., University of Colorado.

Curran, M. L.

1984 The Whipple Site and Paleoindian Tool Assemblage Variation: A Comparison of Intrasite Structuring. *Archaeology of Eastern North America* 12:5–40.

1994 Hampshire Paleoindian Research and the Whipple Site. *New Hampshire Archaeologist* 33–34:29–52.

Curran, M. L., and D. F. Dincauze

1977 Paleoindians and Paleo-Lakes: New Data from the Connecticut Drainage. In *Amerinds and Their Paleoenvironments in Northeastern North America*, ed. W. S. Newman and B. Salwen, 333–348. Annals of the New York Academy of Sciences, vol. 288. New York: Academy of Sciences.

Curran, M. L., and J. R. Grimes

1989 Ecological Implications for Paleoindian Lithic Procurement Economy in New England. In *Eastern Paleoindian Lithic Resource Use*, ed. C. J. Ellis and J. C. Lothrop, 41–74. Boulder CO: Westview Press.

Custer, J. F., and R. M. Stewart

1990 Environment, Analogy, and Early Paleoindian Economies in Northeastern North America. In *Research in Economic Anthropology*, ed. K. B. Tankersley and B. L. Isaac, 303–322. Supplement No. 5. Greenwich CT: JAI Press.

Cwynar, L. C.

1978 Recent History of Fire and Vegetation from Laminated Sediment of Greenleaf Lake, Algonquin Park. *Canadian Journal of Botany* 56:10–21.

Daniel, R. I.

2001 Stone Raw Material Availability and Early Archaic Settlement in the Southeastern United States. *American Antiquity* 66:237–266.

Daniel, R. I., and M. Wisenbaker

1987 *Harney Flats: A Florida Paleo-Indian Site*. New York: Baywood.

Daniels, I. R., Jr.

1996 Early Archaic Settlement in the Southeast: A North Carolina Perspective. In *The Paleoindian and Early Archaic Southeast*, ed. D. G. Anderson and K. E. Sassaman, 84–91. Tuscaloosa: University of Alabama Press.

Dansie, A. J., and W. J. Jerrems

1999 Lahontan Chronology and Early Human Occupation in the Western Great Basin: A New Look at Old Collections. Poster presentation at the "Clovis and Beyond" conference, Santa Fe NM.

Darby, M.

1999 Meat and Wapatos: The Post-glacial Distribution of *Saggitaria latifolia* in North America and the Implications of This with Regard to the Diet of Late Pleistocene, Early Holocene Hunter-Gatherers. Paper presented at the 63rd Annual Meeting of the Society for American Archaeology, Seattle.

Davis, E. L.

1978 Associations of People and a Rancholabrean Fauna at China Lake, California. In *Early Man in America from a Circum-Pacific Perspective*, ed. A. L. Bryan, 183–217. Occasional Papers No. 1. Edmonton: Department of Anthropology, University of Alberta.

Davis, E. M.

1954 The Culture History of Central Great Plains Prior to the Introduction of Pottery. Ph.D. diss., Harvard University.

Davis, L. B.

1971 The Lindsey Mammoth Site (24DW501): Paleontology and Paleoecology. Paper presented at the annual meeting of the Montana Archaeological Society.

Davis, L. B., ed.

1988 *Avonlea Yesterday and Today: Archaeology and Prehistory*. Saskatoon: Saskatchewan Archaeological Society.

Davis, L. B., S. A. Aaberg, W. P. Eckerle, J. W. Fisher, and S. T. Greiser

1989 Montane Paleoindian Occupation of the Barton Gulch Site, Ruby Valley, Southwestern Montana. *Current Research in the Pleistocene* 6:7–9.

Davis, L. B., S. A. Aaberg, and S. T. Greiser

1988 Paleoindians in Transmontane Southwestern Montana: The Barton Gulch Occupations, Ruby River Drainage. *Current Research in the Pleistocene* 5:9–11.

Davis, L. B., and S. T. Greiser

1992 Indian Creek Paleoindians: Early Occupation of the Elkhorn Mountains' Southeast Flank, West-Central Montana. In *Ice Age Hunters of the Rockies*, ed. D. J. Stanford and J. S. Day, 285–321. Niwot: University of Colorado Press.

Davis, M. B.

1969 Climate Changes in Southern Connecticut Recorded by Pollen Changes at Rogers Lake. *Ecology* 50:409–522.

1983 Holocene Vegetational History of the Eastern United States. In *Late-Quaternary Environments of the United States*. Vol. 2, *The Holocene*, ed. H. E. Wright Jr., 166–181. Minneapolis: University of Minnesota Press.

Davis, R. B., and G. L. Jacobson Jr.

1985 Glacial and Early Holocene Landscapes in Northern New England and Adjacent Areas of Canada. *Quaternary Research* 23:341–358.

Dawson, K. C.

1983 A. Cummins Site: A Late Paleo-Indian (Plano) Site at Thunder Bay, Ontario. *Ontario Archaeology* 39:3–31.

deFrance, S., D. K. Keefer, J. B. Richardson, and A. Umire Alvarez

2001 Late Paleoindian Coastal Foragers: Specialized Extractive Behavior at Quebrada Tacahuay, Peru. *Latin American Antiquity* 12:413–426.

DeJarnette, D. L., E. Kurjack, and J. Cambron

1962 Excavations at the Stanfield-Worley Bluff Shelter. *Journal of Alabama Archaeology* 8(1–2): 1–124.

Delcourt, P. A., and H. R. Delcourt

1981 Vegetational Maps for Eastern North America: 40,000 Yr BP to the Present. In *Geobotany II*, ed. R. C. Romans, 123–166. New York: Plenum Press.

1985 Quaternary Palynology and Vegetational History of the Southeastern United States. In *Pollen Records of Late-Quaternary North American Sediments*, ed. V. M. Bryant and R. G. Holloway, 1–37. Dallas: American Association of Stratigraphic Palynologists Foundation.

Deller, D. B., and C. J. Ellis

1984 Crowfield: A Preliminary Report on a Probable Paleo-Indian Cremation in Southwestern Ontario. *Archaeology of Eastern North America* 12:41–71.

1988 Early Paleoindian Complexes in Southwestern Ontario. In *Late Pleistocene and Early Holocene Paleoecology of the Eastern Great Lakes Region*, ed. R. S. Laub, N. G. Miller, and D. W. Steadman, 251–263. Bulletin of the Buffalo Society of Natural Sciences 33, Buffalo NY.

Denbow, J.

1984 Prehistoric Herders and Foragers of the Kalahari: The Evidence for 1500 Years of Interaction. In *Past and Present in Hunter Gatherer Studies*, ed. C. Stirrer, 175–194. Orlando FL: Academic Press.

Dent, R. J.

1979 *Ecological and Sociocultural Reconstruction in the Upper Delaware Valley*. Ann Arbor MI: University Microfilms.

1981 Amerind Society and the Environment: Evidence from the Upper Delaware Valley. In *Anthropological Careers: Essays Presented to the Anthropological Society of Washington during Its Centennial Year, 1979*, ed. R. Landman, 74–85. Washington DC: Anthropological Society of Washington.

1985 Amerinds and the Environment: Myth, Reality, and the Upper Delaware Valley. In *Shawnee Minisink: A Stratified Paleoindian-Archaic Site in the Upper Delaware Valley of Pennsylvania*, ed. C. W. McNett, 123–163. New York: Academic Press.

1995 *Chesapeake Prehistory: Old Traditions, New Directions*. New York: Plenum Press.

Dent, R. J., and B. E. Kauffman

1985 Aboriginal Subsistence and Site Ecology as Interpreted from Microfloral Remains. In *Shawnee Minisink: A Stratified Paleoindian-Archaic Site in the Upper Delaware Valley of Pennsylvania*, ed. C. W. McNett, 55–79. New York: Academic Press.

Descola, P.

1994 *In the Society of Nature: A Native Ecology in Amazonia*. Trans. Nora Scott. Cambridge: Cambridge University Press.

Detwiler, K. R.

1994, 1999, 2000 Field Notes. Excavations at Dust Cave, Alabama. On file at Office of Archaeological Services, University of Alabama Museums, Moundville.

2000 Gathering in the Late Paleoindian: Botanical Remains from Dust Cave, Alabama. Paper presented at the 65th Annual Meeting of the Society for American Archaeology, Philadelphia.

2001 Plant Use during the Late Paleoindian/Early Archaic Transition at Dust Cave. Paper presented at the 58th Annual Southeastern Archaeological Conference, Chattanooga TN.

Dial, S. W., A. C. Kerr, and M .B. Collins

1998 Projectile Points. In *Wilson-Leonard: An 11,000-Year Archeological Record of Hunter-Gatherers in Central Texas*. Vol. 2, *Chipped Stone Artifacts*, ed. M. B. Collins, 313–445. Studies in Archeology 31, Texas Archeological Research Laboratory, University of Texas at Austin and Archeology Studies Program, Report 10, Environmental Affairs Division, Texas Department of Transportation.

Dibble, D. S., and D. Lorrain

1968 *Bonfire Shelter: A Stratified Bison Kill Site, Val Verde County, Texas*. University of Texas at Austin, Texas Memorial Museum, Miscellaneous Papers 1.

Dietrich, P. M., and J. A. Gifford

1996 Early-Middle Archaic Paleoenvironments and Human Populations at Little Salt Springs, Florida. Ms. on file, Rosenstiel School of Marine and Atmospheric Science at the University of Miami.

Dikov, N. N.

1996 The Ushki Sites, Kamchatka Peninsula. In *American Beginnings:*

The Prehistory and Palaeoecology of Beringia, ed. F. H. West, 244–250. Chicago: University of Chicago Press.

1990 Population Migration from Asia to Pre-Columbian America. Paper presented at the 17th International Congress of Historical Sciences, Madrid.

Dillehay, T. D.

1974 Late Quaternary Bison Population Changes on the Southern Plains. *Plains Anthropologist* 19:180–196.

1997 *Monte Verde: A Late Pleistocene Settlement in Chile. Vol. 2, The Archaeological Context and Interpretation*. Washington DC: Smithsonian Institution Press.

2000 *The Settlement of the Americas: A New Prehistory*. New York: Basic Books.

Dincauze, D. F.

1981 Paleoenvironmental Reconstruction in the Northeast: The Art of Multidisciplinary Science. In *Foundations of Northeast Archaeology*, ed. Dean Snow, 51–96. New York: Academic Press.

1988 Tundra and Enlightenment: Landscapes for Northeastern Paleoindians. *Quarterly Review of Archaeology* 9:6–8.

1993a Fluted Points in the Eastern Forests. In *From Kostenki to Clovis: Upper Paleolithic–Paleo-Indian Adaptations*, ed. O. Soffer and N. D. Praslov, 279–292. New York: Plenum Press.

1993b Pioneering in the Pleistocene: Large Paleoindian Sites in the Northeast. In *Archaeology of Eastern North America*, ed. J. Stoltman, 43–60. Archaeological Report No. 25. Jackson: Mississippi Department of Archives and History.

2000 The Northeast. *Common Ground* (Spring/Summer): 34–43.

Dincauze, D. F., and M. L. Curran

1983 Paleoindians as Generalists: An Ecological Perspective. Paper presented at the 48th Annual Meeting of the Society for American Archeology, Pittsburgh.

Dincauze, D. F., and V. Jacobson

2001 The Birds of Summer: Lakeside Routes into Late Pleistocene New England. *Canadian Journal of Archaeology* 25:121–126.

Dincauze, D. F., and M. T. Mulholland

1977 Early and Middle Archaic Site Distributions and Habitats in Southern New England. In *Amerinds and Their Paleoenvironments in Northeastern North America*, ed. W. S. Newman and B. Salwen, 439–456. Annals of the New York Academy of Sciences, vol. 288. New York: Academy of Sciences.

Dixon, E. J.

1999 *Bones, Boats, and Bison: Archeology and the First Colonization of Western North America*. Albuquerque: University of New Mexico Press.

Dobres, M. A., and J. E. Robb

2000 Agency in Archaeology: Paradigm or Platitude. In *Agency in Archaeology*, ed. M. A. Dobres and J. E. Robb, 13–17. London: Routledge.

Dodson, P.

1973 The Significance of Small Bones in Paleoecological Interpretation. *Geology* 12(1): 15–19.

Dolan, E. M., and G. T. Allen

1961 *An Investigation of the Darby and Hornsby Springs Sites, Alachua County, Florida*. Special Publication No. 7. Tallahassee: Florida Geological Survey.

Dragoo, D. W.

1976 Some Aspects of Eastern North American Prehistory: A Review 1975. *American Antiquity* 41:3–37.

Driskell, B. N.

1994 Stratigraphy and Chronology at Dust Cave. *Journal of Alabama Archaeology* 40(1–2): 17–34.

1996 Stratified Late Pleistocene and Early Holocene Deposits at Dust Cave, Northwestern Alabama. In *The Paleoindian and Early Archaic Southeast*, ed. D. G. Anderson and K. E. Sassaman, 315–330. Tuscaloosa: University of Alabama Press.

1998 An Assessment of Use-Wear Traces on Chipped Stone Artifacts. In *Wilson-Leonard: An 11,000-Year Archaeological Record of Hunters-Gatherers in Central Texas*. Vol. 3, *Artifacts and Special Artifactual Studies*, ed. M. B. Collins, 732–743. Studies in Archeology 31, Texas Archeological Research Laboratory, University of Texas at Austin and Archeology Studies Program, Report 10, Environmental Affairs Division, Texas Department of Transportation.

Driver, J. C.

1982 Early Prehistoric Killing of Bighorn Sheep in the Southeastern Canadian Rockies. *Plains Anthropologist* 27:265–271.

1999 Raven Skeletons from Paleoindian Contexts, Charlie Lake Cave, British Columbia. *American Antiquity* 64:289–298.

Dudzik, M. J.

1991 First People: The Paleoindian Tradition in Northwestern Wisconsin. *Wisconsin Archeologist* 72:137–154.

Dunbar, J. S.

1981 The Effect of Geohydrology and Natural Resource Availability on Site Utilization at the Fowler Bridge Mastodon Site (8Hi393c/uw) in Hillsborough County, Florida. In *Report of Phase II Underwater Archaeological Testing at the Fowler Bridge Mastodon Site (8Hi393c/uw)*,

Hillsborough County, Florida, comp. Jill Palmer, J. S. Dunbar, and Danny H. Clayton, 63–106. Tallahassee FL: Bureau of Archives, History and Records Management.

1991 Resource Orientation of Clovis and Suwannee Age Paleoindian Sites in Florida. In *Clovis Origins and Adaptations*, ed. R. Bonnichsen and K. L. Turnmire, 185–213. Corvallis: Center for the Study of the First Americans, Oregon State University.

2002 Chronostratigraphy and Paleoclimate of Late Pleistocene Florida and the Implications of Changing Paleoindian Land Use. Master's thesis, Florida State University.

2006 a Paleoindian and Early Holocene Land Use Options Based on Changing Climate and Resource Availability. In *First Floridians and Last Mastodons: The Page-Ladson Site on the Aucilla River*, ed. S. D. Webb. Dordrecht, The Netherlands: Springer.

2006b Pleistocene-Holocene Climate Change: Chronostratigraphy and Geoclimate of the Southeast United States. In *First Floridians and Last Mastodons: The Page-Ladson Site on the Aucilla River*, ed. S. D. Webb. Dordrecht, The Netherlands: Springer.

2006c Paleoindian Archaeology, Chapter 14. In *First Floridians and Last Mastodons: The Page-Ladson Site on the Avcilla River*, ed. S.D. Webb. Dordrecht, The Netherlands: Springer.

Dunbar, J. S., and C. A. Hemmings

2004 Florida Paleoindian Points and Knives. In *New Directions on the First Americans*, ed. B. T. Lepper and R. Bonnichsen, 65–72. College Station: Center for the Study of the First Americans, Texas A&M Press.

Dunbar, J. S., C. A. Hemmings, P. Vojnovski, S. D. Webb, and W. M. Stanton

2005 The Ryan/Harley Site 8J>E1004: A Suwannee Point Site in the Wacissa River, North Florida. In *Paleoamerican Origins: Beyond Clovis*, ed. R. Bonnichsen, B. T. Lepper, D. J. Stanford, and M. R. Waters, 73–87. College Station: Center for the Study of the First Americans, Texas A&M Press.

Dunbar, J. S., and S. D. Webb

1996 Bone and Ivory Tools from Submerged Paleoindian Sites in Florida. In *The Paleoindian and Early Archaic Southeast*, ed. D. G. Anderson and K. E. Sassaman, 331–353. Tuscaloosa: University of Alabama Press.

Dunbar, J. S., S. D. Webb, and D. Cring

1989 Culturally and Naturally Modified Bones from a Paleoindian Site in the Aucilla River, North Florida. In *Bone Modification*, ed. R. Bonnichsen and M. Sorg, 473–497. Orono ME: Center for the Study of the First Americans.

Ebright, C. A.

1992 *Early Native American Prehistory on the Maryland Western Shore: Archeological Investigations at the Higgins Site.* Report prepared by the Maryland State Highway Administration for the Maryland State Railroad Administration.

Edwards, M., B. Finney, C. Mock, M. Abbott, N. H. Bigelow, V. Barber, P. Bartlein, and K. Kelts

2001 Late-Quaternary Paleohydrology and Paleoclimatology of Eastern Interior Alaska. *Quaternary Science Reviews.*

Edwards, R. A.

1948 An Abandoned Valley near High Springs, Florida. *Quarterly Journal of the Florida Academy of Sciences* 11(4): 325–332.

Elfhick, J., ed.

1995 *Atlas of Bird Migration.* New York: Random House.

Elias, S. M., S. K. Short, and R. L. Phillips

1992 Paleoecology of Late-Glacial Peats from the Bering Land Bridge, Chuckchi Sea Shelf Region, Northwestern Alaska. *Quaternary Research* 38:371–378.

Ellis, C., A. C. Goodyear III, D. F. Morse, and K. B. Tankersley

1998 Archaeology of the Pleistocene-Holocene Transition in Eastern North America. *Quaternary International* 49–50:151–166.

Ely, C. R., D. C. Douglas, A. C. Fowler, C. A. Babcock, D. V. Derksen, and J. Y. Takekawa

1997 Migration Behavior of Tundra Swans from the Yukon-Kuskokwim Delta, Alaska. *Wilson Bulletin* 109:679–692.

Engelbrecht, W., and C. Seyfert

1994 Paleoindian Watercraft: Evidence and Implications. *North American Archaeologist* 15:221–234.

Ensor, H. B.

1992 The Clovis Assemblage from the Belle Mina Paleo-Indian Locality, Middle Tennessee Valley, Limestone County, Alabama. Paper presented at the annual winter meeting of the Alabama Archaeological Society, Montgomery.

Epstein, J. B.

1969 *Surficial Geology of the Stroudsburg Quadrangle Pennsylvania–New Jersey.* Harrisburg PA: Bureau of Topographic and Geologic Survey.

Erlandson, J. M.

1998 Paleocoastal Occupations of Daisy Cave, San Miguel Island, California. Paper presented at 63rd Annual Meeting of the Society for American Archaeology, Seattle.

Erlandson, J. M., D. L. Kennett, B. L. Ingram, D. A. Guthrie, D. P. Morris, M. A. Tveskov, G. J. West, and P. L. Walker

1996 An Archaeological and Paleontological Chronology for Daisy Cave (CA-SMI-261), San Miguel Island, California. *Radiocarbon* 38(2): 355–373.

Erlandson, J., and M. L. Moss

1996 The Pleistocene-Holocene Transition along the Pacific Coast of North America. In *Humans at the End of the Ice Age: The Archaeology of the Pleistocene-Holocene Transition*, ed. L. G. Straus, B. V. Eriksen, J. M. Erlandson, and D. R. Yesner, 278–302. New York: Plenum Press.

Evans, J.

1978 *Paleo-Indian to Early Archaic Transition at the Shawnee Minisink Site.* Ann Arbor MI: University Microfilms.

1985 Paleoindian to Early Archaic Transition at the Shawnee Minisink Site. In *Shawnee Minisink: A Stratified Paleoindian-Archaic Site in the Upper Delaware Valley of Pennsylvania*, ed. C. W. McNett, 221–259. New York: Academic Press.

Eyre, F. H., ed.

1980 *Forest Cover Types of the United States and Canada.* Washington DC: Society of American Foresters.

Faught, M. K.

1996 Clovis Origins and Underwater Prehistoric Archaeology in Northwestern Florida. Ph.D. diss., University of Arizona.

Faught, M. K., and B. Carter

1998 Early Human Occupation and Environmental Change in Northwestern Florida. *Quaternary International* 49–50:167–176.

Fawcett, W. B., Jr.

1987 Communal Hunts, Human Aggregations, Social Variation, and Climatic Change. Ph.D. diss., University of Massachusetts.

Fedje, D.

1996 Early Human Presence in Banff National Park. In *Early Human Occupation in British Columbia*, ed. R. L. Carlson and L. D. Bona, 35–44. Vancouver: University of British Columbia Press.

Fedje, D. W., and H. Josenhans

2000 Drowned Forests and Archaeology on the Continental Shelf of British Columbia, Canada. *Geology* 28(2): 99–102.

Fedje, D. W., J. B. McSporran, and A. R. Mason

1996 Early Holocene Archaeology and Paleoecology at the Arrow Creek Sites in Gwaii Haanas. *Arctic Anthropology* 33(1): 116–142.

Fedje, D. W., J. M. White, M. C. Wilson, D. E. Nelson, J. S. Vogel, and J. R. Southon

1995 Vermilion Lakes Site: Adaptations and Environments in the Canadian Rockies during the Latest Pleistocene and Early Holocene. *American Antiquity* 60:81–108.

Fenenga, F.

1953 The Weights of Chipped Stone Points: A Clue to Their Functions. *Southwestern Journal of Anthropology* 9:309–323.

Ferring, C. R.

1995 The Late Quaternary Geology and Archaeology of the Aubrey Clovis Site, Texas: A Preliminary Report. In *Ancient Peoples and Landscapes*, ed. E. Johnson, 273–281. Lubbock: Museum of Texas Tech University.

2001 *The Archaeology and Paleoecology of the Aubrey Clovis Site (41DN479), Denton County, Texas*. Denton: Center for Environmental Archaeology, Department of Geography, University of North Texas.

Fiedel, S. J.

1996 Blood from Stones? Some Methodological and Interpretive Problems in Blood Residue Analysis. *Journal of Archaeological Science* 23:139–147.

1999a Artifact Provenience at Monte Verde: Confusion and Contradictions. *Scientific American Discovering Archaeology Special Report* 1(6): 1–12.

1999b Older Than We Thought: Implications of Corrected Dates for Paleoindians. *American Antiquity* 64:95–116.

Fifield, T. E.

1996 Human Remains in Alaska Reported to Be 9,730 Years Old. *SAA Bulletin* 14(5): 5.

Figgins, J.

1927 The Antiquity of Man in America. *Natural History* 27:229–239.

1933 A Further Contribution to the Antiquity of Man in America. *Proceedings of the Colorado Museum of Natural History* 12(2): 4–8.

Fisher, D. C.

1987 Mastodon Procurement by Paleoindians of the Great Lakes Region: Hunting or Scavenging? In *The Evolution of Human Hunting*, ed. M. H. Nitecki and D. V. Nitecki, 309–321. New York: Plenum Press.

Fladmark, K. R.

1979 Routes: Alternate Migration Corridors for Early Man in North America. *American Antiquity* 44:55–69.

1983 Times and Places: Environmental Correlates of Mid-to-Late Wisconsinan Human Population Expansion in North America. In

Early Man in the New World, ed. R. Shutler Jr., 13–42. Beverly Hills CA: Sage.

Fladmark, K. R., J. C. Driver, and D. Alexander

1988 The Paleoindian Component at Charlie Lake Cave (HBRf 39), British Columbia. *American Antiquity* 53:371–384.

Flegenheimer, N., and M. Zarate

1997 Considerations on Radiocarbon and Calibrated Dates from Cerro La China and Cerro El Sombrero, Argentina. *Current Research in the Pleistocene* 14:17–28.

Flenniken, J. J., and J. C. Haggarty

1979 Trampling as an Agency in the Formation of Edge Damage: An Experiment in Lithic Technology. *Northwest Anthropological Research Notes* 13:208–214.

Food and Agriculture Organization of the United Nations (FAO)

1974 *Handbook on Human Nutritional Requirements*. FAO Nutritional Studies 28.

Forbis, R. G., W. D. Strong, and M. E. Kirby

n.d. Signal Butte and MacHaffie: Two Stratified Sites on the Northern Great Plains. Ms. on file, National Park Service, Midwest Archaeological Center, Lincoln NE.

Forrest, D. T.

2000 Beyond Presence and Absence: Establishing Diversity in Connecticut's Early Holocene Archaeological Record. *Bulletin of the Archaeological Society of Connecticut* 62:79–100.

Foss, J. E.

1977 The Pedological Record at Several Paleoindian Sites in the Northeast. In *Amerinds and Their Paleoenvironments in Northeastern North America*, ed. W. S. Newman and B. Salwen, 234–244. Annals of the New York Academy of Sciences 288.

Fowler, C. S.

1986 Subsistence. In *Handbook of North American Indians*, W. C. Sturtevant, gen. ed. Vol. 11, *Great Basin*, ed. W. L. D'Azevedo, 64–97. Washington DC: Smithsonian Institution Press.

1996 Historical Perspectives on Timbisha Shoshone Land Management Practices, Death Valley, California. In *Case Studies in Environmental Archaeology*, ed. E. J. Reitz, L. A. Newsom, and S. J. Scudder, 87–101. New York: Plenum Press, 1996.

Fowler, C. S., and N. J. Turner

1999 Ecological/Cosmological Knowledge and Land Management among Hunter-Gatherers. In The *Cambridge Encyclopedia of Hunters and Gatherers*, ed. R. Lee and R. Daly, 419–425. Cambridge: Cambridge University Press.

Fowler, M. L.

1959 Summary Report of Modoc Rock Shelter: 1952, 1953, 1955, 1956. *Illinois State Museum Report of Investigations* 8.

Freeman, S.

2003 Prepared Surfaces: A First Impression. Paper presented at the 60th Annual Meeting of the Southeastern Archaeological Conference, Charlotte NC.

Frison, G. C.

1967 *The Piney Creek Sites, Wyoming*. University of Wyoming Publications 33(1).

1971 The Buffalo Pound in Northwestern Plains Prehistory: Site 48CA302, Wyoming. *American Antiquity* 36:77–91.

1973 Early Period Marginal Cultural Groups in Northern Wyoming. *Plains Anthropologist* 18:300–312.

1976 The Chronology of Paleo-Indian and Altithermal Cultures in the Big Horn Basin, Wyoming. In *Cultural Change and Continuity*, ed. C. E. Cleland, 147–173. New York: Academic Press.

1977 Paleoindian Site and Economic Orientations in the Big Horn Basin. In *Paleoindian Lifeways*, ed. E. Johnson, 97–116. Museum Journal 17. Lubbock: Texas Tech University.

1982 The Sheaman Site: A Clovis Component. In *The Agate Basin Site*, ed. G. C. Frison and D. J. Stanford, 143–157. New York: Academic Press.

1984 The Carter/Kerr-McGee Paleoindian Site: Cultural Resource Management and Archeological Research. *American Antiquity* 49:288–314.

1989 Experimental Use of Clovis Weaponry and Tools on African Elephants. *American Antiquity* 54:766–784.

1990 The North American High Plains Paleoindian: An Overview. *Journal of American Archaeology* 2:9–54.

1991a The Clovis Cultural Complex: New Data from Caches of Flaked Stone and Worked Bone Artifacts. In *Raw Material Economies among Prehistoric Hunter-Gatherers*, ed. A. Montet-White and S. Holen, 321–333. Publications in Anthropology 19. Lawrence: University of Kansas.

1991b *Prehistoric Hunters of the High Plains*. 2nd ed. New York: Academic Press.

1993 North American High Plains Paleo-Indian Hunting Strategies and Weaponry Assemblages. In *From Kostenki to Clovis: Upper Paleolithic–Paleo-Indian Adaptations*, ed. O. Soffer and N. D. Praslov, 237–249. New York: Plenum Press.

1998 Paleoindian. In *Archaeology of Prehistoric Native America: An Encyclopedia*, ed. G. Gibbon, 620–621. New York: Garland.

Frison, G. C., ed.
1996 *The Mill Iron Site*. Albuquerque: University of New Mexico Press, 1996.
Frison, G. C., R. L. Andrews, J. M. Adovasio, R. C. Carlisle, and R. Edgar
1986 A Late Paleoindian Animal Trapping Net from Northern Wyoming. *American Antiquity* 51:352–361.
Frison, G. C., and B. A. Bradley
1980 *Folsom Tools and Technology at the Hanson Site, Wyoming*. Albuquerque: University of New Mexico Press.
1999 *The Fenn Cache: Clovis Weapons and Tools*. Santa Fe NM: One Horse Land and Cattle Company.
Frison, G. C., C. V. Haynes Jr., and M. L. Larson
1996 Discussion and Conclusion. In *The Mill Iron Site*, ed. G. C. Frison, 205–216. Albuquerque: University of New Mexico Press.
Frison, G. C., and D. J. Stanford
1982 Agate Basin Components. In *The Agate Basin Site*, ed. G. C. Frison and D. J. Stanford, 76–135. New York: Academic Press.
Frison, G. C., and D. J. Stanford, eds.
1982 *The Agate Basin Site*. New York: Academic Press.
Frison, G. C., and L. C. Todd
1986 *The Colby Mammoth Site: Taphonomy and Archeology of a Clovis Kill in Northern Wyoming*. Albuquerque: University of New Mexico Press.
Frison, G. C., and L. C. Todd, eds.
1987 *The Horner Site: The Type Site of the Cody Cultural Complex*. New York: Academic Press.
Fritz, G. J., V. D. Whitekiller, and J. W. McIntosh
2001 Ethnobotany of Ku-Nu-Che: Cherokee Hickory Nut Soup. *Journal of Ethnobiology* 21(2): 1–27.
Funk, R. E.
1978 Post-Pleistocene Adaptations. In *Handbook of North American Indians*, W. C. Sturtevant, gen. ed. Vol. 15, *Northeast*, ed. B. G. Trigger, 16–27. Washington DC: Smithsonian Institution Press.
Futato, E. M.
1982 *Archaeological Investigations in the Cedar Creek and Upper Bear Creek Reservoirs*. Report submitted to the Tennessee Valley Authority, Norris, by the Office of Archaeological Research, University of Alabama. Office of Archaeological Research, Report of Investigations 29, University of Alabama, Moundville.
1983 Patterns of Lithic Resource Utilization in the Cedar Creek Reservoir Area. *Southeastern Archaeology* 2(2): 118–131.
1996 A Synopsis of Paleoindian and Early Archaic Research in Alabama. In *The Paleoindian and Early Archaic Southeast*, ed. D. G. Anderson and K. E. Sassaman, 298–314. Tuscaloosa: University of Alabama Press.

Gamble, C. S.
1986 *The Palaeolithic Settlement of Europe*. Cambridge: Cambridge University Press.

Gamble, C. S., and W. A. Boismier, eds.
1991 *Ethnoarchaeological Approaches to Mobile Campsites: Hunter-Gatherer and Pastoralist Case Studies*. Ann Arbor MI: International Monographs in Prehistory.

Gardner, P. S.
1994 Carbonized Plant Remains from Dust Cave. *Journal of Alabama Archaeology* 40(1–2): 192–211.
1997 The Ecological Structure and Behavioral Implications of Mast Exploitation Strategies. In *People, Plants and Landscapes*, ed. K. J. Gremillion, 161–178. Tuscaloosa: University of Alabama Press.

Gardner, W. M.
1974 The Flint Run Complex: Patterns and Process during the Paleoindian to Early Archaic. In The *Flint Run Paleoindian Complex: A Preliminary Report 1971 through 1973 Seasons*, 5–47. Occasional Paper No. 1. Washington DC: Archaeology Laboratory, Catholic University of America.
1983 Stop Me If You've Heard This One Before: The Flint Run Paleoindian Complex Revisited. *Archaeology of Eastern North America* 11:49–59.

Gaudreau, D. M.
1988 The Distribution of Late Quaternary Forest Regions in the Northeast: Pollen Data, Physiography, and the Prehistoric Record. In *Holocene Human Ecology in Northeastern North America*, ed. G. P. Nicholas, 215–256. New York: Plenum Press.

Gaudreau, D. C., and T. Webb III
1985 Late-Quaternary Pollen Stratigraphy and Isochrone Maps for the Northeastern United States. In *Pollen Records of Late-Quaternary North American Sediments*, ed. V. M. Bryant Jr. and R. G. Holloway, 247–280. Dallas: American Association of Stratigraphic Palynologists Foundation.

Gerasimov, M. M.
1958 The Paleolithic Site of Mal'ta (1956–7 Excavations). *Sovyetskayen Etnografiya* 3:28–52.

Gero, J.
1993 The Social World of Prehistoric Facts: Gender and Power in Paleoindian Research. In *Women in Archaeology: A Feminist Critique*, ed. H. du Cros and L. Smith, 31–40. Occasional Papers in Prehistory No. 23. Department of Prehistory, Australian National University, Canberra.

1995 Railroading Epistemology: Paleoindians and Women. In *Interpreting Archaeology: Finding Meaning in the Past*, ed. I. Hodder, M. Shanks, A. Alexandri, V. Buchli, J. Carman, J. Last, and G. Lucas, 175–178. New York: Routledge.

Gillam, J. C.

2002 The Early Archaic Landscape of the Middle Savannah River. Paper presented at the 59th Annual Meeting of the Southeastern Archaeological Conference, Biloxi MS.

Goebel, T., R. Powers, and N. Bigelow

1991 The Nenana Complex of Alaska and Clovis Origins. In *Clovis: Origins and Adaptations*, ed. R. Bonnichsen and K. L. Turnmire, 49–80. Corvallis: Center for the Study of the First Americans, Oregon State University.

Goebel, T., and S. B. Slobodin

1999 The Colonization of Western Beringia: Technology, Ecology, and Adaptations. In *Ice Age People of North America: Environments, Origins, and Adaptations*, ed. R. Bonnichsen and K. L. Turnmire, 104–155. Corvallis: Oregon State University Press.

Goebel, T., M. Waters, and M. Dikova

2002 The Ushki Sites, Kamchatka, and the Pleistocene Peopling of the Americas. Paper presented at the 67th Annual Meeting of the Society for American Archaeology, Denver.

Goldberg, P., and S. C. Sherwood

1994 Micromorphology of Dust Cave Sediments: Some Preliminary Results. *Journal of Alabama Archaeology* 40:56–64.

Goldman-Finn, N. S., and B. N. Driskell

1994 Introduction to Archaeological Research at Dust Cave. *Journal of Alabama Archaeology* 40(1–2): 1–16.

Goldman-Finn, N. S., and R. B. Walker

1994 The Dust Cave Bone Tool Assemblage. *Journal of Alabama Archaeology* 40(1–2): 107–115.

Goldstein, L.

1987 The Context of the Hensler Petroglyphs and Its Implications. *Wisconsin Archeologist* 68:412–418.

Goldstein, L., and R. Kind

1987 The Early Vegetation of the Region. In *The Southeastern Wisconsin Archaeology Project: 1986–1987 and Project Summary*, ed. L. Goldstein, 18–37. Archaeological Research Laboratory, Report of Investigations No. 88, University of Wisconsin–Milwaukee.

Gooding, J. D.

1981 *The Archaeology of Vail Pass Camp*. Colorado Department of Highways, Highway Salvage Report No. 35, Boulder.

Goodyear, A. C.

1974 *The Brand Site: A Techno-Functional Study of a Dalton Site in Northeast Arkansas*. Fayetteville: Arkansas Archeological Survey.

1982 The Chronological Position of the Dalton Horizon in the Southeastern United States. *American Antiquity* 47:382–395.

1983 A Hypothesis for the Use of Cryptocrystalline Raw Materials among Paleoindian Groups of North America. In *Eastern Paleoindian Lithic Resource Use*, ed. C. J. Ellis and C. Lothrop, 1–9. Boulder CO: Westview Press.

1999 The Early Holocene Occupation of the Southeastern United States: A Geoarchaeological Summary. In *Ice Age Peoples of North America: Environments, Origins, and Adaptations*, ed. R. Bonnichsen and K. L. Turnmire, 432–481. Corvallis: Oregon State University Press.

2000 Topper Site: Results of the 2000 Allendale Paleoindian Expedition. *Legacy* 5(2): 18–25.

2006 Evidence of Pre-Clovis Sites in the Eastern United States. In *Paleoamerican Origins: Beyond Clovis*, ed. R. Bonnichsen, B. T. Lepper, D. J. Stanford, and M. R. Waters, 89–98. College Station: Texas A&M University Press.

Gorecki, P. P.

1991 Horticulturalists as Hunter-Gatherers: Rock Shelter Usage in Papua New Guinea. In *Ethnoarchaeological Approaches to Mobile Campsites: Hunter-Gatherer and Pastoralist Case Studies*, ed. C. S. Gamble and W. A. Boismier, 237–262. Ann Arbor MI: International Monographs in Prehistory.

Gosden, C.

2001 Postcolonial Archaeology: Issues of Culture, Identity, and Knowledge. In *Archaeological Theory Today*, ed. I. Hodder, 241–261. Cambridge: Polity Press.

Gould, R. A.

1985 Lithic Procurement in Central Australia: A Closer Look at Binford's Idea of Embeddedness in Archaeology. *American Antiquity* 50:117–136.

Gove, H. E.

1994 The History of AMS, Its Advantages Over Decay Counting: Applications and Prospects. In *Radiocarbon after Four Decades: An Interdisciplinary Perspective*, ed. R. E. Taylor, A. Long, and R. S. Kra, 214–229. New York: Springer-Verlag.

Graham, R. W., C. V. Haynes, D. L. Johnson, and M. Kay

1981 Kimmswick: A Clovis-Mastodon Association in Eastern Missouri. *Science* 213:1115–1117.

Graham, R. W., and M. Kay
1988 Taphonomic Comparisons of Cultural and Noncultural Faunal Deposits at the Kimmswick and Barnhart Sites, Jefferson County, Missouri. In *Late Pleistocene and Early Holocene Paleoecology and Archeology of the Eastern Great Lakes Region*, ed. R. S. Laub, N. G. Miller, and D. W. Steadman, 227–240. *Bulletin of the Buffalo Society of Natural Sciences* 33.

Graham, R. W., and J. I. Mead
1987 Environmental Fluctuations and Evolution of Mammalian Faunas during the Last Deglaciation in North America. In *The Geology of North America*. Vol. K-3, *North America and Adjacent Oceans during the Last Deglaciation*, ed. W. F. Ruddiman and H. E. Wright Jr., 371–402. Boulder CO: Geological Society of America.

Gramly, R. M.
1992 *Guide to the Paleo-Indian Artifacts of North America*. 2nd ed. Buffalo NY: Persimmon Press Monographs in Archaeology.
1993 *The Richey Clovis Cache: Earliest Americans along the Columbia River*. Buffalo NY: Persimmon Press Monographs in Archaeology.
1996 An Embedded Projectile Point Found near Wapakoneta, Auglaize County, Ohio. *Ohio Archaeologist* 46(3): 5–9.

Grayson, D. K.
1984 *Quantitative Zooarchaeology: Topics in the Analysis of Archaeological Faunas*. Orlando FL: Academic Press.
1991 Late Pleistocene Mammalian Extinctions in North America: Taxonomy, Chronology, and Explanations. *Journal of World Prehistory* 5(3): 193–231.

Greenan, D. N.
1985 Investigation on the Possible Use of Phytoliths for Environmental Reconstruction. Ms. in author's possession.

Greene, A. M.
1967 The Betty Greene Site: A Late Paleo-Indian Site in Eastern Wyoming. Master's thesis, University of Pennsylvania.

Greiser, S. T.
1977 Micro-Analysis of Wear-Patterns on Projectile Points and Knives from the Jurgens Site, Kersey, Colorado. *Plains Anthropologist* 22:107–116.

Griffin, J. W.
1974 *Investigations in Russell Cave*. National Park Service Publications in Archaeology No. 13. Washington DC: U.S. Government Printing Office.

Grimes, J., E. W. Eldridge, B. G. Grimes, A. Vaccaro, F. Vaccaro, K. Vaccaro, M. Vaccaro, and A. Orsini
1982 Bull Brook II. *Archaeology of Eastern North America* 12:184–191.

Grimm, L.

2000 Apprentice Flintknapping: Relating Material Culture and Social Practice in the Upper Paleolithic. In *Children and Material Culture*, ed. J. S. Derevenski, 53–71. London: Routledge.

Grinker, R. R.

1994 *Houses in the Rainforest: Ethnicity and Inequality among Farmers and Foragers in Central Africa*. Berkeley: University of California Press.

Gruhn, R.

1988 Linguistic Evidence in Support of the Coastal Route of Earliest Entry into the New World. *Man* 23:77–100.

1994 The Pacific Coast Route of Initial Entry: An Overview. In *Method and Theory for Investigating the Peopling of the Americas*, ed. R. Bonnichsen and D. G. Steele, 249–256. Corvallis: Center for the Study of the First Americans, Oregon State University.

Gryba, E. M.

1983 *Sibbald Creek: 11,000 Years of Human Use of the Alberta Foothills*. Archaeological Survey of Canada Occasional Paper No. 22.

Guilday, J. E., and P. W. Parmalee

1982 Vertebrate Faunal Remains from Meadowcroft Rockshelter, Washington County, Pennsylvania: Summary and Interpretation. In *Meadowcroft Rockshelter and the Cross Creek Drainage*, ed. R. C. Carlisle and J. M. Adovasio, 163–174. Pittsburgh: Department of Anthropology, University of Pittsburgh.

Gumerman, G. J., and D. A. Phillips

1978 Archaeology Beyond Anthropology. *American Antiquity* 43:184–191.

Guthrie, R. D.

1982 Mammals of the Mammoth Steppe as Paleoenvironmental Indicators. In *Paleoecology of Beringia*, ed. D. M. Hopkins, J. V. Matthews Jr., C. E. Schweger, and S. B. Young, 317–326. New York: Academic Press.

1983a Osseous Projectile Points: Biological Considerations Affecting Raw Material Selection and Design among Paleolithic and Paleoindian Peoples. *British Archaeological Review (BAR) International Series* 163:273–294. Oxford: British Archaeological Reports.

1983b Paleoecology of the Site and Its Implication for Early Hunters. In *Dry Creek: Archaeology and Paleoecology of a Late Pleistocene Alaskan Hunting Camp*, ed. W. E. Powers, R. D. Guthrie, and J. F. Hoffecker, 209–287. Anchorage: Alaska Regional Office, U.S. National Park Service.

1990 *Frozen Fauna of the Mammoth Steppe*. Chicago: University of Chicago Press.

Guthrie, R. D., and M. L. Guthrie

1990 On the Mammoth's Dusty Trail. *Natural History* 90(7): 34–41.

Hall, D.

2000 First Americans Probably Were Not Marine Specialists, Scientist Argues. *Mammoth Trumpet* 15(2): 16–19.

Hames, R. B., and W. T. Vickers

1982 Optimal Diet Breadth Theory as a Model to Explain Variability in Amazonian Hunting. *American Ethnologist* 9:358–378.

Hamilton, T. D., and T. Goebel

1999 Late Pleistocene Peopling of Alaska. In *Ice Age Peoples of North America*, ed. R. Bonnichsen and K. L. Turnmire, 156–199. Corvallis: University of Oregon Press.

Hamilton, T. M.

1982 *Native American Bows*. Missouri Archaeological Society Special Publication No. 5.

Hammett, J. E.

1992 Ethnohistory of Aboriginal Landscapes in the Southeastern United States. *Southern Indian Studies* 41:1–50.

Hanebuth, T., K. Stattegger, and P. M. Grootes

2000 Rapid Flooding of the Sund4 Shelf: A Late-Glacial Sea-Level Record. *Science* 288 (5468): 1033–1035

Hannus, L. A.

1986 Report on 1985 Test Excavations at the Ray Long Site (39FA65), Angostura Reservoir, Fall River County, South Dakota. *South Dakota Archaeology* 10:48–71.

1990 Mammoth Hunting in the New World. In *Hunters of the Recent Past*, ed. L. B. Davis and B. O. K. Reeves, 47–67. London: Unwin-Hyman.

Harington, C. R.

1978 Quaternary Vertebrate Faunas of Canada and Alaska and Their Suggested Chronological Sequence. Syllogeus 15, Canadian Museum of Natural Sciences, Ottawa.

Haury, E. W.

1953 Artifacts with Mammoth Remains, Naco, Arizona I: Discovery of the Naco Mammoth and the Associated Projectile Points. *American Antiquity* 19:1–14.

Haury, E. W., E. B. Sayles, and W. W. Wasley

1959 The Lehner Mammoth Site, Southeastern Arizona. *American Antiquity* 25:2–30.

Hawkes, K., K. Hill, and J. F. O'Connell

1982 Why Hunters Gather: Optimal Foraging and the Aché of Eastern Paraguay. *American Ethnologist* 9:379–395.

Hawkes, K., J. F. O'Connell, and N. G. Blurton
1995 Hadza Children's Foraging: Juvenile Dependency, Social Arrangements, and Mobility among Hunter-Gatherers. *Current Anthropology* 36(4): 688–700.

Haynes, C. V., Jr.
1966 Elephant-Hunting in North America. *Scientific American* 214:104–112.
1982 Were Clovis Progenitors in Beringia? In *Paleoecology of Beringia*, ed. D. M. Hopkins, J. V. Matthews, C. E. Schweger, and S. B. Young, 383–398. New York: Academic Press.
1984 Stratigraphy and Late Pleistocene Extinction in the United States. In *Paleoecology of Beringia*, ed. P. S. Martin and R. G. Klein, 345–353. Tucson: University of Arizona Press.
1987 Clovis Origin Update. *Kiva* 52(2): 83–93.
1991 Geoarchaeological and Paleohydrological Evidence for a Clovis-Age Drought in North America and Its Bearing on Extinction. *Quaternary Research* 35:438–450.
1993 Clovis-Folsom Geochronology and Climatic Change. In *From Kostenki to Clovis: Upper Paleolithic–Paleo-Indian Adaptations*, ed. O. Soffer and N. D. Praslov, 219–236. New York: Plenum Press.
2006 The Rancholabrean Termination. In *Paleoindian Archaeology: A Hemispheric Perspective*, ed. J. Morrow and C. Gnecco, 139–163. Gainesville: University Press of Florida.

Haynes, C. V., Jr., M. McFaul, R. H. Brunswig, and K. D. Hopkins
1998 Kersey-Kuner Terrace Investigations at the Dent and Bernhardt Sites, Colorado. *Geoarchaeology* 13(2): 201–218.

Haynes, C. V., D. J. Stanford, M. Jordy, J. Dickenson, J. Montgomery, P. Shelley, I. Rovner, and G. A. Agogino
1999 A Clovis Well at the Type Site 11,500 BC: The Oldest Prehistoric Well in America. *Geoarchaeology* 14(5): 455–470.

Haynes, G.
2002a The Catastrophic Extinction of North American Mammoths and Mastodons. *World Archaeology* 33(3): 391–416.
2002b *The Early Settlement of North America: The Clovis Era*. Cambridge: Cambridge University Press.

Heaton, T. H., S. L. Talbot, and G. F. Shields
1996 An Ice Age Refugium for Large Mammals in the Alexander Archipelago, Southeast Alaska. *Quaternary Research* 46:186–192.

Heidegger, M.
1971 The Thing. In *Poetry, Language, Thought*, 165–186. Trans. Albert Hofstadter. New York: Harper and Row.
1977 Building, Dwelling, Thinking. In *Basic Writings*, ed. D. Krell, 319–339. San Francisco: Harper.

Heinselman, M. L.

1973 Fire in the Virgin Forests of the Boundary Waters Canoe Area, Minnesota. *Quaternary Research* 3:329–382.

Heite, L.

1998 Spear Straightener or Spinning Tool? *Mammoth Trumpet* 13(3): 18–19.

Hemmings, C. A.

1999 The Paleoindian and Early Archaic Tools of Sloth Hole (8JE121): An Inundated Site in the Lower Aucilla River, Jefferson County, Florida. Master's thesis, University of Florida.

2004 The Organic Clovis: A Single Content Wide Cultural Adaptation. Ph.D. diss., University of Florida, Gainesville.

Hemmings, T. E.

1970 Early Man in the San Pedro Valley, Arizona. Ph.D. diss., University of Arizona.

Hester, J. J.

1972 *Blackwater Locality No. 1: A Stratified Early Man Site in Eastern New Mexico*. Fort Burgwin Research Center Publication 8.

Hickman, M., and C. E. Schweger

1991 A Palaeoenvironmental Study of Fairfax Lake, a Small Lake Situated in the Rocky Mountain Foothills of West-Central Alberta. *Journal of Paleolimnology* 6(1): 1–16.

Hicks, B. A., ed.

2004 *Marmes Rockshelter: A Final Report on 11,000 Years of Cultural Use*. Pullman: Washington State University Press.

Hill, M. E.

2002 An Animal for All Seasons: Variations in Paleoindian Bison Bonebeds on the Great Plains. Paper presented at the 60th Plains Anthropological Conference, Oklahoma City OK.

Hill, M. G.

2001 Paleoindian Diet and Subsistence Behavior on the Northwestern Great Plains of North America. Ph.D. diss., University of Wisconsin–Madison.

Hoadley, R. B.

1990 *Identifying Wood: Accurate Results with Simple Tools*. Newtown CT: Taunton Press.

Hoffecker, J. F.

1988 Applied Geomorphology and Archaeological Survey Strategy for Sites of Pleistocene Age: An Example from Central Alaska. *Journal of Archaeological Science* 15:683–713.

Hoffecker, J. F., W. R. Powers, and N. H. Bigelow

1996 Dry Creek. In *American Beginnings: The Prehistory and Palaeoecology of Beringia*, ed. F. H. West, 343–352. Chicago: University of Chicago Press.

Hoffecker, J. F., W. R. Powers, and T. Goebel

1993 The Colonization of Beringia and the Peopling of the New World. *Science* 259:46–53.

Hofman, J. L.

1991 Folsom Land Use: Projectile Point Variability as a Key to Mobility. In *Raw Material Economies among Prehistoric Hunter-Gathers*, ed. A. Montet-White and S. Holen, 335–355. University of Kansas, Publications in Anthropology No. 19.

Hofman, J. L., and E. Ingbar

1988 A Folsom Hunting Overlook in Eastern Wyoming. *Plains Anthropologist* 33:337–350.

Hogue, S. H.

1994 Human Skeletal Remains from Dust Cave. *Journal of Alabama Archaeology* 40(1–2): 173–191.

Holen, S. R.

1995 Evidence of the First Humans in Nebraska. *Museum Notes: University of Nebraska State Museum* 90.

Hollenbach, K. D.

2004 Gathering and Mobility Decisions in the Late Paleoindian and Early Archaic Periods, Northwest Alabama. Paper presented at the 61st Annual Southeastern Archaeology Conference, St. Louis.

2005 Gathering in the Late Paleoindian and Early Archaic in Northwest Alabama. Ph.D. diss., University of North Carolina.

Holliday, V. T.

1997 *Paleoindian Geoarchaeology of the Southern High Plains*. Austin: University of Texas Press.

Holliday, V. T., C. V. Haynes Jr., J. L. Hofman, and D. J. Meltzer

1994 Geoarchaeology and Geochronology of the Miami (Clovis) Site, Southern High Plains of Texas. *Quaternary Research* 41:234–244.

Holmes, C. E.

1996 Broken Mammoth. In *American Beginnings: The Prehistory and Palaeoecology of Beringia*, ed. F. H. West, 312–318. Chicago: University of Chicago Press.

1998 New Data Pertaining to Swan Point, the oldest microblade site in Alaska. *Current Research in the Pleistocene* 15 (21–22).

Holmes, C. E., R. VanderHoek, and T. E. Dilley

1996 Swan Point. In *American Beginnings: The Prehistory and Palaeoecology of Beringia*, ed. F. H. West, 319–322. Chicago: University of Chicago Press.

Holmes, C. E., and D. R. Yesner

1992 Investigating the Earliest Alaskans: The Broken Mammoth Archaeological Project. *Arctic Research of the United States* 6:6–9.

Holmes, W. H.

1892 Modern Quarry Refuse and the Paleolithic Theory. *Science* 20:295–297.

Honigmann, J. J.

1981 West Main Cree. In *Handbook of North American Indians*, W. C. Sturtevant, gen. ed. Vol. 6, *Subarctic*, ed. J. Helm, 217–230. Washington DC: Smithsonian Institution Press.

Hopkins, D. M.

1979 Landscape and Climate of Beringia during Late Pleistocene and Holocene Time. In *The First Americans: Origins, Affinities, and Adaptations*, ed. W. S. Laughlin and A. B. Harper, 15–42. New York: Gustav Fischer.

Hosley, E. H.

1981 Environment and Culture in the Alaska Plateau. In *Handbook of North American Indians*, W. C. Sturtevant, gen. ed. Vol. 6, *Subarctic*, ed. J. Helm, 533–545. Washington DC: Smithsonian Institution Press.

Howard, E. B., L. Satterwaite Jr., and C. Bache

1941 Preliminary Report on a Buried Yuma Site in Wyoming. *American Antiquity* 7:70–74.

Hrdlička, A.

1913 A Search in Eastern Asia for the Race That Peopled America. *Smithsonian Miscellaneous Collections* 60(30): 10–13.

Hubbert, C. M.

1989 Paleoindian Settlement in the Middle Tennessee Valley: Ruminations from the Quad Paleoindian Locale. *Tennessee Anthropologist* 14(2): 148–164.

Huber, J. K.

1995 Vegetational History. In *The Paleo-Indian of Southern St. Louis Co., Minnesota: The Reservoir Lakes Complex*, ed. C. Harrison, E. Redepenning, C. L. Hill, G. Rapp, S. E. Aschenbrenner, J. K. Huber, and S. C. Mulholland, 125–134. Duluth: University of Minnesota.

Hudecek-Cuffe, C.

1998 *Engendering Northern Plains Paleoindian Archaeology*. British Archaeological Review (BAR) International Series S699. Oxford: British Archaeological Reports.

Hudson, J. L.

1991 Nonselective Small Game Hunting Strategies: An Ethnoarchaeological Study of Aka Pygmy Sites. In *Human Predators and Prey Mortality*, ed. M. C. Stiner, 105–121. Boulder CO: Westview Press.

Hughen, K. A., J. T. Overpeck, L. C. Peterson, and S. Trumbore
1996 Rapid Climate Changes in the Tropical Atlantic Region during the Last Deglaciation. *Nature* 380:5154.

Hulse, D. C., and J. L. Wright
1989 The Pine Tree–Quad–Old Slough Complex. *Tennessee Anthropologist* 17(2): 102–147.

Husted, W. M.
1969 *Bighorn Canyon Archaeology*. Smithsonian Institution River Basin Surveys Publications in Archaeology No. 12.

Husted, W. M., and R. Edgar
2002 *The Archeology of Mummy Cave Wyoming*. Lincoln NE: U.S. Department of the Interior National Park Service, Midwest Archaeological Center.

Hyland, D. C., I. S. Zhushchikhovskaya, V. E. Medvedev, A. P. Derevianko, and A. V. Tabarev
2000 Pleistocene Textiles in the Far East: Impressions from the World's Oldest Pottery. Paper presented at the 65th Annual Meeting of the Society for American Archaeology, Philadelphia.

Ingold, T.
1994 From Trust to Domination: An Alternative History of Human-Animal Relations. In *Animals and Human Society: Changing Perspectives*, ed. A. Manning and J. Serpell, 1–22. New York: Routledge.
1999 On the Social Relations of the Hunter-Gatherer Band. In The Cambridge Encyclopedia of Hunters and Gatherers, ed. R. Lee and R. Daly, 399–410. Cambridge: Cambridge University Press.

Irwin, H. T.
1967 The Itama: Late Pleistocene Inhabitants of the Plains of the United States and Canada and the American Southwest. Ph.D. diss., Harvard University.

Irwin, H. T., and H. M. Wormington
1970 Paleo-Indian Tool Types in the Great Plains. *American Antiquity* 35:24–34.

Irwin-Williams, C., H. Irwin, G. Agogino and C. V. Haynes Jr.
1973 Hell Gap: Paleoindian Occupation of the High Plains. *Plains Anthropologist* 18:40–53.

Ives, J. W., A. W. Beaudoin, and M. P. R. Magne
1989 Evaluating the Role of a Western Corridor in the Peopling of the Americas. Paper presented at Circum-Pacific Prehistory Conference, Seattle.

Jackson, L., and H. McKillop
1991 Approaches to Paleo-Indian Economy: An Ontario and Great Lakes Perspective. *Midcontinental Journal of Archaeology* 16:34–68.

Jackson, T. L.
1991 Pounding Acorn: Women's Production as Social and Economic Focus. In *Engendering Archaeology: Women and Prehistory*, ed. Joan Gero and Margaret Conkey, 301–325. Oxford: Basil Blackwell.

Jacobson, G. L., T. Webb III, and E. C. Grimm
1987 Patterns and Rates of Vegetation Change during the Deglaciation of Eastern North America. In *The Geology of North America*. Vol. K-3, *North America and Adjacent Oceans during the Last Deglaciation*, ed. W. F. Ruddiman and H. E. Wright Jr., 277–288. Boulder CO: Geological Society of America.

Jelinek, J.
1975 *The Pictorial Encyclopedia of the Evolution of Man*. London: Hamlyn Press.

Jennings, J. D.
1957 *Danger Cave*. Anthropological Papers No. 27. Salt Lake City: University of Utah.
1989 *Prehistory of North America*. Mountain View CA: Mayfield.

Jerrems, W. J., and A. Dansie
2002 Testing the Clovis Paradigm: Extinct Horses and Human Association. Paper presented at the 67th Annual Meeting of the Society for American Archaeology, Denver.

Jodry, M. A.
1987 Stewart's Cattle Guard Site: A Folsom Site in Southern Colorado. Master's thesis, University of Texas.
1999a Alternate Routes Beyond the Horizon: Certitude, Suspended Disbelief, and Surprise. Paper presented at the "Clovis and Beyond" conference, Santa Fe NM.
1999b Folsom Technological Organization and Socioeconomic Strategies. Ph.D. diss., American University.
1999c Paleoindian Stage. In *Colorado Prehistory: A Context for the Rio Grande Basin*, by M. A. Martorano, T. Hoeffer II, M. A. Jodry, V. Spero, and M. L. Taylor, 45–114. Denver: Colorado Council of Professional Archaeologists.

Jodry, M. A., M. D. Turner, V. Spero, J. C. Turner, and D. J. Stanford
1996 Folsom in Colorado High Country: The Black Mountain Site. *Current Research in the Pleistocene* 13:25–27.

Johnson, E.
1977 Animal Food Resources of Paleoindians. In *Paleoindian Lifeways*, ed. E. Johnson, 65–77. Lubbock: Texas Tech University.
1987 *Lubbock Lake: Late Quaternary Studies on the Southern High Plains*. College Station: Texas A&M University Press.

Johnson, L., Jr.

1991 Early Archaic Life at the Sleeper Archaeological Site, 41BC65, of the Texas Hill Country, Blanco County, Texas. Publications in Archaeology, Report 39. Texas State Department of Highways and Public Transportation, Austin.

Johnson, M.

1999 *Archaeological Theory: An Introduction*. Oxford: Blackwell.

Jones, B. D.

1994 Hunter-Gatherer Adaptations to the Terminal Pleistocene and Early Holocene Environments of Northeastern North America: Effects on Site Visibility. Paper presented at the 34th Annual Meeting of the Northeastern Anthropological Association, State University of New York, Geneseo.

2000 The Late Paleoindian Hidden Creek Site in Southeastern Connecticut. *Archaeology of Eastern North America* 25:45–80.

Josenhans, H., D. Fedje, R. Pienitz, and J. Southon

1997 Early Humans and Rapidly Changing Holocene Sea Levels in the Queen Charlotte Islands–Hecate Strait, British Columbia, Canada. *Science* 277:71–74.

Judge, W. J.

1973 *Paleoindian Occupation of the Central Rio Grande Valley in New Mexico*. Albuquerque: University of New Mexico Press.

Julig, P. J.

1991 Late Pleistocene Archaeology in the Great Lakes Region of North America: Current Problems and Prospects. *Revista de Arqueologia Americana* 3:7–30.

1994 *The Cummins Site and Paleoindian Occupations in the Northwestern Lake Superior Region*. Ontario Archaeological Reports 2. Toronto: Ontario Heritage Foundation.

Justice, N. D.

1987 *Stone Age Spear and Arrow Points of the Midcontinental and Eastern United States: A Modern Survey and Reference*. Bloomington: Indiana University Press.

1995 *Stone Age Spear and Arrow Points of the Midcontinental and Eastern United States: A Modern Survey and Reference*. 2nd ed. Bloomington: Indiana University Press.

Kapp, R. O.

1999 Michigan Late Pleistocene, Holocene, and Presettlement Vegetation and Climate. In *Retrieving Michigan's Buried Past: The Archaeology of the Great Lakes State*, ed. J. R. Halsey, 31–58. Bulletin 64. Cranbrook Institute of Science, Bloomfield Hills MI.

Karafet, T. M., S. L. Zegura, O. Posukh, L. Osipova, A. Bergen, J. Long, D. Goldman, W. Klitz, S. Harihara, P. de Knijff, R. C. Griffiths, A. R. Templeton, and M. F. Hammer

1999 Ancestral Asian Source(s) of New World Y-Chromosome Founder Haplotypes. *American Journal of Human Genetics* 64(3): 817–831.

Kay, M.

1996 Microware Analysis of Some Clovis and Experimental Chipped Stone Tools. In *Stone Tools*, ed. G. H. Odell, 315–344. New York: Plenum Press.

Keefer, D. K., S. D. deFrance, M. E. Moseley, J. B. Richardson III, D. R. Satterlee, and A. Day-Lewis

1998 Early Maritime Economy and El Niño Events at Quebrada Tacahuay, Peru. *Science* 281:1833–1835.

Keeley, L. H.

1980 *Experimental Determination of Stone Tool Uses*. Chicago: University of Chicago Press.

Keene, A. S.

1981 Optimal Foraging in a Nonmarginal Environment: A Model of Prehistoric Subsistence Strategies in Michigan. In *Hunter-Gatherer Foraging Strategies*, ed. B. Winterhalder and E. A. Smith, 171–193. Chicago: University of Chicago Press.

Kellogg, D., and K. Simons, with contributions by T. L. Arpin, A. R. Kelly, L. McWeeney, S. C. Mulholland, and A. E. Spiess

2000 *Phase III Data Recovery Excavations at the Neal Garrison Paleoindian Site (1.8 ME), Eliot, York County, Maine*. Report prepared for Portland Natural Gas Transmission System. West Chester PA: John Milner Associates.

Kelly, R. L.

1988 The Three Sides of a Biface. *American Antiquity* 53:717–734.

1995 *The Foraging Spectrum*. Washington DC: Smithsonian Institution Press.

Kelly, R. L., and L. C. Todd

1988 Coming into the Country: Early Paleoindian Hunting and Mobility. *American Antiquity* 53:231–244.

Keyser, J. D., and C. M. Davis

1985 Lightning Spring and Red Fox: McKean Research in the Grand River Drainage. In *McKean/Middle Plains Archaic*, ed. M. Kornfeld and L. C. Todd, 123–136. University of Wyoming, Occasional Papers on Wyoming Archaeology No. 4.

Knecht, H.

1997 The History and Development of Projectile Technology Research. In *Projectile Technology*, ed. H. Knecht, 3–35. New York: Plenum Press.

Knudson, R.

1983 *Organizational Variability in Late Paleo-Indian Assemblages.* Washington State University, Laboratory of Anthropology, Reports of Investigations No. 60.

2002 Medicine Creek Is a Paleoindian Cultural Ecotone: The Red Smoke Assemblage. In *Medicine Creek: Seventy Years of Archaeological Investigations*, ed. D. C. Roper, 84–141. Tuscaloosa: University of Alabama Press.

Kolman, C. J., N. Sambuughin, and E. Bermingham

1996 Mitochondrial DNA Analysis of Mongolian Populations and Implications for the Origin of New World Founders. *Genetics* 142(4): 1321–1334.

Kornfeld, M.

1988 The Rocky Foolsm Site: A Small Folsom Assemblage from the Northwestern Plains. *North American Archaeologist* 9(3): 197–222.

1994 *Pull of the Hills: Affluent Foragers of the Western Black Hills.* Ann Arbor MI: University Microfilms.

1996 The Big Game Focus: Reinterpreting the Archeological Record of Cantabrian Upper Paleolithic Economy. *Current Anthropology* 37:629–657.

2003 Affluent Foragers of the North American Plains. British Archaeological Review (BAR) International Series 1106. Oxford: British Archaeological Reports.

Kornfeld, M., and J. E. Francis

1991 A Preliminary Historical Outline of Northwestern High Plains Gender Systems. In *Gender in Archeology*, ed. D. Walde and N. D. Willows, 444–451. Proceedings of the 22nd Annual Conference of the Archeological Association of the University of Calgary, Alberta.

Kornfeld, M., and G. C. Frison

2000 Paleoindian Occupation of the High Country: The Case of Middle Park, Colorado. *Plains Anthropologist* 45:129–153.

Kornfeld, M., G. C. Frison, M. L. Larson, J. C. Miller, and J. Saysette

1999 Paleoindian Bison Procurement and Paleoenvironments in the Middle Park of Colorado. *Geoarchaeology* 14(7): 655–674.

Kornfeld, M., G. C. Frison, and P. White

2001 Paleoindian Occupation of Barger Gulch and the Use of Troublesome Formation Chert. *Current Research in the Pleistocene* 18:32–34.

Krajick, K.

2002 Melting Glaciers Release Ancient Relics. *Science* 296:454–456.

Kreutzer, L. A.
1996 Taphonomy of the Mill Iron Site Bison Bonebed. In *The Mill Iron Site*, ed. G. C. Frison, 101–143. Albuquerque: University of New Mexico Press.

Krieger, A. D.
1947 Artifacts from the Plainview Bison Bed. *Bulletin of the Geological Society of America* 58:938–952.

Kuehn, S. R.
1998 New Evidence for Late Paleoindian–Early Archaic Subsistence Behavior in the Western Great Lakes. *American Antiquity* 63:457–476.

Kuehn, S. R., and J. A. Clark
n.d. Analysis of Faunal Remains from Three Late Paleoindian (Lake Poygan Phase) Sites in East-Central Wisconsin. Ms. in author's possession.

Kunz, M. L., and R. E. Reanier
1994 Paleoindians in Beringia: Evidence from Arctic Alaska. *Science* 263:660–662.

Kurtén, B., and E. Anderson
1980 *Pleistocene Mammals of North America*. New York: Columbia University Press.

Kutzbach, J. E., and P. J. Guetter
1986 The Influence of Changing Orbital Parameters and Surface Boundary Conditions on Climate Simulations for the Past 18,000 Years. *Journal of Atmospheric Science* 43:1726–1759.

La Barre, W.
1972 *The Ghost Dance*. New York: Delta.

Labelle, J.
2002 Where's the Fire? Thoughts on Paleoindians' Landscape Use and Feature Abundance in the Great Plains and Rockies. Paper presented at the 60th Plains Anthropological Conference, Oklahoma City.

Lahren, L. A.
1976 *The Myers-Hindman Site: An Exploratory Study of Human Occupation Patterns in the Upper Yellowstone Valley from 7000 BC to AD 1200*. Livingston MT: Anthropologos Research International.

Lahren, L., and R. Bonnichsen
1974 Bone Foreshafts from a Clovis Burial in Southwestern Montana. *Science* 186(4159): 147–150.

Landals, A.
1990 The Maple Leaf Site: Implications of the Analysis of Small-Scale Bison Kills. In *Hunters of the Recent Past*, ed. L. B. Davis and B. O. K. Reeves, 122–151. London: Unwin Hyman.

Lantis, M.
1984 Nunivak Eskimo. In *Handbook of North American Indians*, W. C. Sturtevant, gen. ed. Vol. 5, *Arctic*, ed. D. Damas, 209–223. Washington DC: Smithsonian Institution Press.

Largent, F. B., M. R. Waters, and D. L. Carlson
1991 The Spatiotemporal Distribution and Characteristics of Folsom Projectile Points in Texas. *Plains Anthropologist* 36:323–341.

Larick, R.
1985 Spears, Style, and Time among Maa-Speaking Pastoralists. *Journal of Anthropological Archaeology* 4:206–220.

Larson, M. L.
1990 *Early Plains Archaic Technological Organization: The Laddie Creek Example*. Ann Arbor MI: University Microfilms.
1992 Site Formation Processes in the Cody and Early Plains Archaic Levels at the Laddie Creek Site, Wyoming. *Geoarchaeology* 7(2): 103–120.

Larson, M. L., M. Kornfeld, and D. J. Rapson
1995 *High Altitude Hunter-Gatherer Adaptations in the Middle Rocky Mountains, 1988–1994 Investigations*. Report prepared for the National Science Foundation, Washington DC, Grant #BNS-91095914. Technical Report No. 4. Department of Anthropology, University of Wyoming.

Layton, R. H.
2001 Hunter-Gatherers, Their Neighbors and the Nation State. In *Hunter-Gatherers: An Interdisciplinary Perspective*, ed. C. Panter-Brick, R. H. Layton, and P. Rowley-Conwy, 292–321. Cambridge: Cambridge University Press.

Leacock, E. B.
1952 *The Montagnais "Hunting Territory" and the Fur Trade*. Ann Arbor MI: University Microfilm International.

Leavy, B. F.
1994 *In Search of the Swan Maiden*. New York: New York University Press.

Lee, R. B.
1988 Reflections on Primitive Communism. In *Hunters and Gatherers*. Vol. 1, *History, Evolution and Social Change*, ed. T. Ingold, D. Riches, and J. Woodburn, 252–268. Oxford: Berg.
1992 Art, Science, or Politics? The Crisis in Hunter-Gatherer Studies. *American Anthropologist* 94:31–54.

Lee, R. B., and R. Daly
1999 Introduction: Foragers and Others. In *The Cambridge Encyclopedia of Hunters and Gatherers*, ed. R. Lee and R. Daly, 1–19. Cambridge: Cambridge University Press.

Leidy, J.

1852 Memoir of the Extinct Species of American Ox. *Smithsonian Contributions to Knowledge* 5(3): 1–20.

Lemonnier, P.

1992 *Elements for an Anthropology of Technology*. University of Michigan Anthropological Papers No. 88.

1993 Introduction. In *Technological Choices: Transformation in Material Cultures since the Neolithic*, ed. P. Lemonnier, 1–35. London: Routledge.

Leonhardy, F. C.

1966 *Domebo: A Paleo-Indian Mammoth Kill in the Prairie Plains*. Contributions of the Museum of the Great Plains 1, Lawton OK.

Lepper, B. T.

1999 Pleistocene Peoples of Midcontinental North America. In *Ice Age Peoples of North America: Environments, Origins, and Adaptations*, ed. R. Bonnichsen and K. L. Turnmire, 362–394. Corvallis: Oregon State University Press.

Lepper, B. T., and D. J. Meltzer

1991 Late Pleistocene Human Occupation of the Eastern United States. In *Clovis: Origins and Adaptations*, ed. R. Bonnichsen and K. L. Turnmire, 175–184. Corvallis: Center for the Study of the First Americans, Oregon State University.

Leroi-Gourhan, A.

1981 *Treasures of Prehistoric Art*. New York: Harry N. Abrams.

Levesque, A. J., F. E. Mayle, I. R. Walker, and L. C. Cwynar

1993 A Previously Unrecognized Late-Glacial Cold Event in Eastern North America. *Nature* 361:623–626.

Lewis, H. T.

1980 Indian Fires of Spring. *Natural History* 89(1): 76–83.

1982 Fire Technology and Resource Management in Aboriginal North America and Australia. In *Resource Managers: North American and Australian Hunter-Gatherers*, ed. N. M. Williams and E. S. Hunn, 45–67. Boulder CO: Westview Press.

Lincoln, F. C.

1950 *Migration of Birds*. Washington DC: U.S. Department of the Interior, Fish and Wildlife Service.

Lippincott, K.

1985 Introduction to the Symposium. *Archaeology inMontana* 26(2): 1–4.

Little, E. L.

1980 *National Audubon Society Field Guide to North American Trees, Eastern Region*. New York: Chanticleer Press.

Loendorf, L. L.
1973 Prehistoric Settlement Patterns in the Pryor Mountains, Montana. Ph.D. diss., University of Missouri.

Logan, W. D.
1952 *Graham Cave: An Archaic Site in Montgomery County, Missouri*. Missouri Archaeological Society Memoir No. 2.

Long, R. J.
1977 McFaddin Beach. Patillo Higgins Series of Natural History and Anthropology 1. Beaumont TX: Spindletop Museum, Lamar University.

Lopinot, N. B.
1984 *Archaeobotanical Formation Processes and Late Middle Archaic Human-Plant Interrelationships in the Midcontinental U.S.A.* Ann Arbor MI: University Microfilms.

Lotter, A. F., H. J. B. Birks, U. Eicher, W. Hofmann, J. Schwander, and L. Wick
2000 Younger Dryas and Allerød Summer Temperatures at Gerzensee (Switzerland) Inferred from Fossil Pollen and Cladoceran Assemblages. *Paleogeography, Paleoclimatology, Paleoecology* 159:349–361.

Loy, T. H., and E. J. Dixon
1998 Blood Residues on Fluted Points from Eastern Beringia. *American Antiquity* 63:21–46.

Lundelius, E. L., R. W. Graham, E. Anderson, J. Guilday, J. A. Holman, D. W. Steadman, and S. D. Webb
1983 Terrestrial Vertebrate Faunas. In *Late-Quaternary Environments of the United States*. Vol. 1, *The Late Pleistocene*, ed. S. Porter, 311–353. Minneapolis: University of Minnesota Press.

Lyman, R. L.
1994 *Vertebrate Taphonomy*. Cambridge: Cambridge University Press.

Lyman, R. L., and M. J. O'Brien
2001 The Direct Historical Approach, Analogical Reasoning, and Theory in Americanist Archaeology. *Journal of Archaeological Method and Theory* 8(4): 303–342.

Lynch, T.
1983 The Paleo-Indians. In *Ancient South Americans*, ed. J. D. Jennings, 86–137. San Francisco: Freeman.

Lysek, C. A.
1997 Archaeologists May Overlook Value of Fiber Artifacts. *Mammoth Trumpet* 12(2): 19–21.

Magurran, A. E.
1988 *Ecological Diversity and Its Measurement*. Princeton NJ: Princeton University Press.

Mallouf, R. J.

1989 A Clovis Quarry Workshop in the Callahan Divide: The Yellow Hawk Site, Taylor County, Texas. *Plains Anthropologist* 34:81–103.

1994 Sailor-Helton: A Paleoindian Cache from Southwestern Kansas. *Current Research in the Pleistocene* 11:44–46.

Mandryk, C. A. S.

1992 Paleoecology as Contextual Archaeology: Human Viability of the Late Quaternary Ice-Free Corridor, Alberta, Canada. Ph.D. diss., University of Alberta.

1998 Evaluating Paleoenvironmental Constraints on Interior and Coastal Entry Routes into North America. Paper presented at 63rd Annual Meeting of Society for American Archaeology, Seattle.

Markgraf, V., and T. Lennon

1986 Paleoenvironmental History of the Last 13,000 Years of the Eastern Powder River Basin, Wyoming, and Its Implications for Prehistoric Cultural Patterns. *Plains Anthropologist* 31:1–12.

Marriott, A., and C. K. Rachlin

1975 *Plains Indian Mythology*. New York: Crowell.

Marshack, A.

1972 *The Roots of Civilization*. New York: McGraw-Hill.

Marshall, S. B.

1981 *Artifact Form and Function: Implications of Morphological Classification and Wear Pattern Analysis on Cultural Interpretation*. Ann Arbor MI: University Microfilms.

1985 Paleoindian Artifact Form and Function at Shawnee Minisink. In *Shawnee Minisink: A Stratified Paleoindian-Archaic Site in the Upper Delaware Valley of Pennsylvania*, ed. C. W. McNett, 165–209. New York: Academic Press.

Martin, A. C., and W. D. Barkley

1961 *Seed Identification Manual*. Berkeley: University of California Press.

Martin, L.

1965 *The Physical Geography of Wisconsin*. 3rd ed. Madison: University of Wisconsin Press.

Martin, P. S., and R. G. Klein, eds.

1984 *Quaternary Extinctions, A Prehistoric Revolution*. Tucson: University of Arizona Press.

Martin, P. S., and H. E. Wright, eds.

1967 *Pleistocene Extinctions: A Search for a Cause*. New Haven CT: Yale University Press.

Mason, R. J.

1962 The Paleo-Indian Tradition in Eastern North America. *Current Anthropology* 3:227–283.

1981 *Great Lakes Archaeology*. New York: Academic Press.

1997 The Paleo-Indian Tradition. *Wisconsin Archeologist* 78:78–111.

Mason, R. J., and C. Irwin

1960 An Eden-Scottsbluff Burial in Northeastern Wisconsin. *American Antiquity* 26:43–57.

Mathewes, R. W.

2000 Paleoecology of a Lost World: Postglacial Environments and Biogeography of the Continental Shelf of Western Canada. Paper presented at GeoCanada 2000, Calgary.

Matthews, J. V., Jr.

1982 East Beringia during Late Wisconsin Time: A Review of the Biotic Evidence. In *Paleoecology of Beringia*, ed. D. M. Hopkins, J. V. Matthews, C. E. Schweger, and S. B. Young, 127–150. New York: Academic Press.

May, D. W.

2002 Stratigraphic Studies at Paleoindian Sites around Medicine Creek Reservoir. In *Medicine Creek*, ed. D. C. Roper, 37–53. Tuscaloosa: University of Alabama Press.

McAvoy, J. M.

1992 *Nottoway River Survey. Part I: Clovis Settlement Patterns: The 30 Year Study of a Late Ice Age Hunting Culture on the Southern Interior Coastal Plain of Virginia*. Archeological Society of Virginia Special Publication No. 28. Richmond VA: Dietz Press.

McAvoy, J. M., J. C. Baker, J. K. Feathers, R. L. Hodges, L. J. McWeeney, and T. R. Whyte

2000 *Summary of Research at the Cactus Hill Archaeological Site, 44SX202, Sussex County, Virginia*. Report to the National Geographic Society in compliance with stipulations of grant #6345-98.

McAvoy, J. M., and L. D. McAvoy

1997 *Archaeological Investigations of Site 44SX202, Cactus Hill, Sussex County, Virginia*. Nottoway River Survey Archaeological Research Report No. 2 and Research Report Series No. 8. Richmond VA: Department of Historic Resources.

McBrearty, S., L. Bishop, T. Plummer, R. Dewar, and N. Conard

1998 Tools Underfoot: Human Trampling as an Agent of Lithic Artifact Edge Modification. *American Antiquity* 63:108–129.

McCarthy, M. A., and R. H. Matthews

1984 *Composition of Foods: Nut and Seed Products*. Agriculture Handbook 8-12. Washington DC: U.S. Department of Agriculture.

McCary, B. C.

1975 The Williamson Paleo-Indian Site, Dinwiddie County, Virginia. *Chesopiean* 13:48–131.

1991 *Survey of Virginia Fluted Points*. 2nd ed. Archeological Society of Virginia Special Publication 12. 2nd ed., rev. (originally published 1984).

McDonald, G.

1968 Debert: A Paleoindian Site in Central Nova Scotia. National Museums of Canada, Anthropology Paper 16.

McDonald, J. N.

1981 *North American Bison*. Berkeley: University of California Press.

2000 An Outline of the Pre-Clovis Archeology of SV-2, Saltsville, Virginia, with Special Attention to a Bone Tool Dated 14,510 Yrs BP. Virginia Museum of Natural History. *Jeffersonia* 9:1–60.

McKennan, R. A.

1981 Tanana. In *Handbook of North American Indians*, W. C. Sturtevant, gen. ed. Vol. 6, *Subarctic*, ed. J. Helm, 562–576. Washington DC: Smithsonian Institution Press, 1981.

McKinney, W. W.

1981 Early Holocene Adaptations in Central and Southwestern Texas: The Problem of the Paleoindian-Archaic Transition. *Bulletin of the Texas Archeological Society* 52:91–120.

McLennan, C., and G. Denniston

1981 Environment and Culture in the Cordillera. In *Handbook of North American Indians*, W. C. Sturtevant, gen. ed. Vol. 6, *Subarctic*, ed. J. Helm, 372–386. Washington DC: Smithsonian Institution Press.

McMillan, R. B.

1976 The Dynamics of Cultural and Environmental Change at Rodgers Shelter, Missouri. In *Prehistoric Man and His Environment*, ed. W. R. Wood and R. B. McMillan, 211–235. New York: Academic Press.

McMillan, R. B., and W. E. Klippel

1981 Environmental Changes and Hunter-Gatherer Adaptations in the Southern Prairie Peninsula. *Journal of Archaeological Science* 8(3): 215–245.

McNett, C. W.

1985a Artifact Morphology and Chronology at the Shawnee Minisink Site. In *Shawnee Minisink: A Stratified Paleoindian-Archaic Site in the Upper Delaware Valley of Pennsylvania*, ed. C. W. McNett, 83–122. New York: Academic Press.

1985b Methodology and Research Design at the Shawnee Minisink Site. In *Shawnee Minisink: A Stratified Paleoindian-Archaic Site in the Upper Delaware Valley of Pennsylvania*, ed. C. W. McNett, 21–31. New York: Academic Press.

McNett, C. W., ed.

1985 *Shawnee Minisink: A Stratified Paleoindian-Archaic Site in the Upper Delaware Valley of Pennsylvania.* New York: Academic Press.

McWeeney, L. J.

1985 Rise in Sea Level and Submergence of Archaeological Sites in Connecticut. *Bulletin of the Archaeological Society of Connecticut* 49:53–60.

1991 Macrofossil Identification as a Method toward Archaeo-environmental Reconstruction. *Bulletin of the Archaeological Society of Connecticut* 54:87–97.

1992 Bog Formation Processes at the Flamingo Pingo, South Windsor, Connecticut. Report prepared for Jelle DeBoer, Geological Sciences, Wesleyan University. Ms. in author's possession.

1994 *Archaeological Settlement Patterns and Vegetation Dynamics in Southern New England in the Late Quaternary.* Ann Arbor MI: University Microfilms.

1996a Charcoal Evidence for Human Modification of the Landscape in Southern New England. Paper presented at the 61st Annual Meeting of the Society for American Archaeology, New Orleans.

1996b Does pH Affect Pollen Preservation in the Late Pleistocene Beringian Sediments? Program and Abstracts: Beringian Paleoenvironmental Workshop, Florissant CO.

1997a Paleoenvironmental Reconstruction Using Plant Macrofossils and Microfossils. Paper presented at the 62nd Annual Meeting of the Society for American Archaeology, Nashville TN.

1997b Report on the Charcoal Remains from the Cactus Hill Site, Nottoway River, Virginia. In *Archaeological Investigations of Site 44SX202, Cactus Hill, Sussex County Virginia,* ed. J. M. McAvoy and L. D. McAvoy, Appendix D. Nottoway River Survey Archaeological Research Report No. 2 and Research Report Series No. 8. Richmond VA: Department of Historic Resources.

1998 Pequot Cedar Swamp Paleoenvironment. In *Coastally Restricted Forests,* ed. A. Laderman, 124–141. New York: Oxford University Press.

1999 A Review of Late Pleistocene and Holocene Climate Changes in Southern New England. *Bulletin of the Archaeological Society of Connecticut* 62:3–18.

2000 Determining Human Presence Using Multiple Lines of Evidence for the Cactus Hill Site, Virginia. Paper presented at the 65th Annual Meeting of the Society for American Archaeology, Philadelphia.

2001 The Role of Sediment Analyses in Establishing Human Presence at Early Archaeological Sites. *Current Research in the Pleistocene* 18:44–46.

2002 Archaeological Charcoal Used for Environmental Reconstruction: The Templeton Paleoindian Site, Connecticut, USA. In *The Archaeobotany of Temperate Zone Hunter-Gatherers*, ed. S. L. R. Mason and J. G. Hather, 117–127. London: Institute of Archaeology Publications.

Medsger, O. P.

1966 *Edible Wild Plants*. New York: Collier MacMillan.

Meeks, S. C.

1994 Lithic Artifacts from Dust Cave. *Journal of Alabama Archaeology* 40(1–2): 79–106.

2001 Wandering Around Dust Cave: An Overview of Late Paleoindian and Early Archaic Settlement Patterns in the Middle Tennessee River Valley. Paper presented at the 58th Annual Southeastern Archaeology Conference, Chattanooga TN.

Mehringer, P. J.

1988 Weapons Cache of Ancient Americans. *National Geographic* 174(4): 500–503.

1989 Of Apples and Archaeology. *Universe* 1(2): 2–8.

Mehringer, P. J., and F. F. Foit

1990 Volcanic Ash Dating of the Clovis Cache at East Wenatchee, Washington. *National Geographic Research* 6(4): 495–503.

Meinholz, N. M., and S. R. Kuehn

1995 Late Paleoindian Ceremonialism in the Western Great Lakes: New Information from the Deadman Slough Site. Paper presented at the 40th Midwest Archaeological Conference, South Beloit IL.

1996 *The Deadman Slough Site: Late Paleoindian/Early Archaic and Woodland Occupations along the Flambeau River, Price County, Wisconsin*. Archaeology Research Series No. 4. Museum Archaeology Program, State Historical Society of Wisconsin, Madison.

Mellars, P.

1976 Fire Ecology, Animals Populations and Man: A Study of Some Ecological Relationships in Prehistory. *Proceedings of the Prehistoric Society* 42:15–45.

Meltzer, D. J.

1988 Late Pleistocene Human Adaptations in Eastern North America. *Journal of World Prehistory* 2:1–52.

1993a Is There a Clovis Adaptation? In *From Kostenki to Clovis: Upper Paleolithic–Paleo-Indian Adaptations*, ed. O. Soffer and N. D. Praslov, 293–310. New York: Plenum Press.

1993b *Search for the First Americans*. Montreal: St. Remy Press.

Meltzer, D. J., and M. R. Bever

1995 Paleoindians of Texas: Update on the Texas Clovis Fluted Point Survey. *Bulletin of the Texas Archeological Society* 66:47–81.

Meltzer, D. J., and B. D. Smith

1986 Paleoindian and Early Archaic Subsistence Strategies in Eastern North America. In *Foraging, Collecting, and Harvesting: Archaic Period Subsistence and Settlement in the Eastern Woodlands*, ed. S. W. Neusius, 3–32. Occasional Paper No. 6. Carbondale: Center for Archaeological Investigations, Southern Illinois University.

Meltzer, D. J., L. C. Todd, and T. V. Holliday

2002 The Folsom (Paleoindian) Type Site: Past Investigations, Current Studies. *American Antiquity* 67:5–36.

Miller, K. A.

1993 A Study of Prehistoric Biface Caches from Texas. Master's thesis, University of Texas at Austin.

Miller, N. G.

1973 *Late-Glacial and Postglacial Vegetation Change in Southwestern New York State*. Bulletin 420. Albany: New York State Museum and Science Service.

1988 The Late Quaternary Hiscock Site, Genesee County, New York: Paleoecological Studies Based on Pollen and Plant Macrofossils. In *Late Pleistocene and Early Holocene Paleoecology and Archaeology of the Eastern Great Lakes Region*, ed. R. S. Laub, N. G. Miller, and D. W. Steadman, 33:83–93. Buffalo NY: Buffalo Society of Natural Sciences.

1994 Snapshot Paleobotanical Analyses of Late-Glacial Sediments in the Connecticut River Valley, Northern Vermont to Central Connecticut. *Geological Society of America, Abstracts with Programs, Northeastern Section* 27:69.

Miller, N. G., and G. G. Thompson

1979 Boreal and Western North American Plants in the Late Pleistocene of Vermont. *Journal of the Arnold Arboretum* 60:167–218.

Mithen, S.

1990 *Thoughtful Foragers*. Cambridge: Cambridge University Press.

Moeller, R. W.

1980 *6LF21: A Paleoindian Site in Western Connecticut*. Washington CT: American Indian Archaeological Institute.

1984 Regional Implications of the Templeton Site for Paleoindian Lithic Procurement and Utilization. *North American Archaeologist* 5(3): 235–245.

Moerman, D. E.

1998 *Native American Ethnobotany*. Portland OR: Timber Press.

Molnia, B. F.
1986 Glacial History of the Gulf of Alaska: A Synthesis. In *Glaciation in Alaska: The Geologic Record*, ed. T. Hamilton, K. M. Reed, and R. M. Thorson, 237-265. Anchorage: Alaska Geological Society.

Moore, J. H., and T. L. Willems
1995 *The Paleo-Indian Tradition in Central Wisconsin: A Region Four Study Unit*. Stevens Point: State Archeology Regional Program, State Historical Society of Wisconsin, and the University of Wisconsin.

Morgan, A. V.
1987 Late Wisconsin and Early Holocene Paleoenvironments of East-Central North America Based on Assemblages of Fossil Coleoptera. In *North America and Adjacent Oceans during the Last Deglaciation*. Vol. K-3, *The Geology of North America*, ed. W. F. Ruddiman and H. E. Wright Jr., 353–370. Boulder CO: Geological Society of America.

Morlan, R. E., and J. Cinq-Mars
1982 Ancient Beringians: Human Occupations in the Late Pleistocene of Alaska and the Yukon Territory. In *Paleoecology of Beringia*, ed. D. M. Hopkins, J. V. Matthews Jr., C. E. Schweger, and S. B. Young, 353–382. New York: Academic Press.

Morphy, H.
1993 Colonialism, History and the Construction of Place: The Politics of Landscape in Northern Australia. In *Landscape: Politics and Perspectives*, ed. B. Bender, 205–243. Oxford: Berg.
1995 Landscape and the Reproduction of the Ancestral Past. In *The Anthropology of Landscape: Perspectives on Place and Space*, ed. E. Hirsch and M. O'Hanlon, 184–209. Oxford: Clarendon Press.

Morrow, J. E.
1995 Clovis Point Manufacture: A Perspective from the Ready/Lincoln Hills Site in Jersey County, Illinois. *Midcontinental Journal of Archaeology* 20:167–191.

Morrow, J. E., and T. A. Morrow
1999 Geographic Variation in Fluted Projectile Points: A Hemispheric Perspective. *American Antiquity* 64:215–230.

Morse, D. F.
1975 Reply to Schiffer. In *The Cache River Archaeological Project: An Experiment in Contract Archaeology*, ed. B. Schiffer and J. J. House, 113–120. Arkansas Archaeological Survey Research Series 8.
1997 An Overview of the Dalton Period in Northeastern Arkansas and in the Southeastern United States. In *Sloan: A Paleoindian Dalton Cemetery in Arkansas*, ed. D. F. Morse, 123–139. Washington DC: Smithsonian Institution Press.

1998 Dalton. In *Archaeology of Prehistoric Native North America: An Encyclopedia*, ed. G. Gibbon, 194–196. New York: Garland.

Morse, D. F., D. G. Anderson, and A. C. Goodyear III

1996 The Pleistocene-Holocene Transition in the Eastern United States. In *Humans at the End of the Ice-Age: The Archaeology of the Pleistocene-Holocene Transition*, ed. L. G. Strauss, B. V. Eriksen, J. M. Erlandson, and D. R. Yesner, 319–338. New York: Plenum Press.

Mueggenbourg, H. E.

1991 Excavations at the Blue Hole Site, Uvalde County, Texas, 1990. Master's thesis, University of Texas at Austin.

Mulholland, S. C.

1989 Procedures for Phytolith Analysis. Ms. on file, Archaeometry Laboratory, University of Minnesota, Duluth.

1993 AMS Radiocarbon Dating of Phytoliths. *MASCA* 10:21–23.

Mulholland, S. C., S. L. Mulholland, G. R. Peters, J. K. Huber, and H. D. Mooers

1997 Paleo-Indian Occupations in Northeastern Minnesota: How Early? *North American Archaeologist* 18:371–400.

Mulloy, W.

1958 *A Preliminary Historical Outline for the Northwestern Plains*. University of Wyoming Publications 27(1).

1959 The James Allen Site, near Laramie, Wyoming. *American Antiquity* 25:112–116.

Munn, N. D.

1996 Excluded Spaces: The Figure in the Australian Aboriginal Landscape. *Critical Inquiry* 22:446–465.

Munson, P. J., ed.

1984 *Experiments and Observations on Aboriginal Wild Plant Food Utilization in Eastern North America*. Indiana Historical Society, Prehistory Research Series 6(2).

Nami, H. G.

1996 New Assessments of Early Human Occupations in the Southern Cone. In *Prehistoric Mongoloid Dispersals*, ed. T. Akazawa and E. J. E. Szathmáry, 256–269. Oxford: Oxford University Press.

Neal, L.

1994 A Calf Creek Component from the Lamar Site, 34<SC>br</SC>8, Bryan County. *Bulletin of the Oklahoma Anthropological Society* 40:139–179.

Nelson, R. K.

1973 *Hunters of the Northern Forest: Designs for Survival among the Alaskan Kutchin*. Chicago: University of Chicago Press.

Newman, M. E.

1994 Analyse immunologique d'artefacts lithiques provenant d'un site datant du Paléoindien récent et situé à Rimouski (DcEd-1),

Quebéc, Canada. In *Il y à 8000 ans a Rimouski . . . Paléoécologie et Archéologie d'un site de la culture Plano*, ed. C. Chapdelaine, 287–294. Paléo-Quebec 22. Montreal: Recherches Amerindiennes au Quebéc.

1997 Immunological Analysis of Lithic Artifacts from the Cactus Hill Site. In *Archaeological Investigations of Site 44SX202, Cactus Hill, Sussex County, Virginia*, by J. M. McAvoy and L. D. McAvoy, Appendix F. Nottoway River Survey Archaeological Research Report No. 2 and Research Report Series No. 8. Richmond: Virginia Department of Historic Resources.

Newman, M. E., and P. J. Julig

1990 The Identification of Protein Residues on Lithic Artifacts from a Stratified Boreal Forest Site. *Canadian Journal of Archaeology* 13:119–132.

Nicholas, G. P.

1988 Ecological Leveling: The Archaeology and Environmental Dynamics of Early Postglacial Land Use. In *Holocene Human Ecology in Northeastern North America*, ed. G. P. Nicholas, 257–296. New York: Plenum Press.

1991 Putting Wetlands into Perspective. *Man in the Northeast* 42:29–38.

1994 Prehistoric Human Ecosystems in the Northeast: Interpreting Past Landscapes and Land Use. In *Great Lakes Archaeology and Paleoecology: Exploring Interdisciplinary Initiatives for the Nineties*, ed. R. I. MacDonald, 117–140. Waterloo ONT: Quaternary Sciences Institute, University of Waterloo.

1996 A Light but Lasting Footprint: Human Influences on the Northeastern Landscape. In *The Archaeological Northeast*, ed. M. A. Levine, K. E. Sassaman, and M. S. Nassaney, 25–38. Westport CT: Bergin and Garvey.

1998 Assessing Climatic Influences on Human Affairs: Wetlands and the Maximum Holocene Warming in the Northeast. *Journal of Middle Atlantic Archaeology* 14:147–160.

Novitzki, R. P.

1979 *An Introduction to Wisconsin Wetlands: Plants, Hydrology, and Soils.* Madison: U.S. Department of the Interior, Geological Survey, and University of Wisconsin–Extension, Geological and Natural History Survey.

Nuñez, L., and C. Santoro

1990 Primeros poblaminetos del cono sur de América (XII–IX Milenio A.P.). *Revista Arqueologia Americana* 1:92–139.

Okladnikov, A.

1981 *Art of the Amur: Ancient Art of the Russian Far East.* New York: Harry N. Abrams.

Oldale, R. N., S. M. Colman, and G. A. Jones
1991 Radiocarbon Ages from Two Submerged Strandline Features in the Western Gulf of Maine and a Sea-Level Curve for the Northeastern Massachusetts Coastal Region. *Quaternary Research* 40:38–45.
Oldale, R. N., F. C. Whitmore Jr., and J. R. Grimes
1987 Elephant Teeth from the Western Gulf of Maine, and Their Implications. *National Geographic Research* 3(4): 439–446.
Olsen, S. J.
1990 Was Early Man in North America a Big Game Hunter? In *Hunters of the Recent Past*, ed. L. B. Davis and B. O. K. Reeves, 103–110. London: Unwin Hyman.
Orians, G. H., and N. E. Pearson
1979 On the Theory of Central Place Foraging. In *Analysis of Ecological Systems*, ed. D. J. Horn, G. R. Stairs, and R. D. Mitchell, 155–177. Columbus: Ohio State University Press.
Orr, P. C.
1956 Pleistocene Man in Fishbone Cave, Pershing County, Nevada. *Nevada State Museum Bulletin* 2:1–120.
Overstreet, D. F.
1991a Paleoindian Study Unit: Region 9, Southeastern Wisconsin. *Wisconsin Archeologist* 72:265–366.
1991b Updated Paleoindian Study Unit for Region 7. *Wisconsin Archeologist* 72:201–244.
1993 *Chesrow: A Paleoindian Complex in the Southern Lake Michigan Basin.* Case Studies in Great Lakes Archaeology No. 2. Milwaukee: Great Lakes Archaeological Press.
1998 Late Pleistocene Geochronology and the Paleoindian Penetration of the Southwestern Lake Michigan Basin. *Wisconsin Archeologist* 79:28–52.
Overstreet, D. F., with D. F. Joyce, R. Blazina-Joyce, D. Waison, and K. A. Sverdrup
1993 *FY 1992 Historic Preservation Survey and Planning Grant—Early Holocene Megafauna Exploitation—Kenosha County, Wisconsin.* Reports of Investigations No. 325. Milwaukee: Great Lakes Archaeological Research Center.
Palmer, H. A.
1954 A Review of the Interstate Park, Wisconsin Bison Find. *Proceedings of the Iowa Academy of Science* 61:313–319.
Panshin, A. J., and C. de Zeeuve
1980 *Textbook of Wood Technology*. New York: McGraw Hill.
Panter-Brick, C.
2002 Sexual Division of Labor: Energetic and Evolutionary Scenarios. *American Journal of Human Biology* 14:627–640.

Panter-Brick, C., R. H. Layton, and P. Rowley-Conwy, eds.
2001 *Hunter-Gatherers: An Interdisciplinary Perspective*.Cambridge: Cambridge University Press.

Parfit, M.
2000 Hunt for the First Americans. *National Geographic* 198(6): 40–67.

Parmalee, P. W.
1959 Animal Remains from the Modoc Rock Shelter Site, Randolph County, Illinois. In *Summary Report of Modoc Rock Shelter: 1952, 1953, 1955, 1956*, ed. M. L. Fowler, 61–65. Illinois State Museum, Report of Investigations No. 4, Springfield.
1962 Faunal Remains from the Stanfield-Worley Bluff Shelter. *Journal of Alabama Archaeology* 8:112–114.
1968 Cave and Archaeological Faunal Deposits as Indicators of Post-Pleistocene Animal Populations and Distribution in Illinois. In *The Quaternary of Illinois*, ed. R. E. Bergstrom, 104–113. Special Publication No. 14. Urbana: College of Agriculture, University of Illinois.
1994 Freshwater Mussels from Dust and Smith Bottom Caves, Alabama. *Journal of Alabama Archaeology* 40(1–2): 135–162.

Patterson, L. W.
1985 Distinguishing Between Arrow and Spear Points on the Upper Texas Coast. *Lithic Technology* 14:81–89.

Pearsall, D.
2000 *Handbook of Paleoethnobotany*. 2nd ed. New York: Academic Press.

Perino, G.
1985 *Selected Preforms, Points, and Knives of the North*. Idabel OK: Gregory Perino.

Perry, D.
1999 Vegetative Tissues from Mesolithic Sites in the Netherlands. *Current Anthropology* 40:231–238.
n.d. Vegetative Plant Remains from Site 72. Ms. on file, Mashantucket Pequot Museum and Research Center, Mashantucket CT.

Perry, D., and K. A. McBride
n.d. Understanding Plant Use: The Importance of Parenchymatous Tissues. Ms. on file, Mashantucket Pequot Museum and Research Center, Mashantucket CT.

Peteet, D. M., R. A. Daniels, L. E. Heusser, J. S. Vogel, J. R. Southon, and D. E. Nelson
1993 Late-Glacial Pollen Macrofossils and Fish Remains in Northeastern U.S.A.: The Younger Dryas Oscillation. *Quaternary Science Review* 12:597–612.

1994 Wisconsinan Late-Glacial Environmental Change in Southern New England: A Regional Synthesis. *Journal of Quaternary Science* 9(2): 151–154.

Peterson, J. B., R. N. Bartone, and B. J. Cox

2000 The Varney Farm Site and the Late Paleoindian Period in Northeastern North America. *Archaeology of Eastern North America* 28:113–140.

Petersen, J. B., and D. E. Putnam

1992 Early Holocene Occupation in the Central Gulf of Maine Region. In *Early Holocene Occupation in Northern New England*, ed. B. S. Robinson, J. B. Petersen, and A. Robinson, 13–61. Occasional Publications in Maine Archaeology 9. Providence: Maine Archaeological Society, Maine Historic Preservation Commission, and Brown University.

Peterson, L. A.

1997 *A Field Guide to Edible Wild Plants of Eastern and Central North America.* Boston: Houghton Mifflin.

Peterson, M.

2001 Folsom Mobility and Technological Organization at the Krmpotich Folsom Site. Master's thesis, University of Wyoming.

Peterson, R. T., and L. A. Peterson

1978 *A Field Guide to Edible Wild Plants of Eastern and Central North America.* Boston: Houghton Mifflin.

Petruso, K. M., and J. M. Wickens

1984 Acorn in Aboriginal Subsistence in Eastern North America: A Report on Miscellaneous Experiments. In *Experiments and Observations on Aboriginal Wild Plant Food Utilization in Eastern North America*, ed. P. J. Munson, 360–378. Indiana Historical Society, Prehistory Research Series 6(2).

Pewe, T. L.

1975 *Quaternary Geology of Alaska.* U.S. Geological Survey, Professional Paper No. 835. Washington DC: U.S. Government Printing Office.

Pielou, E. C.

1975 *Ecological Diversity.* New York: Wiley.

Piperno, D. R.

1988 *Phytolith Analysis: An Archaeological and Geological Perspective.* London: Academic Press.

Pitblado, B.

1999 Late Paleoindian Occupation of the Southern Rocky Mountains: Projectile Points and Land Use in the High Country. Ph.D. diss., University of Arizona.

Pond, A. W.

1937 Wisconsin Joins Ranks of Oldest Inhabited Areas in America. *Wisconsin Archeologist* 17:51–54.

Powell, J. P., and D. G. Steele

1994 Diet and Health of Paleoindians: An Examination of Early Holocene Human Dental Remains. In *Paleonutrition: The Diet and Health of Prehistoric Americans*, ed. K. D. Sobolik, 178–194. Center for Archaeological Investigations, Occasional Paper No. 22. Carbondale: Board of Trustees, Southern Illinois University.

Powers, W. R., and J. F. Hoffecker

1989 Late Pleistocene Settlement in the Nenana Valley, Central Alaska. *American Antiquity* 54:263–287.

Powers-Jones, A. H., J. Padmore, and D. D. Gilbertson

1989 Studies of Late Prehistoric and Modern Opal Phytoliths from Coastal Sand Dunes and Machair in Northwest Britain. *Journal of Archaeological Science* 16:27–45.

Prewitt, E. R.

1995 Distributions of Typed Projectile Points in Texas. *Bulletin of the Texas Archeological Society* 66:83–173.

Prufer, O. H.

1962 Fluted Points and Ohio Prehistory. *Explorer* 4(3): 14–21.

Purdy, B. A.

1981 *Florida's Prehistoric Stone Technology*. Gainesville: University Press of Florida.

Puri, H. S., and R. O. Vernon

1964 *Summary of the Geology of Florida and a Guidebook to the Classic Exposures*. Florida Geological Survey Special Publication No. 5. Tallahassee: Florida Geological Survey.

Puri, H. S., W. J. Yon, and W. R. Oglesby

1967 *Geology of Dixie and Gilchrist Counties, Florida*. Florida Geological Bulletin No. 49. Tallahassee: Florida Division of Geology.

Putman, J. J.

1988 In Search of Modern Humans. *National Geographic* 174(4): 438–477.

Randall, A.

2001 Untangling Late Paleoindian and Early Side-Notched Stone Tool Assemblages at Dust Cave, Alabama. Paper presented at the 58th Annual Southeastern Archaeological Conference, Chattanooga TN.

Rapson, D. J., and L. Niven.

2000 Hell Gap Fauna. Paper presented at the 65th Annual Meeting of the Society for American Archaeology, Philadelphia.

Rattner, B. A., N. H. Golden, J. L. Peterson, J. B. Cohen, L. J. Garrett, M. A. Ottinger, and R. M. Erwin

n.d. Biological and Ecotoxicological Characteristics of Terrestrial Vertebrate Species Residing in Estuaries—Mink. www.pwrc.usgs.gov/bioeco/mink.htm. Site accessed September 15, 2001.

Reeves, B. O. K.

1990 Communal Bison Hunters of the Northern Plains. In *Hunters of the Recent Past*, ed. L. B. Davis and B. O. K. Reeves, 168–194. London: Unwin Hyman.

Reher, C. A., and G. C. Frison

1980 *The Vore Site, 48CK302: A Stratified Buffalo Jump in the Wyoming Black Hills*. Plains Anthropologist Memoir 16, pt. 2.

Reinhard, K. J., and V. M. Bryant Jr.

1992 Coprolite Analysis: A Biological Perspective on Archaeology. In *Archaeological Method and Theory*, ed. M. B. Schiffer, 4:245–288. Tucson: University of Arizona Press.

Reitz, E. J., and E. S. Wing

1999 *Zooarchaeology*. Cambridge: Cambridge University Press.

Richard, P. J. H., A. C. Larouche, and N. Morasse

1989 Études floristiques et paléophytogéographiques au Cratère du Nouveau-Québec. In *L'histoire naturelle du Cratère du Nouveau-Québec*, ed. M. A. Bouchard, 315–342. Collection Environnement et Géologie, vol. 7, Université de Montréal.

Richards, H. G.

1939 Reconsideration of the Dating of the Abbott Farm Site at Trenton, New Jersey. *American Journal of Science* 237(5): 345–354.

Richards, M. P., P. B. Pettitt, M. C. Stiner, and E. Trinkhaus

2001 Stable Isotope Evidence for Increasing Dietary Breadth in the European Mid-Upper Paleolithic. *Proceedings of the National Academy of Sciences* 98(11): 6528–6532.

Richings-Germain, S.

2002 The Jerry Craig Site: A Paleoindian Bison Bonebed in the Colorado Rocky Mountains. Master's thesis, University of Wyoming.

Ricklis, R. A., M. D. Blum, and M. B. Collins

1991 *Archeological Testing at the Vera Daniel Site (41TV1364) Zilker Park, Austin, Texas*. Texas Archeological Research Laboratory, Studies in Archeology 12, University of Texas at Austin.

Ricklis, R. A., and M. B. Collins

1994 *Archaic and Late Prehistoric Human Ecology in the Middle Onion Creek Valley, Hays County, Texas*. Texas Archeological Research Laboratory, Studies in Archeology 19, University of Texas at Austin.

Ridington, R.

1999 Dogs, Snares, and Cartridge Belts: The Poetics of Northern Athapaskan Narrative Technology. In *The Social Dynamics of Technology: Practice, Politics, and World Views*, ed. M. Dobres and C. R. Hoffman, 167–185. Washington DC: Smithsonian Institution Press.

Ridge, J. C., M. R. Besonen, M. Brochu, S. L. Brown, J. W. Callahan, G. J. Cook, R. S. Micholoson, and N. J. Toll

1999 Varve, Paleomagnetic, and 14C Chronologies for Late Pleistocene Events in New Hampshire and Vermont (USA). Geographie *physique et Quaternaire* 53(1): 79–106.

Ritzenthaler, R. E.

1972 The Pope Site: A Scottsbluff Cremation? in Waupaca County. *Wisconsin Archeologist* 53:15–19.

Roberts, A., and P. Julig

1997 Palaeo Indian Littoral Adaptations. Paper presented at the 62nd Annual Meeting of the Society for American Archaeology, Nashville TN.

Roberts, F. H. H.

1935 A Folsom Campsite and Workshop. In *Explorations and Field-work of the Smithsonian Institution in 1934*, vols. 61–64. Smithsonian Institution Miscellaneous Collections.

1940 Development in the Problem of the North American Paleoindian. In *Essay of Historical Anthropology of North America*, 51–116. Smithsonian Institution Miscellaneous Collections 100.

Rogers, E. S., and J. G. E. Smith

1981 Environment and Culture in the Shield and Mackenzie Borderlands. In *Handbook of North American Indians*, W. C. Sturtevant, gen. ed. Vol. 6, *Subarctic*, ed. J. Helm, 130–145. Washington DC: Smithsonian Institution Press.

Rolingson, M. A.

1964 *Paleoindian Culture in Kentucky: A Study Based on Projectile Points*. Studies in Archaeology 2. Lexington: University of Kentucky.

Romanoski, S. M.

1984 Fauna from the Averbuch Site. In *Averbuch: A Late Mississippian Manifestation in the Nashville Basin*. Vol. 2, Description, ed. W. E. Klippel and W. M. Bass, 1–46. Report to the National Park Service.

Rood, R. J.

1993 Deception Creek Projectile Points: A Late Paleoindian Type for the Foothill-Mountain Regions. *Southwestern Lore* 59:26–33.

Roosevelt, A. C., J. Douglas, and L. Brown
2002 The Migrations and Adaptations of the First Americans: Clovis and Pre-Clovis Viewed from South America. In *The First Americans: The Pleistocene Colonization of the New Worlds*, ed. N. G. Jablonski, 159–236. Memoirs of the California Academy of Sciences 27.

Roper, D. C., ed.
2002 *Medicine Creek: Seventy Years of Archaeological Investigations.* Tuscaloosa: University of Alabama Press.

Rosenzweig, M. L.
1993 *Species Diversity in Space and Time.* New York: Cambridge University Press.

Rowley-Conwy, P.
2001 Time, Change and the Archaeology of Hunter-Gatherers: How Original Is the "Original Affluent Society." In *Hunter-Gatherers: An Interdisciplinary Perspective*, ed. C. Panter-Brick, R. H. Layton, and P. Rowley-Conwy, 39–65. Cambridge: Cambridge University Press.

Rule, P., and J. Evans
1985 The Relationship of Morphological Variation to Hafting Techniques among Paleoindian Endscrapers at the *Shawnee Minisink Site. In Shawnee Minisink: A Stratified Paleoindian-Archaic Site in the Upper Delaware Valley of Pennsylvania*, ed. C. W. McNett, 211–220. New York: Academic Press.

Rusch, L. A., and J. T. Penman
1984 Transportation Archaeology in Wisconsin: The 1983 Field Season. Ms. on file, State Historical Society of Wisconsin, Madison.

Sahlins, M.
1985 *Islands of History*. Chicago: University of Chicago Press.

Salwen, B.
1978 Indians of Southern New England and Long Island: Early Period. In *Handbook of North American Indians*, W. C. Sturtevant, gen. ed. Vol. 15, *Northeast*, ed. B. G. Trigger, 240–252. Washington DC: Smithsonian Institution Press.

Sanchez, M. G.
2001 A Synopsis of Paleo-Indian Archaeology in Mexico. *Kiva* 67(2): 119–136.

Sanders, T. N.
1990 *Adams: The Manufacturing of Flaked Stone Tools at a Paleoindian Site in Western Kentucky*. Buffalo NY: Persimmon Press.

Sandweiss, D. H., H. McInnis, R. L. Burger, A. Cano, B. Ojeda, R. Paredes, M. del Carmen Sandweiss, and M. R. Glascock
1988 Quebrada Jaguay: Early South American Maritime Adaptations. *Science* 281(5384): 1830–1832.

Sandweiss, D. H., B. Tanner, D. Sanger, F. Andrus, and D. Piperno

2000 Paleoindian-Age Domestic Structure at a Peruvian Fishing Site. Paper presented at the 65th Annual Meeting of Society for American Archaeology, Philadelphia.

Santos, F. R., A. Pandya, C. Tyler-Smith, S. D. J. Pena, M. Schanfield, W. R. Leonard, L. Osipova, M. H. Crawford, and R. J. Mitchell

1999 The Central Siberian Origin for Native American Y Chromosomes. *American Journal of Human Genetics* 64:619–628.

Santos-Granero, F.

1998 Writing History into the Landscape: Space, Myth, and Ritual in Contemporary Amazonia. *American Ethnologist* 25(2): 128–148.

Sassaman, K. E.

2001 Hunter-Gatherers and Traditions of Resistance. In *The Archaeology of Traditions: Agency and History before and after Columbus*, ed. T. R. Pauketat, 218–236. Gainesville: University Press of Florida.

Saunders, J. J.

1980 A Model for Man-Mammoth Relationships in Late Pleistocene North America. *Canadian Journal of Anthropology* 1:87–98.

Saunders, J. J., E. B. Daeschler, and J. L. Cotter

1994 Descriptive Analysis and Taphonomical Observations of Culturally-Modified Mammoths Excavated at "The Gravel Pit," near Clovis, New Mexico in 1936. *Proceedings of the Academy of Natural Sciences of Philadelphia* 145:1–28.

Schoenwetter, J.

1998 Rethinking the Paleoethnobotany of Early Woodland Caving. *Midcontinental Journal of Archaeology* 23:23–44.

Schopmeyer, C. S.

1974 *Seeds of Woody Plants*. Agricultural Handbook 450. Washington DC: U.S. Department of Agriculture.

Schorger, A. W.

1973 *The Passenger Pigeon: Its Natural History and Extinction*. Norman: University of Oklahoma Press.

Schweingruber, F. H.

1978 *Microscopic Wood Anatomy*. 3rd ed. Birmensdorf, Switzerland: Swiss Federal Institute for Forest, Snow and Landscape Research.

1990 *Anatomy of European Woods*. Birmensdorf, Switzerland: Paul Haupt.

Scott, T. M., K. M. Campbell, F. R. Rupert, J. D. Arthur, T. M. Missimer, J. M. Lloyd, J. W. Yon, and J. G. Duncan

2001 *Geological Map of the State of Florida*. Map Series 146. Tallahassee: Florida Geological Survey.

Sellards, E. H.

1938 Artifacts Associated with Fossil Elephant. *Bulletin of the Geological Society of America* 49:999–1010.

1952 *Early Man in America: A Study in Prehistory*. Austin: University of Texas Press.

Sellet, F.

1999 A Dynamic View of Paleoindian Assemblages at the Hell Gap Site, Wyoming. Ph.D. diss., Southern Methodist University.

Shane, L. C. K., and K. H. Anderson

1991 Intensity, Gradients and Reversals in Late Glacial Environmental Change in East-Central North America. *Quaternary Science Reviews* 12:307–320.

Sharrock, F. W.

1966 *Prehistoric Occupation Patterns in Southwest Wyoming and Cultural Relationships with the Great Basin and Plains Culture Areas*. University of Utah, Anthropological Papers No. 77.

Shay, C. T.

1971 *The Itasca Bison Kill Site: An Ecological Analysis*. Minnesota Prehistoric Archaeology Series. St. Paul: Minnesota Historical Society.

Shelford, V .E.

1963 *The Ecology of North America*. Urbana: University of Illinois Press.

Sherwood, S. C.

2001 The Geoarchaeology of Dust Cave: A Late Paleoindian through Middle Archaic Site in the Western Middle Tennessee River Valley. Ph.D. diss., University of Tennessee.

Sherwood, S. C., B. N. Driskell, A. R. Randall, and S. C. Meeks

2004 Chronology and Stratigraphy at Dust Cave, Alabama. *American Antiquity* 69:533–554.

Shiner, J. L.

1983 Large Springs and Early American Indians. *Plains Anthropologist* 28:1–7.

Shoberg, M.

2001 Preliminary Use-Wear Analysis of Lithic Artifacts from the Gault Site. Paper presented at the 59th Plains Anthropological Conference, Lincoln NE.

Shoberg, M., and J. Beers

2004 Use-Wear on Stone Tools from BYU and UT Excavations at the Gault Site. Paper presented at the 69th Annual Meeting of the Society for American Archaeology, Montreal.

Shott, M. J.

1992 On Recent Trends in the Anthropology of Foragers: Kalahari Revisionsim and Its Archaeological Implications. *Man* 27:843–871.

Skinner, M. F., and O. Kaisen

1947 The Fossil Bison of Alaska and a Preliminary Revision of the Genus. *Bulletin, American Museum of Natural History* 89:123–256.

Smith, E. A.
1988 Risk and Uncertainty in the "Original Affluent Society": Evolutionary Ecology of Resource-Sharing and Land Tenure. In *Hunters and Gatherers*. Vol. 1, *History, Evolution and Social Change*, ed. T. Ingold, D. Riches, and J. Woodburn, 222–251. Oxford: Berg.

Smith, E. A., and B. Winterhalder
1992 Natural Selection and Decision Making: Some Fundamental Principles. In *Evolutionary Ecology and Human Behavior*, ed. E. A. Smith and B. Winterhalder, 25–60. Hawthorne NY: Aldine de Gruyter.

Smith, M. O.
1996 Biocultural Inquiry into Archaic Period Populations of the Southeast: Trauma and Occupational Stress. In *Archaeology of the Mid-Holocene Southeast*, ed. K. E. Sassaman and D. G. Anderson, 1:34–154. Gainesville: University Press of Florida.

Sneddon, L. A.
1987 A Late-glacial and Post-glacial Vegetation History of Black Pond, Norwell, Massachusetts. Master's thesis, University of Massachusetts.

Sneddon, L. A., and L. Kaplan
1987 Pollen Analysis from Cedar Swamp Pond Westborough, Massachusetts. *Archaeological Quarterly* (W. Elmer Ekblaw Chapter of the Massachusetts Archaeological Society) 9(2): 1–15.

Snyder, L. M., and P. W. Parmalee
1991 *An Archaeological Faunal Assemblage from Smith Bottom Cave, Lauderdale County, Alabama*. Tennessee Valley Authority, Report of Investigations, University of Tennessee, Knoxville.

Soday, F. J.
1954 The Quad Site: A Paleo-Indian Village in Northern Alabama. *Tennessee Archaeologist* 10(1): 1–20.

Soffer, O., J. M. Adovasio, D. C. Hyland, B. Klima, and J. Svoboda
1998 Textiles and Basketry in the Paleolithic: What Then is the Neolithic? Paper presented at the "Historic-Cultural Contacts of Indigenous Populations of the Pacific Coast of the North-Western America and the North-Eastern Asia" conference. Russian Academy of Sciences, Institute of History, Archaeology and Ethnography of the Peoples of the Far East, Vladivostok.

Soffer, O., J. M. Adovasio, J. S. Illingworth, H. A. Amirkhanov, N. D. Praslov, and M. Street
2000 Palaeolithic Perishables Made Permanent. *Antiquity* 74:812–821.

Solway, J., and R. B. Lee
1990 Foragers, Genuine or Spurious? Situating the Kalahari San in History. *Current Anthropology* 31(2): 109–146.

Sorrow, W. S., H. J. Shafer, and R. E. Ross
1967 *Excavations at Stillhouse Reservoir*. Papers of the Texas Archeological Salvage Project No. 11. Austin: Texas Archeological Salvage Project, University of Texas at Austin.

Spear, R. W.
1986 Late-Quaternary History of High-Elevation Vegetation in the White Mountains of New Hampshire. *Ecological Monographs* 59:125–151.

Spear, R. W., M. B. Davis, and L. C. K. Shane
1994 Late Quaternary History of Low- and Mid-Elevation Vegetation in the White Mountains of New Hampshire. *Ecological Monographs* 64:85–109.

Speiser, E. A.
1958 Akkadian Myths and Epics. In *The Ancient Near East*, vol. 1, An *Anthology of Texts and Pictures*, ed. J. B. Pritchard, 31–86. Princeton NJ: Princeton University Press.

Spencer, R. F., J. D. Jennings, C. E. Dibble, E. Johnson, A. R. King, T. Stern, K. M. Stewart, O. C. Stewart, and W. J. Wallace
1965 *The Native Americans*. New York: Harper and Row.

Speth, J. D.
1990 Seasonality, Resource Stress, and Food Sharing in So-called "Egalitarian" Foraging Societies. *Journal of Anthropological Archaeology* 9:148–188.
1996 Paleo-Indian and Early Archaic Periods Study Unit for Region 5. Ms. on file, Neville Public Museum, Green Bay WI.

Speth, J. D., and K. A. Spielmann
1983 Energy Source, Protein Metabolism, and Hunter-Gatherer Subsistence Strategies. *Journal of Anthropological Archaeology* 2:1–31.

Spielmann, K. A., and J. F. Eder
1994 Hunters and Farmers: Then and Now. *Annual Review of Anthropology* 22:303–323.

Spiess, A. E.
1979 *Reindeer and Caribou Hunters*. New York: Academic Press.
1992 Archaic Period Subsistence in New England and the Atlantic Provinces. In *Early Holocene Occupation in Northern New England*, ed. B. S. Robinson, J. B. Petersen, and A. Robinson, 163–185. Occasional Publications in Maine Archaeology 9. Providence: Maine Archaeological Society, Maine Historic Preservation Commission, and Brown University.

Spiess, A. E., M. L. Curran, and J. R. Grimes
1985 Caribou (*Rangifer tarandus* L.) Bones from New England Paleoindian Sites. *North American Archaeologist* 6:145–159.

Spiess, A. E., D. Wilson, and J. W. Bradley

1998 Paleoindian Occupation in the New England–Maritimes Region: Beyond Cultural Ecology. *Archaeology of Eastern North America* 26:201–264.

Spivey, T., F. Freese, and D. G. Wyckoff

1994 The Frazier Site: A Calf Creek–Bison Association in the Southern Osage Plains, South-Central Oklahoma. *Bulletin of the Oklahoma Anthropological Society* 40:131–137.

Stafford, R.

1991 Archaic Period Logistical Foraging Strategies in West Central Illinois. *Midcontinental Journal of Archaeology* 16:212–245.

Stafford, T. W., Jr., V. S. Sellars, and J. R. Johnson

2002 Chronostratigraphy at Arlington Springs: A Paleoindian Site in Insular California. Paper presented at the 67th Annual Meeting of the Society for American Archaeology, Denver.

Stanfill, A.

1988 Avonlea Projectile Point Manufacture: A Testable Model. In *Avonlea Yesterday and Today*, ed. L. B. Davis, 251–256. Saskatchewan: Saskatchewan Archaeological Society.

Stanford, D. J.

1978 The Jones-Miller Site: An Example of Hell Gap Bison Procurement Strategy. In *Bison Procurement and Utilization: A Symposium*, ed. L. B. Davis and M. Wilson, 89–97. Plains Anthropologist Memoir 14.

1982 A Critical Review of Archeological Evidence Relating to the Antiquity of Human Occupation of the New World. In *Plains Indian Studies: A Collection of Essays in Honor of John C. Ewers and Waldo R. Wedel*, ed. D. H. Ubelaker and H. J. Viola, 202–218. Smithsonian Contributions to Anthropology 30. Washington DC: Smithsonian Institution Press.

1983 Pre-Clovis Occupation South of the Ice Sheets. In *Early Man in the New World*, ed. R. Shutler Jr., 65–72. Beverly Hills CA: Sage.

1984 The Jones-Miller Site: A Study of Hell Gap Procurement and Processing. *National Geographic Society Research Reports* 1975:615–635.

1991 Clovis Origins and Adaptations: An Introductory Perspective. In *Clovis: Origins and Adaptations*, ed. R. Bonnichsen and K. L. Turnmire, 1–13. Corvallis: Center for the Study of the First Americans, Oregon State University.

1998 The First Americans: A New Perspective. Paper presented at the 33rd Annual Symposium of the Archeological Society of Maryland, Crownsville.

1999 Paleoindian Archaeology and Late Pleistocene Environments in the Plains and Southwestern United States. In *Ice Age Peoples of North America: Environments, Origins, and Adaptations*, ed. R. Bonnichsen and K. L. Turnmire, 281–339. Corvallis: Oregon State University Press.

Stanford, D. J., and J. Albanese

1975 Preliminary Results of the Smithsonian Institutions Study at the Claypool Site, Washington County, Colorado. *Southwestern Lore* 41:22–28.

Stanford, D. J., and M. A. Jodry

1988 The Drake Clovis Cache. *Current Research in the Pleistocene* 5:21–22.

Stevenson, M. G.

1982 Toward an Understanding of Site Abandonment Behavior: Evidence from Historic Mining Camps in the Southwest Yukon. *Journal of Anthropological Archaeology* 1:237–265.

1985 The Formation of Artifact Assemblages at Workshop/Habitation Sites: Models from Peace Point in Northern Alberta. *American Antiquity* 50:63–81.

Stewart, A.

1994 Relating Environmental Change to Cultural Behavior in the Late Pleistocene Great Lakes Region. In *Great Lakes Archaeology and Paleoecology: Exploring Interdisciplinary Initiatives for the Nineties*, ed. R. I. MacDonald, 141–154. Waterloo ONT: Quaternary Sciences Institute, University of Waterloo.

Stiner, M. C., N. D. Munro, and T. A. Surovell

2000 The Tortoise and the Hare: Small-Game Use, the Broad-Spectrum Revolution, and Paleolithic Demography. *Current Anthropology* 41(1): 39–73.

Stirling, M. W.

1960 The Use of the Atlatl on Lake Patzcuaro, Michoacan. *Anthropological Papers, Smithsonian Institution Bureau of American Ethnology Bulletin* 173(59): 265–268.

Stoltman, J. B.

1978 Temporal Models in Prehistory: An Example from Eastern North America. *Current Anthropology* 19:703–746.

Stone, J. R., and G. M. Ashley

1992 Ice-Wedge Casts, Pingo Scars and the Drainage of Glacial Lake Hitchcock. New England Intercollegiate Geological Conference, 84th Annual Meeting, Guidebook for Field Trips in the Connecticut Valley Region of Massachusetts and Adjacent States. *Contributions of the University of Massachusetts Department of Geology* 66:305–331.

Storck, P. L., and A. E. Spiess

1994 The Significance of New Faunal Identifications Attributed to an Early Paleoindian (Gainey Complex) Occupation at the Udora Site, Ontario, Canada. *American Antiquity* 59:121–142.

Story, D. A.

1990 Cultural History of the Native Americans. In *The Archeology and Bioarcheology of the Gulf Coastal Plain*, ed. D. A. Story, J. A. Guy, B. A. Burnett, M. D. Freeman, J. C. Rose, D. G. Steele, B. W. Olive, and K. J. Reinhard, 1:163–366. Arkansas Archeological Survey, Research Series 38.

Stothers, D. M.

1996 Resource Procurement and Band Territories: A Model for Lower Great Lakes Paleoindian and Early Archaic Settlement Systems. *Archaeology of Eastern North America* 24:173–216.

Strauss, L., B. Eriksen, J. Erlandson, and D. Yesner, eds.

1996 *Humans at the End of the Ice Age: The Archaeology of the Pleistocene—Holocene Transition*. New York: Plenum Press.

Stright, M.

1999 *Spatial Data Analysis of Artifacts Redeposited by Coastal Erosion: A Case Study of McFaddin Beach, Texas*. Outer Continental Shelf, Minerals Management Service Study 99-0068, U.S. Department of Interior, Minerals Management Service, Herndon VA.

Struever, S.

1968 Flotation Techniques for the Recovery of Small-Scale Archaeological Remains. *American Antiquity* 40:353–362.

1972 The Koster Site: A Stratified Archaic Site in the Illinois Valley. *Central States Archaeology Journal* 37:27–47.

Stuiver, M. T., and B. Becker

1991 High Precision Decadal Calibration of the Radiocarbon Time Scale, AD 1950–6000 BC. *Radiocarbon* 35(1): 1–24.

Stuiver, M. T., and P. J. Reimer

1993 Extended 14C Data Base and Revised CALIB3.0 14C Age Calibration Program. *Radiocarbon* 35(1): 215–230.

Styles, B. W.

1981 *Faunal Exploitation and Resource Selection: Early Late Woodland Subsistence in the Lower Illinois Valley*. Scientific Papers No. 3. Evanston IL: Archaeological Program, Northwestern University.

Styles, B. W., S. R. Ahler, and M. I. Fowler

1983 Modoc Rock Shelter Revisited. In *Archaic Hunters and Gatherers in the American Midwest*, ed. J. A. Phillips and J. A. Brown, 261–297. New York: Academic Press.

Sundstrom, L.
2003 Sacred Islands: An Exploration of Religion and Landscape in the Northern Great Plains. In *Islands on the Plains*, ed. M. Kornfeld and A. J. Osborn, 258–300. Salt Lake City: University of Utah Press.

Surovell, T.
2000 Early Paleoindian Women, Children, Mobility, and Fertility. *American Antiquity* 65:493–509.

Surovell, T., N. M. Waguespack, M. Kornfeld, and G. C. Frison
2001 Barger Gulch Locality B: The Folsom Occupation. *Current Research in the Pleistocene* 18:58–60.

Taçon, P. S.
1999 Identifying Ancient Sacred Landscapes in Australia: From Physical to Social. In *Archaeologies of Landscape: Contemporary Perspectives*, ed. W. Ashmore and A. B. Knapp, 33–57. Malden MA: Blackwell.

Takac, P. R.
1991 Underwater Excavations at Spring Lake: A Paleoindian Site in Hays County, Texas. *Current Research in the Pleistocene* 8:46–48.

Talalay, L., D. R. Keller, and P. J. Munson
1984 Hickory Nuts, Walnuts, Butternuts, and Hazelnuts: Observations and Experiments Relevant to Their Aboriginal Exploitation in Eastern North America. In *Experiments and Observations on Aboriginal Wild Plant Food Utilization in Eastern North America*, ed. P. J. Munson, 338–359. Indiana Historical Society, Prehistory Research Series 6(2).

Tankersley, K. B.
1991 A Geoarchaeological Investigation of the Distribution and Exchange in the Raw Material Economies of Clovis Groups in Eastern North America. In *Raw Material Economies among Prehistoric Hunter-Gatherers*, ed. A. Montet-White and S. Holen, 285–303. University of Kansas Publications in Anthropology 19. Lawrence: University of Kansas Printing Service.
1993 Clovis Mastic and Its Hafting Implications. *Journal of Archaeological Science* 21:117–124.
1994a The Effects of Stone and Technology on Fluted Point Morphometry. *American Antiquity* 59:498–510.
1994b Sheriden: A Clovis Cave Site in Eastern North America. *Geoarchaeology: An International Journal* 12:713–724.
1999 Sheriden: A Stratified Pleistocene-Holocene Cave Site in the Great Lakes Region of North America. *British Archaeological Review* (BAR) *International Series* 800:67–75. Oxford: British Archaeological Reports.

Tankersley, K. B., K. Ford, G. McDonald, R. Genheimer, and R. Hendricks
1997 Late Pleistocene Archaeology of Sheriden Cave, Wyandot County, Ohio. *Current Research in the Pleistocene* 14:81–83.

Tankersley, K. B., and C. S. Landefeld
1998 Geochronology of Sheriden Cave, Ohio: The 1997 Field Season. *Current Research in the Pleistocene* 15:136–138.

Tankersley, K. B., and B. Redmond
1999a Fluoride/Radiocarbon Dating of Late Pleistocene Bone from Sheriden Cave, Ohio. *Current Research in the Pleistocene* 16:107–108.
1999b Radiocarbon Dating of a Projectile Point from Sheriden Cave, Ohio. *Current Research in the Pleistocene* 16:76–77.
2000 Ice Age Ohio. *Archaeology* (Nov./Dec.): 42–46.

Taylor, K. C., G. W. Lamorey, G. A. Doyle, R. B. Alley, P. M. Grootes, P. A. Mayewski, J. W. C. White, and L. K. Barlow
1993 The Flickering Switch of Late Pleistocene Climate Change. *Nature* 361:432–436.

Taylor, R. E., A. Long, and R. S. Kra, eds.
1992 *Radiocarbon after Four Decades: An Interdisciplinary Perspective*. New York: Springer-Verlag.

Thomas, D. H.
1978 Arrowheads and Atlatl Darts: How the Stones Got the Shaft. *American Antiquity* 43:461–472.

Thompson, W. B., B. K. Fowler, and C. C. Dorion
1999 Deglaciation of the Northwestern White Mountains, New Hampshire. *Geographie physique et Quaternaire* 53(1): 59–77.

Thorson, R. M.
1990 Geologic Contexts of Archaeological Sites in Beringia. In *Archaeological Geology of North America*, ed. N. P. Lasca and J. Donahue, 399–420. Centennial Special No. 4. Boulder CO: Geological Society of America.

Thorson, R. M., and R. Webb
1991 Post-glacial Development of the Cedar Swamp. Journal of *Paleolimnology* 6:17–35.

Thurmond, J. P.
1990 *Late Paleoindian Utilization of the Dempsy Divide on the Southern Plains*. Plains Anthropologist Memoir No. 25.

Tighe, E.
1966 *Women's Day Encyclopedia of Cookery #5*. 3rd ed. New York: Fawcett.

Tilley, C.
1994 *A Phenomenology of Landscape: Places, Paths and Monuments*. Oxford: Berg.

Timperley, C. L., P. R. Owen, and E. L. Lundelius Jr.

2003 Preliminary Comments on Faunal Material from the Gault Site, Central Texas. *Current Research in the Pleistocene* 20:117–119.

Todd, L. C.

1983 The Horner Site: Taphonomy of an Early Holocene Bison Bonebeds. Ph.D. diss., University of New Mexico.

1987 Taphonomy of the Horner II Bone Bed. In *The Horner Site*, ed. G. C. Frison and L. C. Todd, 107–198. New York: Academic Press.

1991 Seasonality Studies and Paleoindian Subsistence Strategies. In *Human Predators and Prey Mortality*, ed. M. C. Stiner, 217–276. Boulder CO: Westview Press.

Todd, L. C., M. G. Hill, D. J. Rapson, and G. C. Frison

1997 Cutmarks, Impacts, and Carnivores at the Casper Site Bison Bonebed. In *Proceedings of the 1993 Bone Modification Conference, Hot Springs, South Dakota*, ed. L. A. Hannus et al., 136–157. Occasional Paper No. 1, Archeology Laboratory, Augustana College, Sioux Falls SD.

Todd, L. C., J. L. Hofman, and C. B. Schultz

1990 Seasonality of the Scottsbluff and Lipscomb Bison Bonebeds: Implications for Modeling Paleoindian Subsistence. American *Antiquity* 55:813–827.

Todd, L. C., and D. J. Rapson

1999 Formational Analysis of Bison Bonebeds and Interpretation of Paleoindian Subsistence. In *Le bison: Gibier et moyen de subsistence des hommes du Paleolithique aux Paleoindiens des Grandes Plaines*, ed. J.-Ph. Brugal, F. David, J. G. Enloe, and J. Jaubert, 479–499. Actes du colloque international, Toulouse 1995. Editions APDCA, Antibes.

Todd, L. C., D. J. Rapson, and J. L. Hofman

1996 Dentition Studies of the Mill Iron and Other Early Paleoindian Bison Bonebed Sites. In *The Mill Iron Site*, ed. G. C. Frison, 145–175. Albuquerque: University of New Mexico Press.

Todd, L. C., and D. J. Stanford

1992 Application of Conjoined Bone Data to Site Structural Studies. In *Piecing Together the Past: Applications of Refitting Studies in Archaeology*, ed. J. L. Hofman and J. G. Enloe, 21–35. British Archaeological Reports, International Series 578, Oxford.

Trigger, B. G.

1989 *A History of Archaeological Thought*. Cambridge: Cambridge University Press.

Tunnell, C. D., and J. T. Hughes

1955 An Archaic Bison Kill in the Texas Panhandle. *Panhandle-Plains Historical Review* 28:63–70.

Turner, E. S., and P. Tanner
1994 The McFaddin Beach Site on the Upper Texas Coast. *Bulletin of the Texas Archeological Society* 65:319–336.

Tyldesley, J. A., and P. G. Bahn
1983 Use of Plants in the European Palaeolithic: A Review of the Evidence. *Quaternary Science Review* 2:53–81.

Upchurch, S. B., R. N. Strom, and M. G. Nuckels
1982 *Methods of Provenance Determination of Florida Cherts*. Tampa: Department of Geology, University of South Florida.

Vernon, R. O.
1951 *Geology of Citrus and Levy Counties, Florida*. Geological Bulletin No. 33. Tallahassee: Florida Geological Survey.

Vinson, D. M.
1993 Taphonomic Analysis of Faunal Remains from Trail Creek Caves, Seward Peninsula, Alaska. Master's thesis, University of Alaska.

Waguespack, N. M., and T. A. Surovell
2003 Clovis Hunting Strategy: Or How to Make Out on Plentiful Resources. *American Antiquity* 68:333–352.

Walker, D. N.
1975 A Cultural and Ecological Analysis of the Vertebrate Fauna of the Medicine Lodge Creek Site (48BH499). Master's thesis, University of Wyoming.
1982 Early Holocene Vertebrate Fauna. In *The Agate Basin Site*, ed. G. C. Frison and D. J. Stanford, 270–274. New York: Academic Press.

Walker, R. B.
1997 Late-Paleoindian Faunal Remains from Dust Cave, Alabama. *Current Research in the Pleistocene* 14:85–87.
1998 The Late Paleoindian through Middle Archaic Faunal Evidence from Dust Cave, Alabama. Ph.D. diss., University of Tennessee.
2000 *Subsistence Strategies at Dust Cave: Changes from the Late Paleoindian through Middle Archaic Occupations*. University of Alabama, Office of Archaeological Services, Report of Investigations No. 78.

Walker, R. B., K. R. Detwiler, S. C. Meeks, and B. N. Driskell
2001 Berries, Bones and Blades: Reconstructing Late Paleoindian Subsistence Economies at Dust Cave, Alabama. *Midcontinental Journal of Archaeology* 26:169–197.

Walker, R. B., B. N. Driskell, S. C. Sherwood, S. C. Meeks, and K. R. Detwiler
1999 Recent Investigations at Dust Cave: A Late Paleoindian through Middle Archaic Site in Northwest Alabama. Paper presented at the 64th Annual Meeting of the Society of American Archaeology, Chicago.

Walker, R. B., K. Hill, H. Kaplan, and G. McMillan

2002 Age-Dependency in Hunting Ability among the Ache of Eastern Paraguay. *Journal of Human Evolution* 42:639–657.

Walker, R. B., and P. W. Parmalee

2004 A Noteworthy Cache of Goose Humeri from Late Paleoindian Levels at Dust Cave, Northwestern Alabama. *Journal of Alabama Archaeology* 50(1): 18–35.

Waller, B. I.

1983 *Florida Anthropologist* Interview with Ben Waller. *Florida Anthropologist* 36:31–39.

Walthall, J. A.

1980 *Prehistoric Indians of the Southeast: Archaeology of Alabama and the Middle South.* Tuscaloosa: University of Alabama Press.

1998a Overwinter Strategy and Early Holocene Hunter-Gatherer Mobility in Temperate Forests. *Midcontinental Journal of Archaeology* 23:1–22.

1998b Rockshelters and Hunter-Gatherer Adaptation to the Pleistocene/Holocene Transition. *American Antiquity* 63:223–238.

Walthall, J. A., and B. Koldehoff

1998 Hunter-Gatherer Interaction and Alliance Formation: Dalton and the Cult of the Long Blade. *Plains Anthropologist* 43:257–273.

Watson, P. J.

1976 In Pursuit of Prehistoric Subsistence: A Comparative Account of Some Contemporary Flotation Techniques. *Mid-Continental Journal of Archaeology* 1(1): 77–100.

Watts, W. A.

1983 Vegetational History of the Eastern United States, 25,000 to 10,000 Years Ago. In *Late-Quaternary Environments of the United States.* Vol. 1, *The Late Pleistocene*, ed. S. Porter, 294–310. Minneapolis: University of Minnesota Press.

Webb, C. H., J. L. Shiner, and E. W. Roberts

1971 The John Pearce Site (16CD56): A San Patrice Site in Caddo Parish, Louisiana. *Bulletin of the Texas Archaeological Society* 42:1–49.

Webb, R. S.

1992 Late-Quaternary Water Level Fluctuations in the Northeastern United States. Ph.D. diss., Brown University.

Webb, S. D., J. T. Milanich, R. Alexon, and J. S. Dunbar

1984 A *Bison antiquus* Kill Site, Wacissa River, Jefferson County, Florida. *American Antiquity* 49:384–392.

Wedel, W. R.

1961 *Prehistoric Man on the Great Plains.* Norman: University of Oklahoma Press.

1986 *Central Plains Prehistory.* Lincoln: University of Nebraska Press.

Weigel, R. D., J. A. Holman, and A. A. Paloumpis

1974 Vertebrates from Russell Cave. In *Investigations in Russell Cave*, ed. J. W. Griffin, 81–85. National Park Service Publications in Archaeology No. 13. Washington DC: U.S. Government Printing Office.

Wendt, D.

1985 Paleo-Indian Site Distribution in the Yahara River Basin of Wisconsin. *Wisconsin Archeologist* 66:243–264.

West, F. H.

1996 Beringia and New World Origins II: The Archaeological Evidence. In *American Beginnings: The Prehistory and Paleoecology of Beringia*, ed. F. H. West, 537–559. Chicago: University of Chicago Press.

Wheat, J. B.

1972 *The Olsen-Chubbuck Site: A Paleo-Indian Bison Kill*. Society for American Archaeology Memoir 26.

Wheeler, R. P.

1995 *Archaeological Investigations in Three Reservoir Areas in South Dakota and Wyoming. Part I: Angostura Reservoir*. Reprints in Anthropology 46. Lincoln NE: J and L Reprints.

Whelan, M. K.

1990 Late Woodland Subsistence Systems and Settlement Size in the Mille Lacs Area. In *The Woodland Tradition in the Western Great Lakes: Papers Presented to Elden Johnson*, ed. G. E. Gibbon, 55–76. University of Minnesota Publications in Anthropology No. 4.

Whitaker, J. O., Jr.

1992 *The Audubon Society Field Guide to North American Mammals*. New York: Alfred A. Knopf.

White, J. M.

1983 Late Quaternary Geochronology and Palaeoecology of the Upper Peace River District, Canada. Ph.D. diss., Simon Fraser University.

Whittaker, R. H.

1972 Evolution and Measurement of Species Diversity. *Taxon* 21:213–251.

Wilding, L. P.

1967 Radiocarbon Dating of Biogenetic Opal. *Science* 156:66–67.

Wilke, P. J., J. J. Flenniken, and T. L. Ozbun

1991 Clovis Technology at the Anzick Site, Montana. *Journal of California and Great Basin Anthropology* 13(2): 242–495.

Willey, G. R., ed.

1966 *An Introduction to American Archeology: North and Middle America*, vol. 1. Englewood Cliffs NJ: Prentice-Hall.

Willey, G. R., and J. Sabloff

1993 *A History of American Archaeology*. 3rd ed. New York: W. H. Freeman.

Williams, S., and J. B. Stoltman

1965 An Outline of Southeastern United States Prehistory with Particular Emphasis on the Paleoindian Era. In *The Quaternary of the United States*, ed. H. E. Wright and D. G. Frey, 669–683. Princeton NJ: Princeton University Press.

Williams, T. C., and T. Webb III

1996 Neotropical Bird Migration during the Ice Ages: Orientation and Ecology. *Auk* 113(1): 105–118.

Willig, J. A.

1991 Clovis Technology and Adaptation in Far Western North America: Regional Pattern and Environmental Context. In *Clovis: Origins and Adaptations*, ed. R. Bonnichsen and K. L. Turnmire, 91–119. Corvallis: Center for the Study of the First Americans, Oregon State University.

1996 Environmental Context for Early Human Occupation in Western North America. In *Prehistoric Mongoloid Dispersals*, ed. T. Akazawa and E. J. E. Szathmáry, 241–253. Oxford: Oxford University Press.

Willis, C.

1988 Controlled Surface Collection of the Little River Rapids Site (8JE603): A Stratigraphically Deflated Site in the Aucilla River, North Florida. *Florida Anthropologist* 41(3): 453–470.

Wilmsen, E. N.

1970 *Lithic Analysis and Cultural Inference: A Paleoindian-Case*. Tucson: University of Arizona Press.

1974 *Lindenmeier: A Pleistocene Hunting Society*. New York: Harper and Row.

Wilmsen, E. N., and F. H. H. Roberts Jr.

1978 *Lindenmeier, 1934–1974: Concluding Report on Investigations*. Smithsonian Contributions to Anthropology No. 24. Washington DC: Smithsonian Institution Press.

Wilson, M. C.

1975 Holocene Fossil Bison from Wyoming and Adjacent Areas. Master's thesis, University of Wyoming.

1996 Late Quaternary Vertebrates and the Opening of the Ice-Free Corridor, with Special Reference to the Genus *Bison*. *Quaternary International* 32:97–105.

Wilson, M. C., and J. A. Burns

1999 Searching for the Earliest Canadians: Wide Corridors, Narrow Doorways, Small Windows. In *Ice Age People of North America: Environments, Origins, and Adaptations*, ed. R. Bonnichsen and K. L. Turnmire, 213–248. Corvallis: Oregon State University Press.

Wilson, T.

1889 Ancient Indian Matting from Petit Anse Island, Louisiana. *Annual Report of the U.S. National Museum, 1888*, 673–676.

Wimer, A.

2001 Folsom Sites in Southwestern Wyoming. Master's thesis, University of Wyoming.

Winterhalder, B.

1981 Foraging Strategies in the Boreal Forest: An Analysis of Cree Hunting and Gathering. In *Hunter-Gatherer Foraging Strategies*, ed. B. Winterhalder and E. A. Smith, 66–98. Chicago: University of Chicago Press.

1983a Boreal Foraging Strategies. In *Boreal Forest Adaptations: The Northern Algonkians*, ed. A. T. Steegmann Jr., 201–242. New York: Plenum Press.

1983b History and Ecology of the *Boreal Zone in Ontario. In Boreal Forest Adaptations: The Northern Algonkians*, ed. A. T. Steegman, 9–54. New York: Plenum Press.

1990 Open Field, Common Pot: Harvest Variability and Risk Avoidance in Agricultural and Foraging Societies. In *Risk and Uncertainty in Tribal and Peasant Economies*, ed. E. Cashdan, 67–87. Boulder CO: Westview Press.

1996 Social Foraging and the Behavioral Ecology of Intragroup Resource Transfers. *Evolutionary Anthropology* 5(2): 46–57.

Winterhalder, B., and E. A. Smith

1992 Evolutionary Ecology and the Social Sciences. In *Evolutionary Ecology and Human Behavior*, ed. E. A. Smith and B. Winterhalder, 3–24. Hawthorne NY: Aldine de Gruyter.

Wisner, G.

1998 Ohio Cave, Sealed since Ice Age, Yields Data on Paleo-Americans. *Mammoth Trumpet* 13(1): 1–10.

1999 Channel Island Woman May Be Oldest Yet. *Mammoth Trumpet* 14(3): 1.

Wissler, C.

1916 Material Culture of the North American Indians. *American Anthropologist* 16:447–505.

Witthoft, J.

1952 A Paleo-Indian Site in Eastern Pennsylvania: An Early Hunting Culture. *Proceedings of the American Philosophical Society* 96(4).

Wittkofski, J. M., and T. R. Reinhart, eds.

1989 *Paleoindian Research in Virginia: A Synthesis*. Special Publication 19. Richmond: Archeological Society of Virginia.

Wolf, E. R.

1982 *Europe and the People without History*. Berkeley: University of California Press.

Woodburn, J.

1970 *Hunters and Gatherers: The Material Culture of the Nomadic Hadza*. London: Shenval Press for the Trustees of the British Museum.

1988 African Hunter-Gatherer Social Organization: Is It Best Understood as a Product of Encapsulation? In *Hunters and Gatherers 1: History, Evolution, and Social Change*, ed. T. Ingold, D. Riches and J. Woodburn, 31–64. Washington DC: Berg.

Woods, J. C., and G. L. Titmus

1985 A Review of the Simon Clovis Collection. *Idaho Archaeologist* 8(1): 3–8.

Wormington, H. M.

1949 *Ancient Man in North America*. Denver Museum of Natural History, Popular Series, 3rd ed.

1957 *Ancient Man in North America*. Denver Museum of Natural History, Popular Series, 4th ed.

Wyckoff, D. G.

1995 A Summary of the Calf Creek Horizon in Oklahoma. Bulletin of the *Oklahoma Anthropological Society* 42:179–210.

Wylie, A.

1985 The Reaction against Analogy. *Advances in Archaeological Method and Theory* 8:63–111.

Yesner, D. R.

1996 Human Adaptation at the Pleistocene-Holocene Boundary (circa 13,000 to 8,000 BP) in Eastern Beringia. In *Humans at the End of the Ice Age*, ed. L. G. Straus, B. V. Eriksen, J. M. Erlandson, and D. R. Yesner, 255–276. New York: Plenum Press.

1998 Origins and Development of Maritime Adaptations in the Northwest Pacific Region of North America: A Zooarchaeological Perspective. *Arctic Anthropology* 35(1): 204–222.

2000 Human Colonization of Eastern Beringia and the Question of Mammoth Hunting. In *Mammoth Site Studies*, ed. D. L. West, 69–84. Publications in Anthropology No. 22. Lawrence: University of Kansas.

2001 Human Dispersal into Interior Alaska: Antecedent Conditions, Mode of Colonization, and Adaptations. *Quaternary Science Reviews* 20:315–327.

Young, S. B.

1982 The Vegetation of Land-Bridge Beringia. In *Paleoecology of Beringia*, ed. D. M. Hopkins, J. V. Matthews Jr., C. E. Schweger, and S. B. Young, 179–194. Academic Press, New York.

Yu, Z., and U. Eicher

1998 Abrupt Climate Oscillations during the Last Deglaciation in Central North America. *Science* 282(5397): 2235–2238.

Zeanah, D. W.

2000 Transport Costs, Central Place Foraging, and Hunter-Gatherer Alpine Land Use Strategies. In *Intermountain Archaeology*, ed. D. B. Madsen and M. D. Metcalfe, 1–14. University of Utah Anthropological Papers 122. Salt Lake City: University of Utah Press.

Zhao, A., and D. M. Pearsall

1998 Experiments for Improving Phytolith Extraction from Soils. *Journal of Archaeological Science* 25:587–598.

INDEX

Page numbers in italic indicate illustrations; page numbers with t indicate tables.

LaVergne, TN USA
04 December 2009
166056LV00003B/3/P